The Balkans in the New Millennium

Can the Balkans ever become a peace peninsula like Scandinavia? With enlightened backing, can it make common cause with the rest of Europe rather than being an arena of periodic conflicts, political misrule and economic misery?

In the last years of the twentieth century, Western states watched with alarm as a wave of conflicts swept over much of the Balkan Peninsula of South-East Europe. Ethno-nationalist disputes, often stoked by unprincipled leaders, plunged Yugoslavia into bloody warfare. Romania, Bulgaria and Albania struggled to find stability as they reeled from the collapse of the Communist social system. Greece, the only wholly Balkan state to remain outside the Communist bloc, became embroiled in the Yugoslav tragedy.

This book examines the politics and international relations of the Balkans during a decade of mounting external involvement in its affairs. Tom Gallagher asks what evidence there is that lessons have been learned and applied as the transatlantic engagement with Balkan problems enters its second decade. His book identifies new problems: organised crime, demographic crises of different kinds and the collapse of a strong employment base.

The Balkans in the New Millennium contains chapters on Bosnia, Serbia, Macedonia and Greece as well as on the Kosovo crisis and the relationship between the European Union and the Balkan region. It should appeal to students, researchers and all those with a general interest in Balkan politics.

Tom Gallagher holds the Chair of Ethnic Conflict and Peace at Bradford University, UK. He has published widely on international engagement with South-East Europe and the roles of democracy and nationalism in the region. He is also the author of *Outcast Europe* and *The Balkans after the Cold War*.

Outcast Europe

The Balkans in the New Millennium

In the shadow of war and peace

Tom Gallagher

Routledge
Taylor & Francis Group

LONDON AND NEW YORK

First published 2005
by Routledge
2 Park Square, Milton Park, Abingdon, Oxon OX14 4RN

Simultaneously published in the USA and Canada
by Routledge
270 Madison Ave, New York, NY 10016

Routledge is an imprint of the Taylor & Francis Group

Typeset in Times New Roman by
Newgen Imaging Systems (P) Ltd, Chennai, India
Printed and bound in Great Britain by
Antony Rowe Ltd, Chippenham, Wiltshire

British Library Cataloguing in Publication Data
A catalogue record for this book is available from the British Library

Library of Congress Cataloging in Publication Data
Gallagher, Tom, 1954–
    The Balkans in the New Millennium: in the shadow of war and
peace / by Tom Gallagher.
        p. cm.
    Includes bibliographical references and index.
    1. Balkan Peninsula – Politics and government – 1989– 2. Kosovo
(Serbia)–History–Civil War, 1998–1999–Peace. 3. Yugoslav War,
1991–1995. 4. Former Yugoslav republics–History. I. Title.

DR48.6.G35 2005
949.703–dc22   2004021078

ISBN 0–415–34940–0

Contents

Preface

The Balkan peninsula of South-East Europe and its problems became a dominant factor in European affairs from the early 1990s. Yet the European Union, NATO and the major states shaping the policies of these Euro-Atlantic bodies were slow to get involved despite the issues at stake: the collapse of Yugoslavia into internal warfare as Slobodan Milošević tried to build a Greater Serbia from its ashes, was the first continuous crisis facing the world in the post-Cold War era. It revealed that ethno-nationalist disputes in countries damaged by failed efforts at modernisation along communist lines, were a serious source of instability. A deep-seated instinct in Western capitals was to adopt minimalist measures to contain these problems. In a companion volume entitled *The Balkans after the Cold War: from tyranny to tragedy* (Routledge 2003) I describe the limited attention span of the West and the unwillingness to devote enough energy, imagination and resources to overcome a crisis in Europe's troublesome backward. Border changes, an exchange of populations and accommodation with leaders who had licensed or used massive violence to pursue their goals, were the favoured peace-making instruments applied until 1995. In that year, the Dayton Peace Agreement (DPA) brought to an end the worst of the conflicts that would be seen in the former Yugoslavia, the 1992–5 Bosnian war. But this hastily arranged deal gave nationalist leaderships strong incentives to refine their separatist agendas and ignore or weaken a central state that was supervised by an international administration with uncertain powers.

The flawed Bosnian settlement marked the zenith of American involvement in the region. From the late 1990s onwards, the European Union has acquired increasing responsibility for Western policy in the Balkans while maintaining an often-strained partnership with Washington. This volume examines the international record in the face of fresh crises that have erupted since 1998. These have mainly been located in territories and states belonging to the southern part of the Balkan Peninsula. Arguably, deeper ethnic antagonisms had existed here – ones stretching back longer in time – than could be found further north and west in Bosnia and Croatia, the initial conflict flashpoints after 1990.

It was therefore fortunate that the West was prepared to take Balkan issues more seriously just as conflicts erupted, first in Kosovo in 1998, and later in Macedonia which in some ways, were more complicated than the ones encountered further north in the early 1990s by Western multilateral agencies and states. A period of drift, characterised by a tendency to appease ethnic hardliners because they appeared to represent mainstream popular opinion, gave way to a less cynical and more optimistic outlook about what could be done in the Balkans. Kosovo was the catalyst. In 1999 there was sufficient transatlantic resolve to prevent Milošević completing a strategy of 'ethnic cleansing' (acquiring control of territory through the removal of much of the population) more audacious even than the ones perpetrated in Croatia and Bosnia. A new team in the European Commission that year, showed impressive common ground about the need to prioritise the Balkans and gave the countries and territories of the region the chance to eventually find a place in the European Union as full members. It was hoped that belonging to an entity of twenty-five states by 2004 whose own internal borders counted for less and less would be a catalyst for the relegation of border disputes in South-East Europe and the normalisation of inter-ethnic relations.

The removal of Milošević in 2000 and the need to support a fragile successor regime in Serbia with a tenuous pro-Western agenda, followed by the 2001 crisis in Macedonia, kept the attention of the European Union focussed on the region. Aid programmes were geared towards reconstruction of war-affected states and the rebuilding of infrastructure and the transformation of institutions. As the United States withdrew to the sidelines, the European Union increasingly presides over a fragile peace process first in Bosnia and now in Kosovo. Both territories have remained deeply fractured polities despite being the object of expensive and complicated experiments in state-building directed from the outside. Concentrated assistance has not provided a strong momentum behind economic recovery or the emergence of states with the capacity to effectively tackle major structural problems. The approach of the European Union has all too often been poorly co-ordinated and over-bureaucratised. The reliance on neo-liberal strategies encapsulated by rapid privatisation all too often gives additional leverage to predatory elements who have acquired wealth by their involvement in war or by looting the publicly owned economy. Corruption and organised crime are increasingly recognised as scourges that threaten not just the well-being of South-East Europe but also the security of its neighbours to the west, yet the broader economic strategy promoted by the European Union, the World Bank and IMF has failed to effectively confront these twin menaces. Only Croatia appeared to be well advanced in the European Union integration process by 2004. A range of internal problems prevented Albania, Macedonia and Serbia–Montenegro from making a significant headway. Under international supervision, Bosnia and Kosovo remained aid-dependent territories whose political futures remained unclear (particularly in the latter case). Bulgaria and Romania were poised to join the European Union as full members by around 2007. But particularly in the case of Romania, the enlargement process has not been handled well. It approaches the European Union as a weak and under-performing state with worrying authoritarian tendencies which has not made the best use of pre-accession funds from Brussels. Bulgaria has made more effective progress and could be a model for its western neighbour Macedonia, whose ethnic tensions are likely to be an increasing headache for the European Union which thought it had contained them by the Ohrid Agreement of 2001 imposed on the rival ethnic Macedonian and Albanian camps.

By 2004, the European Union was more closely intertwined with the Balkans than it could have imagined it would be in 1994. But it is still unfamiliar with dealing with weak states, whether ones that have remained at peace, or those parts of ex-Yugoslavia caught up in warfare of differing degrees of intensity. It remains unclear whether the instruments it employs to integrate the post-communist Balkans with the rest of the European Union will actually accomplish that goal or instead, widen the developmental gap between them. Its own willingness to stay engaged remains in question and the return of simplistic solutions such as wholesale border changes or exchange of populations cannot be ruled out.

Chapter 1 examines the role of Greece, the only Balkan state to escape communist rule and a member of the European Union since 1981. It shows how a series of nationalist complexes shared by much of the public and sections of the political elite got it entangled in the disputes of the region. It began the 1990s as the only European country that could be described as an ally of the Milošević regime but, by its close, had emerged as a genuine force for stability in South-East Europe and an enthusiastic advocate of the European Union's more engaged stance towards the region.

Chapter 2 traces the escalation of the dispute between Belgrade authorities and the ethnic Albanian majorities in Kosovo, which was an autonomous province of Serbia, the largest of the republics in communist Yugoslavia. It dwells on the period when Milošević took charge from the late 1980s, showing how repressive policies gave rise to a campaign of passive resistance by the Albanians. Most of the chapter focuses on the response of the international community; its changing approach to the Kosovo question mirrored that towards the Balkans as a whole in the 1990s and beyond. It moved from a position whereby it tacitly recognised Milošević's claim to Kosovo, to one where it insisted on a restoration of local autonomy and an end to state repression as internal violence escalated from 1997 onwards. The scale of the Kosovo crisis prompted Euro-Atlantic institutions to confront Milošević directly over it and be prepared to supervise a peace process with NATO troops and UN international officials.

But as the West switched from diplomacy to contemplating force, mistakes, rivalries and faulty assumptions which had already undermined its role in the Balkans, weakened its effectiveness even as the resolve of Western leaders to finally confront Milošević hardened. Chapter 3 examines the first major armed conflict seen in Europe for over fifty years, fought by NATO and Milošević over Kosovo in the spring of 1999. It shows how both sides greatly misread each other's mood, intentions and tactics. The Atlantic Alliance was unprepared and failed to use its military preponderance to good effect, but Milošević's blunders were of a higher order, particularly the deportation of most Albanians from Kosovo. This strengthened NATO resolve and had a decisive effect on Western public opinion, Milošević suing for peace in the face of a looming ground invasion.

Chapter 4 shows how Milošević's legacy lived on in Serbia following his overthrow in September 2000. A large criminal sector that had emerged from the bloated Serbian security apparatus and the subterranean economy in many ways remained the chief power in the land. A veritable Serbian mafia had benefited from sanctions, the effective collapse of the rule of law, smuggling and the looting of the state. Weak and divided reformers were not in a position to dismantle this shadow power structure. The advice given from the West was often uninspired. A speedy resolution of the Kosovo issue was shelved in favour of enforcing a union of Serbia and Montenegro despite the relative shortage of adherents in both countries. Following the assassination of the main Serbian reformer, Zorin Djindić in 2003, the country appeared polarised between re-emboldened nationalist forces and fragmented reformers. Fresh thinking about how to breathe life into a flagging reform process was far from evident either at home or in the capitals of the European Union as Serbia appeared likely to be a force for instability in parts of the region despite the extradition of Milošević to face war crimes charges in The Hague.

Chapter 5 examines the conflict that quickly erupted in Macedonia, in 2001, following the removal of Milošević. The West had shut its ears to warning rumbles from Macedonia for several years and had assumed that the awkwardly positioned country was somehow robust enough to absorb shock waves from conflicts elsewhere. But there were deep-seated differences about how power should be distributed between the two principal ethnic groups, Macedonians and Albanians. The conflict did not solely arise from manipulation by unscrupulous political figures or criminal groups. Thankfully, the main transnational agencies involved in South-East Europe quickly mobilised to try to broker a peaceful resolution to the crisis. The European Union and NATO got directly involved early and managed to cooperate effectively. This was in sharp contrast to the early 1990s in Bosnia. From late 2001 onwards and in the face of acute majority misgivings, the European Union promoted the adoption of measures that would award the large ethnic Albanian minority and other significant minorities a much greater role in decision-making.

Chapter 6 examines the flawed peace that allowed all but a few of the architects of ethnic cleansing in Bosnia to retain the levers of power and indeed expand their influence. Belatedly, the powers of the central state were greatly augmented and from 1999, there was a concerted drive to spearhead the return of refugees to their home areas. Strong pressure was imposed on Serbian and Croatian separatists to cease undermining the building of a common Bosnian state. But a decade of externally led state-building only confirmed the extent to which Bosnia was a deeply fractured polity.

Both Chapter 6 and 7, looking at Bosnia and Kosovo, examine the shortcomings and complexities of multi-layered international peace-building initiatives, the most ambitious the post-1945 world had seen up until that date. In Kosovo, lessons had been learned from the Bosnian experience but international organisations and participating major states were slow to discard their clashing agendas and management styles. Nearly always, the calibre of the international staff proved as variable as in Bosnia and the turnover was just as rapid. Chapter 7 shows how international shortcomings in Kosovo jeopardised vital peace-building tasks in a territory where ethnic animosity was probably deeper than anywhere else in the Balkans and the economic problems defied easy solution.

Chapter 8 examines the integration efforts of the European Union in the Balkans which, by 2000 had become the testing-ground for its ambitious Common Foreign and Security Policy. It evaluates its deepening engagement with Bulgaria and Romania and asks whether its strategy of offering the similar possibility of full membership to Western Balkan countries over a longer time-scale enjoys much prospect of success. Particular attention is paid to the way the European Union approaches administrative reform and a relaunch of the Balkan economies along market lines. The danger that most of the countries concerned will fall further behind Western Europe through adopting a low-grade strategy crafted in Brussels, important parts of which may be unsuited to their needs, is fully explored; as is NATO's shifting priorities in the region, downscaling its role in the Western Balkans but offering full membership to Romania and Bulgaria in 2004.

A concluding chapter examines the political landscape of the Balkans in the new century. It shows how it has been easier for post-communist forces to stage a comeback than for self-styled reformers to consolidate their position. Many of the political figures who have come to prominence in the Balkans since 1989 have mobilised the traditional, dependent sectors of the population who have low expectations and a pre-disposition for authoritarian solutions. By contrast, younger, modernising groups living in the cities have largely opted out of politics. In some places, this has left the field open to organised crime which has flourished in the shadow of war, economic sanctions and the debilitating long-term effects of the communist system. It was probably in post-2001 Macedonia that the struggle for supremacy between those who preferred a weak state unable to promote national recovery and other forces committed to a state able to gradually bring to heal criminal structures, was at its most intense. The chapter argues that economic recovery will be the essential requirement if inter-ethnic relations are to be normalised in trouble spots old and new, and a form of politics intimately bound-up with protecting human security is to get off the ground in the rest of the region.

Most attention in this volume is given to the states and territories where crises, peace-building efforts and attempts at integration to Euro-Atlantic structures have preoccupied the international community from 1998 onwards. Since 2000, I have visited all the states and territories in the region and I am grateful for the assistance, advice, hospitality and friendship received from many quarters during these trips. I would also like to thank Balkan Academic News, the Bosnian Institute, the Centre for European Policy Studies, the European Stability Institute, the Greek Helsinki Committee, the Institute for War and Peace Reporting, the International Crisis Group, Radio Free Europe/Radio Liberty and Transitions Online for placing a lot of material in the public domain that provided much raw material for this book. Let me finally thank (as I have done in the previous volumes) the librarians, immediate colleagues, fellow Balkanologists, conference hosts, proponents of peaceful and democratic change in the Balkans and friends whose information, advice and assistance with locating materials helped this project to acquire momentum.

Acronyms

AI	Amnesty International
AKEL	Progressive Party of the Working People of Cyprus
AKsh	Albanian National Army
ASAM	Academy of Sciences and Arts in Macedonia
BBC	British Broadcasting Corporation
BSP	Bulgarian Socialist Party
CARDS	Community Assistance for Reconstruction, Development and Stabilisation
CEPS	Centre of European Policy Studies
CIA	Central Intelligence Agency
CSCE	Conference for Security and Cooperation in Europe
DM	Deutschmark
DOS	Democratic Opposition of Serbia
DPA	Dayton Peace Agreement
DPNE	Democratic Party for Macedonian National Unity
DS	Democratic Party
DSS	Democratic Party of Serbia
DUI	Democratic Union for Integration
EC	European Community
EIU	Economist Intelligence Unit
ESDP	European Security and Defence Policy
ESI	European Stability Institute
EU	European Union
EYP	Greek Intelligence Service
FHP	Humanitarian Law Foundation
FRY	Federal Republic of Yugoslavia
FSN	National Salvation Front
FYROM	Former Yugoslav Republic of Macedonia
GDP	Gross Domestic Product
HCNM	High Commission for National Minorities
HDZ	Croatian Democratic Union
HRW	Human Rights Watch
IC	International Community

ICC	International Criminal Court
ICFY	International Conference on the Former Yugoslavia
ICG	International Crisis Group
ICRC	International Committee of the Red Cross
ICTY	International Criminal Tribunal for Yugoslavia
IHF	International Helsinki Federation
IMF	International Monetary Fund
IPTF	International Police Task Force
IWPR	Institute for War and Peace Reporting
JNA	Yugoslav Federal Army
JSO	The Unit for Special Operations
JUL	United Yugoslav Left
KFOR	Kosovo Force
KGB	Russian Secret Service
KPC	Kosovo Protection Corps
KPS	Kosovo Police Service
KTA	Kosovo Trust Agency
KVM	Kosovo Verification Mission
LDK	Democratic League of Kosovo
MEP	Member of the European Parliament
MILS	Macedonian Information and Liaison Service
MPC	Macedonian Orthodox Church
MUP	Ministry of the Interior
NATO	North Atlantic Treaty Organisation
ND	New Democracy
NGO	Non-Governmental Organisation
NLA	National Liberation Army
OECD	Organisation for Economic Co-operation and Development
OHR	Office of High Representative
OLAF	European Office for Combatting Fraud
OSCE	Organization for Security and Co-operation in Europe
PASOK	Panhellenic Socialist Movement
PDK	Kosovo Democratic Party
PDP	Party of Democratic Prosperity
PDsh	Democratic Party of Albanians
PfP	Partnership for Peace
PIC	Peace Implementation Council
PISG	Provisional Institutions of Self-Governance
PLIP	Property Law Implementation Plan
PNTCD	National Peasant and Christian Democratic Party
PRM	Greater Romania Party
PSD	Social Democratic Party
RFE/RL	Radio Free Europe/Radio Liberty
RS	Republika Srpska (Republic of Srpska)

SAA	Stabilisation and Association Agreement
SACEUR	Supreme Allied Commander in Europe
SAP	Stabilisation and Association Process
SBiH	Party of Bosnia–Herzegovina
SDA	Party of Democratic Action
SDP	Social Democratic Party
SDS	Serbian Democratic Party
SDSM	Social Democratic Alliance of Macedonia
SFOR	Stabilisation Force
SNM	Simeon II National Movement
SNSD	Alliance of Independent Social Democrats
SP	Stability Pact
SPO	Serbian Renewal Movement
SPS	Serbian Socialist Party
SRS	Serbian Radical Party
SRSG	Special Representative of the Secretary-General
UÇK	Kosovo Liberation Army
UDF	Union of Democratic Forces
UDMR	Democratic Union of the Hungarians of Romania
UN	United Nations
UNDP	United Nations Development Programme
UNHCR	United Nations High Commission for Refugees
UNMIK	United Nations Interim Administrative Mission in Kosovo
UNPREDEP	United Nations Preventative Deployment Force
UNSC	United Nations Security Council
VJ	Yugoslav Army
VMRO	Internal Macedonian Revolutionary Organization
VRS	Army of the Republic of Srpska

Map 1 Yugoslavia before 1991.

Map 2 Yugoslavia after the break-up.

Geographic names mentioned

Albanian	Serbian
Kosova	Kosova
Decan	Decani
Gjilan	Gnjilane
Mitrovica	Mitrovica
Peja	Pec
Prislitina	Priština
Prizreni	Prizren

Map 3 KFOR peacekeeping sectors in Kosovo from 1999.

Map 4 Republic of Macedonia.

1   Greece

A peace-making role lost
and re-found

In Greece, nationalist energies were channelled away from the Balkans and towards the island of Cyprus, especially during the 1967–74 dictatorship of the Greek Colonels. The year 1981 marked the start of a long political ascendancy of the Panhellenic Socialist Movement (PASOK). It would be in charge of the government except for the years 1989–93 until 2004. Andreas Papandreou, its leader, came to represent the political attitudes of Greece for much of the rest of the world during the fifteen years he held the limelight after 1981. He wished to bury the civil war legacy of the 1940s when the communist-dominated Left was suspected of wishing to place the Greek part of Macedonia in a large communist Slavic state. Papandreou felt that his leftist party with its neutralist Third World orientation would need to strengthen its nationalist credentials (Kofos 1999: 233). This chapter explores the effect of this approach on Greece's relations with its northern neighbours during the fifteen years in which conflict in the former Yugoslavia superseded the Cold War.

In Bulgaria and Romania, ruling Leftists of the Marxist–Leninist persuasion had already been trailblazers in this regard. Like Papandreou, they had a credibility problem because of their failure to make good on their economic promises to their citizens. They provided extravagant doses of 'national communism' in an effort to shore up their popular legitimacy. PASOK's first extended period in office from 1981 to 1988 enabled this 'patriotic' strategy to enjoy important popular success. Turkey was usually the focus of PASOK's 'patriotic' orientation but Papandreou continued to bar the 67,000 refugee Slavs from Greece – who settled mainly in Yugoslavia after the civil war – from returning even for visits unless they signed a document declaring themselves as 'Greeks of Greek origin' (Reuter 1999: 31).

Even before the Yugoslav crisis, alarm was being expressed in sections of the Greek press and the intelligentsia, and by some political figures, about a cultural offensive emanating from Skopje, designed to place in question Greece's entitlement to the Aegean part of Macedonia, which had been under its control since 1913. Intellectuals used Radio Skopje to argue that the concept of 'Macedonianism' extended beyond the southernmost Republic of Yugoslavia. The government in Athens responded by stepping up assistance to archaeologists and by promoting international exhibitions in order to reassert the links of 'Macedonia with Hellenism over three millennia' (Kofos 1989: 257).

The European Union (EU) proved to be an ineffective restraining force over Greece as well-placed individuals and groups started to argue that cultural pretensions in Skopje were becoming a mask for full-blown irredentism. The crisis in Yugoslavia and the collapse of internal borders in 1991–2 raised the possibility that Greece's own borders with the crumbling South Slav state might be called into question. Brussels arguably hadn't thought through the implications of inviting Greece, with its strongly nationalist political culture and difficulties with neighbouring states, to be part of its post-nationalist project. Admittedly, Greece had to fulfil a range of economic, financial and administrative conditions to secure membership. But apparently it was not pressed by its sponsors to promise to behave with realism and restraint over sensitive identity questions.

Perhaps Greece's main west European champion was Valery Giscard d'Estaing, president of France from 1974 to 1981. He saw modern Greece as the inheritor of the ancient civilisations that shaped the humanistic cultures of modern Europe. In 2002, it emerged that he shared some of the Islamophobia of sections of the Greek political elite and public when he said that the adherence of the majority of Turks to Islam disqualified the country from joining the European Union.[1]

Post-Cold War trauma

The Yugoslav crisis first manifested itself in Kosovo where the Serbian regime of Slobodan Milošević cracked down severely on the Albanian population there. He was perhaps inspired by events in Bulgaria where the large Turkish minority was suffering state persecution without undue concern in the rest of Europe. Fear of Serbia's wish for domination prompted Macedonia to pull out of the disintegrating federation in 1991. Despite Slavic-Albanian tensions, Macedonia avoided internal unrest. It was fortunate to have as its founding President a moderate and tactically astute former communist Kiro Gligorov. He was assisted by the fact that Milošević was focusing his attention on expanding Serbian power in the western Balkans.

Towards the rest of the neighbourhood, Bulgaria also behaved in a low-key manner after the removal of Todor Zhivkov in 1989. It failed to revive the territorial claims which had led it to back the wrong side in both world wars. It was the first country to recognise Macedonian statehood. As for Albania, it was too preoccupied with a daunting range of internal problems to look much beyond its borders until the late 1990s (Kola 2003: 383–95).

Instead, it was Greece that reacted with undisguised hostility to the emergence of a Macedonian state on 17 November 1991 (with the promulgation of a new constitution). Nerves had been stretched by the trial-of-strength with Turkey. Following the upheavals in the hitherto frozen communist bloc to its north, it feared a replay of past events. The Internal Macedonian Revolutionary Organization (VMRO) quickly emerged as a major contender for power in Macedonia. It claimed to have descended from the pre-1939 party of the same name, which had often resorted to terrorism in a bid to create an independent Macedonia. As well as expressing anti-Turkish and anti-Albanian sentiments, VMRO reiterated the desire to reincorporate the 'lost' parts of 'the nation' located in Bulgaria and Greece and announced that it wished to hold its second conference in Thessaloniki (Schwartz 2000: 387). The party's young leader, Ljubčo Georgievski even managed to become the first vice-president of the newly independent state. There was an electrifying reaction in Greece to this perceived threat to its northern frontiers which didn't die down after VMRO failed to enjoy any lasting breakthrough. Irredentist dreams were not just harboured by romantic nationalists. Cvitejo Job, a well-connected diplomat from pre-1991 Yugoslavia, recalling the communist leadership in Skopje, has written:

> Not one Macedonian leader out of many whom I personally knew, would even in private admit that 'all Macedonians in one state' is a dangerous pipe dream. Some of these leaders were otherwise very sophisticated, with impressive experience in international relations. But no, they would insist, we must not declare Yugoslav borders as definitely settled, as final. Why should we deprive, they would carry on, future generations the chance of 'amicably reaching progressive solutions'.
>
> (Job 2002: 118)

What can be described as Aegean Macedonia was only acquired by Greece in 1913. Constantin Karamanlis (1907–98), President of Greece from 1990 to 1995, had actually been born a subject of the Ottoman Empire. The Greek Civil War of the late 1940s showed how many Slavic Macedonians were receptive to calls emanating from their co-ethnics in southern Yugoslavia to establish a free Macedonia (Koliopoulos and Veremis 2002: 75). By 1949, the last year of the civil war, Greek Macedonians made up more than 50 per cent of the communist army (Koliopoulos and Veremis 2002: 89). In 1948, the rebels had carried away 28,000 children aged between 2 and 14 and taken them to communist countries. To official Greece this was mass kidnapping, but to an émigré group such as the Macedonian Human Rights Movement of Canada, it was a bid to save them from hunger in which the help of the Red Cross was enlisted.[2] Some reached Austria, Canada, the United States and Australia thanks to Western philanthropic efforts. In adult life not a few enlisted in irredentist movements associated with the VMRO line. In Greece it was widely assumed that such movements were being directed from Skopje in Yugoslav Macedonia in order to destabilise Greece (Koliopoulos and Veremis 2002: 95). For this reason they were exempt from the general amnesty which became law in 1982. It allowed for the repatriation of all political refugees of Greek nationality, a restoration of their human rights and a reinstatement of their property. But those child exiles, who in adult life declared themselves Greek citizens of Macedonian ethnicity, were exempt from the amnesty and could not re-enter Greece until 2003.

The domestic political context also helps to explain this defensive approach by the Athens state to a painful civil war legacy. The eruption of a regional security challenge to the north coincided with a period of political instability at home.

Greek democracy was *not* under threat as in the 1960s, but the political scene was overshadowed by a bitter struggle for supremacy between two fierce rivals: PASOK and New Democracy (ND). PASOK had been forced to relinquish power in 1988 owing to the economic profligacy of Andreas Papandreou who had reneged on promises of economic distribution but had boosted the incomes of the lower-paid by undertaking costly loans.

Greece has been described as '[A] triangle upside down with its peak in the sea and a vulnerable base touching upon four neighbours' (Svolopoulos 1999: 24). This vivid description underlines the vulnerability that its geographical position appeared to bestow. Its advantages vis-à-vis its northern neighbours might have elicited a lower-key response. It was the only Balkan state fully integrated into the Euro-Atlantic economic and security community. There was a developed market economy with Greece having a per capita income of $10,981 (1995) compared with Bulgaria's $1,476 (Ioakimidis 1999: 171). Greece enjoyed military superiority over all its northern neighbours; in the 1990s its annual defence spending exceeded the Gross Domestic Product (GDP) of Albania and Macedonia (Constas and Papasotiriou 1999: 217). It had a record in promoting regional multilaterism which gave it the chance to exercise a leadership role over its post-communist neighbours (Veremis 1999: 34).

All these factors gave it enviable immunity from shock waves further north. But instead worst-case scenarios were stressed, in no small measure due to the domestic political context. Neither of the two electoral titans, PASOK and ND was able to offer economic inducements to voters after the unwise spending sprees of the 1980s. Nationalism was seen as a handy device to prolong their credibility and gain advantage over the other. It was not difficult to mobilise voters on nationalist grounds, given their strength in Greek political culture.

The country had witnessed a long struggle against foreign domination and had been badly affected by both world wars. Threats to Greek sovereignty were seen in the 1970s and 1980s not as emanating from the Warsaw Pact but from the United States. Deep-seated anti-Western and anti-American sentiments existed on both the Right and Left of politics. They were increasingly promoted by the Orthodox Church which enjoyed a pre-eminent place in political life. Since the nineteenth century it had been encouraged to promote the secular values of Greek nationalism. The ministries of religion and education had overseen the official Church (Pollis 1994: 12). Sometimes the state intervened quite blatantly in the Church's affairs as during the Colonels regime. But Greek Orthodoxy recovered from its entanglement with that dictatorship. Indeed its popular influence was growing just as that of national churches elsewhere was declining in the face of post-modern secularism. This influence sometimes appeared to supersede that of the political elite burdened by domestic policy failures.

The constitution of 1975 recognises the Orthodox Church as the dominant religion in Greece. Its prior approval is required for building or repairing a non-Orthodox Church or mosque. The teaching of a course on the Orthodox religion is compulsory at all levels of education.[3] Until 2002, the inclusion of religion in identity documents was normal and an EU regulation requiring its abandonment was complied with only after a fierce struggle led by Archbishop Christodoulos, head of the Church. He mobilised those Greeks fearing change most:

> those who have been worst hit by the demands of a global economy and government cutbacks in the bloated state sector; and those who see the Church as the embodiment of Greece's defensive national identity. A televangelist *par excellence*, he has drawn his support from a heady mix of the marginalized petit-bourgeoisie, unskilled workers, disgruntled civil servants and small-time self-employed people... To many of the archbishop's supporters, the Church is the only bulwark left against the threat of a multicultural, open society, symbolised for them by yuppies who work for multinationals, drive jeeps and wield mobiles like firearms.
>
> (Smith 2001: 141)

Under Christodoulos, the Church could appear less concerned with saving souls than in preparing the ground for the further homogenisation of the Greek nation (Michas 2002: 143). The sizeable population of Catholics, Protestants, Jews, Muslims and Jehovah's Witnesses, comprising 10 per cent of the population, have often not fared well in a climate where Greekness is commensurate with Orthodoxy (Pollis 1994: 12). Until 1997, Greece was the only EU state that did not offer civilian service as an alternative to military service.[4]

In the early 1990s, the Greek Intelligence Service (EYP) commissioned a study into dangers posed by various religious groups. It divided Greeks into 'authentic' and 'non-authentic' ones (Michas 2002: 125). It stated that '[I]t would not be too much to say that any Greek who is not Orthodox is not completely Greek. It then went on to call for a purge of "heretics" from the media and to propose that the Orthodox religion should form the basis of Greek foreign policy and that Greece should create an Orthodox Christian axis in the Balkans...'.[5]

Matching the Orthodox Church in vigilance about threats to national security were journalists and academics who 'chose... to sensationalise the "Macedonian question" with an assortment of distorted historical facts and half-truths' (Kofos 1999: 234). A 'bandwagon' of 'nationalist fundamentalism' gathered speed with historians, archaeologists, theologians as well as journalists in the vanguard. Evangelos Kofos, a Balkan regional policy expert who had been writing on the Macedonian question since before the 1990s, argued that they drew up 'a theoretical framework' for the policy and wider public debates on the revived Macedonian question (Kofos 1999: 250).

What were the chief elements of the Macedonian dispute? The most persistent cause of Greek complaint was the name. Taking *Macedonia* as the title of a new state was seen as a misappropriation of Greek cultural heritage by a Slavic people for a contemporary political end, which was to acquire Western Thrace lying immediately to the south of them. Second, there was the question of the flag. It was deep red with a bright yellow sun in the middle from which sixteen points radiated. This is the Vergina Sun, the emblem of the ancient royal dynasty of Macedonia. It decorated the funeral cask of Philip of Macedonia, which archaeologists discovered on a site south-east of Thessaloniki in 1977. Greece argued that by adorning their flag with this symbol, the Slav Macedonians were expropriating ancient Greek history and laying claim to the region of northern Greece also known as Macedonia (or Western Thrace).[6] There was also the understated but very real anxiety about the way that an independent Macedonia might act as a rallying-point for the inhabitants of northern Greece who still clung to a Slavophone outlook. Slav Macedonians couldn't exist 'for the very simple reason that nobody who is not Greek' can properly be said to exist in a Greece where the ethnic Greek identity enjoyed monopoly status.[7] For the view that the spur to minority consciousness in a country that prided itself on its supposed homogeneity was the essence of the problem, reference can be made to the words of the former Greek Prime Minister Constantine Mitsotakis in 1995: 'I saw from the first moment the problem of Skopje in its true dimensions. What concerned me from the very first moment was not the name of the state. The problem for me . . . was that [we should not allow] the creation of a second minority problem in the area of western Macedonia [in Greece]. My main aim was to convince the Republic [of Macedonia] to declare that there is no Slavomacedonian minority in Greece. This was the real key of our difference with Skopje'.[8]

Only with the greatest reluctance had Greece granted minority status to the Turkish population of Eastern Thrace under the 1923 Treaty of Lausanne. There was a widespread fear that the recognition of minorities was the first step in the dismemberment of a country. The idea that multi-ethnic states were, by their very nature, unviable, became the cornerstone of official policy towards the rest of the Balkans at least in the first half of the 1990s.[9] The view that the multi-ethnic state model was a recipe for break up also had much popular resonance. Was it a good thing for societies to be mixed, asked a Eurobarometer poll in a survey carried out in 2001 after passions had died down. The average for the European Union was a 64 per cent vote in favour of heterodoxy, but in Greece the corresponding percentage was much less at 36 per cent (Michas 2002: 122). Eight years earlier, another Eurobarometer poll on European identity found that a mere 21 per cent of Greeks believed that 'tolerance and respect for others' were important qualities to encourage in their children compared to 48.62 per cent in other EU countries.[10]

Greece, the European Union and the Macedonian dispute

The West, its hands full trying to extinguish the flames of the Yugoslav conflict, slowly realised that one of its own members was heavily embroiled in that bitter dispute. The first realisation came at the end of 1991 when Greece objected to the EU recognition of Macedonia because of the name and symbols being adopted. Other EU states soon became aware of the powerful emotions and group interests driving the view that only the modern Greeks 'were entitled to use the Macedonian name either as a cultural-ethnic or a geographic appellation' (Kofos 1999: 235). Greece had one big advantage. The European Union was keen to obtain overwhelming backing for the Maastricht Agreement that marked an important step in the emergence of common institutions. On 2 May 1992, EU foreign ministers declared their readiness to recognise the Former Yugoslav Republic of Macedonia (FYROM) as an independent state 'under a name which could be acceptable to all interested parties' (Kofos 1999: 239). In June at the Copenhagen gathering of the European Union, the other member states edged closer to the Greek position by saying that they would proceed to recognition 'under a name which will not include the denomination Macedonia' (Kofos 1999: 239). Britain's Douglas Hurd duly travelled to Skopje in July to present Kiro Gligorov with a series of alternative names for his country.[11]

Prime Minister Mitsotakis's EU partners were aware that he was relatively moderate on the thorny Macedonia question but that he was under intense pressure at home, including from members of his own ND party. His foreign minister Antonis Samaras had adopted a hardline over the dispute. In April 1992, he was dismissed by Mitsotakis who took over his portfolio. But he also felt himself obliged to adopt Samaras's maximalist stance in light of his own precarious position: the ND had a tiny majority and there was restlessness among senior colleagues (Kofos 1999: 242). Above all, he could not ignore popular feeling: on 14 February 1992, nearly one million people had demonstrated in Thessaloniki against recognition of the former Yugoslav republic on its terms (Veremis 1999: 35).

EU forbearance towards Greece on this issue began to wane when it emerged that Greece had become a stalwart ally of the Milošević regime in Belgrade, responsible for the bulk of violence in much of Yugoslavia from 1991 onwards. From the end of 1991 onwards, there was accumulating evidence that Greece was ignoring the sanctions that the European Union had imposed on the Belgrade regime. Uffe Ellemann-Jensen, the Danish foreign minister and president of the European Council of Ministers pointed the finger at Greece in this regard on 13 January 1993.[12] But far more offensive to Greek sensibilities were the sharp words he uttered about its stance over Macedonia. He stated that 'It is ridiculous to believe that this small, poor, landlocked country [Macedonia] is any kind of threat'. He believed that it had 'lived up to all the requirements of international law' and expressed the hope that 'the Security Council will very quickly recognise Macedonia and that many of the member states of the Community will support this…'.[13] Apoplectic Greek members of the European Parliament where Ellemann-Jensen had been speaking on 20 January 1993 berated him, one government party member shouting, 'You cannot disguise your hatred for Greece. You are an ethical and moral disgrace to the presidency of the European Community'.[14]

There was also European Community (EC) irritation regarding Greece's then stern attitude to Albania. In June 1993, a Greek Orthodox priest had been expelled from southern Albania where he was accused of inciting the Greek minority there to opt for unification with Greece. In the following month, Athens expelled tens of thousands of illegal Albanian immigrants from Greece; hitherto, they had been tolerated because of their contribution to productivity through being prepared to work for very low wages in the agricultural, construction and tourist industries.[15] Even more inflammatory was the demand of Prime Minister Mitsotakis that Greeks who left Albania in 1944 should have their property restored to them. Mitsotakis referred to the area of Albania where the ethnic Greeks lived as 'Northern Epirus', the name often used by Greek nationalists who felt that it rightly belonged to Greece.[16] Greeks had certainly suffered at the end of the Second World War but so had the Albanian-speaking Chams of western Epirus that came under Greek jurisdiction in 1913. The Christian part of the population would identify with the Greek state, but approximately 20,000 Muslim Chams were forcibly driven across the border to Albania for having allegedly collaborated with the Axis occupiers (Baltsiotis and Embiricos 2001: 147).

Relations with the United States also grew sour over Greece's Balkan preoccupation. Clinton, the 1992 presidential election victor, had been cautious in his remarks about the Macedonian question out of a need not to antagonise the powerful Greek political lobby.[17] Clinton's caution brought forth criticism from US analysts who feared that Greek economic pressure would polarise the feelings in Macedonia.[18] But in April 1993, the United States used its UN Security Council vote to support the admission of Macedonia into the United Nations under the provisional name of the FYROM.

Deep-seated anti-Western and particularly anti-American feelings burst to the surface on both the Left and Right of Greek politics in the face of such perceived insensitivity from Greece's nominal allies. A race ensued between ND and PASOK to mount and ride this nationalist tiger. ND suffered a grievous setback with the defection of Antonis Samaras who, set up an overtly nationalist party, Greek Spring, in June 1993. Hailing from a prominent family in the Greek community in the Egyptian city of Alexandria, embracing nationalism was a useful way for Antonis Samaras to emphasise his Greekness. Kofos has written: 'As a zealot, sensing the approval of the masses at his back, he entered forcefully into the quagmire of Balkan politics' (Kofos 1999: 251).

Greek Spring got its political opportunity when new elections were called in the autumn of 1993 following the collapse of the government. But it was PASOK which was the chief beneficiary of the climate of heightened nationalism and insecurity. The 72-year-old Andreas Papandreou was once again prime minister. He had skilfully massaged nationalist neuroses after spending most of his adult life in the United States where he had pursued a successful career as an economist. He appointed as his deputy foreign minister, Theodoros Pangalos who broke a basic EU rule that officials never insult a partner country, when he described Germany as 'a giant with the strength of a beast and the mind of a spoilt child'.[19] In November 1993, the month this remark was made, Panayotis Dimitras, then a rare critic of the hyper-nationalism evident in Greek public life, described Pangalos as 'a typical example of Greece's former cosmopolitan intellectual elite, becoming steadily more anti-Western'.[20]

A year before his return to office, Papandreou had declared in November 1992 that 'we are faced with the loss of all our foreign policy supports in the region'.[21] Fears built up in Athens of an 'Islamic arc' emerging on its eastern and northern borders as Turkey 'embarked on a systematic process of concluding various agreements with Bulgaria, FYROM, and Albania...' (Triantafyllou 1999: 145). Official insecurity was reflected in responses to minority agitation and even academic scholarship which challenged the state position on ethnic identity. The anthropologist, Dr Anastasia Karakasidou (a Greek national) was reviled in the Greek media and condemned by Greek politicians and diplomats because of her work showing that the Greek provinces of Macedonia, Epirus and Thrace had always been ethnologically complex even in ancient times (Karakasidou 1997). This was perceived as propaganda on behalf of Greece's enemies and the British intelligence service MI6 warned her publisher Cambridge University Press of a risk to British interests in Greece if the book was issued.[22] Cambridge terminated the contract, an internal document expressing concern about the risk of 'terrorist violence'. This prompted the resignation of the Press's editorial board for anthropology, one member arguing that the 'restriction of academic freedom' would 'encourage irresponsible individuals to threaten the safety of scholars'.[23]

A number of trials for crimes of opinion during 1993–4, including those of opponents of government policy on Macedonia and a leader of the Turkish minority, got unfavourable international publicity. In one case, a youth aged 18 was jailed for five years for distributing a leaflet on Macedonia including the words: 'Do not be consumed by nationalism. Alexander the Great war criminal. Macedonia belongs to its people'.[24] Hristos Sideropoulos, a 45-year-old forester, was put on trial in 1994 for making what was considered to be an inflammatory public statement in Copenhagen at a fringe meeting of the Conference for Security and Cooperation in Europe (CSCE) conference seeking to establish common standards for the treatment of minorities. According to the public prosecutor, Ilias Costaras, he violated the criminal code for saying that 'he is a Macedonian and lives in Greek Macedonia, but does not have the right to express that or to use his language, to cherish his customs and traditions of his ancestors'.[25] Mitsotakis, when still Prime Minister, had declared that 'we are the only Balkan country not to have minorities'.[26] As late as 1998, the leader of the Slavophone Macedonian Rainbow Party was facing criminal charges because he had hung a Slavic text outside the party's office.[27] Theodoros Pangalos, by now foreign minister, condemned Rainbow as 'a coalition of Slavomacedonians, Stalinists and homosexuals that got 1,700 votes in the last elections'.[28] He and church figures used the pejorative term of 'Greekling' for those who took up minority concerns. Government pressure and the nationalist climate of society meant that human rights NGOs in Greece were unable to close ranks and work together to safeguard minority rights. This led Panayote Dimitras of the Greek Helsinki Monitor to conclude that 'most human rights defenders…have yet to come to terms with the fact that Greece is not a homogeneous society; that one can be a Greek citizen but have a non-Greek ethnonational identity…'.[29]

Greece and Serbia

Given the hyper-nationalism influencing Greek politics during the first half of the 1990s, it is not surprising that influential political players, as well as much of public opinion, responded positively to Milošević's drive to assert Serbian primacy in what had been Yugoslavia. Neither state had a common frontier, so their interests did not clash, but they had adversaries in common. Opinion in both states was encouraged to view Western states and the organisations associated with them as being viscerally hostile to Greek and Serbian interests. A history of struggle against foreign domination loomed large in the folk culture of both countries. Both had also witnessed state-led cycles of ethnic purification, though nothing in Greece would compare with what was to unfold in Bosnia–Herzegovina from 1992 to 1995 (Pollis 1994: 12). In both states, there was barely concealed official disdain for minorities (though in Serbia at least they were recognised).

Accordingly, Greece and Serbia shared a remarkably similar outlook about how the southern part of the Balkans should evolve politically. A political scientist attached to the University of Athens, P.C. Ioakimidis, has referred to '[T]he *almost* unqualified support Greece gave to Serbia and Slobodan Milošević at the early stages of the Yugoslav crisis' (Ioakimidis 1999: 172). Greece wished Serbia to retain control of Macedonia and Kosovo. It was felt this would reduce the likelihood of irredentist moves from Albania or from Slavophone elements in Macedonia or Bulgaria. Policy-makers also feared that the relinquishment by Belgrade of influence in the southern parts of former Yugoslavia would pro-vide an opportunity for Turkey to re-establish its influence there, raising fears of possible encirclement.

Mitsotakis and Papandreou, with decades of rivalry behind them, nevertheless shared remarkably similar views about Serbia. Mitsotakis declared in 1992 that Milošević 'is very competent...If [his government] were to be destabilised I am not sure this would be good for the peace of the region'.[30] Later, in 1993, he told relatives that when he met the Bosnian Serb leaders, Karadžić and Mladić, both dressed in battledress, they reminded him of the heroes of the Greek war of independence (Michas 2002: 37).

One of Papandreou's advisers, Aris Mousionis, reckons that he saw 'the Serbs as the bearers of the international struggle against the New World Order and the plans of the imperialists' (Michas 2002: 38). In 1994 he lauded Milošević, saying: 'There is hardly a sphere in which our views differ'.[31] A contrast can be drawn with Papandreou's attitude to Spain's moderate socialist Prime Minister, Felipe Gonzalez. He berated him for adopting 'neo-liberalism' and unlike him, showed no desire to speak up for the Serbian opposition in 1996 in the face of overwhelming evidence that Milošević had robbed it of electoral victory through systematic fraud.[32]

Despite Papandreou's uninhibited rhetoric, it was under Mitsotakis that plans were synchronised with Belgrade for a joint pincer-action against the Skopje-ruled state that lay between their borders. It was seen as both an unviable entity and a danger to Greece's national security. Takis Michas has written (with Macedonia in mind): 'Outward intervention in a non-viable state resembled more a case of assisted suicide than outright murder' (Michas 2002: 45).

On 4 September 1991, a meeting was held in Belgrade between Milošević and the then Greek Foreign Minister Samaras. The Serbian leader proposed flooding Macedonia with Serbs from other parts of Yugoslavia and then proclaiming common borders with Greece. No negative reaction ensued from Samaras even though what was proposed amounted to a serious breach of international legality (Michas 2002: 48–50). The Democratic Serbian Party (of Macedonia) did try to create a 'Karadag Republic' where Macedonia's Serbian minority was concentrated but it failed to win sufficient support (Michas 2002: 51). But in early 1992 the Greek foreign ministry adopted a plan that would involve Greece and Serbia in a common effort to destabilise Macedonia. It was known as 'Samaras's Pincer' and involved (a) economic pressure to provoke unrest and (b) military pressure: the Yugoslav army's 3rd division was still in Macedonia (Michas 2002: 52). In May 1991, a Greek intelligence report announcing the presence in Macedonia of a repressed Greek minority, 239, 360 strong, had been leaked. On 2 November 1991, the deputy foreign minister had claimed that there were '150,000 Vlachs of pure Greek consciousness' living in Macedonia. On the same day, the Serbian vice-president declared there were 300,000 Serbs in Macedonia (six times the normally accepted figure). If true, both minorities would make up nearly half the population (Michas 2002: 54). But the arrival in June 1993 of a UN force to prevent conflict on the Macedonian–Serbian border, UN Preventative Deployment Force (UNPREDEP), consisting of 300 US troops, effectively foiled the efforts of sections of the political establishment in Greece and Serbia to carve-up Macedonia between them.

Nevertheless, 'common borders with Serbia' was a customary cry at mass rallies all over Greece that were held between 1991 and 1994 in the shadow of the Yugoslavia conflict (Michas 2002: 48). Greece succeeded in consistently backing the most hardline elements in the Serbian conflict, especially in the breakaway Republic of Srpska (RS), in Bosnia.[33] In July 1993, Karadžić, while on a visit to Greece organised by the Orthodox Church, was guest-of-honour at a rally in Piraeus attended by politicians from all parties as well as prominent trade-unionists.[34] He was later hailed by the Church as 'one of the most prominent sons of Our Lord Jesus Christ working for peace' (Clark 2000b: 123). A Greek Volunteer Guard aided Bosnian Serb hardliners in their war to capture Bosnia. The rationale provided by one of them was that: 'We are fighting for a Greater Greece in a Europe free from Muslims and Zionists' (Michas 2002: 18). A sizeable number of Greek paramilitaries were in Srebrenica when it was stormed in July 1995, Karadžić decorating four of them in September. When a Greek newspaper ran a large spread in August 1995 on the 'heroic' exploits of the Greeks in Srebrenica, the paper's phone lines were jammed with enquiries from young people avid for information on the force.[35] It seemed that the grisly massacre of 7,000 people committed there produced no inhibitions.

Not a single well-known Greek was prepared to condemn Serb atrocities in Bosnia while the war there lasted; none visited Sarajevo to express solidarity with its besieged inhabitants. Not a single Greek journalist was accredited to the Bosnian government. Humanitarian aid convoys from Greece were all meant for Serbia or Serb-held areas (Michas 2002: 19, 34). In 1995, the Greek Serbian Friendship Association collected two million signatures in factories, offices, and streets protesting against the UN indictment of Karadžić on war crimes charges; in the same year, when North Atlantic Treaty Organisation (NATO) finally got tough against the Serb hardliners, Prime Minister Papandreou alerted their leaders about NATO's plans (Michas 2002: 36, 39).

Papandreou (unlike Mitsotakis) even appeared to take seriously overtures from Belgrade about a formal unification of both countries. In December 1994, he said that the idea of a confederation proposed by Milošević was 'interesting'. But President Karamanlis, perhaps influenced by his upbringing in a part of Greece where Greek–Slav tensions had been rife, was distinctly unenthusiastic (Michas 2002: 20). Papandreou saw the Yugoslavia crisis in simplistic terms as one 'nurtured by the two old friends from the Second World War: Germany and the Vatican', a view designed to please many Greeks with both leftist and right wing sympathies (Michas 2002: 35). His detailed grasp of the background to the conflict and the disposition of some of its key actors was shaky. Thus, at a 1993 meeting with Karadžić, he kept calling this pillar of the hardline Orthodox right 'comrade' which can only have baffled or bemused the Bosnian Serb leader (Michas 2002: 24).

Papandreou's most controversial action in the crisis was to impose sanctions on Macedonia for a twenty-month period in 1994–5: it further harmed relations with the European Union and greatly hampered the Greek economy as well as almost driving the Macedonian one into the ground. This move was taken on 16 February 1994, after news reached Athens that the United States was ready to follow the diplomatic example of several EU states and establish diplomatic relations with Macedonia. The United States became a 'traitor' in the eyes of Greeks who were adamant that Clinton had previously promised not to recognise Macedonia.[36] An estimated 70 per cent of Macedonian trade was going through Thessaloniki, including 5,000 tons of oil a day. Milošević had been informed about the sanctions by Athens one week before they were announced. Jacques Delors, the President of the European Commission, said: 'The announcement by the Greek government is not good news for the construction of Europe and it does not reflect a willingness to act as a member of the European family'.[37] More damning was the later verdict of authoritative Greek commentator Thanos Veremis: 'Papandreou's improvisations reintroduced the factor of unpredictability that had marked his earlier years of policy-making at considerable cost to Greece's image abroad' (Veremis 1999: 43).

During Papandreou's last tenure in government (before his death in 1996), a report by the Dutch government into the Srebrenica massacre found that large shipments of arms had been transferred from Athens to the Bosnian Serb forces led by Mladić in 1994–5.[38] Over a longer period, Greece had been a crucial arena for sanctions busting and the laundering of money from Serbia. Already by the spring of 1993, British officials were expressing anger at Greece, and also Cyprus, over their lax approach to the financial sanctions imposed on Serbia.[39] How much of a lifeline Greece had been for the Milošević regime started to emerge after its overthrow in October 2000. The event was quickly followed by the murder of Vladimir Bokan who, for the past seven years, had been Milošević's front man in Greece. The Greek authorities had ignored repeated demands by western security agencies to curtail Mr Bokan's successful flouting of the international embargo on fuel, cigarettes and other goods destined for Serbia which soon made him a multimillionaire. He received Greek citizenship in the record time of two years and worked closely with the Greek security services. However, when he started revealing the extent of the economic cooperation between the Greek authorities and the Milošević regime, he was killed by an assassin's bullet on 7 October 2000.[40]

Cyprus was perhaps even more vital for evading sanctions than Greece, particularly in the financial sphere. The number of Yugoslavia-controlled offshore companies on Cyprus soared from fewer than one thousand to over 7,000 after the imposition of sanctions on Serbia in 1992. As much as $4 billion in foreign currency was transferred from Serbia to Cyprus between 1992 and 1994 according to the Yugoslav central bank governor in the country's first post-Milošević government. A *Financial Times* investigation in 2002 revealed that instead of acting to halt sanctions-busting, 'leading members of Cyprus's close-knit elite facilitated the transactions'.[41] The relationship with Milošević and his regime continued even after Cyprus started accession talks with the European Union in 1998. The *Financial Times* named the persons involved, who included the prominent lawyer, Tassos Papadopoulos, elected President of Cyprus in 2003.[42] Two years earlier, the Cypriot authorities impeded Serbian officials when they tried to trace the route money embezzled by Milošević had taken to Cyprus and beyond.[43]

Greece returns to the mainstream

A less belligerent stance to contentious Balkan issues began to emerge even during the last spell in office of the ageing and unwell Papandreou. As so often in his career, a bombastic exterior concealed a more accommodating private stance. The imposition of sanctions on Macedonia at a time when Greece was holding the EU Presidency had caused fury among larger EU states whose nerves were already strained by deepening Balkan entanglements. Speaking in February 1994, one EU official remarked: '[O]fficially I can say nothing but probably I can tell you there is a great deal of anger about this amazing move by what is the EU's own Presidency'.[44] High-level anger at Greece's wayward stance on the regional crisis burst forth at a dinner of EU leaders on 29 June 1995. Jacques Chirac was the host, France having recently assumed the EU Presidency. He took umbrage when Papandreou argued that the Serbs had sound religious reasons for behaving as they did. Chirac promptly cut him short: 'Don't speak to me of any religious war. These people are without any faith, without any sense of law. They are terrorists'.[45]

In the subsequent months, hopes for a compromise in the bitter dispute with Macedonia grew. On 13 September 1995, the foreign ministers of the two states signed an agreement on the normalisation of relations. They undertook to respect mutual sovereignty and accept the current borders. In return for Macedonia removing the Sun of Vergina from its state symbols, Greece agreed to lift the economic blockade within thirty days, which indeed ended on 14 October. Macedonia was able to join the Council of Europe and NATO's Partnership for Peace under the provisional name of FYROM.

NATO was now taking a tougher line against outbursts of nationalism in South-East European countries as it sought to promote a favourable regional environment for its high-risk Bosnian peace plan. So it would have been strange if discreet pressure had not been put on Greece to retreat from its militant position. There was also discreet pressure from within. A 'silent majority' emerged after 1993, which was mindful of the economic losses and squandered opportunities for advancing Greek economic interests in adjacent Balkan states. The government was discreetly urged to temper its intransigence and lift the embargo on Macedonia (Kofos 1999: 246). Simultaneously, social scientists and more balanced media figures, who were closer to 'international political realities' seized back the initiative from populist historians, emotive journalists and lobbyists. These 'realists' emphasised the need to defend Greece's foreign policy interests at a time of expanding Western involvement in the Balkans to counter radical nationalism.

Dubbed as 'yielders' or 'Euro-addicts' by their nationalist detractors, the realists increasingly prevailed. Questions of heritage and identity ceased to exercise a disproportionate influence over foreign policy. Looking back, two respected commentators have argued that the saga of Greek foreign policy in the first half of the 1990s 'became a case-study of how diplomacy, when driven by an inflamed public opinion, is bound to fail' (Koliopoulos and Veremis 2002: 316). Ironically, much of the pressure for change emanated from the Greek north where businessmen were losing contracts over the embargo. Indeed, the crescendo of protests over Skopje's actions concealed North–South cleavages in Greece which occasionally burst to the surface at sporting and other occasions.

By 1995, it was also becoming apparent that Turkish influence in the Balkans was limited and waning (Constas and Papasotiriou 1999: 231). The Muslim arc threatening to surround Greece was the figment of the imagination of unquiet spirits in the Greek foreign ministry. Mark Mazower wrote in 1994: 'The test for Greeks in the next few years is whether they can develop a more confident and searching sense of themselves and their past'.[46] Common ground among modernisers in PASOK and the ND parties managed to strengthen a new Balkan policy of 'open doors – no walls' (Kofos 1999: 255). It got a vital boost with the emergence as Papandreou's successor in January 1996 of Kostas Simitis. He won two successive general elections and would be the least nationalistic Prime Minster in thirty years. His main goals were bringing Greece into the euro currency zone and acting as a conciliator in the remaining territorial disputes that disturbed the region.[47] The crux of Simitis's policy was 'peace in the Balkans with established borders' (Triantafyllou 1999: 147). He won a mandate for PASOK in elections called not long after his elevation. The failure of the nationalist Greek Spring to gain a footing in parliament was a sign of the new political mood. But it would take another election in 2000 before PASOK's nationalist wing was marginalised and Simitis emerged as the party's undisputed leader.

Ironically, Greek rigidity had boosted the position of those in Skopje determined not to retreat on the name issue. They were encouraged upon seeing that Greece had forfeited the sympathy of its customary allies. In 1997 the government in Skopje told UN mediator Cyrus Vance that it still wished to retain 'the Republic of Macedonia' as its title (Kofos 1999: 249). The ruling Social Democrats, with a shrill nationalist opposition breathing down their necks, now found themselves under the kind of domestic pressure not to give way on a core identity issue that had hampered Mitsotakis in the early 1990s. The VMRO came to power in 1998, but despite its earlier irredentist language, VMRO's victory caused hardly a tremor in Athens. This showed how the temperature had fallen on Greece's own nationalist fever chart. But Greece had cause for concern because it was under VMRO, that mounting instability in Macedonia contributed to the virtual collapse of the state in 2001. The tensions were bi-communal ones, placing Slavs and Albanians at loggerheads, but a desperate economic situation (which Greece had contributed to in the early 1990s) was the background against which they erupted.

A major breakthrough in Greek–Turkish bilateral relations from 1999 onwards was the most hopeful sign that hyper-nationalism was on the wane. An earthquake near Istanbul in August, followed by one that shook Athens in September softened the animosity between the two countries. Both came to each other's aid, Greece dropped its objection to Turkey joining the European Union, and talks over the Cyprus question soon got underway. Such a denouement had appeared unlikely at the start of the year when Abdullah Ocalan, the Kurdish rebel leader, was snatched from the Greek embassy in Kenya by Turkish security officials. Prime Minister Simitis sacked the foreign, interior and public order ministers. But the new foreign minister, Georgios Papandreou, taking over at the height of the Kosovo crisis, showed a strong inclination to move beyond nationalist antagonisms and cooperate with NATO and the European Union to stabilise Balkan flashpoints. Similar figures were found in the New Democracy Party. Shortly before it replaced PASOK in power in May 2004, a leading figure, the mayor of Athens, Dora Bakoyannis told a visiting high-level delegation from Bosnia that Greece had erred in supporting Milošević during his wars in the first half of the 1990s. She stressed that her country bore 'a significant moral responsibility' for actions and omissions that contributed to Bosnia's suffering and she called on Greece to take 'a share of the blame for what happened before and during the conflict'.[48] The daughter of former Prime Minister Mitsotakis, Bakoyannis was busy preparing for the hosting of the 2004 Olympic Games in Athens when she knew the eyes of the world would be on her country. She was well aware that a self-righteous collective mood about the rest of the world still gripped much of the Greek public. It was well captured by the famous composer and politician Mikis Theodorakis upon receiving an honorary doctorate from the University of Thessaloniki in 2000. At the ceremony he said: '[There is an] opposition between two worlds – the Greek and the other. And when I say "the other," I mean collectively the Eastern despotism, the Jewish monotheism, the Roman militarism, and the Western authoritarianism'.[49]

In 1998, the Greek President, Kostas Stefanopoulos, during a visit to Mount Athos, had spoken of 'the vicious threat from the West', a place populated by 'Protestants and Papists'.[50] Religious observance in Greece was among the highest in Europe, and under a trenchantly nationalist, Archbishop Christodoulos of Athens, the identity of Greekness with Orthodoxy had overwhelming adherence.[51] But the most religious political culture in Europe was challenged by a growing wave of cultural diversity. Already by 2001, migrants from Albania, Bulgaria, the former Soviet Union, Africa and Asia made up almost 10 per cent of the population (Margaronis 2001: 131). Their concentration in the black economy boosted a sluggish economic growth rate, but the Albanians in particular were viewed as an unwelcome presence. Insecurity about rising crime fed into a xenophobic discourse in a country with the lowest crime rates in the European Union, but where the police enjoyed higher trust than any other institution.[52] Gradually, protection for minorities in Greece is beginning to match the provisions found in other EU countries, but a court decision in 2001 showed how far it still had to go. Sotiris Bletsas, an architect and promoter of the Vlach language (a Balkan Romance language akin to Romanian) was sentenced by an Athens court to fifteen months in jail for distributing a leaflet listing all the lesser used languages of Europe at an annual gathering of Vlachs. The court decided that by doing so he was defying the national convention that no language other than Greek is spoken by citizens today (Baltsiotis and Embiricos 2001: 145).

Cyprus remains an apple of discord

Despite good intentions, Greece was unable to make the newfound pragmatism of its political elite the basis for a solution of the long-running Cyprus dispute. A UN plan to reunite the island following the occupation of the northern third by Turkish forces in 1974, came tantalisingly close to success in 2004. In 2003 Kofi Annan, the UN Secretary-General, submitted plans for a re-unified federal state that were narrowly approved in the elections in Turkish Cyprus held at the end of 2003. Earlier in the year, thousands from both communities had crossed the UN patrolled Green Line demarcating the two parts of the island to visit homes from which they had been forced to flee in 1974. Reconciliation at popular level raised hopes of a political breakthrough.[53] By early 2004 Günter Verheugen (the EU commissioner enlargement), was hoping that he had persuaded Cypriot leaders to accept the UN plan and throw their weight behind it in a referendum to be held not long before Cyprus joined the European Union as a full member on 1 May. But major political players on the Greek side turned against it. The influential Progressive Party of the Working People of Cyprus (AKEL) communist party opposed it, claiming that the United Nations had not provided enough security guarantees for Greek Cypriots. On 21 April, Russia vetoed a Security Council resolution meant to reassure Greek Cypriots on a technicality, raising speculation that it preferred to see the dispute continue in order to undermine Western security in the Eastern Mediterranean. The President of Cyprus, Tassos Papadopoulos threw aside his ambiguity and emerged as a staunch opponent. Local pro-EU voices, and even leading UN and EU spokesmen were denied access to the news media by the President's supporters during the referendum. Verheugen told the European Parliament on 21 April that he felt 'disappointed' and 'cheated' by the

Greek Cypriot government.[54] On 25 April 76 per cent of Greek Cypriots voted against a UN plan to re-unite Cyprus as a bi-zonal, bi-communal federation. Around 180,000 of them had been forcibly displaced in 1974 and just over half would get their homes back if reunification went ahead. The deal was also criticised for allowing the Turks (who account for some 18 per cent of the island's 800,000 population), to retain 29 per cent of the island.[55] The Greek part of a divided Cyprus duly joined the European Union on 1 May 2004. Having been wrong-footed by a wily nationalist leadership, Verheugen promised a package of measures to end the isolation of the Turkish north given the majority support there for a compromise solution. But Greek Cyprus, having joined the European Union in disputed circumstances, was now capable of vetoing Turkey's membership bid. Internal reforms demanded by Brussels, particularly a reduction in the political influence of the military, had been carried out by Turkey in 2003. The European Union had promised a decision on whether accession negotiations could go ahead by December 2004. The European Union was divided about the merits of including Turkey which, with a population of over 70 million people, would be the second-largest member. The French politician Valery Giscard d'Estaing had declared in 2002 that bringing Turkey in would spell 'the end of the European Union'. He spoke from a strong position, as head of the convention devising a new European constitution. But support for Turkey's inclusion existed in the German and British governments as well as in smaller countries; as an over-whelmingly Muslim but strongly Western state, it was felt capable of bridging the cultural and civilisational divide between Europe and the Middle East. But it remained to be seen if Greece and the Republic of Cyprus would hold out for the European Union remaining 'a Christian Club' or endorse (however reluctantly) a growing popular desire for a normalisation of ties with a neighbour that remained very much a Balkan state owing to its jurisdiction over Eastern Thrace and interest in the welfare of Muslim inhabitants of former Yugoslav states and territories, some of whom still looked to Turkey as a protector.

Conclusion

Like the major Euro-Atlantic states, Greek foreign policy towards the rest of the Balkans was reactive. Rather than spearhead new regional ties designed to sta-bilise the region, it fell back on its traditional alliance with Serbia. Its preference for a strong Serbia dominating the post-Yugoslav space mirrored the attitudes to be found in parts of the British and French foreign policy-making establishments. But Greece persisted in adopting a permissive attitude to the Belgrade regime long after it came to be reviled worldwide, above all for the warfare it promoted in Bosnia from 1992 to 1995, the chief targets being unarmed civilians. There is no evidence that Athens used its direct line of communications to the Milošević regime to urge a more cautious or restrained set of policies on it. Greece undoubt-edly had leverage over Serbia given the manner in which it was prepared to provide banking facilities and allow the importation of oil and other vital com-modities in violation of international sanctions. It could have used its influence to urge a rethink by Milošević on the Kosovo issue, the main inter-ethnic flashpoint in the southern Balkans. But Athens held aloof, no government even issuing an invitation to Ibrahim Rugova, the leader of the Kosovar Albanians who was committed to a strategy of non-violence.

Greece feared that turmoil on its northern borders would threaten its security and enable its principal foe Turkey to establish a decisive advantage over it. It was the Macedonian question which 'held Greek diplomacy captive' for half-a-decade in the 1990s (Triantafyllou 1999: 145). The threat this pitifully weak state posed to Greece was exaggerated out of all proportion mainly due to internal political factors. Populist forces hijacked foreign policy in the Balkan region for a number of years, marginalising professionals who, if given the chance, might have enabled Greece to play a far more constructive role in containing the fall out from the destruction of Yugoslavia.

Rather than an aggressive irredentist challenge from the north, what Greece had most to fear was the existence of weak states threatened by inter-ethnic tensions where the rule of law and good governance were conspicuous by their absence. A succession of weak states from the Adriatic to the Black Sea meant an absence of markets for Greek goods, a flow of illegal immigrants and neighbours where organised crime threatened to cast a darker shadow than anywhere else in Europe, excepting the former Soviet Union. Greece's neurotic stance towards its northern neighbours threatened to exacerbate factors which only served to deepen its own insecurity. If moves synchronised with Belgrade to dismember Macedonia had been followed through, Greece would have found itself with a direct land frontier with Serbia. Given the predatory nature of the Milošević regime and the dominance of criminal elements in the political economy of Serbia, it is hard to see how Greece could have avoided serious destabilisation.

By the mid-1990s, influential players were beginning to realise that Greece had been mistaken to become entangled in the disputes of the region. It had lost valuable time by its emotional and intransigent stance towards puny neighbours like Albania and Macedonia. A calmer and more confident approach might have enabled it to become the dominant political force in the Balkans, perhaps even with a place in the Contact Group of Nations, seeking to stabilise its main trouble spots from 1994 onwards. Greece began to fulfil its positive potential from 1996 onwards under the leadership of Costas Simitis.

Confronted by a serious breakdown in inter-ethnic relations in 2001, the Greek government promised to make a 'significant contribution' to Macedonian reconstruction.[56] Of all Macedonia's neighbours, it was probably the one that caused the least trouble to international mediators seeking to prevent a slide towards full-scale civil war. By now, memories of Greek intransigence were beginning to fade and Greece was at last being recognised as a genuine force for stability in South-East Europe.

George Papandreou's successors devoted more attention than he had to trying to boost Greece's economic performance. It had failed to converge economically with the rest of the European Union unlike Spain and Ireland, other recent entrants.

Greek GDP as a percentage of the EU average actually fell during its first decade of membership. It continued to rely on economic transfers from the European Union more than any other member (Europe Enlarged: 25). A modest recovery after 2000 was helped by the economic opportunities grasped by Greek companies who bought up companies cheaply in their northern neighbours. Real estate, banks, factories, oil refineries and telecommunications were bought up for ridiculous prices. Greece also elbowed Macedonia out of the way to ensure that Thessaloniki (and not Skopje) became the regional centre from which the reconstruction of Kosovo was organised. It naturally benefited by its closeness to Kosovo and Macedonia, the scene of ambitious aid and reconstruction projects after 1999, which Greek companies got a slice of. (Between 1990 and 2000, $3.4 billion was invested by Greek business in other Balkan countries, about 60 per cent of the total.)[57] Complaints about Greek asset-stripping and taking unfair advantage began to be heard further north, but resentment would be greater, in some places, towards West European firms as tariff barriers were dismantled to pave the way for EU expansion into the rest of the Balkans. Trade and investment helped to do what polite EU notes never accomplished and Greece started to put aside its nationalist complexes towards its northern neighbours.

2   The road to war in Kosovo

A history of deepening confrontation

Kosovo had been a longstanding source of bitter enmity between Serbs and Albanians. The dispute had deeper origins than the ones which had dominated the earlier phases of the Yugoslavia crisis from 1991 to 1995. Kosovo (to Albanians it was known as Kosova) was a place crucial for the historical evolution of both peoples and significant in their respective nineteenth-century political awakenings (Cohen 2001: 4). The Serbs predominantly viewed it as their 'Holy Land' or Jerusalem. It had been at the core of their medieval empire. The battle of Kosovo Polje had been fought there in 1389. It was Kosovo that possessed the main religious markers that helped shape Serbian cultural identity, notably the monasteries erected in medieval times. Dobrica Ćosić, a well-known Serbian writer, claimed in 1999 that Kosovo 'is the source of major epic poetry and is the precious receptacle of the Serbs' spiritual identity. It is not a piece of land, it is the Serb identity. With the loss of Kosovo . . . the Serb people has been spiritually mutilated' (Cohen 2001: 4).

Kosovo's exalted status in the Serbian mindset was not very old. It dated from the nineteenth-century emergence of national ideology as a new form of group identity. In an ethnically mixed region like the Balkans, nationalists invariably drew upon history to justify their right to fully control a territory.

Albanians, for their part, often viewed themselves as descendents of the Illyrians and thus descended from some of the oldest residents of the Balkans. Their spokesmen and champions argue that they were already present in Kosovo in the sixth and seventh centuries when Slavic tribes arrived to settle the lands.

In Serbian eyes, the history of Kosovo began with their own arrival and subsequent state-building efforts. Albanians only became a significant element in 1690, when a large part of the Serbian people emigrated under the leadership of Patriarch Arsenije III (von Kohl and Libal 1997: 17). Following the Turkish defeat at the gates of Vienna in 1683, Orthodox Serbs and also Catholic Albanians had heeded a Hapsburg call for the Christian population in the Balkans to rise up and cast aside Turkish overlordship. But the Hapsburg advance into the Balkans was driven back and the Turks tightened their grip on Kosovo. The rate of conversion of Albanians to Islam rose sharply in the eighteenth century. As late as 1610, there had been ten times more Catholics in Kosovo than Muslims (Vickers 1998: 26). Adapting the religion of their overlords increased the status of the Albanians. According to Vickers, 'it marked the first step along the separate road for them and the Serbs' (Vickers 1998: 26).

The Serbian centre of gravity had moved far to the north, to Belgrade, strategically situated at the junctions of the Sava and Danube rivers. The Hapsburgs had allowed the refugee Serbs to settle in the rich southernmost part of the Pannonian plain which had become relatively depopulated during the period of Ottoman control.

The Serbian state that took shape in stages during the nineteenth century saw it as its historic mission to gain control of the lands that had comprised a medieval Serbian empire, irrespective of the demographic changes that had occurred subsequently. Albanians were seen as forfeiting the right to good treatment for having aligned with the Turks. Nor was it forgotten that Muslim Albanians had helped the Turks to defend Kosovo when Serbia sought to capture it in 1876–7. In 1878, it was in Prizren, then Kosovo's largest town, that the Albanians established their first national movement which aimed to forge political unity among them by merging four Turkish administrative units into one political entity (Jelavich 1983: 364–6).

Serbian–Albanian cycles of attack and reprisal only began in earnest with the onset of the twentieth century. In 1903 census figures regarded as being fairly precise because they had been checked and revised by the Austro-Hungarian consulates established in the region, showed that both Christians and Muslims were present in large numbers in both the Serbian and Albanian populations. There were 111,350 Orthodox, 69,250 Muslims and 6,660 Catholic Serbs, a total of 187,200 Serbs. Of the total of 230,000 Albanians, 215,050 were Muslims, 14,350 Catholics and 900 Orthodox (von Kohl and Libal in Elsie 1997: 19). Over one-third of Serbs were Muslims. Their numbers were considerably reduced in the century to come but Slavic Muslims, often known as *gorani*, remained a conspicuous presence in parts of Kosovo and in certain trades.

Despite the preponderance of Muslims among the Albanians, there is no shortage of evidence to suggest that usually, religion has not been central to Albanian identity. According to one Albanian academic writing in 1994: 'Albanians have never been good believers in any religion. Their faith lies in a high traditional morality, not in religious dogmas' (Vickers 1998: 25). The Bektashis, a Shia grouping which made up nearly half of Albanian Muslims, were on the fringes of conventional Islam and some purists even placed them beyond the pale: as part of the Sufi order dedicated to mysticism and meditation, they consumed wine or brandy and permitted women in their ceremonies (Schwartz 2001: 28–9).

Sufi Muslims have been depicted as champions of Albanian nationhood (Schwartz 2001: 20). But the pride of place in the Albanian pantheon belongs to Skanderberg, the fifteenth-century Albanian noble who held the Turks at bay for several decades. His standard, the red banner with the black double-headed eagle has become the national Albanian symbol. In the 1990s, there was even talk of mass conversions to Christianity in order to strengthen the ties of beleaguered Kosovan Albanians with the West (Maliqi 1998: 52).[1]

The turning-point in Albanian–Serb relations occurred in the autumn of 1912, when Kosovo fell to Serbia as Turkey lost most of its remaining European possessions in the face of a combined assault from most of the Balkan states. The brutality of the Serbian takeover appalled a leader of the Serbian Social Democrats, Dimitrije Tucović who had enlisted in the army. Albanian villages were razed to the ground and their inhabitants killed. Tucović later wrote:

> We have carried out the attempted premeditated murder of an entire nation. We were caught in that criminal act and have been obstructed. Now we have to suffer the punishment... In the Balkan Wars, Serbia not only doubled its territory, but also its external enemies.[2]

Tucović believed that the Serbian, Albanian and Montenegrin inhabitants of northern Albania formed a single inter-related regional community, embracing two nations, Serbia–Montenegro and Albania, and three religions, Catholic, Orthodox and Muslim. However, the efforts of a Serbian Socialist (who would shortly perish on the battlefields of the First World War) to promote a supra-regional consciousness over an exclusively nationalist one made little headway. Narrow chauvinism, promoted through the press and the educational system drowned out appeals to repair past bonds of solidarity through identification with socialism. The 1913 Treaty of London, while creating an Albanian state placed more than half of the Albanian population found in present day Kosovo and Macedonia under Serbian rule. Joseph Swire, a British Albanianist, warned: 'There remains in the heart of the Balkan peninsula an ulcer poisoning the European system, and bidding fair to render inevitable a bloody operation' (Swire 1971: 162).

After suffering from persecution in the inter-war years and being subjected to an attempted wholesale deportation to Turkey, the pendulum swung towards the Kosovo Albanians in the early 1940s.[3] Following the Axis defeat of royal Yugoslavia in 1941, most Albanian lands found themselves united under Italian occupation.[4] Albanians retained a localist outlook, being wary of identifying with the cause of their new overlords. Many conquerors had come and gone and history advised against an over-close association with fickle or transitory conquerors. Although the German SS recruited a small 'Skanderberg Division' among Albanians, it has been claimed that Kosovo provided the second-highest rate of survival for European Jews caught up in the Nazi Holocaust, 62 per cent (Schwartz 2001: 84).[5]

Simultaneously, little enthusiasm could be found among Kosovo Albanians for joining the Partisans, the communist-led guerrillas emerging as a formidable resistance force elsewhere in occupied Yugoslavia. Kosovo Albanians distrusted communism as a pan-Slav conspiracy, a fresh attempt to keep them in subjugation (Schwartz 2001: 88). The influence of Russia over communism was not a recommendation. Russia, irrespective of the political system in place, was the country-of-origin of diplomats stationed in the Balkans who had egged on the Serbs in their anti-Albanian pogroms in 1912 (Schwartz 2001: 56). In 1941, the Yugoslav Communist Party had only 270 members in Kosovo of whom just twenty were Albanians (von Kohl and Libal in Elsie 1997: 36). A wing of the newly formed Albanian Communist Party supported Albanian unification. Josip Tito, who installed a communist regime in Belgrade in 1944, would tolerate a common Albanian formation only within an enlarged Yugoslavia.

In 1944–5, a rebellion against the new Yugoslav authorities erupted in the Dreniça region. Nearly 50,000 Albanians may have lost their lives in a bloody pacification drive. In a 1998 meeting with NATO's military chief in Europe, General Wesley Clark, Milošević referred approvingly to the ruthless measures used then to extinguish Albanian insurgency: 'You know, General Clark that we know how to handle these Albanians, these murderers, these rapists, these killers-of-their-own-kind. We have taken care of them before . . . In Dreniça . . . we killed them. We killed them all!' (Clark 2001a: 153–4).

The fly in the communist ointment

Albania and Yugoslavia are the first examples of adjacent communist states deeply at odds over rival national claims. Kosovo was treated with the utmost vigilance and its Albanian population subjected to the tightest of controls during Alexander Ranković's long era as Tito's interior minister. Although an autonomous region in a federal system, Kosovo 'functioned as a satrapy of the Serbian-dominated security forces' (Cohen 2001: 21). Many Albanians were forced to declare themselves as Turks in the censuses of 1953 and 1961, and large numbers were induced to emigrate to Turkey in this period (Islami 1994: 47; Malcolm 1998: 323). A very high birth rate, however, reduced the impact of these population losses. During the Ranković era, Albanians held largely menial positions. In 1953, Serbs and Montenegrins, who comprised 31.5 per cent of Kosovo's active population held 68 per cent of the 'administrative and leading positions in the province' (Cohen 2001: 18). The situation was not greatly different from that in Soviet-ruled Central Asia at this time where a layer of privileged Russians controlled the upper echelons of power in these largely Muslim-populated republics. But Albanians were being taught in their own language in state schools. The literacy rate rose sharply from 37 to 59 per cent between 1948 and 1961 and an ethno-political consciousness also emerged.

In 1967, Tito visited Kosovo for the first time in sixteen years and criticised the situation left by Ranković who had fallen from grace the previous year: 'One cannot talk about equal rights when Serbs are given preference in the factories . . . and Albanians are rejected although they have the same or better qualification' (Malcolm 1998: 324). In 1968, it was announced that the Serbian word for Albanian, 'Šiptar', which had pejorative connotations, would no longer be used. A decade of rising expectations followed. In the long-term, the transformation of Priština University into the primary centre of learning for Albanians across Yugoslavia's territorial boundaries was probably the key event. Until 1970 it had been a branch of Belgrade University. By 1978, four times as many Kosovan Albanians were graduating from university than in 1966. It proved also to be a magnet for Albanians in Macedonia where they continued to suffer discrimination at the hands of the state (though their smaller numbers meant that the Skopje authorities had refrained from taking really severe measures against them).

Despite undeniable improvements, the economic gap between Kosovo and the rest of Yugoslavia widened. Jens Reuter of the *Südost-Institut* in Munich described Kosovo's economic plight as follows:

> The structure of investments made in Kosovo is one of the reasons for the conspicuous lack of jobs. Unemployment should have been fought by investments in labour-intensive industry rather than capital-intensive sectors such as heavy industry and energy. In 1985, unemployment in Kosovo was 3.33 times the Yugoslav average.
>
> (quoted by von Kohl and Libal in Elsie 1997: 51)

Priština, with its garish high-rises, 'banks and sixteen-floor Grand Hotel plonked into a virtually destitute region, and with a population which had grown from 14,000 to 140,000 since the end of the war', looked like 'a ridiculous imitation of Manhattan' (von Kohl and Libal in Elsie 1997: 51). In 1968, tensions arose which Tito's commanding prestige was able to smother. Popular Serbian writer Dobrica Ćosić, had claimed that political pressures were driving Serbs and Montenegrins from Kosovo. In refutation of Ćosić's allegations, it was pointed out that of the 10,000 inhabitants who had left Kosovo annually, 9,000 were Albanians. An under-performing economy was seen as the spur for emigration. Ćosić was expelled from the communist party for encouraging nationalism, but he would enjoy mounting influence in Serbia in the decades to come. The year 1969 also witnessed nationalist demonstrations by Albanians in Kosovo. 'We want a university!' 'Down with Colonialism in Kosovo' and 'We Want a Republic' were the main slogans.

Kosovo's autonomous status was reinforced. It was one of two autonomous provinces linked to, but not ruled by Serbia. It had not been made a republic because the architects of Yugoslavia's federal system reckoned in the mid-1940s that this status should be reserved for nations (*nardodi*) as opposed to nationalities (*naradnosti*), the former having their principal homeland inside Yugoslavia, and the latter outside Yugoslavia (Caplan 1998: 748). In 1971, an amendment to the constitution gave the autonomous provinces equal status with the republics in most forms of economic decision-making and even in some areas of foreign policy (Malcolm 1998: 327). Then when a new constitution was promulgated in 1974 to prepare Yugoslavia for a future after Tito, Kosovo's autonomous status was greatly reinforced. It now enjoyed virtually all the prerogatives of a republic, including its own constitution, courts, bank and an equal voice within the collective federal presidency, the main decision-making arm of the state (Surroi 1998: 145–72).

By 1978, Albanians would make up nearly two-thirds of communist party members in Kosovo (Cohen 2001: 26). Serbs and Montenegrins were losing their previous dominance in the power structure. To what degree a decline in their fortunes was accompanied by harassment and persecution of vulnerable Serbs by newly assertive Albanians has remained a topic of intense controversy. Albanian scholars say that their loss of privileges and an unwillingness to adapt to a new situation from 1966 onwards prompted many Serbs to leave (Islami 1993: 49). Many Serbs argue that emigration was due to a variety of pressures and outright discrimination (Dragović-Soso 2002: 118–19). Two officially authorised studies carried out in 1982–3 and which technically were top secret showed very different conclusions. An investigation by the Kosovo authorities discovered some instances of anti-Serb discrimination but concluded that the main causes of emigration were socio-economic. A study jointly conducted by the Serbian Parliament and a branch of the federal structure asserted that 'emigration was the result of "a political atmosphere and the use of vandal methods with the aim of creating an ethnically pure Kosovo" ' (Dragović-Soso 2002: 119).

Tito's concept of socialist Yugoslavism based on the slogan of *brotherhood and unity* among the peoples of Yugoslavia was challenged in the second half of the 1980s. The backlash emanated from Serbia. Here widely dispersed but previously weakly held sentiments that Serbs had lost out politically owing to Tito's federalist arrangements, were skilfully harnessed by a rising apparatchik, Slobodan Milošević. Once he captured the Serbian political leadership in 1987, the state-controlled media began to depict Kosovo Albanians in a fairly indiscriminate fashion as the collective enemies of Serbia and its people (Thompson 1999: 52–7).

Kosovo's autonomy was wound up in 1989, a state of emergency declared, and the Albanian administrative elite was decapitated. Already by 1983, the proportion of Yugoslav political prisoners that was Albanian was 41.8 per cent of the total (Bellamy 2002: 7; Judah 2000: 40–1). An initial crackdown on Albanian political activity outside the prescribed communist channels had already started in 1981, the year of serious disturbances centred on Priština University. The unrest was spread by nationalist students, one of whose slogans was 'Unification with Albania'. In the eyes of Ramadan Marmullaku (a Kosovan Albanian then in the diplomatic service and who later became a commentator on Albanian affairs), this was a strong indication that the demonstrators were under the influence of Marxist–Leninist groups of Kosovan Albanians operating in Switzerland and Germany. They supported unification with Albania and would have strong influence on co-ethnics radicalised by their position in Yugoslavia until the early 1990s, when the appalling condition of Albania became obvious. Marmullaku even believed that the Sigurimi, the Albanian secret police probably incited the unrest. Up to forty five demonstrators and fifteen policemen were killed, according to figures he obtained from a high-ranking police source at the time (Marmullaku 2003: 305–6).

The events of 1981 crystallised growing distrust between the two main ethnic groupings in Kosovo. The rapid emergence of an Albanian intellectual class with few employment outlets locally, combined with rural overpopulation had produced a combustible mixture. To some degree, Enver Hoxha's Albania represented the Holy Grail for many of the protesters (Judah 2000: 105–6). Cries for a union with Albania came from some of the 1981 protesters who were unaware that the only functioning Albanian state was a vast prison house for much of its population. The local security forces, largely Albanian in composition, obeyed orders to crack down on irredentist or other forms of subversive protest in the aftermath of the riots. Over one thousand Albanians were sentenced to up to fifteen years in jail for their part in the 1981 events (Kola 2003: 158). But Titoist loyalties remained quite pronounced among an Albanian elite, which had clearly advanced since 1968.

From 1981 to 1985, with federally minded officials still in charge in Belgrade, a last effort at narrowing the developmental gap between Kosovo and the rest of the federation was attempted. A sum of $2.5 billion was set aside for investment in Kosovo. Heavy industry was spurned in favour of processing industries and the most backward areas were targeted (Cohen 2001: 28). But even if communist planners had been more successful than before in their modernisation efforts, the high Albanian birth rate would have widened the economic gulf with the rest of the country. Kosovo's population increased by 27 per cent from 1971 to 1981 (Cohen 2001: 25). By the beginning of the 1990s, many Serbs were asserting that the propensity of many Albanians to have large families was part of a deliberate strategy to marginalise them. Kosovo's demographic earthquake saw the Serb minority being reduced from almost 27 per cent of the population in 1953 to around 10 per cent in the mid-1980s (Dannreuther 2001: 16). Many Kosovo Serbs were eager to be enrolled as shock troops by Milošević as he held monster rallies in parts of Yugoslavia, such as the other autonomous province in the federation, Voivodina, and the Republic of Montenegro, both places where he succeeded in seizing control at the end of the 1980s.

In March 1989, the Serbian Parliament, in violation of both the Serbian and the 1974 Federal constitutions, adopted special amendments which deprived Kosovo of its autonomy (International Helsinki Federation (IHF) 1999). A state of emergency was declared following which over fifty people were killed in rioting as the crackdown intensified (Kola 2003: 181, 185). Between 1989 and 1992, 20,000 Albanians served 30–60 day prison sentences (IHF 1999) and in 1991 the Kosovo chief of police admitted that 450,000 Albanians had passed through the hands of the police since 1981 alone (Kola 2003: 182, n. 99).

By 1991, mass sackings had turned the local state almost completely into a Serbian affair:

> Approximately 1,300 employees of Radio & TV Priština lost their jobs. Nearly all broadcasts in the Albania language were terminated. 'Cleansing' of the editorial staff of daily newspapers and magazines followed. Some 80,000 Albanian clerks and civil servants were removed from office. The University of Priština too was 'Serbianised'; it became 'the Holy Sava Academy', named after the Serbian patron saint Sava. In secondary education pupils had to pass an entrance examination in Serbian language and literature. Albanian physicians and nurses were removed from hospitals. Cultural institutions presented purely Serbian productions. Cities, villages and their streets were given Serbian names. Companies and savings of Albanians were confiscated....
>
> (Leurdijk and Zandee 2001)

The most worrying was the denial by the regime of state medical services to the Albanians. A report by the IHF in 1991 pointed out that the dismissal of most ethnic Albanian health workers, the banning of the use of written or spoken Albanian in hospitals, was due to the withdrawal of economic resources for health care, and posed a grave risk to the health of the population.

The Albanian parallel state

Other than gratifying his nationalist followers and his own will to power, the aim of Milošević's strategy still remained unclear. He may have hoped that Albanians would have departed *en masse* if life was simply made too unbearable for them. He may have banked on the eruption of violent protests which would then have been the pretexts for bloody massacres designed to induce mass flight. But the Albanians rejected the armed actions by which they had regularly responded to Serbian oppression in the past. A variety of groups, of which the Youth Parliament of Kosovo was most prominent, persuaded ordinary people 'to keep their tempers'; they managed to sideline Marxist–Leninist groups which had been the main instigators of anti-Belgrade demonstrations in the late 1980s. Their influence was curbed when their imprisoned leader, Adem Demaçi threw his weight behind non-violent resistance rather than on an ill-focussed insurrection (Maliqi 1998: 32).

But the limelight increasingly shone on a new political force which had sprang up and was based largely on the intellectuals and educators who had acquired increasing influence from the 1960s onwards. The Democratic League of Kosovo (LDK) was formed in 1989. At its head was 45-year-old Ibrahim Rugova, the son of a shopkeeper executed by the communists in the mid-1940s.[6] The LDK's goal was independence, but its chosen path was a resolutely political one. On 19 October 1991, the underground Assembly of the Republic of Kosovo, which had been meeting secretly for over a year, announced the results of a referendum held in late September on Kosovo's future. Albanians to the extent of 99.87 per cent had endorsed the sovereignty and independence of Kosovo (Vickers 1998: 251).

On 24 May 1992, elections for a parliament and president were held. The LDK, with 76 per cent of the votes, got 96 out of 100 seats, a number being left vacant for South Slavs who had not voted. Eight monitoring teams from the West observed the elections. Systematic mistreatment from the authorities meant that support for independence was now overwhelming among the Albanians. Albin Kurti, a well-known student leader, declared that living under Serbia was inconceivable: 'why should we if even the Slavs cannot live together' (Kostović 1998: 20). The break-up of the Yugoslav Federation had made autonomy irrelevant. A Kosovo political analyst known for his moderate views and readiness to dialogue with Serbs wrote in 1993 that 'the negative experience with the Serbs will always make them [the Albanians] vote for their freedom and self-determination' (Maliqi 1998: 247). In a 1995 polling survey, none of the respondents favoured the option of being an independent republic within a decentralised Yugoslavia, but they were split on the options: 57 per cent of the Albanians desired outright independence while 43 per cent wanted to join Albania (Mertus 1999: 319).

A passive resistance strategy was pursued by the LDK. Rugova justified it in the following terms: 'The Serbs only wait for a pretext to attack the Albanian population and wipe it out. We believe it is better to do nothing and stay alive than be massacred' (Mertus 1999: 169). There was, of course, the hope that international pressure would reduce the ability of Belgrade to act with impunity in Kosovo. Non-violence was meant to offer a clear contrast with the Serbs in the eyes of the rest of the world; they were to be identified with the use of indiscriminate force. A non-violent struggle was meant to unnerve the stronger opponent and prevent him from acting as he saw fit. This strategy, a very novel one after a century or more of bouts of internal violence, was embraced by the Albanians. One sign of its appeal was the renunciation of the blood feud, a problem that up to 1989 had threatened the lives of up to 17,000 men (Clark 2000a: 60). Anton Çetta, a folklorist with a passion for social reform, had formed a movement to abolish a centuries-old custom under which families of murder victims were obliged to take revenge on the male relatives of the killer. Feuds could start over much lesser issues, such as the killing of a sheepdog or quarrels over water and boundaries. Young men would stay in the family home (the code regulating the feud forbad killings at home), venturing out at the risk of death (Young 2000). Çetta's movement brought peace to around one thousand families who would have been trapped in a cycle of killings.[7]

The passive resistance strategy emphasised that Kosovo was part of the West. Rugova, in particular, appeared keen to banish the view that Kosovo was an Oriental region and he showed little interest in visiting Islamic countries or joining the Organisation of the Islamic Conference which Izetbegović had done in pre-war Bosnia. Mother Theresa, a Catholic Albanian from Macedonia, became a powerful symbol for the LDK. There was a strong urge to show that they were not the Muslim fundamentalists depicted in Serbian propaganda (Clark 2000a: 66).

Parallel institutions were set up, which were meant to provide a concrete expression of Kosovo self-government. Governmental, economic and social institutions were financed from the Albanian diaspora community of Kosovo. It now comprised at least half-a-million people (Judah 2000: 69), most of whom were located in west-central Europe. Bujar Bukosi, a Düsseldorf-based physician who headed the LDK's government-in-exile, was able to persuade most emigrants to donate up to 3 per cent of their income to finance the parallel state. The funds were spent on education, health care, culture, science, sports, agriculture and social assistance. Around 25,000 people were working in these sectors in 1997, on the payroll of the LDK (Dannreuther 2001: 19).

A separate education system would be the flagship of the parallel state. 'Only in education is there a future' was a slogan which had captured the mood in the 1960s in a society which not so long before, had been overwhelmingly illiterate. By 1997, some 18,000 teachers and 330,000 pupils belonged to this alternative education system (Clark 2000a: 99). Salary levels and regularity of pay compared well with Serbia at this time. In addition, there were 14,000 full-time or part-time students by 1996–7 compared with under 20,000 in 1991–2 when Albanians had been expelled from the universities.

In economic terms, the parallel state had achievements to its credit. As a response to mass dismissals, large numbers of people moved into the commercial sector. In 1995, 18,500 small firms were registered in Kosovo compared with 1,733 in 1987. Milošević's crackdown actually placed Kosovo ahead of many parts of ex-communist Eastern Europe in terms of numbers of people developing entrepreneurial experience (Maliqi 1998: 108–9). Albanians also had a long-standing tradition of smuggling to draw upon; they had access to hard currency owing to many families having relatives abroad. Kosovo shops were often better supplied than those in Serbia under a tightening ring of economic sanctions since late 1991 (Neier 1994: 26). But this survival strategy was only able to provide a minimum safety-net for hard pressed people. When Kosovan Albanians had state jobs and access to public services, the per capita income had amounted to only $662 per annum, making it the poorest region in Europe.[8]

The role of women, in what had been an emphatically patriarchal society, underwent some adjustment. But the view strengthened in the 1990s that gender or individual freedom could only come through national freedom. The emergency caused families to regroup in large extended families. Women were pushed further into service roles. The parallel state managed to carve out space vital for Albanian collective expression. But it made surprisingly little use of it. Between 1992 and 1994, there were no public demonstrations of any kind. The LDK preferred passive non-violence to active non-violence (Clark 2000a: 124). Calls to convene parliament openly or hold educational classes openly rather than clan-destinely were opposed. Most of the time, alternative political institutions did not function. If the parliament had convened in broad daylight and the authorities had suppressed it, the publicity which the LDK relied upon to publicise its cause would have been greatly augmented.

The Albanian parallel system was 'physically marginalised, its activities confined to private houses, cafes and restaurants' (Kostović 1998: 21). This has to be borne in mind when considering the hesitancy with which the Kosovo Albanians have responded to the restoration of limited autonomy under United Nations auspices from 2000 onwards. Rugova was recognised by Kosovo Albanians as their President. From his offices in the building of the Writers Union, he behaved as a symbolic or *virtual* Head of State rather than as the leader of a movement in struggle. According to Howard Clark, all the initiatives that made non-violence a viable strategy came from elsewhere (Clark 2000a: 6). Much of what he lacked in political ingenuity was made up for by his right-hand man, a sociology professor Fehmi Agani. Rugova was passive in his approach, sometimes high-handed in his methods, and seemingly content with his figure-head role.[9] But the LDK made sure to observe the rules of a patriarchal society by slotting the heads of Kosovo Albanian families into the party infrastructure (Loza 1998: 29). Women and youth were under-represented in parliament and in other structures of the parallel state. Veton Surroi (born 1961), educated for much of a time in Latin America thanks to his father having been a diplomat in Mexico and Bolivia, sought to appeal to younger people. In 1990, he founded the Parliamentary Party of Kosovo. Shkëlzen Maliqi, a philosopher, for his part founded the Social Democratic Party (SDP). But both found it difficult to weaken the grip of the LDK on Albanian loyalties (Judah 2000: 146–7).

The LDK strove to build up strong international links, starting with members of the US Congress who represented districts with sizeable Albanian constituencies. But despite expressions of sympathy and concern about the Albanian plight, high-level Western bodies viewed Kosovo as an internal Serbian concern through much of the 1990s. Rugova was received in the White House and in other foreign capitals, events that the pro-LDK media characterised as equivalent to official state visits. But it was unable to conceal the fact that Kosovo was only a peripheral issue even when the West grappled with other aspects of the Yugoslav crisis (Vickers 1998: 226).

If more of an effort had been made to reach out to Serbs who rejected hardline positions, it might have boosted the international credibility of the underground state. This was not easy in Kosovo itself where the electoral behaviour of the Serb population showed a high level of identification with some of the most extreme forces in Serbian politics. In Priština, both groups lived side by side in the same communal blocs while leading separate lives. One prominent Albanian commentator wrote in 1993 that 'inter-ethnic relations in Kosovo have … sunk to the lowest ever, practically zero level of communications' (Maliqi 1994: 237). Many Serbs (and Montenegrins) who had filled the jobs of dismissed Albanians were from outside Kosovo and had had no previous contact with Albanians (Ahmeti 1994: 111). Young Albanians as a rule no longer knew how to speak Serbian. A doctor, and adviser to Rugova remarked: 'My children of four and six – all they know of Serbs are the police and killings. My boy keeps asking "when are we going to win"? because only with liberation will they be able to get toys and ice cream'.[10] Ordinary Kosovo Serbs stood by Milošević when urban Serbs closed ranks in huge demonstrations during the winter of 1996–7 in a bid to oust him (Thomas 1999: 402). Forging links with anti-war, human rights and independent media groups in Serbia might have dented the stereotypical image of Albanians that prevailed there. Several Belgrade groups monitoring human rights did consistently speak out about the situation in Kosovo. But the LDK did not see winning hearts and minds in Serbia as part of its strategy (Clark 2000a: 144). It warned off those Albanians who were disposed to enter into a dialogue with Serbs. However, Fehmi Agani was a frequent visitor to Belgrade and, while unswerving in his commitment to independence, saw the need for initiating a Serb–Albanian dialogue.[11]

The LDK firmly refused to take part in Serbian elections. Given their population size, the Albanians were capable of filling 10 per cent of the parliamentary seats in Serbia. Had the LDK run, Milošević and his allies would have been deprived of a majority from 1992 onwards. Prime Minister in the second half of 1992, Milan Panić signalled his willingness to restore Kosovo's autonomy and improve conditions for Albanians (Doder and Branson 1999: 158). But Agani thought self-determination was likelier under Milošević than this enlightened Serbian *émigré* (Judah 2000: 79). Panić got no support from the Albanians when he stood for President at the end of 1992; nor did the United States or its allies throw their weight behind someone who was the most serious internal challenger to Milošević seen in Serbia before 2000 (Doder and Branson 1999: 149–52).

Rugova was never victimised personally by the regime. Veton Surroi believes that 'an equilibrium of interests' accounted for this: Milošević tolerated Rugova for as long as he kept the Albanians quiet, which provided Rugova with the space for what he believed would be a steady if slow advancement of the cause of Albanian independence' (Loza 1998: 28). Nevertheless, the parallel state was an obstacle. The unconventional tactics limited the scope for Serbian aggression and postponed war. It kept the population together and important social structures functioning. Albanian unity made it difficult to disperse the Albanian population and settle South Slavs in Kosovo after a quick 'ethnic cleansing'. It was wrong of José Cutileiro, the Portuguese mediator in the 1992 Bosnia crisis and later head of the West European Union, to claim (as he did in 1999) that Kosovo is a 'dangerous part of the world that has had precious little experience of decency in government'.[12] Rugova, despite his air of lethargy, was a genuinely moderate figure who opposed violence. It placed him apart from many independence-orientated Balkan leaders. He was in fact a refreshing contrast to the implacable hardliners that the Western emissaries had had to negotiate with while in other ethnically riven territories. Yet the West made little effort to reward the Albanians for their non-violent response.

The international non-response

The European Community (EC) peace conference on Ex-Yugoslavia, which convened in The Hague in September 1991, was the first permanent international bid to end the conflict in Yugoslavia which had been raging since the previous summer. It would later become the International Conference on the Former Yugoslavia (ICFY) once the United Nations became part of its negotiating efforts. Its first chairman, Lord Carrington, declined to invite Rugova to send a delegation to take part in the talks process. Indeed, another eight years would have to elapse before an Albanian delegation would be invited to attend a conference on Yugoslavia convened by the international community, as full participants (Bellamy 2002: 22). The European Parliament protested Carrington's decision, made in close conjunction with the British Foreign Office, which he had headed as Foreign Secretary a decade earlier. It called for the full participation of two constitutionally recognised parts of Yugoslavia, whose autonomy had been rescinded by Serbia in 1989 (Voivodina being the other) (Bellamy 2002: 22–3). Concerns were also expressed in the US Congress; in August 1990 the leading Republican politician, Senator Robert Dole, led a group of congressmen to Kosovo and reported adversely on conditions there.

Peace envoys such as Carrington, and his successor Lord Owen, who from August 1992 headed a joint UN–EC peace process, insisted that they were mandated to bring an end to fighting in Croatia and Bosnia–Herzegovina, not to respond to the problems of Yugoslavia in their entirety. But the draft of the peace agreement Carrington released on 23 October 1991 contained the requirement that 'the republics shall apply fully and in good faith the provisions existing prior to 1990 for autonomous provinces', a reference to the autonomy of Kosovo and Voivodina. When Serbia rejected his peace plan, Carrington and his team removed this requirement from subsequent versions, presumably in a bid to secure Milošević's acquiescence (Caplan 1998: 749). The West thus signalled to him its preparedness to support his claim to exercise full sovereignty over Kosovo.

At the London conference on Yugoslavia, convened by the British government in August 1992, a Kosovo delegation was permitted to attend but only as observers. On 17 August Carrington had written to Rugova: 'If you are planning to be in London at the time of the conference', then it would be possible to have some meetings, but it would not 'for practical; and other reasons, be possible to grant your delegation access to the Conference chamber' (Weller 1999: 218, n. 9). But one outcome of the 1992 London gathering was a working group on ethnic and national communities. Its task was to recommend initiatives for resolving ethnic questions in the former Yugoslavia. The German diplomat Geert Ahrens chaired this working group. He wrote in his first report (in November 1992): 'I believe that it is essential for the Peace Conference to be involved in seeking a settlement between the Kosovan Albanians and the Serbian government' (Weller 1999: 89–90). But Lord Owen asked for the exclusion of Kosovo (and also the Sandžak, a mainly Muslim part of Serbia) because these were internal Serbian matters. He feared that a settlement in Bosnia would be imperilled if Kosovo was introduced as an additional issue.[13]

An even shorter-lived initiative involving Ahrens, an envoy who would build up unparalleled experience of the southern Balkans, was the 'Mission of Long Duration to Kosovo, Voivodina and the Sandžak'. The mission had been put together by the Organization for Security and Co-operation in Europe (OSCE). It established a permanent institutional presence in Kosovo and initiated an international relationship with the Kosovan Albanians. But its impact was limited 'by the assumption that either the status of Kosovo had been resolved in Serbia's favour or that it was effectively irresolvable and should therefore be bypassed (Bellamy 2002: 33). Belgrade feared that the Mission of Long Duration could lead to the internationalisation of the Kosovo conflict. One authority had argued that its presence inhibited Serbian 'security' operations in the province (Bellamy 2002: 42). It was quickly expelled after Milošević had smothered Milan Panić's attempt to displace him.

The Kosovo situation received minimal Western media attention. Journalists and NGOs were discouraged by the Serbian authorities from going there. In September 1990, an IHF delegation was detained in Priština, interrogated by the authorities, and had all its documents confiscated. All members were expelled and declared *persona non grata* in Yugoslavia (IHF 1999). Along with Amnesty International (AI) and Human Rights Watch (HRW), the IHF regularly urged international vigilance and action to forestall conflict in Kosovo.

In its 1999 report detailing a decade or more of involvement with Kosovo, the IHF pointed out that it had repeatedly appealed to the OSCE states 'to place the Kosovo situation high on their agenda and urged the European Union and the United Nations to "take immediate steps to prevent the explosion of violence in Kosovo"' (IHF 1999). In April 1992, the IHF sent an open letter to the Conference for Security and Cooperation in Europe (CSCE),[14] the European Commission and the United Nations. It voiced its concern about the increasing distribution of arms to Serbian and Montenegrin paramilitary groups, public threats of violence by leading Serbian authorities, the killings of ethnic Albanians and the positioning of Serbian paramilitary snipers in strategic points in Priština. The IHF again urged the international organisations to put the Kosovo conflict on their agenda to prevent a possible armed conflict and to use international mechanisms to put an end to continuing abuses against ethnic Albanians.

At the CSCE Implementation Meeting on Human Dimension Issues in 1993, the IHF stated that it was 'of the opinion that, had the Serbian President been penalised for pursuing his course in Kosovo, through the use of international sanctions, the tragic warfare in Croatia and Bosnia–Herzegovina might have been prevented'. In 1994, the IHF drew attention to the continuing militarisation and open distribution of arms to the Serbian population and the increasing numbers of draft-age Albanian men fleeing Kosovo. It investigated the situation of draft evaders and deserters concentrated in the Macedonian city of Tetovo and it appealed to European states to give them protection on the grounds that 'it cannot be expected that Kosovan Albanians serve in an army that has occupied their territory since 1989 and has been collectively persecuting ethnic Albanians'. At this time, Rugova and the LDK were behaving in exactly the way that international organisations implored disputants to act elsewhere in the region and got no thanks for it from Brussels, London or Washington. It is no wonder that the IHF and other NGOs could barely conceal their frustrations in their reports on the Kosovo situation (IHF 1999).

The only strong warning from the West to Milošević about his behaviour in Kosovo came from the United States. On 24 December 1992 (in the twilight of his Presidency), President Bush sent a terse one sentence message to Milošević which said: 'In the event of conflict in Kosovo caused by Serbian action, the United States will be prepared to employ military force against Serbians in Kosovo and Serbia proper' (Judah 2000: 74). The Bush administration had received intelligence information that Milošević was planning a major offensive against the Kosovan Albanians, one designed to induce mass flight from the territory (Bellamy 2002: 34). It would have made sense for Milošević to choose that moment to ethnically cleanse Kosovo. The United States was preoccupied with the presidential handover. The new occupant of the White House, William 'Bill' Clinton was seen as a threat and needed to be presented with a *fait accompli* in Kosovo (Bellamy 2002: 34). Bush and his Secretary of State, old Yugoslavia hand Lawrence Eagleburger, were aware that their inaction as Yugoslavia drifted to war had already cast a deep shadow over an administration that should have been seen as triumphant owing to the West's victory in the Cold War. But Clinton turned out to hold similar stereotypical views about the region (though he reiterated Bush's warning to Milošević early in his presidency). On 10 February 1993, he told an audience in Michigan that 'it's no accident that the First World War started in this area. There are ancient ethnic hatreds that have consumed people and led to horrible abuses' (Bellamy 2002: 50).

For most of Clinton's time in the White House, the United States urged restraint on the Serbs while 'turning both a blind eye to human rights abuses and accepting Belgrade's constitutional claim' (Bellamy 2002: 50). A warning issued by the UN's Tadeusz Mazowiecki early in 1995 that the human rights situation in Kosovo was deteriorating did not deter international peace-makers in the Balkans (from 1994 they were known as the Contact Group, representing the United States, Russia, Britain, France and Germany) from announcing a planned 2-month suspension of sanctions on Serbia to strengthen peace prospects (Bellamy 2002: 52).

The impact of the Dayton agreement on Kosovo

Military setbacks for hardline Serbs in Bosnia following NATO's aerial intervention in September 1995 paved the way for the Dayton peace conference in November of that year. Most Western diplomats were adamant that Kosovo, the issue which had catapulted Milošević to power, was not one he could easily compromise on and that to overload the talks agenda was to risk their collapse. Once agreement was reached on Bosnia, it was thought necessary to encourage Milošević to stay in his 'peace-making' mode so as to ensure the successful implementation of the Dayton accord (Caplan 1998: 750). But the West scarcely exhausted the strong bargaining position it had vis-à-vis Milošević. Obtaining the lifting of sanctions which were pulverising the Serbian economy was then his key objective. He could have been asked to put a stop to repression and restore meaningful autonomy to Kosovo while guarantees were extended that it would remain part of a genuinely federal Yugoslavia. In turn, an effort could have been made to persuade the LDK that, in return for Western assistance, it must open up communications with Serbian interlocutors, something which it had shrunk from doing.[15] Just one of numerous initiatives that could have been undertaken would have been for Western universities to support the alternative education system. Such an initiative could have been co-ordinated by the European Union or OSCE, but no steps of this kind were taken.

The 1995 Dayton agreement which turned Bosnia–Herzegovina into several ethnic statelets under a loose and rather contrived federal roof gave out all the wrong signals to Kosovo Albanians. It suggested that ethnically based territorial arrangements in the Balkans enjoyed legitimacy in Western eyes and that only the application of force to achieve self-determination could secure the top-level attention of the West.[16]

Dayton sharply undercut Rugova's appeal at home. Hitherto, he had been categorical in his belief that international society would take Kosovo into consideration when it intervened in the Balkans (Bellamy 2001: 54). While Bosnia staggered towards an uneasy peace, repression was stepped up in Kosovo. Mass arrests of Albanians were carried out, beginning in March 1995 with the detention of some 260 former officials of the interior ministry, mainly ex-policemen. These arrests continued as the eyes of the world were on the Dayton process, many detainees being ill-treated or tortured (IHF 1999).

Carl Bildt, the first head of the UN administration in Bosnia, thought the Atlantic democracies needed to prioritise the search for a solution in Kosovo to prevent a major crisis erupting and he made his concerns public upon stepping down from his post in May 1997 (Sell 2000: 277). In early 1996, Gehrt Ahrens had begun shuttle diplomacy between Belgrade and Priština to try and build common ground, but he obtained no high-level backing and no international organisation was even prepared to pay for his flights (Bellamy 2002: 57). Efforts to bring Milošević's Serbia in from the diplomatic and economic cold were carried out with no apparent heed being given to the situation in Kosovo. The West failed to insist on any special status for Kosovo Albanian and, in April 1996, the European Union formally recognised the Federal Republic of Yugoslavia (FRY) in return for a relatively minor concession by Milošević – he had finally regularised ties with Macedonia (Caplan 1998: 750).

The FRY had been recognised by the European Union 'even though it failed to meet the political conditions for recognition that the other new states in the region had to meet before recognition' (Bellamy 2002: 59). The European Union merely noted at this time that it 'considers' that better relations between the FRY and the international community will depend, *inter alia*, on a 'constructive approach' by the FRY to the granting of autonomy for Kosovo (Caplan 1998: 750). Facing no Western sanctions over Kosovo, Milošević, in September 1996, had no qualms about ending cooperation with the UN Special Rapporteur for Human Rights for Ex-Yugoslavia, Elisabeth Renn (Bellamy 2002: 60). He also refused to implement an agreement, brokered in 1996 by the San Egidio Catholic religious community, normalising education; if acted upon, it would have led to the reopening of Kosovo schools for Albanians (Cohen 2001: 232). Meanwhile, no solution appeared in sight for the university question. Priština University contained 19,000 students, not just Serbs but also Greeks, the cost of whose studies was far less than it would have been at home. Only 2,000 students were actually drawn from Kosovo's embattled Serbs. But regular demonstrations were held in Priština (with solidarity actions in Belgrade) vehemently opposing any educational openings to Kosovo Albanians. One of the most popular slogans at these gatherings was: 'Don't even give them pencils' (Clark 2000a: 157). It wasn't just ethnic antagonism but the fear that an outlet for obtaining degrees (often by recourse to bribing professors and administrative staff) was in danger of being blocked off, that fuelled the protests (Salitu 1998: 23).

On 1 October 1997, 20,000 protesters attended a march in Priština calling for Albanians to have access to educational institutions. The march was peaceful but it embraced the concept of active non-violence rather than the passive form associated with the LDK. Albin Kurti, one of the main leaders, declared openly that 'Rugova's policy blocks the energy of the people and if you block that energy, their anger is going to explode.... He is just looking towards the international community. But he should do it the other way. He should organize the Albanian population here and demonstrate, and then the international community would be naturally attracted to deal with the problem of Kosovo' (Loza 1998: 30).

Rugova had miscalculated by declining to endorse what proved to be the first Albanian demonstration in Priština in five years. It led to dissension within the LDK, and Bujori Bukoshi, the leader of the government-in-exile, turned against him; the daily satellite TV news broadcast to Kosovo that he controlled, began attacking Rugova (Judah 2000: 133–4). Bukoshi had been shocked by the European Union's 1996 decision to recognise FRY: 'we weren't expecting it and it was a fatal mistake' (Judah 2000: 125). Brussels followed this up in early 1997 by granting Serbia trade preferences, effectively removing the last remnants of the EU sanctions (*Under Orders* 2000: 35). The United States still maintained its 'outer wall' of sanctions, Serbia being denied access to the IMF and the World Bank.

The West's apparent willingness to give Milošević a free hand in Kosovo fatally weakened the non-violent movement and led to a surge in support for armed resistance by Albanians (*The Kosovo Report* 2000: 59). According to Alex Bellamy, the violence to come in 1998 'was therefore not inspite of international efforts in Kosovo but because of them' (Bellamy 2002: 66).

The Kosovo Liberation Army (Ushtria Çlirimtare e Kosovës: UÇK), the organisation that would transform the nature of the Albanian resistance in 1998, first began to be heard of in 1996. It seems to have emerged in Switzerland, one of the centres of the Albanian Diaspora. *Émigrés* made up the most radicalised part of the Albanian population and it is no surprise that it was among them that the UÇK made its first appearance. For a while, many Albanians in Kosovo suspected it might be a provocation dreamt up by Belgrade in order to unleash more repression (*The Kosovo Report* 2000: 51). Until 1997, active armed groups were miniscule and certainly had no permanent base within Kosovo. But next door in Albania, the Berisha government had been toppled in a popular revolt after the collapse of a large pyramid savings scheme. The state temporarily disintegrated, which led to the looting of army and interior ministry arms depots. With the demise of Berisha, Rugova lost an ally who had usually endorsed his non-violent strategy. As for the UÇK, it gained an inexhaustible supply of weapons. It now also became possible to organise training facilities in northern Albania, near the border with Kosovo. This was also a period when Germany decided to repatriate 130,000 Kosovans, now that it had restored ties with Belgrade (*The Kosovo Report* 2000: 59).

The throwing of grenades at the gates of Serb refugee camps on 11 February 1996 marked the first organised violence attributable to the UÇK (*Under Orders* 2000: 31). Two years later, the United Nations released figures showing that the UÇK had been responsible for 31 attacks in 1996, 55 in 1997 and 66 in the first months of 1998 (Halberstam 2001: 397). On 24 September as these were mounting, the Contact Group (now augmented by Italy) broke its silence on Kosovo. It declared: 'we do not support independence and we do not support maintenance of the *status quo*. We support an enhanced status for Kosovo within the Federal Republic of Yugoslavia', but under the condition that 'such a status should fully protect the rights of the Albanian population in accordance with OSCE standards and the UN Charter' (Leurdijk and Zandee 2001: 28). The international community remained committed to a political settlement of the Kosovo question within the political framework of FRY. But, in the aftermath of the crisis in Albania and confronted with seemingly unstoppable violence in Kosovo, this part of the Balkans for the first time during the prolonged regional crisis, becomes the primary object of its attentions.

The UÇK felt that Kosovo was not on the international agenda because Albanians did not control any territory. Dreniça became an early stronghold. This hilly region in central Kosovo was inhabited almost entirely by ethnic Albanians and had been the focal-point of an anti-communist uprising in the mid-1940s (*Under Orders* 2000: 155). From late 1997, men in uniforms began to appear openly at the funerals of soldiers and sympathisers, sometimes with tens of thousands of people in attendance.

The West wakes up to Kosovo

The fear that an explosion in Kosovo would trigger a massive refugee flow heading in the direction of Western Europe, concentrated the minds of senior government officials there. On 16 February 1998 the German Foreign Minister Klaus Kinkel expressed his worry about the fact that between 500 and 2,000 Kosovo Albanians were arriving in Germany every month. He advocated 'extended autonomy' for Kosovo within Serbia, falling short of independence.[17] In December of the previous year, he and his French counterpart, Hubert Vedrine, had visited Belgrade to persuade Milošević to accept third-party mediation in Kosovo, but he had simply refused to see them (Bellamy 2002: 65). He would adopt a similar approach to Felipe Gonzalez, the former Spanish Prime Minister, after his appointment as the EU's Kosovo mediator early in 1998 (Judah 2000: 153).

At an EU–US summit in Washington in December 1997, Western states, for the first time, collectively condemned Serbian methods in Kosovo and resolved to promote human rights there.[18] But the United States and the European Union failed to synchronise their responses as the situation on the ground in Kosovo worsened. In Belgrade, on 23 February 1998, Richard Gelbard, the US envoy charged with overseeing the implementation of the Dayton agreement, offered concessions allowing Yugoslavia to increase its diplomatic presence in the United States and obtain landing rights there for the national airline.[19] More significantly, he declared that the UÇK was 'without any question a terrorist group' and the United States condemned the unacceptable violence carried out by such groups in Kosovo' (Dannreuther 2001: 19). Gelbard's remarks were criticised because of the possibility that they would be seen in Belgrade as a justification for stepping up violence. On 3 March Gelbard altered his tone and stated: 'President Milošević is well aware that the United States will not tolerate violence, and violence will be met by the most dire consequences imaginable. That will be the end of his government without any question'; he added that in a telephone conversation, he had offered the Serbian leader two choices: 'one choice is to rejoin the international community . . . the other way however is the road to the end of his government'. He also stated that the Albanians must solve the Kosovo problem themselves through dialogue with the Serbs and not expect 'any rescue from outside'.[20] This was a thoroughly confusing statement which resulted in Gelbard being dropped as the Clinton administration's chief Balkan troubleshooter. On the same day, in a gesture that pointed to a lack of transatlantic coordination, the European Commission's political committee concluded that the Kosovo issue could not be regarded as an internal matter of FRY. Trade preferences were withdrawn from Belgrade because it was failing to meet minimum human rights criteria (IHF 1999).

Two days later, on 5 March 1998, a massacre at Danji Prekaz in the Dreniça valley was carried out by the Serbian paramilitary police, the Ministry of the Interior (MUP). Fifty-one people were killed, including Adem Jasari, a founder member of the UÇK and twenty-eight members of his extended family. This was a catalytic event, which pushed Kosovo towards the top of the Western policy-making agenda. US concessions to Serbia, granted as recently as 23 February, were rescinded. In Rome on 7 March, Madeleine Albright, the US Secretary of State, declared: 'We are not going to stand by and watch the Serbian authorities do in Kosovo what they can no longer get away with doing in Bosnia'.[21] Two days later, at a meeting of six of her European colleagues in London at Lancaster House, she told the assembly: 'History is watching us. In this very room our predecessors delayed as Bosnia burned and history will not be kind to us if we do the same' (Daalder and O'Hanlon 2000: 24).

Albright, who had arrived in the United States in 1948 as an 11-year-old refugee from Czechoslovakia, had seen events in Yugoslavia through the prism of 1930s Europe. Milošević was an opportunistic tyrant seeking fresh conquests by exploiting the irresolution and short attention-span of democratic leaders. Her father, Josef Korbel, a high-level official in the Czechoslovak foreign ministry, had actually been ambassador in Belgrade in 1948, when he persuaded his British counterpart to give him and his family British visas so as to make good their escape from the communist bloc (Halberstam 2001: 379). When Albright declared in Rome on 7 March that 'we have a broad range of options available to us', she was running ahead of her governmental colleagues back in Washington, but she had a kindred spirit in General Wesley Clark, the US general in charge of NATO's military command in Europe. To the chagrin of many in the Pentagon, he had grown 'absolutely certain' by early 1998 that 'Milošević could not be stopped without the use of force' (Halberstam 2001: 396).

For much of 1998, the US political establishment would be embroiled in the scandal involving President Clinton and Monica Lewinsky, a young intern in the White House who claimed he had conducted an affair with her. It led to an impeachment bid in Congress, where the Republicans had a majority after which there were grave doubts about Clinton's version of the controversy. Little thought appears to have been given by an embattled administration to what steps needed to be taken if Kosovo was to draw back from outright war. Aaron Rhodes, the executive director of the IHF emphasised the need for tangible improvements to occur in the lives of Kosovan Albanians to avoid this outcome. He wrote on 18 March 1998: 'a "meaningful dialogue" proposed by the Contact Group could only take place … if the complex array of Serbian policies that have pauperised the Albanians in Kosovo were removed. The dialogue would work only if the two sides had equal rights' (IHF 1999).

A lull in fighting coincided with the holding of parliamentary and presidential elections in Kosovo on 22 March. Rugova hoped to acquire fresh legitimacy for his leadership in the event of any internationally brokered talks with Belgrade. Owing to a boycott by other Albanian forces, the LDK was virtually alone in the contest. But Rugova and LDK candidates loyal to him won comfortably on a high turnout of 80 per cent of adult Albanians. The LDK's links to family networks in rural Kosovo were still in good order and there appeared to be no convincing alternative figures representing a more radical viewpoint (Loza 1998: 23). Adem Demaçi, a veteran of Serbian jails, who was known as 'the Albanian Mandela', headed a rival coalition of Kosovo parties and NGOs. He advocated a more forceful strategy but, his proposal, known as 'Balkania' for an independent Kosovo possessing confederal links with Serbia and Montenegro appealed to few fellow Albanians (Caplan 1998: 757; Judah 2000: 132).

In Serbia, Milošević was also turning to the ballot box to shore up his position in Kosovo. On 31 March, UN Security Council resolution 1160 had imposed a 4-week deadline for the withdrawal of special MUP forces, the granting of access to humanitarian organisations and the admission of an OSCE mission to Kosovo. The resolution branded the UÇK as terrorists and confirmed Kosovo as part of Serbia, but it found that the crisis there presented a threat to international peace and security (Bellamy 2002: 76). To reinforce his view that Kosovo was a wholly internal matter for Serbia, Milošević called for a referendum on international mediation in Kosovo on 23 April 1998. A 94.73 percentage of voters supported the government stance on a 73 per cent turnout (but Montenegro boycotted the poll). This was a higher turnout than was customary in Serbian elections and it showed the continuing ability of Milošević to manipulate popular feelings on the issue of Kosovo. An opinion poll published in the opposition newspaper *Naša borba* showed that these were hardly moderate ones. About 42 per cent of the Serbs surveyed wanted to see the Albanians expelled from Kosovo, whether forcibly or peacefully, whereas 27 per cent of those polled thought the best solution was to extend cultural autonomy to the Albanians of Kosovo; some 6 per cent preferred to partition the province with 3.3 per cent favouring its upgrading to republican status on par with the two remaining republics making up the remains of the Yugoslav federation. Only 1.8 per cent of respondents favoured granting Kosovo independence (Ramet 2001: 37).

Milošević naturally drew encouragement from the disarray in US policy-making circles as the Monica Lewinsky affair grew worse in mid-1998. From May he found himself negotiating with the familiar figure of Richard Holbrooke. With his Bosnian experience, he believed that an acceptable deal could be wrung out of both Milošević and the Kosovo Albanians. His re-emergence was a setback for Madeleine Albright, by now quite convinced that only the imminent threat of force would compel Milošević to make a significant climb-down in Kosovo (Daalder and O'Hanlon 2000: 69). But Holbrooke's goal of a negotiated settlement faced acute difficulties. A chasm separated both sides, with neither being content with a half-way-house where both groups shared an autonomous province. Too much had occurred since Kosovo's autonomy had been revoked in

1989 for that to be simply resurrected. In this harsh context, the Contact Group was at a loss to know what proposals to make about the future of the territory. In mid-1998 it did authorise Christopher Hill (an Albanian speaker and the US ambassador to Macedonia) to begin a process of indirect negotiations through shuttle diplomacy (Weller 1999: 219). But the lack of a clearcut leadership structure on the UÇK side and Rugova's growing marginalisation made it difficult to know who to negotiate with on the Albanian side.[22]

In June 1998, the Americans held direct talks with individuals who claimed to have authority over the fighting men of the UÇK. They were wrong-footed when a uniformed fighter entered the room in Rahovec where Holbrooke was meeting UÇK commanders and sat next to him for a photo which was transmitted worldwide (Kola 2003: 341). By now, the UÇK claimed to control about 30–40 per cent of Kosovo. According to HRW, Serb civilians in areas under UÇK control 'were harassed and terrorised into leaving by assault, kidnappings, and sporadic killing' (*Under Orders* 2001: 42). The taking of hostages and extra-judicial killings continued until the start of 1999. According to the International Committee of the Red Cross (ICRC), ninety-seven Serbs who went missing in 1998 were still missing by May 2000 (Judah 2000: 158–9; *Under Orders* 2001: 13).

Serbia may have allowed the UÇK to fan out across a large part of Kosovo in order to catch it in the open once it mounted a counter-offensive. This was a ruthless operation carried out in July–August 1998. By mid-August, some 20,000 Kosovo families had been driven from their homes according to the head of the United Nations High Commission for Refugees (UNHCR).[23] She claimed that many parts of western and central Kosovo had become depopulated as around 10 per cent of the population was displaced. Indeed, by now Kosovo was the scene of one of the five largest refugee crises in the world: Angola, the Congo, Sierra Leone and Colombia only surpassed it (Garton-Ash 2000).

Serbian brutality should not excuse the UÇK for pursuing reckless military tactics that rebounded terribly on civilians. In the summer of 1998 they attacked the Serbs, inviting retaliation, and then leaving civilians at the mercy of Serbian forces. One of the biggest such fiascos occurred when the UÇK tried to take the city of Rahovec in July 1998. Hashim Thaçi, the rising star of the UÇK; admitted that everything had been calculated, including civilian suffering. It was 'a sacrifice that had to be made to secure NATO intervention' (Kola 2003: 341).

Milošević was emboldened by apparent Western disarray. Eight years of dealing regularly with West European (and not a few US) politicians had convinced him that they were a malleable breed that he could easily wear down or confuse. But it was from Western Europe, particularly Britain (the Western country he most liked to do business with during the 1990–7 premiership of John Major) that he would find his stoutest adversary over Kosovo. Prime Minister Tony Blair expressed his belief in the need for outside humanitarian intervention if a government was systematically ill-treating its own people. In June 1998, he told the House of Commons that Britain would not tolerate an intensification of conflict in Kosovo: 'I don't believe we could afford to have a situation of disorder spreading in that part of the world and I think this is a clear enough message to

Mr Milošević' (Bellamy 2002: 86). Blair's seriousness was shown by his decision to ask the Defence Ministry to investigate options for acting unilaterally (Bellamy 2002: 87). In July, Emyr Jones Parry, the political director of the Foreign Office, met Milošević in the company of his German and Austrian counterparts. They told him of the devastation they had seen in Kosovo. Milošević (who had rarely visited Kosovo during his years of power) disputed their eyewitness testimonies. This prompted his guests to say, according to the Briton: 'Mr President, it is either that your people are not telling you of the things we have seen or you are choosing to ignore them', to which he gave no answer. On his departure, Jones Parry said to Milošević: 'If you carry on like this, the British government will take military action against you within the next six months' (Judah 2000: 170).

Trying to fend off impeachment, President Clinton was scarcely as forthright as Blair or his senior officials. His administration rejected the deployment of ground troops out of hand in the summer of 1998 and did not reconsider this decision until January 1999 (Daalder and O'Hanlon 2000: 55). Quite possibly, the Russian stance in mid-1998 caused Milošević more frustration than Washington's. At a meeting with President Yeltsin on 16 June, he agreed to all but one of the demands of the Contact Group which had been issued four days earlier. They were to:

- cease all action in Kosovo and withdraw security forces;
- enable international monitoring and allow for the unimpeded access of monitors;
- facilitate the return of refugees and displaced persons;
- seek rapid progress in the dialogue with the Kosovo Albanian leadership.

The Contact Group had warned that if these conditions weren't met, 'there will be further measures to halt the violence and protect the civilian population, including those that may require the authorisation of a UN Security Council Resolution'. This was a thinly veiled reference to the authorisation of air-strikes. But according to Alex Bellamy, the day after Milošević's meeting with Yeltsin, the tanks of the VJ (Yugoslav Army) were employed against villagers in Kosovo, thus breaking his word to the Russian leader: 'Russian policy perceptions changed' as shown by Resolution 1199 adopted by the Security Council on 23 September (Bellamy 2002: 93). It was passed under Chapter VII of the UN Charter which authorises the Security Council to permit the use of force to maintain 'international peace and security' (Wheeler 2000: 1); though the wording was carefully ambiguous, it announced further action and additional measures if its demands for an end to violence were not met.

During the summer and early autumn of 1998, both the US State Department and the British Foreign Office had 'conducted a sustained and multi-facetted diplomatic offensive' to secure agreement among the NATO allies on the use of force' (Bellamy 2002: 88). In June Javier Solana, Secretary-General of NATO, had told a closed door meeting of defence ministers that the Serbs were mocking the Alliance with a slow-motion offensive aimed at keeping NATO off the scent. He quoted the joke of a Serbian diplomat that just 'a village a day keeps NATO away'.[24] Solana, a Socialist who had spent more than half of his life under an implacable dictatorship in his native Spain, made the case for air-strikes against Serbian military targets at another gathering of NATO defence ministers in Portugal on 23–24 September 1998. He argued that following its numerous warnings and threats, the Alliance's credibility was now on the line (Daalder and O'Hanlon 2000: 43). On 10 October, the North Atlantic Council, NATO's highest permanent political body, gave the go-ahead for air-strikes if Serbia continued to withhold its compliance from NATO demands centred around the mistreatment of civilians.

Between 5 and 13 October, Holbrooke was locked in negotiations with Milošević. Earlier that year, he had described the Serbian leader as 'a serviceable villain' who could be induced to do a deal over Kosovo. Representing the Contact Group, his mission was an exercise in coercive diplomacy. Milošević was left in little doubt that NATO air strikes were imminent unless he failed to heed the Contact Group's terms for ending the conflict in Kosovo (Cohen 2001: 243). To reinforce Holbrooke's position, he took with him General Michael Short who would have led NATO air operations in the event of conflict. 'So you're the one who will bomb us', he said to Short. He replied: 'I've B52s in one hand and U2s (high altitude surveillance aircraft) in the other. It's up to you which I'm going to use' (*War In Europe* 2000).

Milošević agreed to accept a team of 2,000 civilian observers in Kosovo who would be under the direction of the OSCE (Roberts 1999: 113). The role of the Kosovo Verification Mission (KVM) was to ensure that the FRY fulfilled its commitment to stop its crackdown in Kosovo. Belgrade would guarantee the security of its personnel and their complete freedom of movement. The other main points of the deal were:

- Non-combat aircraft will provide aerial verification of compliance under a formal agreement to be signed between NATO and FRY.
- US mediator Christopher Hill will continue his efforts to promote a political settlement acceptable to both sides.
- It is agreed that Kosovo will remain part of Serbia.
- The outer wall of economic sanctions will remain in place.[25]

At a press conference on 28 October when Holbrooke introduced some of the international officials meant to ensure compliance towards the agreement, he characterised his achievement with Milošević as part of the Clinton administration's 'decision to make the United States a resurgent presence in Europe... working in close partnership with our NATO allies...' (Cohen 2001: 243). Hitherto, whenever the conflict had escalated, there had been a lack of coordination not only between NATO member-states but within different branches of government of several of them, notably the United States itself, and also within the wider Contact Group (Judah 2000: 144). Unfortunately, the KVM was not destined to mark a new departure. The OSCE could put only 1,300 of the projected 2,000 verifiers into the field. They were unarmed and thus in a weak position to enforce the cease-fire (Judah 2000: 188). The head of the KVM, William Walker, was a contested figure. He had recently been head of the UN transitional mission in Eastern Slavonia, preparing the way for its reintegration with Croatia after several years of Serbian occupation. This had gone well, but he had an earlier controversial period of time as UN ambassador to El Salvador when Washington was backing a hardline regime to suppress leftist rebels. Judah has written that: 'Assuming then that his past must presuppose a close relationship with the Central Intelligence Agency (CIA), the Serbian authorities were deeply suspicious of Walker (Judah 2000: 189). His mission was soon impaired by a running feud with his deputy, a French diplomat Gabriel Keller, a former charge d'affaire (and future ambassador) in Belgrade (Bellamy 2002: 103).

Moreover, the agreement had been made with Belgrade and not the UÇK. Both sides refused to sit down and discuss the draft agreement Ambassador Hill had drawn up in mid-September. Under it, Kosovo would function as part of Yugoslavia for three years, with its own assembly, government, judiciary and local police force. But crucially, the plan said that any change of status would have to be by mutual agreement, which left vague as to how the political dispute between Serbs and Albanians could be resolved (Weller 1999: 219).

Narrow options

There was now an emerging transatlantic consensus that the threat of force needed to be clearly laid out in order for Milošević to significantly moderate his behaviour. But the Atlantic democracies were still mired in confusion about what should be the political strategy behind these tough tactics. Even if Serbia could be induced or compelled to grant full separation to Kosovo, there were at least two major problems. First, it could destabilise much of the southern Balkans; it might raise the expectations of the large Albanian minority in Macedonia and give it an excuse to join with its co-ethnics in Kosovo and Albania itself to demand a greater Albania. Albania, it turned out, was actually a force for moderation as the crisis escalated. Following the 1997 upheaval, it was fully absorbed with restoring a functioning state and trying to find a consensus between polarised parties. When Fatos Nano, head of the ex-communist Socialists and Prime Minister in 1997–8, met Milošević at a summit of Balkan heads of government in Crete in 1997, he was conciliatory over the issue of Kosovo.[26] In February 1998, he criticised Belgrade's retrograde policies in Kosovo but said it was still an internal affair of Yugoslavia.[27] But countries like Greece and even Bulgaria, still unsure of the permanence of their own borders, would not have regarded an Albanian unification drive with equanimity.

Second, independence for Kosovo, whereby a territory broke away from one of the six republics established in communist Yugoslavia, might set a precedent for Bosnia–Herzegovina, encouraging Serbs and Croats in the loveless federation created at Dayton in 1995, to break away and align with their respective kin states. This was a near unanimous West European position, the only significant dissenter being William van Eekelen, the former Dutch foreign minister who, from 1989 to 1994 was Secretary-General of the West European Union. He expressed his unhappiness about the proliferation of 'small perhaps unviable states' but couldn't see why Kosovo could be denied its right to statehood since it had been granted to the equally small Slovenia in 1991.[28]

Partition was also ruled out. It had been floated as an idea in 1996 by Aleksandr Despić, President of the Serbian Academy of Sciences (Maliqi 1998: 158). He proposed that talks start 'with those who are insisting on the secession of Kosovo about a peaceful and civilised separation and demarcation' (Veremis and Kofos 1998: 36). But both Serbs and Albanians felt entitled to most of Kosovo's territory. Moreover, the fate of its most precious economic asset, the Trepca mines in the north-east (as well as Serbian religious sites located mainly in the west and centre) was bound to be the subject of fierce dispute. Again, there was the fear of the precedent that might be set in Bosnia, whose *formal* partition at least had been averted at Dayton. This left far-reaching autonomy as the least worst option, but Serbs and Albanians remained poles apart on the nature and extent of it. In 1997 Gazmend Pula, head of the Kosovo Helsinki Committee had privately advanced the 'Three Republic' solution whereby Kosovo would remain within Yugoslavia as an equal republic alongside the two others remaining in the federation. Even though a strong case could be made for arguing that would enable the Albanians to obtain *de facto* independence, Pula as an NGO official, lacked the political clout to promote it in an atmosphere increasingly hostile to such compromise measures (Judah 2000: 94–5).

The Contact Group could have been more energetic in trying to carve out a middle way. It could have pushed Milošević to deliver concessions that brought a rapid improvement in the lives of Albanians, while speaking with a common voice to the Albanians that autonomy with international guarantees offered them less hardship and insecurity than independence for an awkwardly placed and heavily populated territory lacking the means to easily support itself. One interim measure that could have been more energetically pursued would have been the deployment of an international ground force in Kosovo to protect the civilian populace. There were undoubted obstacles. Albright and Holbrooke both acknowledged that NATO ground troops were essential to monitor the cease-fire, but Congress wouldn't give authorisation for their deployment. Robert Dole, the US politician who had been supportive of the Kosovo Albanians since 1990, remarked that 'Kosovo was maybe the first casualty of the Lewinsky affair' (*War In Europe* 2000). But he was a Republican elder statesman who had recently been Senate house leader; he and other multilateralists in the Republican Party could have sought to overcome Senate inhibitions about sending US troops to Kosovo as part of a NATO force.

Russia could have been made more use of in order to persuade Milošević to accept a compromise (Judah 2000: 224). In the end, the Contact Group (with Russia a member), supported the double negative, approving 'neither of independence nor the maintenance of the status quo' (Daalder and O'Hanlon 2000: 38).[29] The nature of the six-nation Contact Group, with its emphasis on detailed consensus before a new initiative could be taken, often resulted in lowest common denominator policies or, in a word, a fudge. Moreover, there were other international organisations involved (the UN, NATO, the OSCE and the EU being the most prominent) and a sometimes complex set of national interests to contend with. The outcome was sometimes a lack of consistency in the diplomatic response and a slow reaction to events on the ground when a single-minded and highly professional approach was needed in order to avert total crisis (*The Kosovo Report* 2000: 133). There was also the syndrome of fighting the last war, basing conflict prevention in Kosovo around lessons learnt in Bosnia, without properly realising that there were differences between the Kosovo and Bosnia questions that required qualitatively different responses.

The nature of the UÇK presented problems for international negotiators. It was a myriad of armed groups which meant that it wasn't easy for it to be integrated into the diplomatic process. There were times when clearly more could have been done to restrain the UÇK. In June 1998, the United States reversed its position and initiated dialogue with some of its representatives, hoping to exercise a moderating influence over it, The US State Department spokesman, James Rubin, tied himself in knots by explaining in late June that an organisation which had some members who committed acts of terrorism was not necessarily a terrorist organisation.[30] Local forces inevitably exploited such ambiguity and perhaps the United States could have made it publicly plainer as to what its links with the UÇK entailed and extricated concessions from its admittedly loosely structured leadership in return for opening a communications channel. It is certainly striking that Holbrooke made no effort to deliver a general appeal to the Albanian populace about the need for realism or moderation. If, at a public meeting arranged for him to speak to large numbers of Kosovo Albanians, he had pointed out the real danger they faced by adopting militant options and the benefits that were likely to arise by choosing moderation, it could have strengthened the position of the LDK and given the Americans more leverage over the UÇK, but such forward thinking was conspicuous by its absence. The Americans retained a preference for operating through state and paramilitary forces which deployed violence.

Milošević's intentions and mood

Milošević's position hardened as the Kosovo conflict intensified. With Albright formulating foreign policy, the second Clinton administration was ceasing to view him as indispensable for the implementation of western peace plans in the Balkans. Second thoughts about the wisdom of having him as the main local guarantor of the Bosnian peace mounted as it appeared increasingly stalled. He was well-aware of the deep-seated Western aversion to using force, especially in the Balkans where many still insisted that no critical interests were at stake. His habit of refusing to see figures such as the Secretary-General of NATO or top foreign ministers when they came to Belgrade may have been a sign of his deep-seated contempt for them and what they represented. There were events occurring in the West which may also have strengthened his belief that he could stay one step ahead of them in the war of nerves over Kosovo. It cannot just have been

Milošević who, upon seeing the United States grotesquely embroiled in the Lewinsky affair, concluded that this was an enfeebled superpower which had lost its way despite its military strength. He is likely to have derived comfort also from the return to office of the German Social Democrats in October 1998. A coalition with the strongly pacifist Greens was formed. Although it gave its backing to NATO's threat of air-strikes within days of taking office, Milošević could reasonably have expected such a government to be a weak link in any NATO push against him.

He already had plenty of evidence that Western states could be made to dance to his tune not just by threats but also by economic inducements. Italy's Foreign Minister Lamberto Dini argued longer than any other top Western official that Milošević was a guarantor of stability in the Balkans. In 1999, Italy was the only Western power not to close down its embassy in Belgrade, an indication that Dini valued his channel of communications with Milošević (Morelli 2001: 69). Dini was soon talking of the need for 'an exit strategy' when NATO finally confronted Milošević in the spring of 1999. Italy had closer economic ties with Serbia than any other major Western country. In 1997, Telecom Italia (and its Greek counterpart) had beat French and German competitors to win a $1 billion stake in Telecom Serbia. Among other things, the extra cash helped him to buy votes in elections held that October (Caplan 1998: 753).[31]

Despite his poor relations with Yeltsin, Milošević may have expected high-level diplomatic and material assistance from the Russians if a confrontation with NATO materialised. One source argues that influential elements in Russian politics were telling him this in early 1999 despite Russian reluctance to use its veto in the Security Council in 1998 when its Western members had proposed tough measures to contain the Kosovo crisis (Bellamy 2002: 150). Russia was grappling with its own insurgency in Chechnya, a largely Muslim territory with a beleaguered Russian minority. It was determined not to internationalise the problem, so there were seemingly plenty of grounds for both Belgrade and Moscow to adopt a common perspective opposed to humanitarian intervention in internal disputes. Milošević could expect even stronger backing at the United Nations from China. In the early 1990s, it had been absorbed with the fallout from the Tien Anmen square massacre of May 1989 when a bloody crackdown against pro-democracy students had ensued. Since then, the state had gone to enormous lengths to inculcate a defiant nationalism among educated youth to prevent a similar reoccurrence in the future. China was determined to block any strong UN measures designed to allow the use of force against the Serbian regime. So the disposition of Russia, an ex-communist state falling back on nationalism for legitimacy, and China, a pseudo-communist one deploying nationalism even more blatantly to allow a privileged leadership, to control its populace, appeared to provide Milošević with important international protection.

Of undeniable importance in pushing Milošević towards outright intransigence, were his mounting domestic troubles. By 1998 he had lost control of Montenegro to an ex-ally pushing for independence so that the Yugoslav federation increasingly existed in name only. The army chief, General Momčilo Perisić had emerged as a powerful figure in his own right in Serbia. He had reassured anti-Milošević students in Belgrade during the 1996–7 protests against his regime that the army would not be used against them and, a year later, he opposed a crackdown on the wayward leadership in Montenegro (Cohen 2001: 252).

A conspicuous retreat by Milošević from a long-held position that Kosovo was an inalienable part of Serbia, might have spelled the beginning of the end for him. The pro-democracy demonstrators who mobilised in such large numbers on an almost nightly basis in the winter of 1996–7 never assailed him over war crimes in Bosnia or his extended crackdown in Kosovo. Instead, a section of the marchers insulted him by shouting 'Slobo is a Turk', a modern-day slur usually aimed at Bosnian Muslims. Sometimes when busloads of heavily armed riot police arrived at the scene, 'the protestors response was to suggest that the police were focussing on the wrong target. "Go to Kosovo! Go to Kosovo!" they would scream'.[32]

The neo-fascist Serbian Radical Party (SRS) had risen to being the second largest party in the state by, among other things, flaunting a policy promoting the destruction of the Kosovan Albanians. Its leader, Vojislav Šešelj, in a chilling article that appeared in his party's newspaper on 14 October 1995, unveiled a plan meant to solve the Kosovo question once and for all. It began with 'the revision of citizenship rights'. The Albanians would be required to possess a citizenship certificate 'something none of them of course have' or else face expulsion. 'Such a measure would first and foremost affect the educated portion of their population so that the rest would not be able to organize resistance and could be easily manipulated'. Then comes the 'revision of land ownership laws'. Land that had 'in one way or another ended up in the hands of the Albanians' would be 'given back to its Serb owners or their successors'. Finally, radical measures would need to be applied to realise the goal of 'changing the ethnic structure of the population'. The 'colonisation of Kosovo' should be 'carried out quickly and conclusively'. Serb settlements should be expanded until they squeezed out the Albanian enclaves. Water and electricity should be cut off to make the lives of the Albanians 'unbearable'.

Fraternisation should be discouraged: 'If Serbs from neighbouring enclaves start to patronise Albanian businesses, incidents or beatings and violence must be prompted in these areas'. Albanian leaders should be humiliated or made the target of violence: 'Important political figures should be eliminated by traffic accidents and jealousy killings or by infecting them with the Aids virus when they travel abroad.... Through adequate propaganda, such events can create the sense of an intolerable percentage of virus carriers, which could be used to isolate large groups of Albanians and would promote a stereotype of Albanians as an infected people'.[33]

That such goals could be publicly advocated shows the depth of Serbian animus towards Kosovo Albanians both at the elite and the popular level. There seems to have been no adverse response from Western leaders when Šešelj joined the government in April 1998 as deputy-premier of Serbia. Milošević was seeking to shore up his domestic position in the face of a looming showdown with the West. In October, he removed Jovica Stanišić, his intelligence chief who had criticised his lurch to the ultra-right. In November, the head of the army, General Perišić was next to go. Both men had been fully involved in Serbian aggression against other republics earlier but, by 1998, they 'represented saner voices in the Belgrade power structure' now dominated by 'a red–brown' coalition of the Socialists and ultra-nationalists (Cohen 2001: 257). By the early winter of 1998, Milošević may already have made his choice to expel much of the civilian population from Kosovo. He must have realised that the UÇK 'was becoming too strong and too popular within ethnic Albanian society for him to defeat using classic counter-insurgency techniques' (Daalder and O'Hanlon 2000: 13).

Holbrooke had declared afterwards that he had not expected the cease-fire monitored by the KVM to survive beyond March 1999. It was destined to break down long before then. Serbian force levels in Kosovo failed to be reduced to the levels agreed with Holbrooke (Bellamy 2002: 106). A 2 November 1998 deadline for a political agreement also passed unnoticed. Ambassador Hill's proposals of meaningful autonomy for Kosovo within Yugoslavia was rebuffed by the UÇK, elements of which obstructed the movements of the KVM (Gow 2003: 273–4, 277). From November, an increase in attacks on Serb civilians and security forces was also noticeable (Bellamy 2002: 111). But for several months, the deployment of the KVM monitors had created a sense of security that encouraged displaced Albanians to return to their homes. The likelihood of the Kosovo winter claiming many victims among the population was significantly reduced. This must be viewed as a real achievement of the KVM (Daalder and O'Hanlon 2000: 49).

But a fresh upsurge of serious fighting occurred in mid-December. Serbian forces moved out of their garrisons without prior notification. Interior Ministry units, known as the MUP, ones that had been required to withdraw from Kosovo, soon returned (Daalder and O'Hanlon 2000: 61). On 14 and 15 December, the MUP ambushed units, killing many guerrillas. Soon after, masked gunmen burst into a Serb student café in Peç and killed six young Serb civilians (*Under Orders* 2001: 289). Despite the return of Holbrooke, the cease-fire had collapsed by 24 December 1998.

Despite a shortage of personnel, the fragile peace had not given way due to any inadequacies of the KVM. Instead, the gulf separating the two sides had proved impossible to bridge and the Atlantic democracies failed to invest enough time and effort to ensure that the cease-fire lasted into 1999. The killings on 15 January 1999 of at least forty-five Albanians from the village of Raçak became the symbol of the October agreement's collapse. Belgrade may not have expected a strong Western response; after all, there had been plenty of other Raçak's the previous year (Ignatieff 2000: 60). But Walker and a team of monitors turned up and con-demned the massacre as 'an unspeakable atrocity' and he 'did not hesitate to accuse the government security forces of responsibility' (Daalder and O'Hanlon 2000: 64). A rattled Milošević tried to expel Walker and refused to allow Judge Louise Arbour, the head of the International Criminal Tribunal for Yugoslavia (ICTY), to enter FRY to investigate what he claimed was a propaganda event fabricated by the UÇK (Sell 2002: 294). The initiative now swung from Holbrooke with his preference for cutting a deal with Milošević, to Albright, the US Secretary of State who, for nearly a year, had shown growing readiness to confront him. In December 1998, she had her spokesman, James Rubin declare publicly that 'Milošević has been at the center of every crisis in the former Yugoslavia over the last decade. He is not simply part of the problem; Milošević is the problem' (Ignatieff 2000: 16). Albright now sought to build an inter-departmental consensus in the US administration for her plan for an ultimatum linked to the threat of force, in order to obtain acceptance in Belgrade of a political settlement (Bellamy 2002: 124). In August 1998, Alexander Vershbow, the US ambassador to NATO had already cabled to the State Department that Kosovo should be turned into an international protectorate through the use of force if necessary (Daalder and O'Hanlon 2000: 55). But support remained lukewarm in the Pentagon and, in some ways, it proved easier to enlist the backing of European officials not previously favourable to US-led coercive diplomacy.

By 28 January 1999, German Foreign Minister Joschka Fischer was ready to state publicly that force should be taken into consideration: 'I am not a friend of using force, but sometimes it is a necessary means of last resort. So I am ready to use it if there is no other way. If people are being massacred, you cannot mutter about having no mandate you must act' (Daalder and O'Hanlon 2000: 75). According to Fischer, the 1995 Srebreniça massacre in Bosnia had convinced him that appeasement would lead only to further mass graves (Rudolf 2000: 135). On 29 January, Tony Blair and Jacques Chirac issued a joint statement declaring that they were 'willing to consider all forms of military action, including the dispatch of ground forces necessary to accomplish the implementation of a negotiated settlement...' (Daalder and O'Hanlon 2000: 75).

Against the background of the worsening Kosovo situation, the European Union was taking the first steps to create its own military force. The initiative stemmed from Tony Blair, reportedly influenced by the United Nation's total failure to impose its will on the prolonged crisis in Bosnia (Deighton 2000: 63). Emerging from a summit between Blair and Chirac, the St Malo declaration of 8 December 1998 said:

> the European Union must have the capacity for autonomous action, backed by credible, military forces, the means to decide to use them, and a readiness to do so, in order to respond to international crises...acting in conformity with our respective obligations to NATO.
>
> (Deighton 2000: 63)

Within NATO, views were hardening on the ground that only the deployment of a large NATO-led force on the ground could make any real difference to the situation (Roberts 1999: 113). For some time, its Secretary-General, Javier Solana had advocated a tough approach towards Milošević and he had the consensual skills to obtain majority support for this position (Hendrickson 2002: 244). After much hesitation and debate, the strategy of unarmed intervention was discarded in favour of one of coercive diplomacy (Bellamy 2002: 130). On 28 January, the North Atlantic Council revealed that it had given Solana authorisation to mount air-strikes against targets on FRY territory if the Belgrade authorities continued aggressive actions threatening a humanitarian catastrophe and were a threat to peace and security in the region. The statement also declared that 'NATO will take all necessary measures in case of a failure by the Kosovan

Albanian side to comply with the demands of the international community' (Weller 1999: 222–3).

A key turning-point was the statement issued by UN Secretary-General Kofi Annan after he met with the North Atlantic Council on 28 January. He urged the NATO countries to build on the lessons of Bosnia and 'further refine the combination of force and diplomacy that is the key to peace in the Balkans and elsewhere'. He went on to say that the 'bloody wars of the last decade have left us with no illusions about the difficulties of halting internal conflicts – by reason or by force – particularly against the wishes of a government of a sovereign state. But nor have they left us with any illusion about the need to use force when all other means have failed. We may be reaching that limit, once again, in the former Yugoslavia'.[34]

The Rambouillet Conference

With the Lewinsky affair having at last subsided, the United States announced on 27 January that a strategy to resolve the Kosovo crisis by 'combining diplomacy with a credible threat of force' had been agreed with Washington's allies, and would be implemented through the Contact Group (Weller 1999: 221). The centrepiece of the strategy was a peace conference which, under the auspices of the Contact Group, got underway at the chateau of Rambouillet near Paris, on 6 February 1999. They were to be closed-door proximity talks in which mediators shuttled between the delegates of the two opposing sides. Only once, on 14 February, did the delegates actually meet in one room.

On 28 January, NATO's Solana had already set out the goals of the conference organisers. They were to be: a settlement that 'will provide an enhanced status for Kosovo, preserve the territorial integrity of the Federal Republic of Yugoslavia and protect the rights of all ethnic groups' (Weller 1999: 221). These were put to the Belgrade delegation as well as a variegated delegation from the Kosovan Albanians drawn mainly from the LDK and the UÇK. The uncooperative mood of the Serbs was shown when they tried to prevent the participants from leaving the country, thus delaying the start of the conference. Once both sides were assembled, mediators laid out ten non-negotiable principles:

- An immediate end to violence.
- Peaceful settlement of the conflict through dialogue.
- The agreement would be an interim one for the period of three years.
- There could be no unilateral change to this interim status.
- The territorial integrity of Yugoslavia and its neighbours must be respected.
- The rights of members of all national communities must be respected.
- There would be free and fair elections in Kosovo, supervised by the OSCE.
- Neither party should prosecute anyone for crimes related to the Kosovo conflict (with the exception of the ICTY).
- There would be an amnesty and release of political prisoners.
- There would be international involvement and full cooperation by the parties on implementation (Bellamy 2002: 131–2).

The Serbian delegation was a low-level one, which most of the time refused to engage in serious negotiations. Milošević absented himself, but made sure that a rare consensual figure, such as Kosovo's leading Orthodox churchman, Bishop Artemije, was kept away from Rambouillet (Judah 2000: 201). The delegation spent much of the time merry-making through the hours of darkness, which deprived the Albanian delegation, on an adjoining floor, of much sleep (Ignatieff 2000: 56). The nature of the delegation was a sign that it was not there to engage in a meaningful talks process. It was strengthened by the arrival of the Serbian Head of State, Milan Milutinović on 11 February, accompanied by professional negotiators and constitutional experts (Weller 1999: 226–7).

By now both sides were thoroughly familiar with the Contact Group's peace plan. Its core was as follows: the UÇK was to be demilitarised over a four-month period; the Serbian military would leave within six months, leaving 2,500 troops for border duties; the existing police would be phased out over two years; a NATO-led force of around 30,000 strong, authorised by the United Nations, would provide security in Kosovo (Cohen 2001: 263).

The plan provided for the restoration of Kosovo's autonomy but left the issue of its future status for reconsideration after a period of three years of an interim administration run by the OSCE. The idea of a referendum on Kosovo's future, whose results would be binding, was promoted by the Albanians but spurned by the Serbs. In the end, the Contact Group mediators said there would be an international conference followed by a referendum, without making it clear if the results would decide the future status of the territory (*The Kosovo Report* 2000: 155).

The large number of Albanians by now incarcerated in Serbian gaols, was an issue ignored by the international negotiators. The IHF wrote to them in February expressing concern that only two pages of what became known as the Kosovo Interim Agreement were devoted to human rights and fundamental freedoms. It also urged that a general amnesty, foreseen by the agreement, be extended all the way back to 1981 (IHF 1999).

The fragmented nature of the Albanian delegation slowed the talks down. Many of its members had previously never met one another. The LDK made up only one-third of its members (Weller 1999: 227). Hashim Thaçi, the most prominent member of the delegation, was elected by the entire delegation to be its chief representative rather than Rugova, who, in most Albanian eyes, was still President of Kosovo (Weller 1999: 227). Thaçi was reluctant to sign the ten principles; he feared he would be disowned by militants back in Kosovo (Kola 2003: 353). The arrival of a tough-talking Madeleine Albright in the second week of talks did not lead to a breakthrough. She declared: 'Let me say that if the talks crater because the Serbs do not say "Yes," we will have bombing. If the talks crater because the Albanians do not say "Yes," we will not be able to support them and in fact will have to cut off whatever help they are getting from outside' (*War In Europe* 2000). Deadlock was only broken by Veton Surroi, publisher of *Koha Ditore*, the leading Albanian daily. He realised that it was important not to be seen to be refusing to sign. He proposed that the delegation should make its choice after a 2-week period of consultation with the people (Judah 2000: 217). The

Serbian delegation also agreed to a talks moratorium which would last from 24 February to 15 March.

To obtain Serbian consent for the plan, the French and British foreign ministers, Hubert Vedrine and Robin Cook, told the Serbian media that 'the Kosovan Albanians will have to give up their demand for independence'. This alienated the Kosovan Albanians without moving the Serbs closer to signing the agreement. Milošević showed no willingness to enter the negotiations. He even refused to see Ambassador Hill when he arrived in Belgrade on 17 February to back up the Anglo-French initiative (Bellamy 2002: 139).

In the event, it turned out that opinion in Kosovo was more accommodating than Thaçi had feared (Judah 2000: 220). The issuing by Serbia of arrest warrants for eight top UÇK leaders on 9 March did not harden their position. The Kosovan Albanian delegation signed on 18 March. They had clearly moved the furthest despite earlier awkwardness. They had shelved their demand for independence and had accepted the disarming of the UÇK. This was in return for a promise of a referendum in three years on the future of Kosovo and a guarantee that a NATO-led peace-keeping force would ensure that the Serbian security forces complied with the cease-fire and pulled back from Kosovo (Bellamy 2002: 206) It was an Albanian decision based on popular consultation and in which a civilian figure like Surroi had proven far more effective than the untested guerrillas of the UÇK.[35]

When the talks resumed on 15 March, the Serbs presented counter-proposals. They did not even accord Kosovo the autonomy it enjoyed from 1974 to 1989. The Russian mediator, Boris Mayorski was shocked that 'whole chapters that had taken months of work, were simply crossed out and replaced with other clearly unacceptable paragraphs or nothing at all' (Judah 2000: 222–3). Milošević refused to take heed of the threat of air-strikes which were emanating from the NATO camp in the dying days of the conference. Nor did he try to play for time or try to wear down the Contact Group by procedural manoeuvres. Holbrooke had returned to Belgrade on 10 March but had gotten nowhere. Milošević's obduracy exposed his lack of interest in genuine negotiation and compromise.

Critics of the Rambouillet process and NATO's subsequent air campaign against Serbia have singled out Annexe B of the implementation chapter of the Rambouillet accord to offer some justification for Milošević's behaviour during the negotiations. It allowed NATO the use of airports, roads, railways and ports in the rest of Yugoslavia. It also gave NATO personnel immunity from prosecution in Serbia and Montenegro. Critics of the Western approach described this as a form of colonisation or a provocation designed to ensure that Milošević would say no at Rambouillet and thus ensure that NATO's air-strikes could get underway.[36] Some even alleged (without offering any back-up evidence) that it required Serbia 'to accept free market principles' (Fouskas 2003: 46). The language of Annexe 2 may have been insensitive given what was at stake in Rambouillet. However, it is similar to that found in any agreement between NATO and a country hosting its troops. NATO's rights in Serbia would be transitory and the clause was felt to be necessary so as to avoid the sort of harassment experienced by the UN force in Bosnia from 1992 to 1995 which prevented it effectively fulfilling its mandate.[37]

Croatia had signed an agreement giving NATO such transitory rights in 1995 and so indeed had Serbian-controlled Yugoslavia, when it signed the Dayton Accord in 1995.[38] So NATO's rights outside Kosovo were transitory, aimed at securing the most efficient logistical routes to the province (Bellamy 2002: 138). Moreover, the Serbian side never actually raised Annexe 2 during the negotiations, directing their opposition instead at the deployment of a NATO-led force *inside* Kosovo (Daalder and O'Hanlon 2000: 14–15). Had the Serbs complained about this annexe, there is a strong likelihood that NATO would have watered it down. One senior British officer said: 'You don't think we would have bombed Serbia for this reason alone do you?' (Daalder and O'Hanlon 2000: 87).

The peace talks were suspended on 18 March as Milošević brushed aside warnings of air-strikes and instead built up his troop levels in Kosovo. According to the OSCE, whose monitors were still in Kosovo, the period from 6 to 23 February had seen 'a significant build-up of VJ forces throughout Kosovo leading to the arming of civilians and the training of reservists, the arrival of anti-aircraft weapons, the digging of tank pits and the preparation of demolition explosives along key routes in from the south and an increase in military air activity' (*Under Orders* 2000: 112). On 19 March, the internal monitors started to be pulled out of Kosovo. This was done with haste due to fears that Yugoslav forces might seal their exit routes and leave them effectively as hostages. On 20 March, Holbrooke arrived once more in Belgrade. By now reports were already emanating from Kosovo that large numbers of civilians were being driven from their homes. The UNHCR would soon estimate that between 13 March, when he had reconvened, the peace talks and 20 March, around 20,000 Albanians had been subjected to ethnic purging (Bellamy 2002: 156).

Talks between Holbrooke and Milošević on 22–23 March got nowhere (Judah 2000: 227). Milošević refused to accept the peace plan or back down from his military offensive in Kosovo. Holbrooke conveyed the talks failure to NATO Secretary-General Solana who, on 23 March, gave the go-ahead for air operations against military targets in territory controlled by Milošević. His unwillingness to negotiate at Rambouillet enabled NATO to argue that it had exhausted all diplomatic options (Wheeler 2000: 283).

Conclusion: why confrontation prevailed

A number of factors made NATO decide that confrontation with Milošević was now unavoidable. There was the resolve not to allow a repetition of the state-led violence and human displacement seen in Kosovo in 1998. For Albright and Blair, refusal to appease a leader with Milošević's track-record of cruelty and duplicity was a matter of principle. The US Secretary of State was also burdened by her failure, as US ambassador to the United Nations, to support speedy international intervention to prevent genocide in Rwanda in 1994 (Rieff 2002: 161).

Albright represented the members of the Clinton administration 'who had already been through a long, agonizing first war with Milošević over Bosnia...' (Halberstam 2001: 442). Interventionists had possessed little clout than vis-à-vis realists who felt that events in the Balkans did not pose a threat to Western security interests. That view had since lost credibility, even though it was still a majority one in the Pentagon. In April, NATO was due to mark its fiftieth anniversary. With an authoritarian leader running amok in a territory located in the heart of Europe, it was feared that the Alliance's credibility would be in tatters if he succeeded in having his way.[39] The appointment of the United Nation's first Human Rights Commissioner in 1998 signified an increasing concern with protecting the rights of vulnerable groups in repressive states and a declining concern with interfering in a state seen to be systematically violating such riots. There was now a post-Rwanda, post-Bosnia desire to show that the western powers were sincere about halting serial patterns of human rights abuses at least where it was politically and militarily feasible.

The Contact Group nations (with Russia on board most of the time), had hoped that Milošević could be persuaded to accept a Dayton-type solution for Kosovo. Yugoslav sovereignty would not be abrogated, nor would the West follow this up with an attempt to drive him from office.[40] But the comparison with Dayton was misplaced in many respects. In 1995, Milošević had moved to halt Serbian resistance in Bosnia with the conflict stalemated and his survival threatened by sanctions. By contrast, the Rambouillet talks had been convened at an early stage of the conflict in Kosovo at a time when Milošević had a reasonable expectation that he could emerge on top. Serbian forces in Kosovo were not under threat of military defeat; indeed they had inflicted heavy losses on the UÇK in mid-1998. Moreover, Milošević had far more at stake in Kosovo than in Bosnia which was peripheral to overall Serbian identity. The nationalist ideologues who had been in the ascendant for over a decade insisted that Serbia would be maimed if it lost Kosovo. Having presided over a series of defeats that had shrunk Serbia's size, he was much weaker politically in 1999 than in 1995. Whatever his own feelings about Kosovo, he must have known that if he let go without a strong fight, the knives would be out for him from his numerous political enemies.

In the past, the West had greatly exaggerated the hold Milošević had over Serbia. This explains why the United States had turned its back on Milan Panić in 1992 and was lukewarm in support of those who comprised the marathon Belgrade protests in 1996–7 (something Holbrooke privately described as a mistake two years later) (Ignatieff 2000: 30). Not only were NATO leaders non-plussed by Milošević's unwillingness to do a deal over Kosovo, but also they were unprepared for the drastic means he would apply in a bid to outwit them when confrontation ensued in March 1999. Milošević in turn probably failed to anticipate a stern reaction from NATO to human rights violations in Kosovo. He had dealt with dozens of Western officials in the first half of the 1990s who had shown scant concern for the victims of the terror he had unleashed first in Croatia and then in Bosnia. He probably had sources of intelligence deep inside the NATO system able to tell him about the confusion and unpreparedness which reigned over what to do about Kosovo. Even in their absence, he cannot have been unaware of decisions like that taken by the Pentagon as the Paris talks collapsed, to send the aircraft carrier USS *Theodore Roosevelt* away from the Adriatic and into the Persian Gulf (Clark 2000: 425). General Klaus Naumann, the chairman of NATO's Military Committee remarked about the situation in mid-1998 that 'If he had learnt that the politicians were making statements and nothing was happening in terms of military preparations, then he would have concluded that it was all a bluff' (*War In Europe* 2000). So both the sides on the verge of waging the first major armed conflict seen in Europe for over fifty years, greatly misread each other's mood, intentions and tactics. The evidence suggests that Milošević was more self-confident than his foes. The defence analyst James Gow has argued that he in fact sought to provoke aerial bombing. He assumed that the poor state of operational planning in NATO and severe disunity would ensure short-term or even token air-strikes. Meanwhile, this would be the perfect cover to carry out an ethnic cleansing operation that dwarfed any seen elsewhere in Yugoslavia (Gow 2003: 207).

3 Milošević and NATO collide over Kosovo

Europe at war: international repercussions

NATO air-strikes began at 8 p.m. GMT on 24 March. Forty targets were hit in Serbia and Montenegro, mainly air defence systems and related facilities, with thirteen NATO countries participating. On the same day, NATO announced five specific objectives that it hoped to achieve:

- A verifiable halt to all Serb military action and an immediate halt to violence and oppression.
- The withdrawal of all Serb military, police and paramilitary forces.
- The stationing of an international military force in Kosovo.
- The unconditional and safe return of all refugees and displaced persons and unhindered access to them by humanitarian aid organisations.
- Credible assurance of work towards a political settlement based on the Rambouillet accords (Bellamy 2002: 159–60).

Despite later denials, there was a palpable feeling within NATO that a small amount of bombing would induce Milošević to come back to the negotiating table. Madeleine Albright illustrated such a feeling when she declared on 24 March that 'I don't see this as a long-term operation. I think it is something that is achievable in a relatively short period of time' (Dannreuther 2001: 33). NATO did have plans for a multi-phased aerial campaign in which the targets would gradually escalate until strategic targets in Belgrade itself were being hit (Cohen 2001: 281). US airforce general, Michael Short, who was NATO's principal commander of operations, was opposed to this 'philosophy of incrementalism'. He decried the 'reluctance to grab him [Milošević] by the throat and shake him'. He said:

> I'd have gone for the head of the snake on the first night. I'd have turned the lights out on the first night. I'd have dropped the bridges across the Danube. I'd have hit five or six political–military headquarters in downtown Belgrade. Milošević and his cronies would have waked [*sic*] up the first morning and asked what the hell was going on…Questioning would have started right away: 'If this is what the first night is like what's the rest of it going to be like?'
> (Cohen 2001: 282)

But among US policy-makers and legislators in the Congress, there was no appetite for such a potentially devastating strike. One analyst has written that the Kosovo conflict 'was fought by an essentially uninterested country, orchestrated by a divided government where the consensus was, at best, extremely flimsy...' (Richardson 2000: 146). It was not just over Kosovo that the Clinton White House was viewed as 'an administration that lives and breathes ambiguity and vacillation'.[1] Clinton himself was described by one former top NATO diplomat, who often dealt with him, as 'utterly ill-equipped by training and temperament to handle national security issues'.[2] On his visits to the White House in 1999, Britain's Tony Blair was struck by how much time Clinton could find 'to sit around watching videos, drinking beer, and shooting the breeze' (Rawnsley 2001: 271). His Defence Secretary, William Cohen, an ex-Republican Senator, had told Clinton before taking up his appointment: 'I voted against your Bosnia policy'. For him the Balkans was a notorious geopolitical cemetery and he remained consistently wary of greater activism by the United States in the region (Halberstam 2001: 441). He faithfully reflected the Pentagon worldview. When General Wesley Clark, NATO's Supreme Allied Commander in Europe (SACEUR) warned the US army chief that the United States might shortly be embroiled in a war situation in Kosovo and that preparations for extra resources should be made, he got the reply: 'But we don't want to fight there' (Clark 2001a: 166–7).

Republican Senators such as Robert Dole and John McCain urged robust action including, if necessary, NATO ground troops. McCain declared in early April 1999: 'In Pyongyang, and Baghdad and Tripoli, they are paying close attention and if a military establishment that was defeated by the Croatian army prevails, one led by a Balkan thug, we will be vulnerable to many challenges in many places'.[3] But more representative of the Republican majority in Congress was Senator Trent Lott who urged that 'peace be given a chance'. The Congress was increasingly wary of US military undertakings with a humanitarian purpose, including in the Balkans (Daalder and O'Hanlon 2000: 2).

To shore up his domestic front, Clinton declared in a television address hours before the start of NATO air attacks: 'I do not intend to put our troops in Kosovo to fight a war' (Cohen 2001: 276). Such a disclosure was widely condemned as a major blunder. It removed the element of surprise concerning what NATO might do in the future and made it far likelier that Milošević would sit out the first wave of bombings, expecting the resolve of his opponents to peter out. General Klaus Naumann, the chairman of NATO's Military Committee said in 2000: 'I do not hesitate to say that all those politicians who ruled out the use of ground forces, made it easier for Milošević to calculate his risk, and this may have encouraged him to make the attempt to ride it out, and by this we prolonged the war' (*War In Europe* 2000).

Milošević was hoping that NATO disunity and a lack of resolve would act in his favour. Security leaks from inside NATO were enabling him to gain vital information about NATO missions and targets (Sell 2001: 303). Already in October 1998, a French officer at NATO headquarters had given key parts of the air operations plan to the Milošević regime (Clark 2000a: 175).

It is also reasonable to assume that Milošević was relying on Russian pressure to cause the NATO air campaign to quickly end. Prime Minister Evgeny Primakov had shown his displeasure by ordering that the plane taking him to the United States be turned round in mid-flight as news of the impending bombing reached him. Soon after, an angry President Yeltsin suspended relations with NATO, withdrawing Russia's military representative from its headquarters (Buckley 2001: 160–1). He warned that 'we have extreme measures in reserve…but we have decided not to use them. On the moral level, we are superior to the Americans'.[4]

On 24 March Russia tabled a UN resolution condemning NATO bombing of Federal Republic of Yugoslavia (FRY). NATO action was seen as aggression against a sovereign state which had not attacked another sovereign state as Iraq did when it invaded Kuwait in 1990. It was therefore entitled to respect of its sovereignty under the UN Charter, as explicitly stated in Article 2.4.[5] On the other hand, NATO members like Britain and the United States claimed that the Alliance had the right to act against FRY without specific Security Council authorisation. They pointed to previous resolutions, particularly 1199 passed on 23 September 1998, which categorised Serbian actions in Kosovo as a threat to international peace and security, thereby transcending the sovereignty issue. It was difficult to argue that Kosovo still remained an internal Yugoslav matter given Milošević's audacious decision to export much of its population to neighbours who were reeling from the consequences (Ignatieff 2000: 78).

Britain argued in the 24–26 March UN debate that the use of force was 'an exceptional measure to prevent an overwhelming human catastrophe' and that it was in conformity with existing Security Council resolutions (Wheeler 2000: 279). Supporters of this position argued that the regional and international threat posed by Serbia's action allowed action by third parties under Article 31 of the UN Charter. They referred to Article 52 which allows for action by regional bodies provided such actions are consistent with UN aims.[6] They were also able to draw upon general international law to justify NATO's action. Under it, conventions pertaining to human rights, genocide and protection of civilians in wartime, made military intervention on behalf of the Kosovo Albanians lawful due to overwhelming humanitarian necessity (Henrikson 2000: 52).

As the debate on the legality or otherwise of NATO's action gathered pace, it was clear that there was a contradiction between the entitlement of states to have their sovereignty respected and the rights of individuals and groups within states to international protection. Unlike Britain, Germany did not argue that a legal basis for international humanitarian intervention existed. Günter Verheugen, then a leading figure in the Berlin government admitted that it posed a challenge to international law and that the UN Security Council was being contravened. But he went on to assert that the right of veto in the Security Council gives its permanent members the moral responsibility to uphold core norms of human behaviour. And where they cannot or won't, unilateral humanitarian intervention is justified on moral grounds even if the law is violated (Wheeler 2000: 277–8). From this standpoint, Slovenia, then on the Security Council, argued on 24 March that the Security Council 'had the primary but not exclusive responsibility for the maintenance of international peace and security' (Wheeler 2000: 279). Rudolf Scharping the German Defence Minister, was one of the few leading western officials who argued that international law should be developed so that human rights violations on the scale of Kosovo's should be treated as a legitimate basis for force (Guicherd 1999: 27). In the event, Russia's resolution was defeated in the Security Council on 26 March. Six non-Western states joined with Slovenia in opposing it. Seven members, constituting a majority, were prepared to legitimise the use of force on humanitarian grounds in a context where there was no explicit Security Council resolution. This was a historic development, but the countries responsible for NATO's Kosovo operation, thereafter showed little enthusiasm to try and reform the UN Charter to shift the balance away from state sovereignty towards human rights.

The United Nations remained very much on the sidelines for the duration of the Kosovo conflict. Sonja Biserko, a leading Serbian human rights activist, believes that Milošević wanted to force the West back to the negotiating table on his terms. A scenario much favoured in Belgrade government circles was: 'a conference...along the lines of the 1878 Congress of Berlin, involving all the regional players. And, if Serbian negotiators have their way, it would be a time for territorial swapping. The key deal would be the partition of Kosovo, hiving off a southern strip from Yugoslavia in exchange for some of Bosnia'.[7]

Lord Owen, the controversial EU negotiator during the Bosnian wars, threw his weight behind such a conference, declaring on 5 June 1999 that the redrawing of existing boundaries should not be excluded from its agenda. He recommended that the whole of Kosovo be allowed to leave Serbia on condition that the eastern parts of Bosnia's Republic of Srpska (RS) take its place.[8] Owen's plan got an angry response from Carlos Westendorp, a former Spanish foreign minister, who was then the UN's High Representative in Bosnia. Westendorp[9] argued that it would encourage disaffected minorities in Macedonia and Voivodina, as well as the large Muslim population in Serbia's Sandžak district, to think about linking up with their ethnic kin in neighbouring territories:

> If we give up on the notion of multi-national states, then those who perpetrate ethnic cleansing have won. This is a disastrous, morally repugnant message we cannot afford to send...
>   ...if any of the elected officials in Bosnia–Herzegovina had suggested Lord Owen's solution, I could have, with the powers given to me by the international community, removed them from office for obstructing the peace process.
>
> (Westendorp 1999)

Milošević appears not to have realised that a significant change of outlook towards the Balkans had occurred among European leaders. Owen, with his preference for partition plans, was now yesterday's man, condemned to pursue a lucrative business career in the Russian oil industry. Eleven of the fifteen governments of EU states were now controlled by social democratic parties, governing alone or in coalition. Among them were Britain, France, Germany and Italy. Many of these parties had a long tradition of opposition to the Leninist version of socialism that emphasised class struggle at the expense of individual human rights'. They recalled how in East European countries that fell on the wrong side of the Iron Curtain after 1945, 'social democrats were among the first victims of the communist regimes'.[10] Rather than back ever-stronger measures to compel the Serbs to pull back from Kosovo, Milošević assumed that the ruling European Left would splinter and NATO's unity would collapse.

Operation Horseshoe: the ethnic cleansing of Kosovan Albanians

The first assaults on Albanian communities began immediately after the Kosovo Verification Mission (KVM) departed on 20 March. Militarily inactive towns and villages, as well as Kosovo Liberation Army (UÇK) strongholds, were subject to indiscriminate attacks (Gow 2003: 210; *Under Orders* 2001: 112). A systematic effort at deporting Kosovo Albanians got underway which acquired the name of 'Operation Horseshoe'. It was attractive to Milošević for several reasons, not least because of the difficulty in distinguishing UÇK fighters from Albanian civilians. After NATO's air attacks began, 'the character and intensity' of the Serbian campaign changed. On 24 March, the full-scale eviction of Albanians in several cities got underway. From 24 to 26 March, an operation unfolded to secure the southwest border with Albania which involved large-scale displacement accompanied by the killing of civilians' (*Under Orders* 2001: 112). The killings were more limited than in Bosnia during 1992 and were used 'principally to strike fear among ethnic Albanians to make them flee the country' (Daalder and O'Hanlon 2000: 101). Within three weeks of the start of NATO bombing, 525,787 refugees from Kosovo poured into neighbouring countries, according to the United Nations High Commission for Refugees (UNHCR). Several hundred thousand more were internally displaced, on top of those who had already been forced into the woods and hills in 1998 and the first two months of 1999 (*Under Orders* 2001: 4).

Natasha Kandić of the Humanitarian Law Foundation (FHP), based in Belgrade, went to Kosovo as soon as the conflict began in March to act as an eyewitness to the unfolding of 'Operation Horseshoe'. She described how, between 26 and 28 March, 20,000 Albanian residents from the city of Pecs (Peje in Albanian) were given often no more than 10 minutes to abandon their homes. More than thirty individual murders were committed, usually at random 'to make as many people as possible join the column of the banished'.[11] The FHP, the only Serbian NGO to investigate war crimes during the conflict, identified the main perpetrators of violence as paramilitary units 'established by orders from a very high level' and attached to regular forces.[12] Loot was an incentive for many of the paramilitary forces to be in Kosovo:

> Endless witnesses and victims told Human Rights Watch how government forces robbed them of valuables, including wedding rings and automobiles, either at their homes or along the road during their expulsion. Police, soldiers and especially members of paramilitary units threatened individuals with death if they did not hand over sums of money, usually demanding German marks.
>
> (*Under Orders* 2001: 9)

The government forces did not behave in a uniform manner towards Albanians in this period. Speaking of Pecs (Peje), Natasa Kandić[13] wrote:

> There is not a single piece of evidence that young soldiers participated in violence: The Albanians even speak about having seen in various places they were passing through during banishment young men in uniform with sadness in their faces ... From their soldiers' bag they pulled out and gave them their own rations of food, bread, liver-paste ... They usually told the banished persons: 'I know nothing, do not think I am doing anything here. I am forced to be here'. They were soldiers doing regular military service.
>
> (AIM 1999)

Human Rights Watch also generally absolved soldiers from responsibility at least for individual crimes. Its 2001 report described the typical Serb method of implementing Operation Horseshoe:

> Typically, as told by witnesses from all over Kosovo, the army and special police forces surrounded a village and shelled it from a distance. Regular and special police forces then moved in, swept the village and gathered the villagers in a centralized location. Men were separated from women and children for interrogation about the UÇK. Regular police and paramilitaries then looted the village, as well as stealing whatever the villagers carried with them and destroying their identity documents. The village was then left to the police, paramilitaries, and local Serb militias, who looted and burned the remains. The women, children, and elderly men were often expelled, and men with suspected ties to the UÇK were sometimes executed.
>
> (*Under Orders* 2001: 63)

Human Rights Watch also documented the common practice of 'identity cleansing':

> refugees expelled towards Albania were frequently stripped of their identity documents and forced to remove the licence plates from their cars and tractors before being permitted to cross the border. Before reaching the border, many Albanians had their personal documents destroyed, suggesting the government was trying to block their return.
>
> (*Under Orders* 2001: 6)

According to the UNHCR, government forces expelled 862,972 Albanians from Kosovo and several hundred thousand more were internally displaced. More than 80 per cent of the entire population of Kosovo – 90 per cent of Kosovan Albanians – were displaced from their homes (*Under Orders* 2001: 4). Paramilitary forces told their Albanian victims to 'Go to NATO!' Unable to thwart the NATO air attacks, they appeared to be taking their vengeance on Albanians who had looked to NATO for deliverance. But the systematic nature of the expulsions contradicted the theory that they were a spontaneous eruption of Serb fury.

James Gow, a British defence analyst who has published widely on the Balkans, had warned the previous autumn that mass ethnic cleansing 'was in the pipeline and that the emptying of Kosovo should be anticipated' (Gow 2003: 209, n. 8). The West had not expected such a brazen undertaking but nor had Milošević apparently anticipated that the resulting biblical images transmitted on television would stiffen NATO determination to confront him and swing public opinion in most of western Europe behind NATO. Discomfited by the international reaction to his deportation efforts, Milošević briefly brought them to a halt in early April. Trainloads and buses of Albanians, some of which were already at the border, were pulled back, only for the deportations to resume days later (Gow 2003: 213–14). Men were often removed from the convoys, several tens of thousands ending up in makeshift prisons. James Gow is in no doubt that their potential as human shields against NATO attacks led the Serbs to opt for mass detentions of people it had no evidence were UÇK fighters (Gow 2003: 140).

The NATO mood

The depopulation of Kosovo made it very hard for the UÇK to operate as an effective insurgent force capable of blending into a supportive civilian population. Indeed, it would not play a significant role in the unfolding conflict (Gow 2003: 263). No one in NATO making political and military decisions appears to have predicted that Milošević would have done something as audacious as Operation Horseshoe. Britain's Defence Minister George Robertson wrote after the war: 'While we had anticipated that the offensive could involve operations against the UÇK, and violent repression of the civilian population, we could not have predicted the full horror and extent of the brutality, which was to include scenes reminiscent of the 1930s and 1940s' (Robertson 1999: 9). Joschka Fischer regretted not taking the Serbian leader at his word when he told him before the conflict that he would empty Kosovo in weeks (Bellamy 2002: 164). He also boasted to the German Foreign Minister: 'I can stand death – lots of it – but you can't', a sign of his low opinion of his West European adversaries (Daalder and O'Hanlon 2000: 94).

It is clear that they and their US partners were taken unawares by Milošević's response to their air assault. The UNHCR had received no advance warning from any Western government about the need to prepare for a mass exodus of people (Judah 2000: 240). NATO would have been in a perilous position if Milošević had successfully resisted his wish to drive out the Albanians and had, instead, hunkered down and restrained his military and paramilitary forces during the bombing' (Daalder and O'Hanlon 2000: 4). The Alliance's policy of keeping aircraft 15,000 feet above sea-level limited the effectiveness of its bombing operations and led to numerous accidental killings of civilians. This stemmed from Washington's desire to avoid military casualties at almost any cost. But with the methods being employed, NATO had proven utterly powerless to halt Milošević's mass expulsions. This much was admitted by General Klaus Naumann, Chairman of NATO's Military Committee whose retirement came up during the latter stages of the conflict. He stated in early May: 'Quite frankly and honestly we did not succeed in our initial attempt to coerce Milošević through air strikes to accept our demands, nor did we succeed in preventing the FRY from pursuing a campaign of ethnic separation and expulsion'. He judged that the decision to mount light strikes 'cost time, effort, and potentially additional casualties, the net result being that the campaign is undoubtedly prolonged'.[14] General Mike Short, the commander of the air operation, strongly criticised his superior, Wesley Clark for concentrating on military targets in Kosovo: 'It was going to take a lot of sorties to kill [*sic*] a tank and there was an enormous risk of hitting the wrong target as we knew refugees were moving around in . . . their environment' (*War In Europe* 2000).

Several NATO states, particularly France, initially blocked Short's wish for a blitzkrieg on 'command and control' targets in Serbia itself. The military campaign was hampered by excessive caution and a growing list of blunders which produced civilian casualties. It would have been difficult to maintain NATO unity in the absence of Milošević's chilling attempt to expel the Albanians *en masse.*

Probably due to its relative proximity, public opinion in Western Europe was more affected than it was in the United States by the scenes of refugees pouring out of Kosovo in distressed circumstances. These dominated news bulletins during the first month of the conflict. Undoubtedly, they had an effect on public opinion in countries where there had been a disinclination to support American-led military operations. In France, support for participation in the Kosovo operation stood at 59, 73 and 67 per cent on 26 March, the second week of April, and the third week of May according to an aggregate of polls. Some polls showed fairly consistent support for a ground invasion if air-strikes proved insufficient: they ranged from a high of 65 per cent in the second week of April to a low of 55 per cent in the third week of May (Macleod 2000: 124).

In Germany, polls in April showed that 60 per cent of the public felt it right to bomb Serbia; an even higher number believed it was right for the *Bundeswehr* (German armed forces) to take part; but support for the overall military campaign would drop to 52 per cent in May (Rudolf 2000: 136). Initially, Chancellor Schröder faced difficulties from Oskar Lafontaine, chairman of the Social Democrats and also Minister of Finance. Lafontaine refused to release funds that Defence Minister Scharping needed to cover the *Bundeswehr's* activities in the Balkans. Upon his resignation on 11 March 1999, Schröder faced no further anti-war challenge from within the SPD (Ramet and Lyon 2001: 91). Even 57 per cent of Green supporters were pro-intervention (a figure that would slump to 38 per cent in May). At the Greens annual conference on 13 May, Joschka Fischer persuaded his party to reject a resolution demanding the unilateral halt to NATO attacks (Rudolf 2000: 138). The troika of Schröder, Scharping and Fischer 'articulated a new position for the German Left . . . confidently conceived' as 'German military action without militarism' (Ramet and Lyon 2001: 91). Thus a weak link in the NATO armour that Milošević might have expected to give way, actually held. The same was true of Italy, the Western country with closest contact to Albanians; they comprised the most unpopular immigrant group, blamed for theft, armed assaults and the growth of prostitution (Clark 2001b: 123). A left-of-centre coalition counted on public fears of a fresh tidal wave of refugees (after the one that had occurred during the 1997 crisis in Albania) to obtain acquiescence for Rome's support of NATO. Prime Minister Massimo d'Alema, an ex-communist, proved to be no ideological soul-mate of Milošević. He revealed himself to be a nimble tactician in sidetracking the pacifism to be found in the red, green and Catholic coalition. It was Dini his Foreign Minister, previously defender of a privileged role for Milošević as a guarantor of Western security, who found it hard to confront him. At the Rambouillet talks, the Americans discovered he had been passing on drafts prepared by the Western negotiators to the Serbian President, Milan Milutinović.[15] He remained in telephone contact during the war with Milošević and had to be talked out of accepting an invitation from him to go to Belgrade during the war (Clark 2002: 124; Morelli 2001: 63, 69).

Only Greece showed widespread popular sympathy for the Serbian side. A poll in late May showed that 69 per cent of Greeks wanted Clinton tried for war crimes but only 14 per cent believed Milošević should face international sanctions for his role in the repression and expulsion of Kosovo Albanians. The Greek press homed in on NATO's 'atrocities' while ignoring the suffering of Albanian refugees.[16] A poll taken in April 1999 revealed that 52 per cent of Greeks were against the admittance to Greece of fleeing Albanian refugees (Michas 2002: 80). In the same month, twenty judges from Greece's highest administrative court announced that NATO was committing war crimes by violating Serbian sovereignty but was silent about Serbia's behaviour towards Albanians. Earlier, on 2 March, soldiers and sailors had joined a march to the American embassy in Athens despite it being illegal for armed forces personnel in Greece to participate in any kind of political activity (Michas 2002: 82–3). Nevertheless, despite mollifying pro-Serb public opinion, the government of Kostas Simitis did not move to halt NATO's action which it was technically entitled to do under the terms of NATO's Atlantic Charter (Garton-Ash 2000).

Except in Greece, a country where ties of friendship with Serbia had long been fostered by church and state, ethnic expulsions diverted attention from the legality of the conflict. Greek opinion saw it as America's war, but NATO was engaged in a conflict that the United States was distinctly half-hearted about. Public support for the war initially stood at around 60 per cent in most polls with more than 50 per cent of Americans supporting the use of ground forces if necessary. But towards the end of the conflict, even US popular backing for air-strikes alone began to significantly fall back. There was thus a contrast between American opinion and that of the public in most European NATO states which remained generally supportive of the war (Daalder and O'Hanlon 2000: 161).

Hostility to the conflict in US military circles and in much of Congress made Clinton hesitate about a ground war. One of his fears was that if Pentagon critics could not kill the idea before it left the drawing-board, they would leak the plans in an effort to make them inoperable (*War In Europe*).[17] If the West had been forced to return to the negotiating table, it is likely that Milošević would have insisted on only a fraction of the pre-war Albanian population being allowed to stay. Serbian officials told one western diplomat in April 1999: '500,000 or 600,000 Albanians are no problem for us'. The Serbian position at this time was that only Albanian citizens able to prove that they were citizens of Kosovo, could return. But this would be a difficult feat for many Albanians given the care Serb officials had taken to destroy their identity papers as they left Kosovo.[18]

Milošević's hopes and intentions

The expulsions were therefore meant to serve the goal of a Kosovo demographically transformed in Serbia's favour. There were also supplementary objectives. Milošević hoped to divide the Kosovo Albanians. To this end, Rugova was shown on television on 1 April engaged in apparently cordial talks with Milošević at the height of the deportations. It appeared to confirm the harsh view of a fellow advocate of non-violence, Veton Surroi that he is 'Jell-o all the way through' (Ignatieff 2000: 27–8). Rugova reportedly agreed that the Kosovo problem should be settled by peaceful means but, in his defence, he said later that he had been forced to meet with Milošević. He was eventually allowed to leave for Italy with his family. Afterwards Rugova was reluctant to endorse NATO bombing to the bafflement of the organisation (Kola 2003: 360). Meanwhile, on 7 May, the family of Fehmi Agani, the brains of the Democratic League of Kosovo (LDK), reported that he had been taken off a train and killed by the Serbian police. The decision was made in Belgrade about which high-profile Albanian leaders should be targeted or left alone (Ignatieff 2000: 55). His killing can be seen as a bid to further weaken the LDK in face of the UÇK, a radical force which Belgrade appeared more comfortable in dealing with. Certainly Rugova's equivocal stance increased the resentment of militants and probably stoked the atmosphere that led to the killing of important people around him when Kosovo was freed from Serbian control.

Milošević also strove to export the conflict to neighbouring territories in order to dissipate NATO's offensive capability. The commander of the army in the RS was instructed from Belgrade to launch a guerrilla war against the NATO-led Stabilisation force in Bosnia, but he refused to obey (Bellamy 2002: 163; Judah 2000: 255). This was yet another example of Milošević's readiness to sacrifice the interests of Serbs elsewhere in order to further his own ends. Under cover of war, he would dearly have loved to remove Milo Djukanović, his increasingly assertive rival in Montenegro. The Montenegrin leader refused to follow Belgrade's lead in declaring a state of emergency, expelling foreign journalists, and severing formal links with the leading states of NATO.[19] The sister republic in the Yugoslav Federation was largely spared NATO bombing and Albanian refugees were welcomed on to its territory. NATO also used informal channels to warn Belgrade that any move against Djukanović would be resisted by force if necessary.

Turning to Albania, Milošević may have hoped that this fragile state would have collapsed under the weight of refugees. It was the country whose borders most were forced across and it had barely recovered from its destabilising crisis in 1997. Even though aid agencies were unprepared to cope with the multitudes, desperately poor citizens improvised and opened their homes to co-ethnics in their hour of need. Thanks to Hoxha's rigid isolationism, they had had little or no contact with Kosovan Albanians who were thus a totally unknown quantity. Yet, ingrained traditions of hospitality immediately came into play and the response of ordinary Albanians, mostly very badly off, was strikingly impressive in its generosity. It is difficult to avoid contrasting transborder Albanian solidarity at the human level with its absence among the wider Serbian nation. In Serbia, the abstract concept of Kosovo was an electrifying one for many people, but relatively few were prompted to visit the territory and even fewer were ready to assist Kosovo Serbs when the tide turned decisively against them later in 1999 (Bozo 2001: 38–40).

The arrival of a large part of the Kosovo population in Albania could be seen as 'the forced introduction of the two main parts of the nation to each other' (Kola 2003: 362). But the contrasts in living conditions and overall outlook did not create the sense of one people according to one Albanian source (Kola 2003: 362–3).

Albanians in Macedonia responded much like their co-ethnics in Albania to the refugee wave, but the authorities in Skopje displayed barely concealed hostility to Albanian refugees (Drezov 2001: 64). Customs officials left them in no-mans-land for days or sometimes pushed them back into Kosovo (Judah 2000: 252). On 26 March, members of the ethnic Serb minority attacked the US embassy in Skopje and, soon after, 19 British soldiers from an elite regiment were beaten up after quarrelling with 5 waiters at a Skopje restaurant.[20] Only on 4 April did Macedonia agree to admit refugees to camps that were to be hastily erected by NATO troops. The willingness of many Slav Macedonians to adopt a strongly pro-Serbian attitude would have repercussions that extended beyond the Kosovo conflict. It suggested that the previous 'widespread perception of interethnic harmony may have been little more than good PR for international consumption'.[21]

For the duration of the armed conflict with NATO, Milošević was in a commanding political position at home. Both he and his wife's party United Yugoslav Left (JUL) were joined in government by their longstanding foes, Šešelj's Radicals and Vuk Drasković's Serbian Renewal Movement (SPO). An atmosphere of defiant anti-Western solidarity pervaded the country in the early weeks of the war. Even a figure like the Serbian sociologist Aleksa Djilas, son of the veteran dissident Milovan Djilas, accepted much of Milošević's world-view of the conflict. He claimed that NATO's real interest in Yugoslavia was not in stopping ethnic purging and promoting democracy but in its 'own prestige and expansion in South-Eastern Europe and throughout the world'. He praised the Serbian media which he believed do not serve up 'such open and blind lies' as do CNN and British and German television'.[22]

The Serbian media had in fact been under severe restrictions since the previous autumn.[23] A law passed in October 1998 fined journalists up to $64,000 for printing unprovable material – what the government viewed as 'lies' – and if the newspaper could not pay the fine, the police had the right to confiscate an editor's private property. The law seems to have been directed in particular at Slavko Curuvija who had become Milošević's most outspoken press critic. His *Dnevi Telegraf* (Daily Telegraph) was published in Montenegro after it had been suppressed in Belgrade. The police had duly turned up at his home after a fine was imposed and confiscated his own belongings with the exception of a family bed and a few chairs. Curuvija condemned NATO's air-strikes in outspoken terms but, as soon as they started, the pro-government daily *Politika Ekspres* carried a commentary claiming that people like Curuvija who 'asked NATO to bomb, must be happy now'. The editor of the paper said it had been written on the suggestion of Dragan Hadzi Antić, a senior figure in the press group the paper belonged to and an intimate of the Milošević family. The article was read out on all state television prime-time news broadcasts prompting Curuvija to remark 'Every fool now has a licence to kill me'.[24] Curuvija, who was 49-year-old duly murdered on 11 April in a professional killing while he and his wife walked their dog in Belgrade.[25]

But there were outspoken Serbian voices still prepared to defy Milošević. Natasa Kandić, who had been documenting human rights violations in Yugoslavia since 1992, has already been mentioned. She had jumped into a taxi soon after the NATO bombing started, and persuaded the driver to take her to Kosovo. She wished to help the local staff of the office in Priština of the Humanitarian Law Centre, (the NGO she headed), to escape.[26] She was also concerned about the fate of ethnic Albanian human rights lawyer, Bajram Kelmendi with whom she had worked. He was murdered along with his two sons on 26 March after being arrested by the Serbian police (*Under Orders* 2001: 128).

Sonja Biserko, a human rights activist who argued that 'Milošević...has only followed and expressed the collective consciousness of much of the Serbian elite – especially within the security forces', fled Belgrade a week into the NATO bombing.[27] She argued in April 1999 that 'we have a situation where everybody knows what is going on but they are all in denial and looking for excuses. It's an absolute catastrophe. My country's history over the past two hundred years has been annulled'.[28]

Lawrence Eagleburger, the former US Secretary of State, who knew both Serbia and Milošević, wrote in April 1999 that the Serbian leader 'may plan the strategy, but the Serbian people are the willing instruments of his terror'.[29] Daniel Goldhagen, author of a book about pre-1945 Germany and the Jews (claiming that many Germans had been only too happy to see their extermination) argued that the same genocidal impulse existed among the Serbs.[30] He advocated an international occupation of Serbia in order to extirpate the destructive inheritance of ultra-nationalism. A fellow North American academic, Janusz Bugajski argued instead that 'the international focus should be on dismembering Yugoslavia into three more viable states'. He anathemised Serbia for lacking a 'critical mass of support for ousting the ruling clique'.[31] But cracks were starting to appear in the united Serbian front hardly a month into the war. Vuk Drasković, holding the post of vice-premier, exclaimed on 26 April that the government should start 'telling the truth' about what was happening in Kosovo and make people aware that the security forces were engaged in wholesale ethnic cleansing and that was the reason why they were being bombed (Bellamy 2002: 181).

Drasković was summarily dismissed from the government for airing these heretical thoughts. They had been made immediately after NATO's fiftieth anniversary summit held in Washington from 23–25 April. No celebrations were held and the mood among the nineteen members was downbeat. A series of controversial incidents involving 'collateral damage', military terminology for civilian casualties, had weakened the resolve to continue among some leaders. The worst was an air attack on a convoy of Albanian refugees on 14 April in which seventy-three were killed, the pilot believing mistakenly that it was a military convoy. A similar incident occurred on 14 May when an attack on a military target in Koriša killed approximately eighty Albanian displaced persons (who may have been used as human shields); on the 30th of that month, an attack on a bridge resulted in eleven civilian deaths. Amnesty International (AI) (in a report on the conduct of the war) alleged that NATO repeatedly gave priority to pilot safety at the cost of civilian lives (AI 2000). On 4 May, Mary Robinson, the UN High Commissioner for Human Rights warned NATO that it might be held responsible for war crimes after the bombing of two buses.[32] She said that NATO would be expected to observe the principles of legality and proportionality in its offensive. But she failed to persuade the Serbian authorities to let her visit Kosovo and see what conditions were like; foreign journalists had been expelled not only from Kosovo but also from Serbia. It is not unreasonable to surmise that Milošević had calculated that any sympathetic reportage of Serbia under bombing would be eclipsed by accounts of destruction and repression which were being perpetrated with industrial intensity on the ground. The propaganda battle would thus go against his regime if the conduct of his forces could be glimpsed close up.

Blair asserts his will

Among NATO leaders, Milošević's deportation of the Albanians produced the most forthright response from Tony Blair, Prime Minister of Britain since 1997. Domestically, Blair was starting to acquire a reputation as an opportunistic politician only prepared to take a chance if it could earn him votes or it suited his or his country's vital strategic interests.[33] But over Kosovo he threw caution to one side and throughout the conflict he exhibited a deep-seated conviction that Milošević must be stopped, even if ways of doing that appeared elusive. On 23 March he had echoed Clinton in saying: 'We do not plan to use ground troops in order to fight our way into Kosovo'.[34] But the treatment of the Albanians, which Blair likened to the Nazi holocaust, appears to have profoundly influenced him. At the start of April he was depicting the conflict as one 'between good and evil; between civilization and barbarity'. He made a pledge to the Albanians that Clinton had shrunk from making: 'We will make sure that you are able to return to your homes, and live in peace'. Before the NATO summit, he was already convinced that speedy preparations must be made for a ground operation to undo Milošević's handiwork in Kosovo. He tried to make the case to a sceptical American public and policy-makers, most notably at a speech in Chicago on 22 April. Speaking at the city's Economic Club, he argued that humanitarian values and the defence of national interests coincided over Kosovo: '...our actions are guided by a...subtle blend of mutual self-interest and moral purpose in defending the interests we cherish...'. He warned his American audience of isolationism, telling them that 'we cannot turn our backs on conflicts and the violation of human rights, within other countries if we still want to be secure'.[35]

At the Washington summit, Blair's argument for a plan to be made for a ground invasion fell on deaf ears. The German government felt its collapse would be imminent if the conflict escalated to that critical stage. Chancellor Schröder told Blair that the British 'liked fighting' but since 1945 Germany had become 'fundamentally pacifist' (Rawnsley 2001: 274). President Chirac later claimed that he and Blair had disagreed over his call for ground troops (Macleod 2000: 122). Afterwards Blair told Clinton: 'You must get a plan... we just cannot lose on this' (*War In Europe* 2000). Serbia had declared its own temporary ceasefire in order to encourage NATO doubters to press for a peaceful exit from the crisis. But Blair's absolute refusal to do a deal with Serbian leader unless he agreed to the Rambouillet terms was reflected in the words of the British journalist Philip Stephens:[36]

> To compromise with Mr Milošević would be to rob NATO...of moral credibility and moral authority. Serbia would have secured in a few short weeks the victory that eluded the Soviet empire for four decades. Mr Blair understands that. Let us pray Mr Clinton does too.
>
> (*Financial Times* 1999)

Unhappy with the quality of information he was getting from an intelligence service which was not known for accurately predicting developments in the Balkans, Blair sent Paddy Ashdown, the leader of the Liberal Democratic Party to the Kosovo border to gather intelligence. Ashdown, an ex-British Marine was by now an old Balkan hand who had been one of the first Western politicians calling for Milošević to be confronted. In his confidential report to Blair, he began: 'You think you are winning this war. I think you are losing it' (Rawnsley 2001: 267). On 3 May Blair became the first elected Western leader to fly out to the Kosovo borders. Observing the tent city hastily erected for refugees, he declared: 'This is obscene. It's criminal. Just criminal. How can anyone think we shouldn't be stopping this' (Rawnsley 2001: 276).

Well into May 1999 both Blair and his foreign secretary, Robin Cook, were intervening in US domestic politics to secure a change of opinion on how to prosecute the war. Cook lobbied key members of Congress, met with the editorial boards of influential newspapers, and appealed directly to the American public in a series of media interviews (Richardson 2000: 153). British newspapers, inspired by Mr Blair's Office in London's No. 10 Downing Street, began to say that the Prime Minister was frustrated by the President's dithering over ground troops. When the *New York Times* gave coverage to this on 18 May, Blair found himself on the receiving end of 'a Clintonite explosion of rage' for 'breaking ranks' (*War In Europe* 2000). He rang Blair to tell him to 'get your people under control'. But in a 90-minute conversation, the President calmed down. He conceded that 'we have to concentrate not on public opinion but on winning' (*War In Europe* 2000); Blair also secured a promise from him that in a speech that evening he would say that no options 'were off the table' (meaning ground troops) (Rawnsley 2001: 285).

Blair had an ally in General Wesley Clark, NATO's military chief in Europe who believed that Milošević's fourth war in the Balkans must be his last. Downing Street permitted Clark to receive details of private telephone conversations between Blair and Clinton so that he would have an advantage over the Pentagon sceptics unwilling to commit ground troops (Richardson 2000: 154). Clark was also sustained by his civilian boss, the Spaniard, Javier Solana. He shielded him from some of the more arduous demands of Alliance members about the choice of targets and came to support the ground war option (Hendrickson 2002). He used his diplomatic skills and impressive work ethic to convince key Alliance players, dubious about the Kosovo enterprise, that NATO must prevail.

Ironically, General Clark's greatest difficulties were not with devotees of compromise in Europe but with his own Pentagon. In his memoir of the conflict, he revealed that his superiors in Washington kept him from seeing the President, with the Secretary of Defence supporting such restrictions (Clark 2001a: 337). Clark got permission from the White House to start the early preliminary paperwork on the use of ground troops, but the top-brass in the Pentagon refused to give him their support when he presented his case to them on 19 May (*War In Europe* 2000).

Russia: the indispensable intermediary

White House support for the Blair–Clark position on how to prosecute the war was starting to firm up in the last days of May (Halberstam 2001: 462). But Clinton hadn't abandoned the idea of using Russia as an intermediary to compel Milošević to accept the terms of the Contact Group. Russia's willingness to co-operate with the United States in this way had appeared distinctly improbable at the start of the conflict. On 9 April Yeltsin had delivered a belligerent speech in which he said: 'They simply want to seize Yugoslavia . . . We cannot allow this to happen' (Bellamy 2002: 175). On 16 April, the lower house of parliament, the State Duma, voted to include Yugoslavia in the still unrealised union of Russia and Belarus.[37] In one opinion poll 67 per cent of Russians said they would personally do anything to help Serbia, 42 per cent being prepared to go there as a volunteer.[38] But feelings had subsided a month after the conflict began. Would-be volunteers who turned up at the offices of the ultra-nationalist leader Vladimir Zhirinovsky were disenchanted to find that they were being asked for nearly $500 before they could join up with the Serbs.[39] After independent TV channels showed pictures of the suffering of Kosovo Albanian refugees, strong feelings began to subside. The section of the electorate committed to democracy, began to see that a pro-Serb and anti-American policy worked in favour of the communists. But Andrei Piontkowski, a Moscow policy expert, said that 'some of them do not understand that it is not possible to aid Milošević, who at the end of the twentieth century is defying all the greatest values of Western and European civilization, and at the same time defend such values in Russia'.[40] There was also the danger of an internal rift in Russia itself. Many of the leaders of the 20-million strong Muslim population took a firm stand in the conflict: 'Confronted with the euphoric nationalist mobilisation of volunteers to join the battle on the Serb side, they immediately warned that they too would send volunteers to help the Albanians. The possibility of a war between Russian citizens on the territory of a third state caused such consternation that signing up volunteers and dispatching them to Serbia was put off indefinitely'.[41]

The political elite also returned to pragmatism. As early as 25 March Prime Minister Primakov stated that Russia would not allow its indignation over the air-strikes to do serious harm to economic relations with the West: 'There will be no isolationism'.[42] Russia made its living largely by selling raw materials to the West. Moreover, most of the Russian political elite kept its money in Western banks or owned property in the West, advantages they were loath to put at risk.[43]

On 25 April Yeltsin phoned Clinton as the NATO summit was ending, resuming ties that had been frozen since the start of the conflict. The threat of impeachment by the Duma, which had been hanging over him for some months, had subsided and his removal of Primakov strengthened his hand vis-à-vis nationalists (Bellamy 2002: 175–6). It was by now clear that NATO was unlikely to split over its actions in Kosovo. The resolve of key Western players to prevail over Milošević was also unmistakable. Even before the bombing, it had been made abundantly clear to Moscow by Strobe Talbott, an old Russia hand and the deputy Secretary of State that Washington would take grave exception if it sold the latest missiles to Serbia (Ignatieff 2000: 109). Russia's 'economic lifeline to the West' would be affected, a veiled threat bound to be taken seriously by the Russians who would in fact gain economically (through being offered cheap credits by the IMF denied to counties like Romania) for their constructive attitude to the crisis (Halberstam 2001: 475).

In his telephone conversation with Clinton, Yeltsin offered to launch a negotiating process to end the conflict. His chief mediator would be Victor Chernomyrdin, who had been his Prime Minister from 1993 to 1996 and was a powerful (and wealthy figure) in the Russian energy industry. By the time of the summit of the G-8 nations in Bonn, Germany on 6 May, Russia was coming close to accepting NATO's demand that all Serbian security forces would have to quit Kosovo and be replaced by an international military force sanctioned by the UN (Bellamy 2002: 185–6). It was also agreed that his partner in the mediation initiative would be the Finnish President, Martti Ahtisaari. The Russians were happy with this arrangement. Despite Finland having been a supporter of NATO's action, Finland was a neutral nation with whose leaders they had long been on good terms (Daalder and O'Hanlon 2000: 169). Ahtisaari had acquired considerable experience, mediating in protracted disputes, having been the UN's mediator in Namibia. Moreover, Finland was due to accede to the EU Presidency in July, so he would be seen as representing its interests also.

But the diplomatic process was overshadowed by the bombing of the Chinese embassy in Belgrade on 7 May (the target having been the building controlling Federal Procurement) (Gow 2003: 287). Many observers in the West believed the embassy had been deliberately targeted and various conspiracy theories were advanced, especially by those firmly against the NATO campaign. Peter Gowan, a Marxist British academic resolutely opposed to the war, argued that the bombing was deliberately meant to antagonise China and prompt a nervous Taiwan to buy more arms from the United States.[44] But the overwhelming evidence points to a mapping error by the Central Intelligence Agency (CIA) which failed to take into account the Chinese move to a new embassy in Belgrade in 1997. Outraged students who had been indoctrinated with nationalist propaganda ever since the 1989 Tian An-men square massacre, demonstrated for days. The communist leadership's self-image evoked parallels with Serbia's. China was a particular victim of modern history at the hands of external aggressors and needed to be allowed its rightful place in the modern world. Towards that end, concern about the human rights of individuals or ethnic minorities should not be elevated above the requirements of state sovereignty (Yahuda 2001: 197, 203).

China calmed down after receiving swift apologies from Washington. By now NATO was well into a new phase of the conflict. At its Washington summit, the go-ahead had been given to target the infrastructure of FRY in Serbia itself, such as bridges, refineries, fuel depots and political buildings that contributed to the war effort in Kosovo. General Clark increased his room to manoeuvre by excluding other nations from decisions about sorties involving only US planes (Rawnsley 2001: 278). The day after the Chinese embassy bomb, on 8 May, a bomb intended for an airfield exploded instead over a crowded market in the southern city of Niš killing at least sixty people. The high casualty-level had been caused by a cluster bomb, not banned under international law, but capable of causing high civilian casualties outside a combat zone. Their high dud rate means that unexploded canisters or bomblets pose an acute danger to human life and, later, between June 1999 and mid-March 2000, fifty-four people were killed in Kosovo by unexploded cluster bombs and landmines (AI 2000).[45] Some targets were near to buildings like hospitals and Solana later admitted in an interview that had bombs landed there instead of at a nearby target, in all likelihood it would have meant an abrupt termination of the war (*War In Europe* 2000).

The most controversial incident by far arising from the offensive against Milošević's 'command and control' system was the bombing of the main Serbian television building on 23 April. Sixteen people were killed. Blair, who had been arguing weeks earlier within NATO for attacks to be mounted against the Serbian 'propaganda machine' had, on the advice of government lawyers, disallowed the participation of British aircraft (Rawnsley 2001: 273). The lawyers considered it a breach of the Geneva Convention and it was widely condemned by many human rights bodies. On 17 May 1999 Solana wrote to AI defending the action, saying that television building's facilities 'are being used as radio relay stations and transmitters to support the activities of the…military and special forces, and therefore they represent legitimate military targets'.[46] James Gow argues that having had advance warning of the attack, the authorities actually increased the number of people in the building, one aim being to profit from the adverse publicity resulting from it being bombed. There was worldwide condemnation of the deaths, but the disabling of the Serbian media headquarters meant that the government lost its ability to control the flow of information to the Serbian populace (Gow 2003: 299).

That NATO survived both these questionable incidents without splintering was bound to have demoralised Milošević, one of whose own residences had been subject to a devastating attack. On 27 May, he and most of the rest of the world were taken by surprise when, along with five associates, he was indicted by the UN's International Criminal Tribunal for Yugoslavia (ICTY) for war crimes committed in Kosovo since 1 January 1999. It was the first indictment for war crimes of a serving head of state. Pressure appears to have been exerted on Chief Prosecutor Louise Arbour *not* to issue the indictment, but it was resisted (Gow 2003: 295–6, n. 20). US State Department sources felt it would place in danger the Russian–Finnish peace initiative (Ignatieff 2000: 119). Henry Kissinger argued that it would simply make Milošević more obdurate (Bellamy 2002: 197). But the indictment could also be read as a clear warning that his adversaries were not going to be brushed off with a paper peace, which had happened during Milošević's previous wars. It might well also have increased Milošević's sense of encirclement. Certainly James Gow believes, it was a surprise move that for Milošević was a psychological blow, undermining his belief that he could manipulate his less astute Western opponents and ultimately arrange a peace with them that left him essentially unscathed (Gow 2003: 296, 301).

Milošević would also find that the Russian attitude, bitterly critical of NATO in public, masked an increasingly ambiguous position. On 27 May, Chernomyrdin, Russia's special envoy in the Balkans, had published an article in the *Washington Post* in which he asserted that 'the United States lost its moral right to be regarded as the leader of the free democratic world when its bombs shattered the ideals of liberty in Yugoslavia';[47] he further warned that he would urge President Yeltsin to freeze all American–Russian relations unless the bombing stopped. The next day, on 28 May, Chernomyrdin held a 9-hour session with Milošević. By now the Russians had ample evidence that the NATO alliance were unlikely to split or abandon its offensive as long as Serbian forces remained in Kosovo. It would be surprising if Chernomyrdin had not been conveying his assessment of the Western mood to his Serbian interlocutors. After further days of wrangling over the form of words to deliver to Milošević, the Russians had agreed by 1 June to support a text calling for the withdrawal of all Serbian forces from Kosovo (Talbott 2002: 325). On 2 June, Ahtisaari obtained the verbal consent of Milošević. There were some delaying procedures: he would have to consult with parliament, a body very much under his thumb. He invited Ahtisaari to dinner only to be told that he might better use the time to discuss practicalities and next steps with colleagues (Ahtisaari 2001: 178).

On 3 June Milošević agreed to a total Serbian withdrawal. Given his reputation for stonewalling and the fact that the Serbian forces had only been lightly touched by NATO action during most of the conflict, Milošević's capitulation remains a mystery. Ahtisaari believed Chernomyrdin's endorsement of the American and Finnish conditions was a crucial factor in leading him to back down. But he may well have been given cause to hope that the Russians would salvage the Serbian position by establishing control of a part of Kosovo with their own troops. Zbigniew Brzezinski, a former US Secretary of State, believes that 'Milošević's sudden acquiescence was part of a desperate double-cross attempt engineered jointly by Belgrade and Moscow . . . to outwit NATO' by splitting Kosovo, gaining for 'frustrated Russia a significant boost in international prestige'.[48] Most Serbs were located in the north-east of Kosovo and a Russian protective presence could have salvaged some of Milošević's battered reputation. The Chief of Staff of the Russian army overrode the objections of civilian ministers and there was a bid to carve out Russian sector in Kosovo that might have been the basis for partition (Talbott 2002: 345). On 13 June Russian forces had entered Kosovo at 6.20 a.m. while NATO had gone in at 10.00 a.m. It was supposed to have been the other way round. Around 200 Russian soldiers took up defensive positions at Priština airport, barring the arrival of NATO forces. Taken unawares, Western military officials disagreed about how to respond. General Michael Jackson, newly appointed head of the UN force in Kosovo refused to carry out the order of General Wesley Clark, the NATO commander in Europe, to establish control of the airport. Russia was already asking Romania, Hungary and the Ukraine for use of their airspace to send cargo aircraft loaded with supplies and as many as 10,000 reinforcement troops to Priština (Talbott 2002: 346). The United States persuaded these countries to deny permission to over-fly their airspace. Strobe Talbott, the US deputy Secretary of State believes there was a risk of serious confrontation if Russian troops had landed to reinforce the unit already on the ground. He has even stated that Russian troops could have been blasted out of the air if they illegally entered Romanian or Hungarian air space. Before the Russians backed down, he called the Russian ambassador in Washington to say that there was the 'possible precondition for a genuine confrontation between the United States and Russia. (Talbott 2002: 346). Secretary Albright believed it was possible that the Yugoslav ambassador in Moscow – Milošević's brother – had cooked up a deal with elements in the Russian military to pave the way for a partition of Kosovo (Albright 2003: 423). For another week, Moscow continued to demand a separate Russian sector in Kosovo but, on 18 June, Russia reluctantly agreed that its troops would be dispersed within the US, French and German zones being set up in Kosovo. NATO's deepest engagement with the Balkans was about to begin.

Conclusion: Kosovo breaks the ideological mould

Opponents of the conflict were drawn from the anti-American Left, pacifist ranks, and also Right-wingers with an isolationist outlook committed to a defence of state sovereignty. The possibility that 'Operation Horseshoe' had been long in the making was discounted by many NATO critics. They saw the bombing campaign as responsible for the atrocities carried out on the ground.[49] Media supporters of the NATO intervention riposted by arguing that if this indeed was the case, then it was possible to argue that Hitler had been provoked to countenance the Holocaust by Allied aggression from 1939 onwards.[50]

One correspondent[51] to *The Guardian* wrote in the following terms on 18 June 1999:

> I wish the supporters of the war had the imagination to put themselves in Serb shoes. Your country is being bombarded by the biggest war machines since Nazi Germany. Your house has been destroyed. Your place of work pulverised. Your family or neighbours blown to pieces. The Muslims who live in your country are cheering on the bombers. In this situation would none of your readers be tempted to engage in ethnic cleansing?
>
> (*The Guardian* 18 June 1999)

This letter elicited the following reply from Maurice Hill three days later: 'The true implications of many of your readers letters are made clear by a slight alteration to the letter from Anthony Knight (18 June)'. By changing Serb to German and Muslims to Jews, it reads: 'I wish the supporters of the war had the imagination to put themselves in German shoes. Your country is being bombarded by the biggest war machine... Your house has been destroyed. Your place of work pulverised. Your family or neighbours blown to pieces. The Jews who live in your country are cheering on the bombers. In this situation would none of your readers be tempted to engage in ethnic cleansing'?[52]

Milošević enjoyed much residual sympathy among parts of the Western Left on account of his regime's Socialist rhetoric (Hoare 2003: 548–9). Regis Debray, the French intellectual responsible for promoting the legend of Che Guevara, wrote to President Chirac in the following terms: 'Mr Milošević has... been elected three times... He respects the Yugoslav Constitution. There is no single party... No political prisoners... People can criticise him in public and they do...' (Debray 2000: 321).

Harold Pinter, the British playwright and prominent critic of Blair's stance over Kosovo, described Milošević's actions against the Kosovan Albanians as 'standard counter-insurgency'.[53] Tariq Ali drew a parallel with Western counter-insurgency in South-East Asia (Ali 2000: xiii). The Irish journalist Fergal Keane riposted: 'I would suggest that Stalin' vast population clearances in the Caucasus or his actions against the Cossacks would be a more appropriate comparison'.[54]

Right-wing commentators in British publications such as *The Times* and *The Spectator* complained of 'liberal imperialism'. They were described as decrying 'the half-baked, emotional, romantic, moralistic, impoverished... pursuit of liberal values'.[55] Left-wing commentators such as Peter Gowan also used 'liberal imperialism' as a term of approbation. They insisted that NATO's involvement in Kosovo had absolutely nothing to do with humanitarian impulses and was all about defending the West's geopolitical interests in the region. This was a war of expansion by NATO (which two years previously had rejected applications for membership from several pro-Western Balkan states), a war designed to push United States power right up to the borders of Russia, or an attempt to usher in an aggressive new world order (Gowan 2000: 3–45). For another likeminded scholar, the Kosovo war was about establishing security in the Balkans to enable oil from the Caspian Sea to be transported across the region to Western markets (Fouskas 2003: 59). But such critics usually failed to acknowledge the fact that American intervention in the region had occurred with extreme slowness during the 1990s and that the US political interests most linked with aggressive capitalism, Right-wing US Republicans, were those keenest to disengage from the Balkans as speedily as possible.

Not a few critics of NATO intervention viewed foreign territories like Kosovo entirely in terms of their relations with the United States. It had no intrinsic interest except as a subject of US foreign policy.[56] Noam Chomsky, the most influential of the critics, was keen to shift the blame for Kosovo's misfortunes from Milošević to the direct and indirect machinations of a rogue superpower (Chomsky 1999). The language he used to describe Milošević's actions was tepid compared to what he reserved for the United States. Marko Hoare reminds us that:

> Twenty-five years ago Noam Chomsky and Edward S. Herman complained of the poor image conveyed by the Western media of the Khmer Rouge regime in Cambodia. They wrote that What filters through to the American public is a seriously distorted version of the evidence available, emphasising alleged Khmer Rouge atrocities and downplaying or ignoring the crucial US role, direct and indirect, in the torment that Cambodia has suffered.[57]
>
> (Hoare 2003: 547)

The criteria for judging Milošević or the UÇK was based on their relationship with the United States and it was the Kosovan Albanians who were found wanting. What might, in another context, have been a national liberation struggle had instead become a campaign of reactionary gangsterism against a legitimate government. According to the Irish writer, Colm Breathnach:[58]

> Such selective thinking bears an uncanny resemblance to the Reagan/Thatcher school of human rights which deemed that only victims of Communist regimes were worthy of support and assistance while victims of Right-wing regimes, such as the East Timorese who were slaughtered in their hundreds of thousands, were expendable. Whether it is articulated by right or left this viewpoint is in total contrast to the belief in universal values of human liberty and equality which constitutes the very core of socialism. Surely, it is incumbent on those who call themselves socialists to support the right of all those who are downtrodden regardless of the ideology of their oppressor.
>
> (*The Irish Times* 14 April 1999)

This writer was echoing the views of Leon Trotsky who opposed the Marxist tendency to demonise 'counter-revolutionary nations' when he had been a journalist covering the Balkan wars of 1912–13. He 'wrote passionately about the atrocities committed by the Balkan Christian states against the Albanians and other Balkan Muslims' (Hoare 2003: 558). In his despatches, he decried Russian liberal supporters of the Serbian and Bulgarian war drive of bearing their share of responsibility for the 'ripped-open bellies of Turkish children and the necks cut through to the bone of aged Muslims' (Trotsky 1980: 286).

Both the 'realist' Right and the far-Left doubted the claim that Kosovo might be a principled intervention by NATO because it was highly selective. The playwright Harold Pinter doubted that principles were in play at all given Western unwillingness to do much about the Kurds being persecuted by a NATO member, Turkey (Pinter 2000: 328). In response, Timothy Garton-Ash conceded that: 'Well, of course there are double standards – multiple standards in fact. Yet it's also true that we can't intervene everywhere. Because I don't prevent a murder in Brooklyn, it doesn't mean I shouldn't try to stop one in Camden. Duties are related to distance: strongest to those nearest'.[59]

The American writer Susan Sonntag asked whether Kosovo revealed that 'European lives, European suffering are more valuable, more worth protecting, than the lives of people in Africa, the Middle East, and Asia'? Without hesitation, she stated that 'to care about the fate of the people in Kosovo is Eurocentric, and what's wrong with that? If several African states had cared enough about the genocide of the Tutsis in Rwanda . . . to intervene, under the leadership of Nelson Mandela say, would we have called this Afrocentric'?[60]

More temperately, the London *Observer* had declared earlier: '. . . to those who criticise the war because the West has not done the same thing in Kurdistan, Chechnya or Tibet, thus displaying allegedly inconsistent standards, we say so what? Is one right action to be excluded because the action cannot be made universally? We have to live in the world as it is not some utopia. The argument is absurd'.[61]

The Kosovo conflict produced a sharp debate mainly conducted on the international Left about the ethics of intervention. Detractors saw it as an insidious exercise of American power. But, as Christopher Caldwell has remarked: 'the Nato intervention in Kosovo . . . proved alarmingly unpopular in the United States. For Americans, Kosovo reinforced the lessons learned in Somalia seven years earlier: no humanitarian interventions where they are not in the national interest. Europeans drew the opposite conclusion from Kosovo. They assumed humanitarianism had replaced national interest as a guiding principle'.[62]

But European leaders failed to display the stamina that might have enabled the United Nation to regularise the rules for humanitarian intervention. The Kosovo conflict had been a nerve-racking confrontation won not by overwhelming military strength or good judgment, but largely through luck. Both Milošević and NATO had drifted into war relying on false assumptions that were based on incomplete intelligence. Milošević was the one who blinked first, but the NATO states soon showed by their neglect of their peace-building responsibilities in Kosovo how peripheral it was to their overall security interests (contrary to what Noam Chomsky and others insisted).

4 Macedonia
Internal dangers supplant external ones

'Macedonia' refers to a territory whose boundaries and identity is often a matter of fierce dispute. In its least problematic form, it refers to an ancient kingdom which reached its apogee under Philip II and Alexander III. Next, it refers to a historically established but ill-demarcated territory partitioned in 1913 between Greece (which acquired 'Aegean Macedonia'), Serbia ('Vardar Macedonia') and Bulgaria ('Pirin Macedonia'). After 1990 the term acquired new resonance with the establishment of the independent Republic of Macedonia based on the republic in the former Yugoslav federation that had emerged from 'Vardar Macedonia' in 1945 (Cowan 2000: xiii).

The fledgling state retained a precarious peace for nearly a decade after it reluctantly opted for independence in 1990 to avoid being caught up in the violent disintegration of Yugoslavia. It was arguably the most distinctive part of the Balkans in ethnic terms. Two groups; the dominant Slavic Macedonians and the Albanians may have comprised over 80 per cent of the population, but there were numerous minorities including Roma (gypsies) and Turks, and Slavic Muslims who contributed to its distinctiveness. The new state enjoyed a strategic location in the heart of the southern Balkans but it was neglected by the powers that were struggling to contain violent conflicts further north. Nervous or resentful neighbours were preoccupied by the sudden appearance of a frail-looking state that had the capacity to plunge this part of the Balkans into serious conflict if either they or internal political forces took a wrong step. But although buffeted by a Greek embargo and the loss of markets in the rest of former Yugoslavia, and by quarrels involving the two main ethnic groups, it remained intact until the chief agent of disorder in the region, Slobodan Milošević ceased to be a menace to peace in 2000. Then in 2001 the cumulative effects of adjacent conflicts in Kosovo and Southern Serbia, elite machinations, grassroots frustrations over economic collapse, and inter-ethnic enmity spilled over into a serious confrontation between Macedonians and Albanians. This chapter examines the driving forces behind a simmering dispute and why a destructive conflict was only avoided by the narrowest of margins.

Macedonian self-rule under Tito

When Tito's Partisan forces unveiled their blueprint for a future Yugoslav state at their assembly in Jajce in 1943, the existence of a separate Macedonian nationality was acknowledged; instead of being deemed the southern part of Serbia, Macedonia was to be a distinct entity within the federal arrangements envisaged for the country under communist rule. Most inhabitants had been wary of those who had exercised state power in what, hitherto, had been the most contested territory in the Balkans. The Ottomans, and the Serbs who had controlled Macedonia during the era of royal Yugoslavia (1918–41), had scarcely been known for the justness of their rule. The occupations by Bulgaria in both world wars were remembered for their severity despite the ethnic and linguistic ties of the Slavic population in both countries. Greece was hardly a pole of attraction given the determined measures it had taken to assimilate the Slavophone population in the southern part of Macedonia which it had acquired in 1913.

Macedonia remained the most ethnically varied territory in the Balkans. But the numerically superior Slavs (among many of whom a Macedonian identity had gradually displaced a local or primarily religious identity since the birth of nationalism in South-East Europe after 1870) were the decisive element. They were the ethnic group whom the Partisans were courting with their 1943 promise of self-rule in a peace-time Yugoslavia; Slavic Macedonians, hitherto wary of Tito's intentions, joined the Partisan movement in large numbers (Perry 1997: 230). By 1946, with Yugoslavia transformed into a communist state, a separate Macedonian nationality was officially deemed to exist and Macedonia became one of Federal Yugoslavia's six constituent republics. An amorphous group identity was being transformed into a national one by affirmative state action. This was not an unusual state of affairs in twentieth-century Europe; elites in charge of a state had often sought to mould national identity according to their state-building purposes. Often the identity being promoted via the classroom and the official media has been an unwelcome one as the centralising state tried to suffocate minority consciousness that might weaken the primary national identity. It is possible to argue that this was the position before 1941 as efforts were made to impose a Serbian identity on the major part of Macedonia located within Yugoslavia since 1918.

Tito's strategy was very different. He aimed to promote a balanced set of identities within his multinational federation. The stability of communist rule seemed to rest on avoiding the hegemony of any one group. It suited his purposes to differentiate the Slavs living in Macedonia from Bulgarians and Serbs. The confusion that existed about collective identity before 1945, as Macedonia was the object of differing national claims appeared to be over. In the decades to come most Slavs from Macedonia grew to assume that their national identity was Macedonian. A literary language was established in 1947. In 1967, during a renewed burst of decentralisation, the creation of a Macedonian Academy of Sciences and a separate (autocephalous) Macedonian Orthodox Church (MPC) were meant to strengthen Macedonian self-identity.

But perhaps the main source of legitimacy was provided by the economic prosperity and material security that were features of most of Tito's long rule (1945–80). Although Macedonia remained far behind republics to the north in terms of economic development, it was greatly affected by urbanisation and industrialisation. This was part of the communist transformation process, but it was carried out under traditional and informal mechanisms. Members of the ethnic majority now found that they had the opportunity to fill the main positions in a state that was growing rapidly in size as it acquired many economic functions. Centuries long experience of foreign rule had made them wary of the state and its officials. Naturally, there was a strong 'need to identify service providers who could be trusted' (Janev 2003: 312). Accordingly, it was not the 'peasants' or 'the workers' but people from these backgrounds, creating networks of relations and friends, who benefited from the 'socialist revolution'. Kinship lay behind recruit- ment and the allocation of resources right across Yugoslavia, but it was particu- larly true of Macedonia. A fledgling nationality previously submerged and, in some minds, previously non-existent, needed to demonstrate its authority. Minorities were not actively persecuted. Indeed, there were elaborate mechanisms designed to allow them to express their cultural identity. But it was Slavic peasants comfortable with their Macedonian identity who benefited disproportionately from the urbanisation process. They mobilised on a kinship basis (Janev 2003: 310). The second-largest ethnic group, the Albanians, would eventually do the same as their numbers increased and their collective identity became more pronounced towards the close of the communist era.

The reaction to Yugoslavia's break-up

As in many other nations that had only recently acquired the attributes of a state, a conspicuous and often noisy intellectual elite was encouraged to stress Macedonia's ancient lineage. Sometimes neighbours that contained parts of historic Macedonia, Bulgaria and Greece, were reminded of this in no uncertain fashion and it was not hard to detect irredentist sentiments in radio broadcasts and cultural exhi- bitions and symposiums (King 1973: 187–219). But Macedonia was unprepared for full statehood when the federation was plunged into crisis in the late 1980s by the effort of Slobodan Milošević to re-centralise Yugoslavia around Serbia. There was no groundswell of enthusiasm for independence when Slovenia and Croatia took that path after 1990. Macedonia had done well economically out of Yugoslavia due to the steady transfer of resources from north to south. Its future prosperity appeared bound up with the survival of at least an economic union which would preserve an all-Yugoslav market. Nevertheless, beyond the small Serbian minority making up just over 2 per cent of the population, few relished falling into Belgrade's exclusive orbit. In line with the rest of Yugoslavia, multi-party elections were held in 1990. In fact they took place in three rounds on 9 November, 25 November and 9 December. The first round was characterised by 'massive irregularities' and the overall result was confusing (Szajkowski 2000: 255). A nationalist movement, the Internal Macedonian Revolutionary Organization (VMRO) emerged as the largest party while being far short of a governing majority. The former communists, grouped mainly in the Party of Democratic Change never lost the initiative and Kiro Gligorov, was elected state President by parliament in January 1991. He worked hard in subsequent months to try to prevent Yugoslavia's break-up by floating a con- federal plan. A poll in April 1991 found that 60 per cent of Macedonians preferred a restructured Yugoslavia of sovereign republics (Ackermann 2000: 58). But on 9 September of that year a referendum on independence was held once it was clear that Yugoslavia was well on its way to collapse. The question did not rule out some revival of the Yugoslav entity in the future: 'Are you for a sovereign and independent state of Macedonia, with the right to enter in a future alliance of sovereign states of Yugoslavia'? (Szajkowski 2000: 250–1). Of the registered electorate 75.74 per cent took part with 95.26 per cent voting in favour.

Despite the massive plurality, there was foreboding about going it alone. Macedonia was located in a historically volatile region which would soon turn into a war zone – the wars to the north inching ever closer to it as the 1990s progressed. Its neighbours Greece, Bulgaria, Serbia and Albania, which became known as 'the four wolves' on account of what were seen as their unfriendly or even predatory intentions, were a source of unease at differing times. Greece not Serbia was the most troublesome (see Chapter 1). Economic restrictions and full-blown sanctions imposed by Athens in 1994–5 underscored Macedonia's economic fragility: it could hardly claim to be able to defend itself militarily; its democratic system was a makeshift one and there was a high level of partisan politics; on occasion, there were high levels of inter-ethnic tensions. Not surprisingly, predictions ran high that the second smallest former Yugoslav republic would soon be consumed by violence that it seemed ill-prepared to fend off.

Kiro Gligorov

But Macedonia had one vital asset, an elected leader who commanded international respect and was a force for internal consensus; few other Yugoslav republics being able to claim as much. Kiro Gligorov was President for eight years (1990–8). His abilities and influence waned, especially after an assassination bid in 1995, but in the early years of his rule, it is no exaggeration to say that Macedonia's fate was intimately bound up with his own. This is all the more remarkable since few of its citizens had probably heard of him until the eve of independence.

Aged 73 in 1990 and an economist by training, Gligorov had spent most of his professional life operating at the federal level in Belgrade. He had been among the architects of a scheme for market reforms in the mid-1960s which Tito had renounced. In the 1970s he found himself speaker of the federal parliament. His career then went into eclipse until he got involved in a new federal effort to liberalise the economy at the end of the 1980s (Perry 1997: 246–7). In 1990, the Macedonian communists were keen to prove that they could relaunch themselves on a democratic path. Gligorov's pragmatic reputation made him an asset in that regard and he was invited to return to join a committee for social reforms. During the elections of that year, Gligorov delivered speeches on behalf of the ex-communists. He helped to check the advance of the inexperienced and volatile VMRO. Liberal-minded figures invited him to run for President; they included Vasil Tuporkovski, Macedonia's representative on the Yugoslav federal presidency who had done much to try to avert Milošević's wrecking plans. Gligorov had always encapsulated moderate behaviour and shunned radical rhetoric. Unlike

VMRO he did not seek to exploit or misuse historical events. He was ready to pursue the path of accommodation but careful not to lose touch with majority opinion (Rusi 1998: 59).

The hostility of Greece towards the emergence of an independent Macedonia delayed EU recognition and prevented EU-sponsored organisations from offering economic assistance. But other international developments assisted the independence drive. The collapse of the Soviet bloc and the restoration of independence to the Baltic and other states meant that Macedonia's declaration of independence occurred in a favourable European (if not local) environment (Roudometof 1996: 285). However, Macedonia needed to remove itself from the orbit of a shrinking Yugoslav state under Milošević's control. The Serbian leader refused to recognise the old administrative border as the new frontier and claimed areas of strategic importance within Macedonia. Gligorov and the Yugoslav Federal Army (JNA) negotiated directly about the forces withdrawal to Serbia. On 21 February 1992 an agreement was signed setting 15 April as the deadline for a complete pull-out (Ackermann 2000: 83). This was a big concession, one that Russia failed to make, since it continued to station troops in many parts of its 'Near Abroad'. But Belgrade was over-extended and needed all the troops it could muster for military operations further north. It is quite possible Milošević believed that Macedonia could not survive on its own and 'therefore no energy needed to be spent trying to keep it within crumbling Yugoslavia' (Mehmeti 1998: 58). Nevertheless, the nature of the withdrawal confirmed the breach between the two South Slav units; letters to UN negotiators and leading ambassadors protested 'the rough and uncivilised way' in which the JNA removed or dismantled 'complete sets of equipment, modern electronic devices and systems, and reserves of fuel and medicines' as well as machinery belonging to Macedonia (Ackermann 2000: 83).

In November 1992, Macedonia successfully appealed to the United Nations for peace-keepers to be deployed in a preventive capacity along its northern frontier. Within less than a month, the United Nations authorised what would be the first preventative deployment of UN peace-keepers in UN history and in 1993 US and Scandinavian troops arrived to make up the UN Preventative Deployment Force (UNPREDEP).

A fragile state

Gradually, the perceived threat to Macedonia's survival shifted from the external to the internal domain. In particular, the large Albanian minority was increasingly unhappy with its position. Albanians had boycotted the 1991 referendum on independence. They felt that their position was being sharply eroded in the new state. The Albanian community was reduced to the status of an ethnic minority. Albanian was no longer recognised as an official language. Even the previously recognised right of Albanians and other national minorities to fly their flags on certain public occasions was removed under the 1991 Constitution.

A diminution of the Albanian position had been taking place even before the rise of ethnic Macedonian nationalism characterised by the early successes of

VMRO. In 1989 the previous constitution had been reworded so that the Yugoslav republic of Macedonia was redefined as a 'nation-state of the Macedonian people' in place of the previous 'a state of the Macedonian people and the Albanian and Turkish minorities' (Poulton 1995: 172). Albanians boycotted the census two years later. Their spokesmen complained that the forms were written in Macedonian to which only a few explanations in Albanian were added. They also suggested that manipulation of the figures was likely since the census commission was composed of ethnic Macedonians only (Reuter 1999: 35). A further census held in 1994, under international supervision, saw Albanians participate, but their leaders claimed that over 1,000,000 Albanians resident in Macedonia were left out of the statistics after a restrictive citizenship act was adopted in 1992.[1]

Albanians in Macedonia lived in a crescent-shaped region that began in Kumanovo in the north-east, stretching through the capital Skopje to Tetovo in the north-west, then reaching south along the border with Albania to Debor, Gostivar and Struga (Perry 1997: 251–2). By the end of the twentieth century, around 20 per cent of people in Skopje would be ethnic Albanian (Gruevski 2004). In 1988, there had been demonstrations by Albanians in Kumanovo and Gostivar, claiming their rights as guaranteed by the 1974 constitution (Poulton 1995: 130). In 1990 two thousand Albanians demonstrated in Tetovo for a greater Albania without any violence occurring. Much earlier, in 1968, demonstrations had occurred in Tetovo, the largest mainly Albanian city, demanding that Albanian areas of Macedonia be joined with Kosovo to form a seventh republic within Yugoslavia (Poulton 1995: 126). Albanian strength in Tetovo clearly concerned the authorities. It was reported in 1988 that the birth rate there was three times the national average (Poulton 1995: 125). In the same year laws were passed meant to restrict further migration by ethnic Albanians to the city (Islami 1994: 35). In a controversial move, the Tetovo local authorities demolished the walls around numerous Albanian dwellings – 'traditional protection from prying eyes' – arguing that they interfered with 'urban progress' (Perry 2000: 276).

Different branches of the state were concerned with the growth of Albanian nationalism in the 1980s; people were 'detected' distributing leaflets and making 'hostile verbal statements', but no mass arrests followed as in Kosovo (Poulton 1995: 131). No Albanian counterpart to VMRO sprung up possibly because the Albanians lacked an intellectual leadership; nearly all Albanians destined for higher-level education went to Priština University in Kosovo from 1970 to 1989. Islam, not secular nationalism, was the main collective influence shaping the outlook of Albanians in Macedonia. So a contrast can be drawn with Kosovo which, back in the 1880s, had been the birthplace of Albanian nationalism. Anxieties about religious indoctrination occasionally cropped up; indeed in the late 1980s the authorities made it illegal for Muslim youth aged 15 or under to receive a religious education and attempts were made to block the construction of mosques (Poulton 1995: 132). But ultimately Islam was seen as less subversive to the Yugoslavia state than secular nationalism. The appeal of Albania soon faded once Albanians from Kosovo and Macedonia started to visit it in the post-communist era.

There was no shortage of economic grievances harboured by Albanians in Macedonia. But those grievances most vocally expressed were ones centring on language, symbols and territorial autonomy. The Party of Democratic Prosperity (PDP), the dominant Albanian political voice until the mid-1990s, sponsored a referendum in January 1992 in support of the cantonisation of Macedonia. Of those who voted (an estimated 92 per cent of Albanians) 74 per cent supported this proposal for territorial autonomy, but the state declared the vote illegal (Perry 1997: 253).

There was also deep resentment that the law on higher education (from the Yugoslav era) still in force, did not allow for the creation of any institutions with a curriculum in a language other than Macedonian, or so-called world languages (Kemp 2001: 193). After Priština University was closed down in 1989 and turned into a Serbian institution, a void had been created that led to increasing demands for higher education taught in Albanian. The politics of the community increasingly centred around the question of an Albanian-language university with government resistance to this demand straining inter-ethnic relations.

The united political front of Albanians collapsed in 1994 when the primacy of the PDP was challenged by a splinter force which eventually became the Democratic Party of Albanians (PDsh). Its demands were radical ones: equal status for the Albanian language, much wider access to Albanian-language secondary and tertiary education and the right to be named as a co-nation of Macedonia, together with ethnic Macedonians, and not as an ethnic minority (Szajkowski 2000: 253). Its leaders were Arber Xhaferi, a former journalist based in Priština who maintained close links with Albanian leaders from Albania and Kosovo and Menduh Thaçi, a former dental student who became a figure of great wealth thanks to his role in the informal economy. Thaçi was quoted by the London *Observer* of 27 February 1994 as warning: 'If Macedonians go on refusing Albanian demands, there will be bloodshed here...Only Albania and Albanians hold the key to stability here'. Xhaferi and Thaçi's party soon went on to control the main local government bodies in all towns with a strong Albanian presence except Skopje: the more integrated Albanians of the capital remained loyal to the PDP which had places in the cabinet from 1992 to 1998.

In ethnic Macedonian eyes, the PDP and many urban-dwelling Albanians were usually moderate, outward-looking and unencumbered with ties with Albanians elsewhere. They were 'Albanci' to whom ethnic Macedonians gave the benefit of the doubt in contrast to the more pejorative term 'Siptarite', whose holders were seen as likely to be involved in drug-trafficking, guns and prostitution and very often having a village background or else hailing from Kosovo.[2] At least there were no current tensions based on historic antagonisms. Albanian lords had dominated Slavic Macedonians in Ottoman times, but these memories were not politicised in the way that occurred in Serbia or Bosnia (Perry 2000: 287). Indeed Macedonian nationalism was late in developing; it flourished under communism when an ethos of 'brotherhood and unity' had been stressed. The national church, often an incubator of divisive historical memories, was weak unlike in Serbia. Those who seemed to covet Macedonia in the state-building era were not Turks or Albanians but fellow Slavs in Serbia and possibly Bulgaria (which refused to recognise the existence of a separate Macedonian *nation* until 1999).

The strong commitment to a multi-ethnic Macedonia was shown by the success that the pro-Yugoslav formation, the Alliance of Reform Forces, enjoyed in the 1990 Macedonian elections where it got 9.2 per cent of parliamentary seats (Perry 2000: 233). Ethnic peace was assisted by the presence of other numerous minorities which could act as a buffer between ethnic Macedonians and Albanians.

Turks, Roma and Slavic Muslims

The 1981 census showed that 85 per cent of all ethnic Turks in Yugoslavia were located in Macedonia where they comprised 4 per cent of the population. Their high numbers suggested a local tradition of tolerance towards the group which had once acted as an overlord. Many spoke Turkish and Albanian fluently as well as Macedonian. One could even find members of the same family who identified themselves differently, some as Turks others as Macedonian, in order to access themselves to different patronage networks; little friction was reported between them and the Macedonian majority (Perry 2000: 254).

Macedonia was also an island of relative tolerance for the Roma (gypsy) population. The Roma town of Šuto Orizari, outside Skopje, was set up after the 1963 earthquake which had devastated the city. It acquired 35,000 inhabitants and had its own elected council, sending a deputy to parliament. It enjoyed a higher standard of living than many Macedonian villages (Poulton 1995: 140). Later, President Gligorov was to show sympathy towards the often difficult situation of the socially submerged Roma and he was always careful to explicitly recognise them as equal citizens of the state (Poulton 1995: 191). At times, Gligorov seemed to play the role of Tito, acting as an arbiter between the two large discordant groups in his multi-ethnic state and championing the interests of lesser minorities in the hope that they would play a balancing role.

Living mainly in western Macedonia were 40,000 Muslims known as Torbeši. These Macedonian-speaking Slav Muslims are largely agricultural. It seems that they wish neither to identify with ethnic Macedonians nor with their fellow Muslim Albanians (Perry 2000: 256). During the years of warfare further north, Serbo-Croatian speaking Muslim refugees arrived from Bosnia whom the authorities were reluctant to recognise as a separate group distinct from the Torbeši. To complicate matters further, there were already a similar group known as the Gorani, living in hilly districts of western Macedonia and extending into the Sar Planina area of Kosovo. They shared the same customs as Torbeši but saw themselves as a separate group (their identity being based primarily on religion and village customs) (Poulton 1999: 117).

Ethnic Macedonian anxieties

The heterogeneity of the minorities reduced the likelihood that a homogenous and intolerant nationalism would take root among the ethnic majority. Nevertheless, many ethnic Macedonians feared being overtaken by the Albanians. In the census of 1948, they had made up 17.1 per cent of the population; in the census of 1991 this had increased by nearly 6 per cent, which didn't seem an excessive rise (Perry 1997: 276, n. 13). Many Macedonians nevertheless believe that Albanian families invariably have 6 to 8 children, but by the late 1990s the average size of the Albanian family was 2.5 children. There was, however, a much lower Macedonian birth rate (1.7 children per family); not a few Macedonians were, and are, convinced that Albanians are deliberately out-breeding them in order to take over Macedonia. But, given the current statistics, it would take another sixty years for the two populations to reach parity.[3]

Further, Macedonian unease is stoked by trans-frontier pan-Albanian links. Informal organisations with an economic or religious character transcend international boundaries. The popular majority view holds that the solidarity springs from a shared ideal to create a greater Albania. But there is no shortage of evidence that the solidarity is non-ideological and stems from kinship and other ties that have rarely been politicised (Kola 2003: *passim*). Nevertheless, the authorities feared that Albanian numbers in Macedonia would be boosted by the arrival of co-ethnics fleeing the Serbian crackdown in Kosovo. Against this background, a citizenship law was introduced in 1992 which decreed that non-Macedonians resident in the republic for less than fifteen years would only be eligible for citizenship if they could prove a regular source of income and if they were above 18 years of age; those who did not meet these stipulations were likely to face deportation (Bugajski 1994: 111).

A major test of community relations was provided by the 1994 elections. Macedonia faced economic sanctions by Greece and there were signs of growing Albanian radicalism. VMRO fought on a platform which 'had a confrontational approach towards Serbia and ethnic Albanians in Macedonia'. Nevertheless, despite suffering economic privations and insecurity about the future, most ethnic Macedonians refused to be pulled in a radical direction (Ackermann 2000: 59).

Albanian perspectives

Albanians in Macedonia found it difficult to identify positively with the Macedonian state. By the end of the 1990s, they held down only 10.2 per cent of state jobs despite making up 22.7 per cent of the population (according to the 1994 census). In the sensitive area of law and order, they were under-represented. In the mainly Albanian cities of Tetovo and Gostivar, they constituted 17 and 12 per cent of the police; within the interior ministry, a paltry 8.7 per cent of employees were Albanian. Turning to the armed forces, they comprised 2.9 per cent of officers and defence ministry personnel, although Albanians constituted between 16 and 26 per cent of military recruits.[4]

In state-controlled enterprises and their privatised successors, Albanians were also often under-represented even in areas where they constituted the majority.[5] Faced over a long period by ethnic Macedonians with better-organised kinship structures, they were obliged to develop their own, being frozen out of the state. One way they built up their economic position was by emigrating to central Europe and further afield. Remittances were sent back to families and sometimes savings were invested in retail businesses at home. This enabled a private sector to take off in Albanian areas in the consumer sector. It gave Albanians greater experience in the private sector than the ethnic majority which found it difficult to shake off its dependence on a shrinking state sector. Enterprising Albanians were thus in a better position to adjust to the onset of privatisation, but the sharp economic downturn faced by Macedonia in the 1990s meant that it was a flimsy prosperity which only a minority of Albanians benefited from.

Albanians depended on group solidarity for survival. Since they got few benefits from the state, there were few incentives to learn the Macedonian language which the constitution decreed was the sole official one. A 1994 poll revealed that only 4.2 per cent of the Albanians considered it necessary to know the language of another ethnic group inhabiting the same area (Gaber 1997: 108). Opposition to inter-marriage was also a longstanding impulse. In 1974, a study of villages in western Macedonia showed that 95 per cent of Albanian heads of households would not permit their sons to marry a girl from another ethnic background (Poulton 1995: 132). A 1995 survey showed that unhappiness about mixed marriages continued to be high among both ethnic Albanians and Macedonians (Szajkowski 2000: 253).

In 1993, 86 per cent of Albanian respondents were prepared to tell pollsters that they felt second-class citizens. In a similar 1994 poll this figure had gone down to 42 per cent, perhaps influenced by the fact that members of the PDP were now included in the coalition government. But 87 per cent still felt that they suffered discrimination on political or legal grounds (Gaber 1997: 111).

Education was crucial for upward mobility, above all in the state sector. Here Albanians had fallen behind ethnic Macedonians. In 1992–3 the latter made up 63.6 per cent of those attending primary school, 88.0 per cent of those in secondary school and 91.4 per cent of those enrolled in university. In the same period, only 27.3 per cent of Albanian children were enrolled in primary school and 7.2 per cent in secondary school; in 1993–4 only 2.8 per cent of the republic's students were Albanian (Janev 2003: 308). The state was adamantly opposed to higher education in Albanian seeing it as a seedbed for irredentism. But the language of instruction in primary and secondary schools in mainly Albanian-inhabited areas was Albanian. Moreover, there was resistance in patriarchal and strongly religious Albanian households, found in rural areas, to the idea of providing girls with an education. (This might explain why the Albanian-owned textile factory in ethnically mixed Kicevo, the town's largest employer, had a completely Macedonian female workforce.)[6]

It was far from easy for the state to pursue a policy of affirmative action designed to reduce some of these glaring discrepancies. Macedonia was preoccupied with multiple challenges to its security and even survival in the 1990s. Above all, the majority was not in the mood to make concessions to Albanians because it faced growing adversity. The GDP fell by 9.9 per cent in 1990, 12.1 per cent in 1991, 14 per cent in 1992, 21.1 per cent in 1993, 8.4 per cent in 1994 and 0.4 per cent in 1995 (Perry 1997: 262). This was an annual economic contraction of 10 per cent in the first half of the decade. Real salaries were going down in the public administration and the mishandling of privatisation schemes in the mid-1990s would further depress the living standards of the majority (Rusi 1998: 60). Owing to its lack of international recognition in the years immediately after independence, Macedonia was denied access to international financial markets. Unemployment reached 36 per cent of the insured population in 1993 (Hislope 2004: 136). Gligorov would have been testing his credibility with ethnic Macedonians to destruction if he had argued in favour of a redistribution of jobs and opportunities to ethnic Albanians against such a grim background.

The politics of the Macedonian majority also made it difficult to respond magnanimously to Albanian complaints. No party commanded an overall majority and the opposition was dominated by the vocal nationalists of VMRO.[7] It enjoyed strong backing from ethnic Macedonians living abroad, which like many diasporas, had a romantic and often militant attitude to the homeland. Many of its voters were found in areas containing large numbers of Albanians (Perry 1997: 242).

Macedonia is not the only territory in the Balkans where members of a national majority who find themselves a local minority, have supported hardline nationalists. Concessions to Albanians would have been denounced as treason by VMRO. Gligorov told Albanian politicians in the mid-1990s: 'if you want to improve some of the ethnic rights, then you have to convince the [Slavic] Macedonian population that that is good, and that it is to the benefit of the country, and of the [Slavic] Macedonians as a nation. All this requires time, preparation, argumentation, patience' (Ackermann 2000: 93).

Papering over the cracks

Bogdan Szajkowski is not alone among scholars when he wrote of the Albanians: '[t]heir language, customs, social organizations, and traditions have very little, if anything, in common with those of their Slav and Greek neighbours' (Szajkowski 2000: 252). But in Macedonia, while a community apart, they did not face a backlash from the Slavophone majority. A pan-Slavic front could only emerge with difficulty owing to intense Serbian–Macedonian differences. Besides these, the ethnic Macedonian political camp itself was riven by sharp antagonisms. In 1994, when VMRO did badly in the first round of parliamentary elections, it boycotted the second round on 30 October. Conference for Security and Cooperation in Europe (CSCE) observers considered the poll valid despite minor irregularities, but with a 57.5 per cent turnout, clearly many in the majority community had heeded VMRO's call for mass abstentions (Perry 1997: 237).

VMRO's great rival was the successor of the League of Communists, the Social Democratic Alliance of Macedonia (SDSM). Since 1992 it had governed not just with smaller parties but also with the Albanian PDP. This was quite a bold move that boosted the government's credibility internationally where the inability of majority and minority to share power was often seen as one of the chief sources of the Balkans troubles. But it was a loveless marriage based on a 'balance of mistrust between ethnic groups' which it has been claimed was the same formula that prevailed in communist Yugoslavia (Mehmeti 1998: 58). Along with the other coalition partners, the PDP benefited in numerous ways from its membership of government. A deal-making culture grew up which afforded short-term stability in inter-ethnic relations while creating long-term difficulties. Kim Mehmeti, an often outspoken ethnic Albanian commentator believed the state of inter-ethnic relations became a hostage to 'business arrangements between the ruling parties'.[8] Perhaps inevitably Albanian politicians tended their own core interests and neglected wider Albanian community concerns, causing restlessness especially among the young.[9] This attitude only intensified in 1998 when the most radical of the Albanian parties, the PDsh, surprised commentators by forming a coalition government with VMRO – Democratic Party for Macedonian National Unity (DPNE). Before long another disenchanted Albanian commentator was writing: 'It is no secret that some of the leading lights' in that coalition 'are among the richest individuals in the country'.[10] Mehmeti himself would bluntly state in 2001 that 'political elites are building "brotherhood and unity", raking in fortunes in dodgy business deals, while the two largest communities in the country grow further apart'.[11]

The need to create democratic institutions which functioned to the benefit of many in the two main communities was neglected. Gligorov cannot escape responsibility for this state of affairs (although he was in retirement by the time the most flagrant looting of the state got underway). Foreign threats gave him an excuse for doing relatively little domestically. He projected the image of Macedonia as 'a model of peace and security in the Balkans' (Gligorov 1995: 5–14); he managed to convince many that Macedonia was 'an oasis of peace and moderation under his wise governance' (Rusi 1998: 59). Major foreign governments and transnational bodies were all too ready to accept such a complacent reading of the situation; it encouraged them to believe that Macedonia was not a potential flashpoint even though their neglect of this strategically placed Balkan country, in many ways increased its instability.

External responses

The Atlantic democracies were slow in offering a constructive response to Macedonia's problems. But once the UNPREDEP force was installed, they had a vested interest in ensuring its success. British and French intelligence services took an early interest in Macedonia (Phillips 2004: 66). The small number of Western diplomatic missions represented in Skopje sometimes intervened very directly in local politics, especially in order to strengthen their wider peace-keeping role in the region. Writing of the EU diplomatic corps, one commentator acerbically claimed that it 'has a function in Skopje akin to that of colonial governors of dependent territories' (Pettifer 1999: 141). He also claimed that most diplomats rarely, if ever, visited the Albanian-inhabited areas (but this didn't prevent them exhibiting distrust for the radical PDsh) (Pettifer 1999: 142). Despite such Western tutelage, Macedonia received direct financial assistance of only $124 million from the European Union up to the mid-1990s.

Under the auspices of the CSCE (from 1994 the Organization for Security and Co-operation in Europe (OSCE)), there were two useful exercises in preventative diplomacy that undoubtedly helped to calm the situation in Macedonia at specific moments. The first was the 'Working Group' chaired by the retired German diplomat, Geert Ahrens. He periodically visited the country from October 1991 to early 1996. He took up the cause of smaller minorities while rejecting territorial demands from ethnic Albanians (either for autonomy or complete statehood), arguing that Macedonia's small size did not allow for sweeping devolution. But it has been claimed that he 'enjoyed the trust of all contending groups' (Ackermann 2000: 112); his advocacy helped to ensure that Albanian-language secondary school classes doubled. He got the government to agree to Macedonia being designated as 'a state of citizens'. But a 'gentleman's agreement' on the display of national symbols involving the interior ministry and ethnic Albanian leader collapsed (Ackermann 2000: 111).

Indeed, disagreement over the use of the flag of the Albanian community (identical to that of the Albanian state) on public buildings would lead to the most serious internal confrontation in Macedonia before the Albanian uprising that would occur in 2001. For several months in 1997, the mayors of Tetovo and Gostivar had been flying this flag next to the Macedonian one on flagpoles in front of their town halls. After the constitutional court decided that the law on flags was being violated, the flags were taken down on 9 July 1997. In the rioting that followed in Gostivar, two Albanians were shot dead.

Almost immediately on the scene was Max van der Stoel, a former Dutch foreign minister, who headed the OSCE's High Commission for National Minorities (HCNM). Since its foundation in 1993, he had interposed himself between alienated minorities and recalcitrant governments drawn from the ethnic majority in a range of post-communist states. He looked for methods to accommodate and integrate ethnic diversity into state structures (Gallagher 2002: 36). This was an approach that only slowly acquired appeal in the first half of the 1990s as the West responded to violent conflict in the Balkans by promoting partition and the transfer of populations. Van der Stoel commented in 1999 that:

> It often amazes me to think that the annual budget of my office is approximately the same as two Tomahawk cruise missiles. One E-2c Hawkeye early warning reconnaissance and command airplane costs approximately ten times the entire expenditure of my office since it opened...

> (Kemp 2001: 132)

Van der Stoel visited Macedonia more than fifty times during his period as the OSCE's HCNM. His main challenge was to try and persuade the authorities to accommodate the Albanian aspiration for a university in their own language. He also sought to persuade Albanians to seek this goal by legal means. One Albanian demonstrator had been killed on 17 February 1995 in clashes with police coinciding with the opening of a so-called Albanian university in Tetovo. His efforts to create a state-funded higher-education institute in Albanian which would train teachers and provide training in business management and public administration, fell foul of arch-conservative intellectuals in the Academy of Sciences and Arts in

Skopje; meanwhile Fadil Sulejmani, the rector of the unrecognised Tetovo University saw it as a diminution of his project (Kemp 2001: 194).

Van der Stoel's visit to Gostivar in the aftermath of the 1997 riots may have helped to deflate tensions, but the two Albanian mayors involved were given draconian prison terms for defying the state on a key symbolic issue (they were released under a 1999 amnesty). One Western analyst warned that 'the fact that such blatant violence could erupt on such a small symbolic pretext, illustrates the basic...instability of the...state, where the new national identity has to be enforced in a highly coercive way' (Pettifer 1999: 143). As for Van der Stoel, he was hampered by the lack of high-level support from powerful states in the OSCE for his conflict prevention approach in potential trouble spots like Macedonia. Even when the emphasis switched from partition to restoring the equilibrium of troubled ethnically mixed states, he warned (in 1999):

> we are now pouring millions of euros into South-East Europe by way of post-conflict rehabilitation. Would not a fraction of these resources and efforts, invested at an earlier stage, have helped to prevent the malaise we now find ourselves in?
>
> (Kemp 2001: 132)

The West was exercising a holding mission in Macedonia. There was no strategy for alleviating the country's internal problems. The effects on Macedonia of the major initiatives taken by the Atlantic democracies in the region were rarely thought through. Perhaps the key initiative was the November 1995 Dayton conference. It was narrowly focussed on ending the Bosnian war and imposing a tenuous peace. The impact on the mood of Albanians in Kosovo, who had clung to a non-violent strategy in the hope of being rewarded by the West was not taken into account. If the smouldering Kosovo situation became a full crisis, Macedonia could not possibly avoid the damaging fall-out.

VMRO gets its place in the sun

The Dayton conference was preceded by an attempt on the life of President Gligorov on 3 October 1995. He was seriously wounded in a car bomb explosion and it took him several months before he could return to lighter duties. The attack had been preceded by an anti-corruption drive in the summer of 1995 in which four deputy ministers were sacked (Perry 1997: 248). The privatisation process (initiated under IMF pressure) had provided rich pickings for the Skopje elite (with Serbs benefiting as well as ethnic Macedonians). Skopje was also an important staging post on the heroin trail from Turkey to Italy. The different drug gangs sought to influence politics in their favour and there is no doubt that a stable country under a respected leader like Gligorov was inconvenient for their activities. Various theories circulated about who tried to slay the President, but it is interesting that none suggested major Albanian involvement.

In the absence of Gligorov's role as an arbiter, the coalition known as the Alliance for Macedonia fell apart. Stojan Andov, the leader of the Liberals (and a former

Yugoslav ambassador to Iraq in the 1980s) attempted to position himself as Gligorov's successor but failed. Andov held the influential post of parliamentary speaker from 1991 to 1996 and again during the crisis of 2001. The PDP remained in government (despite the 1997 Gostivar riot) but a period of unfettered SDSM rule ensued until the 1998 parliamentary elections.

There were modest hopes that a proper renewal of politics could get underway. VMRO drew up a pragmatic electoral manifesto. Contentious nationalism was sidelined. VMRO slammed the SDSM for corruption and promised to root it out. An electoral alliance 'For Change' was concluded with a small moderate party. After two rounds of voting, this alliance secured 58 out of 120 seats in November 1998. In an unexpected move, the most radical of the Albanian parties, the PDsh was invited to join the new government. This was seen as a very hopeful sign. Writing just prior to the elections, Duncan Perry was sanguine about the future:

> Reckless behaviour and irresponsible actions, which until now have not been frequent, are unlikely to grow. Macedonia's citizens seem instinctively to know that stability profits all and that it is in everyone's interest to allow the new Macedonian state to evolve, not explode.

(Perry 1997: 274)

Kosovo: a radicalising agent

But the new government under VMRO's leader, Ljubčo Georgievski, was soon overtaken by the Kosovo crisis in spring 1999 when NATO confronted Milošević as his forces drove out most of the disputed territory's Albanian population. Under pressure from ethnic Macedonians, the government was disinclined to offer sanctuary to the refugees and local confrontations flared up with NATO forces in Macedonia. Those Albanians who got through were welcomed into Albanian homes. By contrast the Slavic majority found it hard to empathise and feared drowning in a sea of Albanians if they were unable quickly to go back to their homes. No less than 114,000 ethnic Albanians crossed into Macedonia during that traumatic spring. Van der Stoel was so concerned with the potential effect that, on 12 May 1999, he issued a formal warning for the first time in his six years heading the OSCE's HCNM: 'the increase of the population ... by more than 10 per cent within a few weeks, resulting in a major change of the inter-ethnic balance, is proving to be too big a burden for the country' (Kemp 2001: 191–2).

Nearly all the deportees returned as NATO forced Milošević to quit Kosovo. But the failure of the West to completely disarm Albanian insurgents produced a growing security threat on Macedonia's porous border with Kosovo. The United Nations did not renew UNPREDEP's mandate. When diplomatic relations were established with Taiwan in return for major investment, China vetoed UNPREDEP's extension just as the Kosovo conflict was erupting. It was a major setback for Macedonian diplomacy, occurring just as Gligorov, now aged 82, was retiring. The mood was a sour one as the race for his successor got underway in late 1999. Seen as a prisoner of Albanian interests, VMRO was in an awkward position. The two main contenders now abandoned their normal platforms. The SDSM's Tito Petkovski's electoral strategy was one of confrontation with Albanians. His rival, VMRO's Boris Trajkovski was described at the time as post-nationalist, pro-Europe and anti-communist. On 31 October 1999, Petkovski was the clear winner with 32.71 per cent, ahead of his VMRO rival who garnered 20.9 per cent.[12] In the run-off, VMRO was now dependent on Albanian parties who were raising demands for autonomy it had always vociferously ruled out. It was bound to be troubling that its opponents had stolen their nationalist clothes.

If the Albanians abstained, it would confirm their alienation from the political system. If less than 50 per cent of the population turned out, the election would in fact be invalid. There was also the danger of a disputed count. With VMRO overtaking the SDSM in the concluding ballot, the loser complained of systematic vote-rigging especially in Albanian areas. But no hard evidence was forthcoming and when a re-run occurred in much of western Macedonia on 23 December, the result was almost identical to the previous one.[13]

The post-Gligorov era had got off to a destructive start. His own party, the SDSM had revealed that it was prepared to abandon inter-ethnic cohabitation in order to cling on to its primacy. It denounced the governing parties as being ready to break up the state and it boycotted the inauguration of President Trajkovski. Many in the majority felt disenfranchised: the candidate most of their votes had gone to who had a clear first round lead, was beaten. Against a background of territorial insecurity and growing unemployment, it is dangerous when an ethnic majority feels it is losing control.

Corruption increases frustrations

It was the media that stepped into the post-Gligorov political vacuum. It fanned the growing mistrust of the public towards the main political forces, placing particular emphasis on corruption. By the year 2000, there was mounting evidence that the fractured political elite was closing ranks to smother corruption allegations. Only a short time before, Prime Minister Georgievski had promised that anti-corruption legislation would be a top priority for his new government, but it was shelved. A parliamentary session held in March 2000 aired the alleged misdeeds of the previous government, some of whose members were accused of handing lucrative state contracts to their relatives and allies. But Andov, the parliamentary speaker, cut the debate short. His lame excuse was that time needed to be found to celebrate International Women's day. Such a self-serving response encouraged widespread mistrust in the ability of the political process to generate solutions to a wide range of problems. The media returned to the fray, the influential *Makedonija Denes* claiming that political parties were in league with racketeers; in an anti-Albanian move, it argued that 70 per cent of the profits went to the PDsh and the rest to VMRO.[14] Later, the PDsh leader Xhaferi would excuse Albanian participation in corruption as 'logical when "the Slavs" dominate the state sector. What are we to do if we don't participate in it'.[15]

Increasingly well-documented accounts of the looting of the state under VMRO surfaced in the media. According to Radio Free Europe, state institutes or enterprises were hollowed out in a particular way: '...a member of a particular party is appointed director of a state institution or a state-owned enterprise. Then he fills positions within the organization or the company with other party members until the whole thing "belongs" to the respective party. Then either the institution or the company is used as a sinecure for deserving party members, or its resources are exploited on behalf of the party until the institution or company is bankrupt'.[16]

One neat illustration of this practice was the way that VMRO introduced large numbers of civilians, in effect party activists, into the defence ministry after 1998. Their knowledge of military affairs was slight which undermined the army's weak capacity when a full-blown crisis occurred in 2001.[17]

Newspapers locked in a circulation war as poverty diminished the amount of readers, increasingly emphasised conspiracy theories. President Trajkovski was branded a puppet that had been imposed on an unwilling Macedonia as a result of a conspiracy involving the international community and Albanian leaders.[18] Much was made of the fact that he belonged to the country's tiny Protestant community and therefore he shared the same faith as the US ambassador, Christopher Hill; the latter had played an active role in the Dayton negotiations and he was even more influential in futile negotiations to avert conflict in Kosovo. It was not hard to depict him as the puppet master in Macedonia. The anti-NATO sentiment was growing. It had surfaced in the summer of 1999 in Kumanovo when several Danish soldiers stripped off and jumped into the town fountain. Perhaps the troops assumed that in line with Balkan under-development, social habits were lax. But it was a wrong perception and residents appalled at their behaviour beat them up.[19]

It would be wrong to assume that the picture in Macedonia was one of unrelieved gloom. In the autumn of 1999, state television started broadcasting a children's television drama series. Based around the lives of two families, one Macedonian and one Albanian who lived in a mixed neighbourhood. 'Nashe Maalo' (Our Neighbourhood) was partly devised by the Macedonian branch of 'Search For Common Ground', a Washington DC-based NGO dedicated to conflict prevention. Aiming to bridge the gap between Macedonian and Albanian children, it gave young viewers the chance to learn basic vocabulary in both languages, and it proved immensely popular.[20] It was a rare example of effective cooperation between international and local NGOs in Macedonia (with US ones often being viewed as an arm of the US administration) (Ackermann 2000: 161).

Van der Stoel of the OSCE also worked effectively with education experts to produce a bill on higher education which was meant to deal with most Albanian grievances. It was passed into law on 25 July 2000, but there was huge sensitivity around the issue. In May, thousands of students, teachers and parents had poured onto the streets of the town of Bitola to protest at government plans to provide an Albanian language class at a local secondary school; there was a fear that it would be a magnet drawing Albanians to this mainly ethnic Macedonian town and the government quickly cancelled the plan.[21] A year earlier, Paulo Teixeira, the head of the EU's delegation to Macedonia, warned in August 1999 that 'the international community doesn't realise the deep divisions that exist in this society'.[22]

Balkan normalisation tips Macedonia over the edge

The danger from Milošević's Serbia had united the two main groups in Macedonia in a loveless marriage. Macedonia's fragile stability was shattered when this threat rapidly appeared to recede. In 1999, Belgrade's repression of the Kosovar Albanians ended with the imposition of NATO control under a UN mandate. This was followed by the removal from power of Milošević in the autumn of 2000. He was replaced by a coalition government composed of moderates initially keen to mend fences with neighbours and normalise relations with the West.

Minus the common threat from the north, Albanians began to compare their situation critically with that of their previously downtrodden co-ethnics in Kosovo; as self-determination loomed, they had not only caught up with, but also appeared to be racing ahead of them. Despite the PDsh being in government, there was no sign of their main grievances (mainly economic ones despite the clamour of intellectuals for a university) being met. Fewer than 20 per cent of Albanians of working age were formally employed.[23] A sense of relative deprivation was increasingly evident. Pent-up frustrations could be endured with less stoicism. There were many such examples, such as the way hostile state inspectors thwarted business ventures or the tendency for the water supply to Albanian villages to be inadequate or non-existent.[24] But Albanians no longer feared that undue defiance might spell catastrophe for them. By taking up arms in the mid-1990s their brothers in Kosovo had offered a potent example. The uprising against Serbian rule had also involved Albanians in Macedonia thanks to kinship ties and porous borders (Rusi 2002: 30). One of them who shortly would acquire fame had even longer involvement with Albanian militancy: as a student at Priština University, Ali Ahmeti had been involved in nationalist protests and was also a founder and fundraiser for the Kosovo Liberation Army (UÇK) in the mid-1990s (Rusi 2002: 30).

During the winter of 1999–2000 there had also been fighting in the Presovo valley, a mainly Albanian inhabited area of Serbia proper which was adjacent to north-west Macedonia. It was brought under control by joint action taken by NATO and the Serbian military. This produced resentment among Albanian fighters who retreated to the isolated Macedonian valley around the village of Tanusevci.

A parallel has been drawn with Greek Macedonia after 1945, where grinding poverty and over-population, on top of the violent upheavals of the Second World War, prompted young men from the Slavic minority to join the ranks of the communist insurgents in Greece's civil war.[25] In the contemporary state which had adopted the name of Macedonia in 1990, rural poverty was not confined to Albanians but, being significantly less urbanised, they felt it more strongly. The 1994 census showed that 59.80 per cent of the ethnic Macedonian population were town or city-dwellers but 60 per cent of the Albanian population were rural (Janev 2003: 308). Previously, emigration had been available to Albanians; it meant that the Diaspora could support families previously struggling at the margins of existence. But this outlet was increasingly closed as EU states took steps to restrict further immigration and indeed repatriate Albanians.

Embattled Macedonians

Ethnic Macedonians were increasingly traumatised by the events of the late 1990s. Significant numbers began to believe for the first time that a Greater Albania was a threat to their existence. In the past, Albania had been seen as too problem-ridden to be a pole of attraction for a Greater Albania. But after years of relegation, those in Kosovo where the dream of unification had first emerged in the late nineteenth century, were now a power in the region. The UÇK, although partially disarmed, appeared a menacing armed force whose reach extended into Macedonia.

Many ethnic Macedonians feared that the secession of Albanian areas was now only a matter of time. The views held by many in the Serbian minority (2 per cent of the population) about the Albanians began to attract a wider audience. The divisions between the Slavophones of Macedonia, real in Milošević's time, began to diminish.

Mounting economic insecurity reinforced political worries. Ethnic Macedonia domination of the public sector was no longer a comforting symbol of their over-all primacy. By the end of 2001, 1,678 state companies had been privatised, leaving 89 still in state hands plus a few large utilities such as the electricity company.[26] Many redundancies had occurred and the nature of the sell-offs had been far from transparent.[27] It was an open secret that governing politicians had benefited, including Albanian ones. An Albanian source says that one PDsh member of Georgievski's government was nicknamed 'Mr Ten Per Cent' – the percentage going to him from privatisation deals'.[28] Turning to the public administration, average salaries had fallen by 75 per cent from the early 1990s onwards.[29] By January 2001, unemployment rates were almost identical for both main ethnic groups, affecting 46.3 per cent of Macedonians and 47.2 per cent of Albanians (Hislope 2004: 137). But this did not produce the reaction that they were all in the same boat and that inter-ethnic solidarity was needed to make Macedonia viable. Many Macedonians chose to equate Albanian success in commerce with criminal proclivities. Albanians for their part saw the state and the sources of employment it provided as 'no go areas' for them, particularly galling for young people less willing than before to be appeased by token concessions to Albanians.[30]

Neither community now exhibited any real confidence in the ability of the political process to address their problems. Nobody approaching Gligorov's stature was on the horizon and indeed, by the end of the 1990s, some of his own statements were hardly designed to soothe frayed inter-ethnic relations.

Tanusevci lights the powder keg

It was no surprise that it was Albanians who took up weapons to advance their claims. Frustrations had simmered longest among them and the regional transformation occasioned by the collapse of Serbian power in Kosovo seemed to offer a window of opportunity to alleviate their grievances. Nor should the location of the outbreak of Albanian insurgency have been a surprise.

Tanusevci lies high in the Black Mountains (Crna Gora/Karadak) adjacent to Kosovo. Although only 24 kilometres from Skopje, it is a world away from the capital. There was no bus service and the nearest services were in the Kosovo settlement of Viti, an hour away on foot. The border through the Black Mountains had never been properly demarcated and most villagers considered themselves Kosovan Albanians. Tanusevci's remoteness enabled it to be used by the UÇK. In 2000, it became a transit-point for weapons destined for the Presovo valley, 30 kilometres to the north-east.

Few Albanian ministers sought to end Tanusevci's isolation. One exception appears to have been Professor Abdulhenaf Bexheti, minister of transport in the mid-1990s who paid several visits while he was in government. Behxeti discovered that the villagers were never provided with Macedonian identity papers and that all their educational, health and business affairs were with Kosovo. He believes that the authorities in Skopje should have anticipated trouble when they signed and ratified a treaty with Yugoslavia in early 2001, defining their two countries' common border.[31] This allowed the Macedonian authorities to patrol the frontier and police the flow of goods and people, leading to clashes with armed men controlling smuggling operations (Ordanoski 2002: 39).

The urban priorities of successive Macedonian governments meant that the needs of a place like Tanusevci never flitted across their radar screens. In its defence, the VMRO-led government argued that the crisis would not have arisen if the Kosovo-Macedonian border had not been more effectively patrolled by international forces. This point was made forcefully by the economist Vladimir Gligorov. He compared NATO's refusal to accept responsibility for sometimes-identical Albanian guerrillas operating in both Kosovo and Macedonia to the way that Serbia used to disavow the actions of proxy forces operating in Bosnia.[32] The finger of blame was directed in particular at the Americans who had direct responsibility for the sector of Kosovo adjacent to this sensitive border. On 18 March, Premier Georgievski accused both the United States and Germany of refusing to admit that Kosovo was the source of the insurgency, lest any admission exposed Western failings there.[33] To press the point home, when President Bush was visiting US soldiers in Kosovo during July 2001, the Macedonian authorities closed all border crossings with Kosovo.

It is clear that the West had been taken by surprise by the Macedonian flare-up and that its strategy in the southern Balkans had hardly allowed for such a contingency. Moreover, in the first months of the new Bush administration, there were strong hints from Washington that the United States was going to pull out of the Balkans since the new Republican President did not view the region as crucial for its security.[34] Such clumsy thinking gave Western governments and agencies some responsibility for the conflict in Macedonia. But the VMRO government was unsuccessful in its attempt to be seen as a blameless victim of Western neglect and local conspiracies. Soon allegations were surfacing that it had encouraged a security vacuum on part of the border to allow illegal trafficking (whose continuation it has been claimed was a condition for cooperation with the PDsh).[35] It was an open secret that Menduh Thaci, the PDsh deputy leader (but actually the party's chief guiding force), had extensive cross-border business interests. He damned the Tanusevci rebels, claiming that these fellow Albanians were connected with the Serbian and Russian secret services and were nothing more than criminals and smugglers.[36] There was widespread speculation that the PDsh leadership (in collusion with VMRO) offered a large sum of money to the insurgents to desist in order to save the face of the hardpressed Macedonian army (and presumably to allow commerce once more to flow).[37]

Much more seriously, it has been claimed that a corrupt governing elite drawn from both main communities sought to trigger a conflict, knowing that it would lead to a formal division of the country, reflecting the way that the economic spoils had already been divided up. A former interior minister in the VMRO-led government claimed that he had been asked to turn a blind eye to the preparations of Albanian fighters by Premier Georgievski of VMRO and his ethnic Albanian governing partner Xhaferi of the PDsh and that the government had been behind the unexplained release of terrorist suspects active near the border.[38] Fazli Veliu, a longstanding Albanian militant (who is Ali Ahmeti's uncle), had been arrested in Germany in 2000 and faced extradition to Macedonia because of his alleged role in a small bombing incident in Kicevo, his home town (Rusi 2002: 21). But, inexplicably, the Skopje authorities declined to pursue extradition proceedings and Veliu was released.[39]

VMRO leaders refused to disavow pro-partition views during the 2001 crisis and openly backed them (along with their PDsh counterparts) afterwards.[40] Georgievski's controlling faction of VMRO was inclined towards merging much of the state with Bulgaria. Both Macedonia and Bulgaria had regularised ties in February 1999, Sofia recognising the Macedonia nation and language; in previous years, the two states had been unable to sign any agreements since they could not agree on a formula to describe the languages involved (Bulgaria until then insisting they were in fact the same language) (Giatzidis 2002: 153).

The idea that a country's elected leaders would seek to demolish their state from within to suit ideological or commercial needs, appears far-fetched but it might appear less so if it is recalled that 'central secession' was what Milošević strove to achieve in the early 1990s in order to build a Greater Serbia from the ashes of Yugoslavia.[41] Intellectuals in Serbia were among the chief promoters of partition in order to create homogeneous ethnic units. It also proved the case in Macedonia; Georgi Efremov, chairman of the Academy of Sciences and Arts in Macedonia (ASAM) argued during an early stage of the 2001 crisis argued that the best way of ending Macedonian–Albanian strife was to carve-up the country into two entities. Albanians would settle in Gostivar, Tetovo and Debor which would later join Albania. In exchange, Albania would hand over to Macedonia the town of Pogradec and the surrounding area near Lake Prepsa where a small Macedonian minority lived; all this would be accomplished within three months.[42]

Among the few political leaders who didn't denounce the partition plan were Georgievski and the influential parliamentary speaker, Andov. Crvenkovski, the former Prime Minister and leader of the SDSM, described it as 'an incitement for civil war and suicide for Macedonia'; he bluntly accused VMRO of working to hand over parts of Macedonia to Bulgaria.[43] Indeed the closeness of ties between VMRO and the centre-right Bulgarian government was shown by the speed with which Sofia dispatched arms to Skopje, President Petur Stoyanov stating that the government should consider also sending troops.[44]

A wake-up call for the West

By March 2001, fighting which had previously been confined to remote north-western areas, spread to the environs of Tetovo.[45] On 13 March, the PDsh organised a demonstration in Skopje that attracted around 10,000 people, proclaiming 'we are not terrorists'. But the next day, 3,000 attended a rally organised in Tetovo, comprising young ethnic Albanians who condemned the moderate approach of the PDsh.[46] Initially Western officials in the area assumed the unrest to be a spill over from Kosovo. Christopher Dell, head of the US diplomatic mission in Priština, publicly chided Kosovo Albanians for committing 'a violation of our trust' by allowing the movement of extremists over the border: 'Is abandoning the hope of self-government forever really the price you want to pay to protect thieves and murderers?'[47] Martti Ahtisaari, instrumental in persuading Belgrade to withdraw Serbian forces from Kosovo in 1999, warned that international sympathy for Albanians was now eroding fast.[48] But as the fighting moved some distance from the border, it soon became clear to dazed international officials that whatever spill over there was from Kosovo, there was enough momentum from within Macedonia to keep the conflict alive.

In fact, it was by no means easy to establish the role of Albanians in Kosovo. Separate Albanian demonstrations in Priština had supported armed action by their co-ethnics in Macedonia and called for purely peaceful action to overcome injustices. Statements and also private utterances from Kosova Albanian politicians (and also former UÇK commanders who had entered politics or joined the new police force), revealed an underlying concern that Albanian militancy to the south would result in the West slamming the brakes on self-determination for Kosovo (Rusi 2002: 30). But there was also evidence that Ramush Haridanaj, an opposition politician in Priština and ex-guerrilla chief, had played an important role in assisting the insurgents of the National Liberation Army (NLA) (Rusi 2002: 30).

On 16 March, Carl Bildt, the UN's special envoy to the Balkans, delivered a sombre warning: 'What is at stake here is not only Macedonia... [but] really everything that we have been trying to do in the Balkans: democracy, people living together, inter-ethnic cooperation'.[49] The danger of a political vacuum appeared a real one with armed groups on both sides of the ethnic divide replacing the politicians. NATO was particularly worried by the influx of arms from the former Soviet Union, particularly the Ukraine. Georgievski had warned in March: 'Macedonia will not be choosy about its allies if preservation of territorial integrity is threatened'.[50] Vladimir Putin's remark on 23 March that Macedonian events reminded him of Chechnya and that the unrest must be dealt with 'in a robust manner' was bound to cause some unease in NATO capitals.[51] NATO sought to preserve common ground with the Skopje government by using similar language to denounce the insurgents. George Robertson, NATO's Secretary-General denounced the shadowy military force that was starting to be known as the NLA, as 'a bunch of murderous thugs' (Hislope 2004: 143). The most outspoken Western official was the British ambassador to Skopje, Mark Dickinson who viewed the NLA to be 'mendacious terrorists' and who declared on Macedonian television: I believe in the Macedonian security forces and I believe they will defeat the terrorists... The only thing that can bring the terrorists victory is if the people under the influence of stress, rage and emotions, that I perfectly understand this time, take the law into their hands.[52]

Initially Western officials saw no place for the NLA in peace efforts. Instead, NATO threw its weight behind the idea of a grand coalition: with all the main parties included, it was hoped that they would not outbid each other in terms of militancy. On 30 March the SDSM's Crvenkovski warned that if Georgievski did not permit a wider coalition, his party would launch street protests with the aim, if necessary, of toppling the government. A month of hard bargaining ensued with strenuous prodding from Robertson of NATO and Javier Solana, the EU's commissioner for security and foreign policy, before the grand coalition was formed in early May. This task was complicated by the fact that on the eve of the fighting, there had been a full-scale crisis when the SDSM accused VMRO of tapping the phones of its leaders. Competition for posts, rather than any wider concerns, dominated the protracted negotiations.[53]

Within a month of the conflict capturing international attention, the Georgievski government was receiving strong signals from NATO and the European Union about the need to reform the political system and make it more responsive to Albanian concerns. US Secretary of State Colin Powell, on a trip to Europe in mid-April said: 'this is the time to show what a multi-ethnic government can do, to start to look at those points of irritation that exist within your society'.[54]

Inter-ethnic relations become a victim of conflict

After the fighting had spread to Tetovo on 14 March, a lull occurred for around ten days until the authorities issued an ultimatum to the NLA to disarm or leave the country. On 25 March, government forces began to shell villages above Tetovo, 11,000 refugees were created, but the NLA could not be dislodged. The crisis then flared up with renewed intensity on 28 April when eight soldiers were killed in an ambush near Tetovo. Fighting resumed, but worryingly, it was accompanied by rioting on 1–2 May in Bitola, the south-western city where four of the soldiers came from. Mobs destroyed about 100 homes, shops and restaurants owned not just by ethnic Albanians but by Turks and Slavic Muslims.[55]

Similar violence occurred on 6 June when three more soldiers from the city were killed. This time a religious element was added to the flames when the Orthodox bishop, Petar, delivered a violent graveside oration. The Holy Synod of the MPC then met and demanded a military solution to the crisis: a lively debate was won by radicals who insisted that 'Macedonia should be militarily liberated from those who threaten our lives and possessions' as a precondition for further talks.[56] In a swift response, the leadership of the Islamic Religious Community of Macedonia accused the MPC of 'promoting civil war and bloodshed'. Accusations went back and forth about the number of religious buildings destroyed: each group suggesting that all the blame lay on one side.[57]

It was reported that almost all the Albanian population in Bitola of around 10,000 left it and the surrounding Lake Prespa region.[58] The city had already been devastated by the economic fall-out from the Yugoslav conflict, notably the sanctions imposed by Greece on Macedonia in the first half of the 1990s. It had enjoyed close ties with Greece, being only 20 kilometres from the main city of north-west Greece, Florina.[59]

The most significant outcome of the new round of fighting was the shifting of the military theatre close to Skopje itself; insurgents seized villages north of the city of Kumanovo on 3 May, less than an hour's drive north of the capital. With a population of 100,000 it was the most mixed urban centre in the country; there were plentiful numbers of Serbs, Roma and Vlachs as well as ethnic Macedonians and Albanians. There was a history of both co-existence and tension, but there would be no repetition of the Bitola events. The mayor, Slobodan Kovacevski played an extremely responsible role, calling on Macedonians and Serbs not to destroy Albanian shops or homes.[60] The peace held even when the water-supply was cut off for 40 days owing to an NLA operation (Petruseva and Devaja 2002: 85). Like Bitola, Kumanova had become economically derelict; once known across Yugoslavia for providing tubes, metallurgical products and shoes, all these factories had gone bankrupt. The mayor managed to gather around him other local leaders who made successful appeals for restraint: 'our frequent meetings with NGO representatives, branches of the political parties and the town's youngsters were the key to preserving the stability of the town'.[61] Even with fighting nearby, the mayor recognised that the long-term answer was as much economic as political: 'the economy here is zero. If we can improve the citizens' standard of living, we reduce the possibility of ethnic tension...'.[62]

International involvement

But, in the first three months of the conflict, the international community was trying to find a cost-free solution that did not burden it with fresh economic or security commitments. The West initially backed efforts by the government to regain territory seized by the NLA, in return for necessary reforms. But the readiness of NATO and the European Union to throw their weight behind the Georgievski government waned after the intransigence of its leading members became apparent. Their lack of compunction about seeing civilians fall victim to clumsy and increasingly desperate military efforts against the rebels reduced the willingness of key Western players to stand by them.

The NLA numbered over two thousand men by the summer of 2001 (Ahmeti claimed five thousand) (Ordanoski 2002: 38). Gradually, the European Union and

NATO came to be mollified by the organisation's 'moderate' public position; no revision of borders or exchange of populations was envisaged. It was claimed that arms had been taken up as a last resort: 'we are fighting because all other peaceful ways to avoid segregation, discrimination, and oppression, have been exhausted' (Rusi 2002: 23).[63] By late March it had emerged that the NLA wished to decentralise rather than break up the Macedonian state. It demanded that Albanian be made an official language, that its speakers enjoy equal status with ethnic Macedonians in the constitution, and that the number of posts available to Albanians in the public service (including the security ones) be considerably increased.[64]

Ali Ahmeti gradually emerged as the NLA's guiding force. There have been claims that he was thrust into the limelight by Western bodies familiar with Kosovo and determined to find a moderate figure to negotiate with.[65] This is a process not dissimilar from the one discerned in Kosova itself in 1998–9 where Hashim Thaci was encouraged by the Americans to act on behalf of the dispersed insurgent bands of the UÇK.

One of the first signs that the West saw both the government and the insurgents at fault came with a statement by Wolfgang Petritsch, the UN's High Commissioner in Bosnia, on 29 May. 'At the core of the difficulties in Macedonia', he argued, 'is the belief that deep-rooted conflicts can be solved by military means...Such attitudes are the result of a lack of experience with the democratic process of compromise'.[66] It was soon followed by the elaboration of a peace plan devised by Robert Frowick, a US diplomat active in the region since the early 1990s. On 21 March, he had been appointed special envoy to Macedonia by the OSCE. Believing that peace prospects could be furthered by facilitating a common Albanian negotiating position, this was consummated by the signing of the Prizren declaration in May 2001. It marked the start of formal cooperation between the Albanian parties (then in the government) and the NLA (Rusi 2002: 45). By early June, Frowick had devised a plan that envisaged: (1) a ceasefire; (2) the redress of the main Albanian grievances. But Georgievski and his allies took umbrage, angry with Frowick for stitching together what appeared to be a pan-Albanian front and outraged that his plan allowed insurgents a seat at the negotiating table (Ackermann 2002: 112).[67]

Frowick also appears to have extended his OSCE brief and was quickly withdrawn from the Macedonian scene (Ackermann 2002: 112; Phillips 2004: 119–20). But, in its essentials, Frowick's plan was indistinguishable from the next one put on the table, this time by the EU's Javier Solana.[68] Ambassador Mark Dickinson, then acting as Solana's representative, had also been critical of it (Rusi 2002: 26). If it had enjoyed strong support from the diplomatic corps and, above all, forthright US backing, it has been claimed that Frowick could have brought much of the ethnic Macedonian leadership on board.[69] As it was, Georgievski was probably aware of Frowick's lack of clout (the OSCE had only given him one assistant), and the Prime Minister cried foul, not fearing adverse consequences.

Fighting around Kumanovo in June and close to Tetovo since March had led to the displacement of large numbers of people from both of the contending communities. The Macedonian Red Cross registered over 37,000 internally displaced people (by mid-July another 70,000 had fled Macedonia, 62,000 to Kosovo). Nearly all of the latter were Albanians but the NLA offensive had forced out Macedonians from villages around Tetovo, and from Aracinovo, less than 10 kilometres from Skopje.

Aracinovo was captured by the NLA on 8 June and appeared to give them a stranglehold over much of Macedonia. It was within shelling distance of the capital and threatened the main airport, as well as the country's oil refinery, and it gave them control of Kumanovo's water supply (Ackermann 2002: 113). In the previous two decades, it had gone from being a mainly Macedonian village to a largely Albanian one, the population swelled by the influx of immigrants from Kosovo. In ethnic Macedonian eyes, it became the most visible stronghold of Albanian criminals.[70]

From this point on, the atmosphere became ugly, raising fears of outright civil war. The government was under heavy pressure from a bellicose media. Newspaper editors and television stations that did not take a sufficiently hardline position received death-threats.[71] Zlatko Dizdarević, a Bosnian journalist observing the conflict, noted: 'With few exceptions, Macedonian journalists seem to have lost all sense of responsibility, actively stoking a drama which could have a very bloody finale...If anything, the media is far ahead of the man-in-the-street when it comes to war-mongering and it is words...which are pushing the population to the fever-pitch required for an all-out war'.

He then went on to make the telling point that 'it is doubly ironic that this is happening in a town chock-full of international forces and foreign NGOs which have poured money into training "independent" journalists'.[72]

Indeed, before the 2001 crisis erupted another source had made the highly pertinent observation: 'If [the] wealth of Macedonia were to be measured by the number of NGOs, it would certainly rank high among...developed countries. But, if this social activity would be evaluated by its "productiveness", it would certainly be qualified as one of the many unproductive "branches" in this country'.[73]

On 22 June government forces deployed artillery, tanks and helicopter-gunships in a bid to re-take Aracinovo.[74] NATO put pressure on the government to halt the offensive. When Solana flew in on 23 June, a fighter aircraft flew over-head which was seen as a deliberate attempt to intimidate him.[75] Both NATO and the European Union were aware that Macedonian forces stood little chance of retaking the town and that the only outcome was likely to be heavy military and civilian casualties that were bound to raise passions even further. For several months, government forces had been unable to dislodge rebels from villages they had occupied. The army's crack commando unit, the Tigers, practically mutinied when they were ordered to storm one village. They refused to go in, saying that the army couldn't provide cover and they would take heavy casualties.[76] But one achievement of the Macedonian forces was to prevent Albanian insurgents estab-lishing 'liberated zones' along the entire border with Kosovo and part of that with Serbia (Ordanoski 2002: 38).

The West tries to avert disaster

Solana achieved a ceasefire on 26 June after applying unspecified intense 'political pressure' with US diplomatic backing.[77] The European Union was able to play the economic card. In April 2001, Macedonia had signed a Stabilisation and Association Agreement (SAA) with the European Union. It was meant to prepare the country for EU membership by, among other things, laying down the provision for EU financial aid and providing for free trade with the European Union.[78] VMRO politicians, who had adopted a proprietorial attitude to state funding were disinclined to see the loss of such EU pre-accession aid. For its part, the European Union (along with NATO) increasingly saw the Macedonian government as just as much an aggressor as the NLA; it noted that on several occasions, government forces had been the first to break a cease-fire agreed by both sides.[79] Chris Patten, the EU commissioner for foreign affairs, told Macedonian foreign minister Ilinka Mitreva in 'an open and frank discussion' in Luxemburg on 25 June that the European Union would provide no more aid to Macedonia until there was a political settlement.[80] At a closed door meeting of EU foreign ministers that day, Mitreva was told that the behaviour of the Macedonian security forces reminded them of the conduct of the Russian forces in Chechnya.[81] Faced with such pressure, the government agreed that the NLA in Aracinova be allowed to withdraw under international auspices. Georgievski admitted that after facing stiff resistance from Albanian fighters, seizing the town would take at least ten days and could result in substantial losses.[82]

But the government-controlled media was incensed that the army was being pulled back and rebels allowed safe-passage under Western supervision.[83] On the evening of 25 June, shortly after it emerged that the fighters were being bussed to Kosovo with their weapons, a crowd of around 5,000 people stormed parliament. They included army reservists with kalashnikov rifles. Some in the mob shouted 'Albanians to the gas chambers' and demanded the resignation of President Trajkovski who was seen as the most moderate of the ethnic Macedonian leaders.[84] If a well-known hardliner, like parliamentary speaker Stojan Andov, had declared himself leader of the country, a coup could have succeeded according to many observers.[85] The country was effectively leaderless until the President addressed the country 24 hours later. But not a few hardliners were motivated by economic interests as well as ideological zeal and it was difficult to see how they could have stabilised the situation if a coup had unfolded. Andov, when Yugoslav ambassador to Iraq in the 1980s, is quite likely to have known Evgenii Primakov, Russia's Middle East envoy, once more a power in the Kremlin. But it is likely Russia would have hesitated before being sucked into the Macedonian quagmire.

All of Macedonia's neighbours had largely behaved with restraint. The pragmatic Simitis government in Greece was concerned with its transport links to central Europe and the fate of its growing investments in Macedonia;[86] it behaved with circumspection throughout the crisis. Albania condemned extremist actions by its co-ethnics elsewhere and Bulgaria's offer of military assistance was soon retracted when it appeared that this might heighten tension.

President Trajkovski condemned the rioters and said that peaceful dialogue with the Albanians was the only way ahead.[87] He welcomed President Bush's move to cut off funds from US-based émigrés to Albanian guerrillas and his banning of their leaders from visiting the United States.[88] As early as the end of May, Trajkovski had revealed dovish views when he signalled his preparedness to introduce an amnesty for the insurgents who would be allowed to exit safely to Kosovo. The measure would not, however, apply to the organisers of the insurgency and to individuals who killed Macedonian soldiers or police.[89] Such views placed him at loggerheads with the hardline interior minister Ljubce Boskovski and also with the ethnic majority as a whole. Trajkovski lacked a strong power-base and had been unable to arbitrate in the way his predecessor Gligorov had done in crises far milder than this one.[90] Opinion polls showed that most ethnic Macedonians believed that the West was actively siding with the NLA in the conflict. The fact that most of the fighters and weaponry appeared to be entering Macedonia from Kosovo just reinforced this view.[91]

An ethnic Macedonian viewpoint urging new thinking was very much an isolated one in the summer of 2001: 'Macedonians are going to have to reinvent themselves. They need to realise that they cannot hide behind that hazy communist concept of "brotherhood and unity". One small example of this illusion of unity is that the great majority of Macedonians, including me, were unaware that the mainly Albanian population of Lipkovo [near Kumanovo] had never had running water despite the fact that it's located right next to a reservoir'.[92]

A gleam of hope was provided from the village of Lopate, near one of the frontlines. When the fighting began, this mixed village set up a crisis committee and began a joint night watch of their properties. The aim according to one committee member was to 'preserve confidence in each other and stop people panicking'.[93]

Despite his weakness, President Trajkovski was the figure the international community was relying on to try and prevent the majority taking extreme measures in order to try and escape from the crisis. Premier Georgievski showed his increasing anti-Western bias in a television address on 26 June when he lashed out at allegedly corrupt Europeans who were 'benefiting from narco-trafficking'.[94] His interior minister and close ally, Ljubce Boskovski, continued to demand an all-out offensive and he even set up a paramilitary force known as the Lions, loyal to VMRO and himself, that became locked in struggle with the SDSM-controlled defence ministry over the legality of the group.[95]

Three months of shuttle-diplomacy by Solana and Robertson had convinced them that averting civil war and inching towards an internal settlement could only be achieved by an external force interposing itself between armed ethnic rivals. On 27 June, NATO agreed to send a 3,000-strong military mission to supervise the disarming of Albanian rebels following a political settlement which the main parties to the conflict would be induced to endorse. On 29 June, the Bush administration overcame its aversion to being further involved in the Balkans by appointing James Pardew as its special envoy to Macedonia.[96] But it was the European role that proved crucial. On 25 June, Francois Leotard, an ex-French defence minister, was appointed the European Union's special envoy. Immediately, he declared that the Macedonian government 'must talk with the leaders of the guerillas' (Hislope 2004: 144). International contacts with the Albanian fighters suggested that their leaders were pragmatic despite the recourse to arms. The guerrillas emphasised that they were fighting for civil rights not the dismemberment of Macedonia or a greater Albania.[97] They had a recognised leader, Ali Ahmeti, who, by the summer, had managed to convince Western officials, such as the NATO envoy Hansjorg Eiff that his word could be trusted (Rusi 2002: 31).

This was in contrast to the disarray to be found on the ethnic Macedonian side with competing and overlapping power-centres, extremist rhetoric and actions sanctioned by the Prime Minister and the interior minister, and private agendas concealed behind the furious nationalist rhetoric. The patience of Solana and Robertson was sorely tried by the posturing and even insults coming from Premier Georgievski who had a tendency to abandon ceasefires as soon as the two international arbiters flew out of Skopje. But at least there were grounds for hoping that VMRO's hold on power was slackening. Back in government, the SDSM appeared more moderate and elections were due by 2002. Opinion polls also suggested that the country was not totally split along ethnic lines. A poll published in the Skopje bi-monthly *Forum* on 27 July showed that 61 per cent of those interviewed preferred a peaceful outcome to the crisis. However, while a military solution enjoyed no Albanian support, 30 per cent of ethnic Macedonians preferred to settle things by arms rather than a negotiated agreement.

It is normal when a majority is under pressure to concede to minority demands for the greatest degree of intransigence to emanate from its ranks. Of the recipients from both groups 60.5 per cent said they could live together in the future, but 22 per cent of Macedonians ruled out peaceful coexistence against 40 per cent of Albanians who didn't answer the question or said they didn't know.[98]

The tortuous road to Ohrid

On 7 July, the international mediators presented a framework document to the parties in the 'unity' government. It was meant to be the basis for a peaceful resolution of the crisis. While emphasising total commitment to Macedonia's territorial integrity, it recommended a revision of the Constitution and the strengthening of local government. It also urged increased or equivalent representation of ethnic Albanians in the public administration and remaining state enterprises and emphasised the need for the provision of the Albanian language in official spheres.[99]

Initially, the Albanian parties insisted that Albanians be elevated to the status of a 'constituent people'. But they backed down in return for the undertaking that the constitution would cease to accord one people, the ethnic Macedonians, a privileged position, and would become a civil document.[100] On the Macedonian side, there was a willingness to accept most of the provisions in the framework document, except for those that allowed the Albanian language to be used for official purposes in parliament and in municipal forums where the population was more than 20 per cent Albanian. Many ethnic Macedonians were convinced that after the elevation of this language, many Albanians would refuse to communicate in Macedonian. It is reckoned that 90 per cent of Albanians are proficient in Macedonian while less than 2 per cent of Macedonians speak Albanian. Macedonians also feared that in districts where they were a minority, they would lose public posts if they couldn't speak Albanian.[101]

The ceasefire signed on 5 July to allow negotiations to proceed, had only been fitfully observed. It collapsed completely after 18 July when the NLA launched attacks on villages north of Tetovo that were largely Macedonian, but surrounded by ethnic Albanian settlements. An estimated 20,000 ethnic Macedonians and Albanians fled from the Tetovo area, some of them directly expelled by the NLA. Once again, on 24 July, parliament was stormed. Anti-western rhetoric from top officials was stepped up. On the same day, government spokesman Antonio Milososki accused the EU and US envoys of deliberately siding with the NLA, saying that 'NATO is not our enemy but is the friend of our enemy'.[102] The embassies and consulates of the European Union, United States and leading West European states were attacked on 24 July by mainly young protestors whose anti-western shouts were punctuated by calls for Russian assistance. The Russian foreign minister, Igor Ivanov, had appeared to provide moral support for hardliners in Skopje on 18 July when he denounced external pressure on the Macedonian government.[103] Earlier, fearing that weapons would pour into Macedonia from the ex-Soviet Union, Condoleeza Rice, the US National Security advisor, had flown to the Ukraine to strongly urge the Kiev government to cease all arms shipments (Hislope 2004: 145).

On 26 July, a new ceasefire was announced, with the chief peace negotiators, Lord Robertson and Javier Solana returning to try and relaunch negotiations. Never had a Balkan crisis attracted so much concentrated attention from the Atlantic democracies and their collective bodies. For the European Union in particular, it was a crucial test. Since the late 1990s, it had assumed increasing responsibility for crisis management in the Balkans. If Macedonia plunged into endemic conflict, it would be a disaster for the common foreign and security policy which the European Union was attempting to launch.

After the latest ceasefire, the NLA withdrew from recently seized villages around Tetovo while the government promised that the army would exercise restraint. But the hardline interior minister added a complicating factor by announcing that he had gathered evidence to charge leading NLA members, including Ahmeti, with crimes against humanity.[104]

Concentrated international pressure finally led to the Macedonian and Albanian representatives in government signing what became known as the Ohrid Agreement on 13 August 2001. It incorporated the framework proposals on the table for the previous six weeks and was designed to usher in an era of genuine, as opposed to cosmetic power sharing between the two main ethnic groups. Parliament was to amend 15 articles in the constitution which the ethnic Albanians say institutionalise inequality, including a reference in the preamble to the lead status of the 'Macedonian nation'. Central power was to be ceded to local municipalities. Changes to the structure of the police were to be made to encourage a much greater Albanian presence. Albanians were to be granted a quasi-veto over the choice of judges, laws on local government, use of language, education, and the display of symbols. Albanian was to be used as an official language in communication with government offices and in plenary sessions of parliament. The supremacy of Macedonian symbols was much reduced by allowing the free use of Albanian symbols, such as their flag. Finally, the special status in the constitution awarded to the Orthodox Church was to be ended.[105]

But the omens were not good. Prime Minister Georgievski stormed out of the Ohrid gathering when Arber Xhaferi's answers to journalists were translated into English but not Macedonian.[106] More worryingly, one hour after the signing Georgievski announced a military offensive against Albanian fighters in the hills around Tetovo. Ethnic Macedonians had been shocked by an attack on a military convoy in a village near Skopje on 12 August in which ten soldiers were killed. Attacks on Albanians where they constituted a minority flared up once more, including in Skopje. Of the 100 or so deaths in the entire conflict, no less than 35 occurred shortly before the signing of the Ohrid Agreement.

But however much they fumed and threatened VMRO hardliners knew that they were in a corner. The soldiers who were deployed at the start of the conflict were inadequately trained and 'barely able to hold a rifle, let alone shoot it', according to an EU Military monitor.[107] The rebels were able to field equivalent military numbers and the armed forces had been unable to push them back. Paramilitary forces were being recruited which gave a dangerous edge to the situation, but they were unlikely to be militarily decisive and were more bound up with the need for VMRO power-brokers to conserve their influence and material wealth acquired since entering government.

From 27 August 2003, some 4,500 British-led troops were engaged in collecting NLA weapons and ammunition in NATO's Operation 'Essential Harvest'. President Bush said on 14 August that if the NLA proved obdurate, it might find that they were labelled as terrorists and all necessary assistance would, in that case, be given to defeat them. Already, Carla del Ponte, the chief prosecutor of the UN tribunal for the Former Yugoslavia warned all sides that they were being watched closely. Although not a formal party to the agreement, the NLA welcomed it. In the aftermath of seven months of intermittent and often sharp conflict, it announced its disbandment. For his part, the President, declared a wide-ranging amnesty in September. But the most difficult challenge would be to ensure that a traumatised Macedonian majority, ill-led by bellicose nationalist politicians, ratified a treaty that made them the leading partner rather than the dominant force in their state.

Conclusion

What is surprising about the armed internal crisis of 2001 is not that it erupted but that it took so long for ethnic Macedonia and Albanian disagreements to spill over into prolonged violence. Warfare close to the country's borders and economic frustrations impoverishing most of the population had strained nerves since the early 1990s. It is very difficult for a majority to accommodate minority demands when the state is constantly buffeted by such severe pressures. Moreover, there were deep-seated and genuinely felt differences about how power should be distributed between the two principal ethnic groups. The conflict did not solely arise from manipulation by unscrupulous political figures or from criminal groups seeking to destabilise politics for their own economic ends. If there was any conspiracy in 2001, it is likely not to have been the primarily element fuelling the resulting violence.

In much of Eastern Europe there is no tradition of a peaceful and voluntary retreat of the majority in the face of a large minority's call for a formal recognition of its strength in the society. In Western Europe, multi-ethnic states like Spain and bi-national ones like Belgium may have witnessed sweeping decentralisation in the 1970s, but this was against a background of economic contentment and regional stability of the kind lacking further east. Macedonia was fortunate that the intransigence of its ethnic hardliners was often diluted by their economic opportunism (but unfortunate that moderate-sounding parties, especially on the Albanian-side, did not show more statesmanship or take more risks in trying to reduce the potential for conflict). Macedonia also succeeded in avoiding complete polarisation on ethnic lines thanks to cross-cutting rivalries in both major communities. A bruising battle for dominance had been waged between two ethnic Macedonian parties, VMRO and the SDSM. Their rivalry intensified during the 2001 crisis which reduced the risk of all-out conflict along ethnic lines. But there was a real danger that armed vigilante groups could have usurped the role of the state during those tense months.

It was Albanian vigilantes who had ignited the immediate crisis and if the conventional political forces had been sidelined and the military eclipsed by paramilitaries, the danger of Macedonia fragmenting as Lebanon had done during its long civil war from 1976 to 1988 was a real one. But time would show that the Albanian insurgency, however much ordinary people suffered from its consequences, was not a wholly destructive process. It was a challenge to the Macedonian state in its existing form, not a bid to dissolve it. The aim was to end the hegemony of the largest ethnic group rather than dismantle the country. It would not take long before it became clear that the within the NLA, there was a strong urge to improve the quality of political representation of the Albanian community. There were also less idealistic goals held by important players in what was a heterogeneous movement. But it was widely recognised that Albanians had been ill-served by parties whose leaders spent far more time acquiring wealth (sometimes by doubtful means) than advancing the interests of their voters.

The chief international actors engaged in the Balkans soon came to see that it was too simple to view the conflict as one between a responsible government and a completely illegitimate guerrilla force. NATO's Secretary-General Robertson and the EU's Solana were on a sharp learning curve as the crisis intensified. The West had shut its ears to warning rumbles from Macedonia for several years and had assumed that the country was somehow robust enough to absorb shock waves from conflicts elsewhere. The complacency of UN Interim Administrative Mission in Kosovo (UNMIK) and Kosovo Force (KFOR) in Kosovo enabled diehard UÇK elements to act as external patrons, providing important services for Albanian rebels in Macedonia (Hislope 2004: 18). Nevertheless, the main transnational agencies involved in South-East Europe quickly mobilised to try to broker a peaceful resolution to the crisis. The European Union and NATO got directly involved early and managed to cooperate effectively. This was in sharp contrast to the early 1990s in Bosnia.

From late 2001 onwards, the European Union worked diligently for the adoption of measures that would award the large ethnic Albanian minority, and other significant minorities, a much greater role in decision-making. Amendments to the Constitution in November 2001, and the adoption of a law on local self-government in January 2002, represented important progress towards that objective. In March 2002, an amnesty allowing Albanian militants who had renounced violence to avoid criminal charges and to play a role in public life was also approved by the Government. In September 2002 Ali Ahmeti, leader of the rebel NLA during the 2001 Albanian revolt, emerged as a major political figure, when his newly established Democratic Union for Integration (DUI) trounced rival ethnic Albanian parties in the legislative election. The main winner of the election was an alliance led by the SDSM, which subsequently formed a coalition Government with Ahmeti's party. Ahmeti showed himself to be a moderating influence committed to a single Macedonia, a hopeful and surprising development in light of his militant origins.

From afar, it might have seemed that the optimum conditions for improving strained inter-ethnic relations appeared to exist in post-2001 Macedonia. Moderate forces had prevailed in both the main communities and there were smaller minorities of Turks, Roma and various Muslim Slavs committed to a united Macedonia. The 2002 census, whose results were only published in December 2003, revealed that no great shift in the respective size of the ethnic Macedonians and Albanians had occurred since the previous one in 1994. But the scale of underlying mutual distrust remained high. Politics appeared still to be a zero-sum game in which one group gains at the expense of another. The proposed revision of local government boundaries in order to create larger units to which important administrative powers could be decentralised, stirred a hornet's nest of resentment and insecurity in 2004. This was exploited by VMRO's Ljubčo Georgievski, defeated in the 2002 elections, but determined to sabotage efforts by his successor as party leader to work within the framework of the Ohrid Agreement. The Albanian parties which lost in that election also pursued a radical discourse and were in a strong position to capitalise on any failure by Ali Ahmeti to consolidate his new party or deliver tangible benefits to expectant Albanian voters. So further anxious years lay ahead for Macedonia before it could hope to put the turmoil and violence of 2001 behind it. The prospect of a common state emerging which enjoyed the allegiance of all major ethnic groups was, in no small measure, bound up with the quality of support it could rely on from the European Union and the pace of European integration in South-East Europe.

5 Serbia from 2000

Milošević's poisonous legacy

The crumbling of a power-base

Milošević's hold over Serbia appeared in no danger of weakening after NATO's occupation of Kosovo. Indeed, there was no shortage of Western critics who argued that by bringing war directly to Serbia with air-strikes on part of the civilian infrastructure, the leaders of NATO had thrown Milošević a lifeline. But defeat undermined his position. Many nationalists believed he had sacrificed Serbia's territorial integrity to shore up his own position. One group he had used for bloody missions, but which he had gradually lost control of as its size mushroomed, also had cause to reassess its ties with Milošević. This was the large criminal sector that had emerged from the bloated Serbian security apparatus and the subterranean economy. A veritable Serbian mafia had benefited from sanctions, the effective collapse of the rule of law, smuggling and the looting of the state. The West's confrontation with the man who had been their patron gave their own activities an unwelcome degree of exposure and notoriety. It is unlikely that the mafia felt that their operations would be under threat from any power-shift within Serbia. So a change at the top could enable their illicit economic activities to be pursued in a more predictable manner.

The already desperate plight of ordinary Serbs also worsened perceptibly during the Kosovo conflict. A collapse in real wages occurred with the average in November 1999 representing just over 50 per cent of the corresponding figure for November 1998 (Dyker 2003: 602). By now the GDP per head was only marginally higher than in Albania's and behind all other countries in the region (Uvalić 2001: 179). Grim resignation appeared to be the dominant reflex in Serbian society. But one exception was the youth movement *Otpor* (Resistance) which was formed in October 1998 by fifteen friends at the Belgrade University in response to the crackdown on the university Milošević had just launched (Collin 2001: 175). Otpor was a total contrast to the hierarchical parties that were the norm in Serbia. It 'became a kind of urban vigilante sect…with no leaders, no hierarchies, no voting procedures and no set ideology other than the replacement of the President' (Collin 2001: 175). Serbian youth had been the social group which was least receptive to Milošević's nationalist–populist message, but he saw no imminent threat from Otpor and prepared to dig in politically. Constitutional changes adopted in

July 2000 introduced direct elections to the federal presidency and allowed him to seek another term. Federal presidential and parliamentary elections took place on 24 September and were boycotted by Montenegro, the junior partner in the increasingly loveless federation. In Serbia however, eighteen opposition parties formed a coalition known as the Democratic Opposition of Serbia (DOS). Vojislav Koštunica, head of one of the numerous smaller parties, the Democratic Party of Serbia (DSS), was chosen as DOS's presidential candidate. Koštunica was an unabashed nationalist who had been purged from Belgrade University in the mid-1970s for criticising policies that appeared to advance minority concerns at the expense of Serbian ones. But he had kept his distance from the Milošević regime and appeared uncorrupted by his years in politics. Opposition strategists hoped that Koštunica would appeal to nationalist as well as to liberal opinion.

The Serbian opposition had bowed to American pressure to find an electable candidate. US Secretary of State Madeleine Albright had told her officials that she wished Milošević gone from power by the time her term of office ended in 2002 (*The Fall of Milošević*, Part 3: 2001). A sum of $30 million from US sources went to the opposition in the pre-election period. It was used to purchase cell phones and computers for DOS's leadership and to recruit and train an army of 20,000 election monitors. External backing also enabled Otpor to launch a sophisticated marketing campaign with posters, badges and T-shirts. By the eve of the elections, it consisted of 20,000 activists organised into 'action teams' in 120 towns across Serbia (Collin 2001: 208). Otpor's rallying-cry was 'He's finished'! A lot of university students, especially from provincial Serbia were in fact quiescent because of their reliance on patronage from the state, and Otpor's most enthusiastic members were high-school students who were arrested in their hundreds in confrontations with the police, or for just wearing an Otpor T-shirt. The detention of school children lost Milošević critical support. The fact that he allowed his unpopular wife, and the leader of her own pseudo-Left party, United Yugoslav Left (JUL), to substitute for him on the campaign trail showed how far he had misjudged the popular mood. DOS's slick election machine calculated that Koštunica had won a narrow outright majority, dispensing the need for a second round. A prudent Milošević might have accepted defeat, confident in the knowledge that his control of the media, the courts, the security forces and the Serbian parliament would have enabled him to isolate and neutralise his opponents, in control of only a small segment of the power apparatus. Zorin Djindić, the best-known DOS figure, revealed that it was decided to provoke Milošević by claiming an even bigger voting figure of 57 per cent (*The Fall of Milošević*, Part 3: 2001). Milošević's party riposted, claiming victory for their man and the Serbian Electoral Commission eventually declaring that Koštunica had won 48 per cent and Milošević 40 per cent of the vote. DOS decided to boycott the second round and provoke a popular revolt in a bid to topple Milošević. It's leaders could not envisage Milošević bowing out whatever the result, and they had their own armed groups in the event of confrontation with state forces (*The Fall of Milošević*, Part 3: 2001). But the state machine was not Milošević's to command as it had been in the past. His order for the suppression of a strike in the Kolubara mine, which provided much of Serbia's electricity, were not carried out by either the army or the police. Demonstrators from all over Serbia swept past roadblocks, half a million converging on Belgrade on 5 October, and 4,000 heavily armed police confronting them. Police buildings and key installations were seized by the crowd. An emblematic figure was Joe Djukić, the owner of a sand and gravel business in Čačak who had fallen victim to the corruption of the Milošević era. His digger machine smashed into the headquarters of Serbian television (Collin 2001: 222).

The next day Milošević, deserted by the institutions of state that normally did his bidding, acknowledged Koštunica's victory. It was a dramatic change replete with moving imagery that easily surpassed those which made the downfall of communism in Gdansk, Prague and Riga epoch-making events in the late 1980s. But the extent of the power-shift was deceptive. The forces around Milošević, without which he could not have pursued his murderous policies, were left substantially intact. They had regrouped rather than defend him in what might possibly have been an extremely bloody last stand, leading to a Serbian civil war and perhaps even external military intervention. They had strong cards to play in their relations with DOS which was hard-placed to carry out a transformation of the state. Indeed, time would quickly show that there were elements in DOS far from committed to root-and-branch change. This realisation might well have prompted the feared Milorad 'Legija' Luković, the head of the interior ministry's Unit for Special Operations (JSO), previously regarded as Milošević's praetorian guard, to abandon his former master.

Events would quickly reveal the extent to which organised crime had penetrated to the heart of Serbia's principal state institutions. A relentless struggle would have been required to be launched in the aftermath of DOS's victory to try and destroy the influence of a mafia establishment, in alliance with and often merging into, the security and political worlds. But DOS had no such plans. Djindjić had needed to strike up alliances with a part of the mafia in order to be able to survive and confront Milošević.[1] He even gave permission for Milošević's racketeering son Marko to leave the country for Russia, despite the existence of an arrest warrant for him. Sometimes resolute leaders have succeeded in taming extremist groups opposed to democracy. Charles de Gaulle managed to do it in his struggle with the French far-Right over Algeria in the early 1960s but he almost paid with his life. There is a belief that before Djindjić's own assassination in 2003, he was poised to move against the main criminal groupings nurtured by the former regime, but this would only have been possible with the active support of international forces. However, there was no coherent strategy or sense of urgency in Western capitals about containing ultra-nationalist forces linked with criminal groups or about how to promote the recovery of Serbia and its integration with mainstream Europe.

Regional openings

The most resolute international intervention was seen in the Presovo valley of southern Serbia where Albanian insurgents launched attacks on Serbian forces in the second half of 2000. Albanians are the overwhelming majority of the population in this desperately poor but strategically placed area: it carries vital road and rail links from Serbia to Macedonia and Greece. A decade of ill-treatment from the authorities and the galvanising effect of a perceived Albanian victory in Kosovo, enabled a military offshoot of the Kosovo Liberation Army (UÇK) to take root. But the military behaved with restraint and NATO sought its cooperation to contain the insurgency. The Yugoslav Army (VJ) was allowed to operate in the security zone along the border with Kosovo set up after the 1999 conflict. Cross-border raids diminished and Nebojša Čović, deputy prime minister in Djindjić's government moved decisively to address some of the main grievances of the local Albanians.

Čović represented the Serbian side in the negotiations over the future of Kosovo, an issue on which he adopted an increasingly hawkish stance. But if Western governments had announced, when Milošević was still in power, or at the moment of his removal that Kosovo was destined for independence, it is quite possible that the issue would have gradually faded from Serbian politics. Noel Malcolm wrote in late 2000 that 'the Serbian people could have accepted such a political *fait accompli* as the final loss inflicted on them by Milošević's policies; they would then have drawn a line under it, and got on with building a normal politics in post-Milošević and post-Kosovo Serbia. Instead the unresolved position of Kosovo will poison Serbia for years to come'.[2]

A strong tendency to overestimate Serbia's importance in the region still existed (thanks in part to the fact that most Western diplomatic missions and emissaries carried out their work in Belgrade). This view encouraged 'Serbian exceptionalism – the belief, rather widespread among Serbs, that their unique qualities and history entitle them to privileged treatment'.[3] Sonja Biserko, a Serbian human rights campaigner, complained that the West exaggerated Serbia's geostrategic significance which prevented her country confronting its immediate problems.[4] Djindjić complained about alleged Western parsimony towards Serbia, declaring in November 2001 that 'if Serbia loses enthusiasm now, there will no longer be a country which could act as a locomotive which, if it keeps up the pace, will pull the entire region towards Europe'.[5] Yet by 2000, the GDP per head in Serbian was down to $1,200 and the country was slipping towards a Third World position if the social indicators were to be believed.[6]

But one important obstacle to normalising relations in the region was overcome in the early months of DOS's tenure when the Yugoslav Federation accepted that it was not the sole successor state of the former Yugoslavia. This realistic stance broke the impasse that blocked the division of property and hard currency reserves (*After Milošević* 2001: 237). It also paved the way for the resumption of transport links between Serbia and Croatia which had been largely severed for nearly a decade.

Persisting with a loveless marriage: Montenegro and Serbia

Following the removal of Milošević from the Yugoslav scene, pressure soon began to be exerted on Montenegro by the West to retreat from pro-independence positions in order for a more accommodating Belgrade government to be allowed to strengthen its position. In the summer of 2001, the government of President Milo Djukanović had decided to boycott the Yugoslav federal elections which resulted in an overwhelming defeat for Milošević. Thus it was no longer represented in the federal institutions, a fact which made the federation even more nominal. Since being elected in 1997 Djukanović and his allies had gradually succeeded in taking over most of the functions previously exercised by the federal state which by 2000 enjoyed a continuing presence only through the army and air-traffic control.[7] In November 1999, growing economic separation was underlined when a dual currency system was introduced, with both the Deutschmark (DM) and the Yugoslav dinar as legal tender.[8] No monetary collapse or panic ensued and it was now easier for Montenegro to assume control over the regulation of customs at its borders and the collection of duties and taxes within them.[9]

On 31 October 2001, Djukanović publicly stated that he was still committed to a loose union of Montenegro and Serbia only as two internationally recognised and independent states. DOS was not keen to accede to Podgorica's maximalist demands. To do so could stimulate demands for equivalent treatment from Voivodina and other areas such as the Sandžak where many felt that they had been shoring up bankrupt centralism while getting little in return.

The West had little enthusiasm for nurturing new states in the region and the fact that it had actively assisted Montenegro in its bid to remove itself from Milošević's state control was conveniently forgotten. On 13 October President Clinton's Balkan envoy, James O'Brien said bluntly that 'the US does not favour independence for Montenegro'.[10] Later, on 2 February 2001, Colin Powell, US Secretary of State under the new administration of President George W. Bush, refused to see Djukanović when he was in Washington.[11]

But it would be the EU's reaction that would be the most critical one. The demise of Tudjman and Milošević coincided with the European Union acquiring far greater visibility in the Balkans. The United States has downgraded its role in the region, especially since the change of administration in Washington at the end of 2000. This means that the European Union has assumed much greater responsibility for crisis management, the EU Commissioner for External Relations admitting that the Balkans would be a critical test for the Common Foreign and Security Policy gradually taking shape.

The bulk of aid to Montenegro had come from Brussels and it was the European Union which the Montenegrin government was aspiring to join. Thus it was bitterly disappointing when, on 22 January 2001, EU foreign ministers issued a statement in Brussels saying that Montenegro must see its future in a federation with Serbia and not take any action unilaterally.[12] The European Union was afraid that independence for Montenegro might encourage separatist or irredentist moves in those adjacent or nearby territories thus complicating immensely the international peace-keeping role in the Western Balkans. A less pressing but no less important concern is not to encourage the rapid growth in the number of small states in the region just at the time when the European Union is seeking to dilute the primacy of 'the sovereign nation-state' among its own sixteen members.[13]

Djukanović called early parliamentary elections in Montenegro on 22 April 2001 in the hope that they would give him a clear mandate for the path to independence. But, in the event, his Victory for Montenegro coalition got only two per cent more votes than 'Together for Yugoslavia', the alliance of his unionist opponents. Djukanović was able to form a majority government only with the help of the even more pro-independence Liberal Alliance, along with Albanian deputies.

Beginning in November 2001, the European Union brokered continuing talks between Belgrade and Podgorica. Javier Solana, the EU's Foreign Affairs Commissioner, made it clear that independence was not on the European Union's agenda: already grappling with a European Union likely to be nearly doubled in membership by 2010, the appetite in Brussels for having more 'micro-states in the accession pipeline' was virtually non-existent.[14] Nevertheless, Djukanović fought a tough rearguard action determined to preserve Montenegro's economic sovereignty. On 14 March 2002, a framework agreement was signed, providing for a 'Union of States' to be known as 'Serbia and Montenegro'. The term Yugoslavia seemed ready to join other names like Czechoslovakia and the Soviet Union 'in the dustbin of history'.[15]

Under the accord, the two republics were to 'maintain separate economies, but share foreign and defence policies, and elect a joint presidency and legislature (in which Montenegro would be guaranteed equal representation to Serbia)'.[16] Montenegro was also given the option of holding a referendum on independence after three years.

A second blow to the proponents of independence was a decision taken in the European Commission to try and rewrite the terms of the March 2002 agreement so as to reduce the amount of economic separation between the two union partners. Chris Patten, the EU External Affairs Commissioner told Djukanović on 3 July that both parts of the federal state must harmonise their customs and tariffs, at which the Montenegrin leader flew into a rage.[17] He complained on 20 August 2002 that 'a destabilising anti-reform coalition supported by certain bureaucracies of the European Union...has tried to...force Montenegro into a tighter Serbian orbit'.[18] This viewpoint enjoyed some international endorsement. The International Crisis Group (ICG), a think-tank concentrating on strategies to reconstruct the western Balkans on a viable long-term basis and with influential global political actors among its board members, is probably the best-placed critic of such a forced marriage. It has accused the European Union of trying to alter the balance of forces in Montenegro in order to breathe life into a union (dubbed by its critics 'Solania' after the EU's security commissioner) which it sees as unviable and a source of further instability. Nevertheless, a constitutional charter for the new federated state was announced on 8 December 2002.[19]

Clearly, the decline of an external threat reduced the coherence of the pro-independence lobby and Djukanović has lost his usefulness for the European Union following the removal from power of Milosević. Parliamentary elections held on 20 October 2002 nevertheless gave Djukanović's coalition an outright majority. This was despite the Liberals running separately and despite the controversial role of the British ambassador in Belgrade, Charles Crawford. He strongly encouraged the pro-Yugoslav parties and the Liberals to cooperate in a bid to oust Djukanović. The ambassadors of two other large EU states initially joined Crawford in assisting the Montenegrin opposition, 'but drew back when they concluded he had gone too far'.[20] The turnout was a high 77.2 per cent but the campaign was generally peaceful despite the high stakes. The pro-independence camp proved stronger than in the 2001 parliamentary elections but it was still an inconclusive verdict regarding what the political future of Montenegro should be.

Soon after, Djukanović decided to switch jobs. The Prime Minister was selected as the presidential candidate of his party and Djukanović stepped into his post which, under the constitution, is where the fulcrum of power really ought to be. But a series of scandals concerning the alleged involvement of top state officials in human trafficking and the smuggling of tobacco in the 1990s tarnished the government's reformist credentials. It is clear that Djukanović sees the joint state structures as transitional and he is unwilling to give them any more force than is necessary to avoid EU displeasure.[21] From 2002 his strategy was to dig in for a long siege until political conditions enabled him to revive the independence option.

The new union can probably only be made to work through constant international engagement. Serbia was unenthusiastic and the Djindjić government used up valuable time and political capital humouring Brussels over it; time and energy that should have been used to try and dismantle the old regime structures.[22] In relation to Serbia, the West did try to keep the popular appetite for change alive in the immediate aftermath of September 2000. Elections for the Serbian parliament alone were due at the close of 2000 and the European Union gave DOS what has been described as a €200 million 'peace dividend' to boost its prospects. This included funds for a special road-building programme and for food supplies, the United States purchasing imported electricity for the Serbian grid (*After Milošević* 2001: 59). The Federation was also quickly accepted as a full member of the Balkan Stability Pact, the Organization for Security and Co-operation in Europe (OSCE) and the European Bank for Reconstruction and Development.

Djindjić in the saddle

On 23 December 2000, DOS won 65 per cent of the vote in the Serbian parliamentary elections, with only 14 per cent going to Milošević's Socialists (SPS). Djindjić's position as Prime Minister was strengthened but it was increasingly impossible to hide the divergences with Koštunica, the Federal President. Before the election, he declared openly that the hasty removal of people from leading positions in the state and the army undoubtedly 'runs counter to state interests'.[23] He refused to agree to the removal of Nebojsa Pavković, Chief of the General Staff, who had previously been linked with ruthless action against the Albanians in Kosovo during 1998–9.[24] On the eve of a visit to Russia in October 2000, Koštunica had described the United States as one of 'the totalitarian societies of this century'.[25] He continued to berate British leaders for their prominent role in NATO's Kosovo campaign, and applauded their opponents in the media and the anti-war movement, such as Simon Jenkins and Harold Pinter.[26] Both the United States and the European Union downplayed the difficulties Koštunica regularly made rather than confronting him directly. Instead, pressure continued to be exerted on Djindjić who did not share the Yugoslav President's ingrained nationalism, 'without giving him political cover for his actions'.[27]

The main highlight of Djindjić's thirty months in charge of Serbia was the detention of Milošević and his extradiction to face the International Criminal Tribunal for Yugoslavia (ICTY) in the Hague. Djindjić was left in no doubt that substantial Western economic support depended on Milošević being removed as an active player in Serbian politics. Understandably, he feared that a backlash might ensue once his adversary was taken into custody. But a series of revelations from the media were meant to show the population that Milošević really had a case to answer. Sections of the media began to report how bodies taken from mass graves in Kosovo had been placed in a container lorry and dumped in the river Danube in eastern Serbia during 1999. On 13 June 2001, Serbian television broadcast footage of the exhumation of hundreds of bodies of Albanians from a police training compound only a short distance from Belgrade.[28] By now, Milošević was already in custody, arrested on 1 April on corruption charges. On 28 June, he was taken from the central prison in Belgrade and extradited to The Hague where, on 3 July, he was formally charged with crimes against humanity.

Western complacency and nationalist revival

But the West failed to coordinate its stance on the war crimes issue. Western officials remained silent when Koštunica claimed soon afterwards that Milošević had been kidnapped from his Belgrade prison.[29] His refusal to apologise for war crimes committed by Serbs and his insistence that Serbs were primarily victims in the recent wars produced an awkward silence from Western leaders (*After Milošević* 2001: 42). By the end of 2002, Carla del Ponte, the Swiss lawyer who was The Hague Tribunal chief prosecutor, was displaying open frustration at what she saw as the absence of insufficient EU pressure on both Serbia and Croatia to arrest and hand over leading indictees. Linking continued financial help with cooperation with the The Hague process had yielded up middle-ranking suspects but the figure suspected of committing the worse crimes, Ratko Mladić remained at large. (In 2002 high-placed government sources told the ICG that he lived openly in Belgrade protected by over seventy VJ soldiers under the command of Pavković, the army chief.[30] Earlier, Graham Blewitt, del Ponte's deputy stated that Mladić lived in Belgrade under the 'full protection' of the authorities.)[31]

The army was the main branch of the state protecting war crimes suspects. Milošević received documents and information from individuals and groups inside the army for use in his defence.[32] Technically under the control of the federal government, the VJ was a law unto itself. Slobodan Krapović, a federal defence minister with some reforming ideas met fierce resistance and was forced out in December 2001.[33] The military was a bastion of 'conservative old-style

Serbian nationalism', retaining significant public trust.[34] A Serbian human rights group observed that it was regarded as 'a discrete social and political entity entitled to intercede, to speak its mind, to protect, and defend, but hardly ever as a body serving the needs of the society and the citizens'.[35] Pavković, its head, acted as a political contender, giving frequent interviews and engaging politicians in running debates in the media.[36]

DOS was unwilling to move against the criminal networks Milošević had used to try and achieve his goals on the killing-fields of Bosnia and Kosovo and in the domestic political arena. No criminal cases were brought against former members of the regime even though their criminal actions had been well-documented.[37] Fear was a strong deterrent factor. Those who genuinely tried to make changes faced the real risk of assassination from powerful elements within the forces supposed to be protecting them or else answerable to them. Reformers also had to take account of the secret editorial and financial control that figures linked to organised crime had over a section of the media. Publications linked to the flourishing underworld demonised reformers and whipped up an atmosphere hostile to change.[38]

Djindjić: ambiguous reformer

Djindjić rarely displayed such fear in public. Since being a teenager he had challenged the orthodoxies of the Tito era and had made a successful academic and business career in Germany before returning to Serbia in the early 1990s.[39] But he had also been a nationalist, identifying with brutal Serbian irredentism in Bosnia until 1994. Thereafter, he seemed to realise his mistake, influenced perhaps by formative experiences abroad denied to most of his fellow citizens. But in office he moved cautiously, even taking decisions that may have helped the criminal structures to remain powerful contenders. He opposed capable reformers if he thought they posed a threat to his own position. He grew increasingly wary of G-17, a think-tank that had provided a reform programme for DOS in 2000, especially after it became a political party in 2002. The poor showing of G-17's Miroslav Labuć in the inconclusive Serbian presidential elections of October 2002 stemmed in part from efforts by Djindjić to undermine his campaign.[40] His government was also locked in dispute with the National Bank of Serbia, headed by Mladjin Dinkić, also from G-17. The Bank 'appeared to be the only institution in Serbia that functioned properly'.[41] The hard-won stability of the banking and monetary system was secured and Dinkić fought against financial crime, particularly money-laundering. Against this background, the Paris Club of sovereign creditors agreed, in November 2001, to write off two-thirds of the debt owed by the Federation to its lenders, one of the most generous debt forgiveness deals with a defaulted borrower.[42] It was G-17 technocrats who also turned the privatisation agency into an effective engine of reform. The conclusion of major privatisations in the tobacco, petroleum retailing and brewing sectors in the second half of 2003 greatly eased pressure on the budget. The state sold stakes in more than 800 companies in 2003, generating proceeds of $1.07 billion.[43]

If Djindjić failed to bond effectively with his most ardent reformers, he relied on an extremely heterogeneous support base where the commitment to true reform was often hard to detect. He had needed to make allies with former Milošević allies in order to survive his duel with his predecessor. One of the most controversial Djindjić friends was Vladimir 'Beba' Popović, a former Milošević fundraiser who became the DOS government's unofficial propaganda minister.[44] Instead of enjoying freedom to operate after years of punitive restrictions, the independent media faced further harassment (but of a more subtle kind) from Popović. In one of his most questionable decisions, Djindjić agreed to allow the main television stations that had championed Milošević to keep their licences provided they switched sides. There was no effort to place the media on a proper legal footing and throw it open to new competition or to bids for the main frequencies and channels.[45] In the absence of proper regulation, the independent media faced reprisals in the form of raids by tax inspectors and other government agents if they repeatedly strayed into sensitive areas. Here was an area vital for maintaining public confidence in the government where it was decided that Milošević-era media constraints had their uses. The media was also cowed by the constant threat of law-suits from Milošević cronies and anti-reform wings of the government who were also able to rely on a compliant judiciary.

Judicial reform was conspicuous by its absence during the years of DOS rule. The courts were still packed with appointees who had become used to ruling in favour of the Milošević regime and who were often closely involved with some of its most discredited elements. It did not come as a shock that the sentences handed down in 2002 in the trial of former state security agents accused of the assassinations of four well-known Serbs in 2000 were very light. One of the defendants, Rade Marković, head of the Serbian security police until 2001, got a mere seven years. (Earlier, on a visit to Brussels, Koštunica had interceded with Chris Patten to try and get Marković's name removed from the European Union list of Serbs banned from entering the Union.)[46]

During the first assassination attempt on Djindjić on 21 February 2003, the suspect was released by a compliant judge after 24 hours even though he had attempted to crash a stolen lorry into the Prime Minister's car and had a long criminal record.[47]

Those figures at the top of the justice and interior ministries were disinclined to engage in anything beyond cosmetic reforms. If they had been substituted by more purposeful figures, it is difficult to see how they could have made headway against entrenched conservative bureaucracies. It was often difficult to find relatively clean figures in branches of the state deeply implicated in the Milošević regime's criminal policies. But there were still baffling appointments, such as that of Sreten Lutić, who became assistant minister of the interior in charge of criminal investigations in January 2001. Not long before, he had cracked down energetically against activists from Otpor as Milošević clung to power. Troops under his command had also been responsible for some of the bloodiest actions against Albanians in Kosova.[48]

Reforms stall

Powerful and entrenched interests from the Milošević era were able to block reform within months of DOS coming to power. One of the most committed reformers, Yugoslav Foreign Minister Goran Svilanović had warned in October 2002 that Milošević-era informal power structures had formed around Koštunica and Djindjić and were pushing the pair increasingly into confrontation.[49] The numerous smaller parties in the DOS coalition were also manipulated by these power structures, the government finding it increasingly difficult to pass laws despite the size of its majority. The need for the Democratic Party (DS) and other parties in DOS to find funds for elections also enabled groups thought to be their natural enemies to re-establish their influence.[50]

No major economic reforms were approved by the Serbian parliament in 2002 and there was little progress on European integration, which Brussels had offered in return for meaningful change. Instead, the reform camp was preoccupied with a growing power-struggle between Djindjić's DS and Koštunica's DSS. Relations had soured at the time of Milošević's 2001 extradition with the DSS complaining that legal formalities had not been observed. The DSS appeared an increasing anomaly within the DOS coalition. A small party prior to 2000, its ranks had been swelled by defectors from parties which found it hard to come to terms with the loss of power. At local level former Serbian Socialist Party (SPS) and JUL directors of state-owned enterprises hoped to keep their jobs by switching to the most congenial of the new coalition forces.[51] By September 2001 the DSS was publicly accusing its DOS adversaries in the government of being involved in criminal activities; claims that it was unable to substantiate.[52] Koštunica's party was expelled from DOS in July 2002 and both opposed each other in the Serbian presidential elections held on 29 September 2002. These had been brought forward to allow the extradition to The Hague of the Serbian President, Milan Milutinović (who had been indicted along with Milošević in May 1999). With no candidate obtaining an outright plurality, a second round was held on 13 October. Koštunica won but the result was invalidated because the turnout was less than the 50 per cent required. In a third attempt to elect a Serbian president, on 8 December 2002, the low turnout meant the post remained vacant, being filled temporarily by the parliamentary speaker.[53]

The ballot box had failed to underwrite political stability. Caught up in internecine party warfare and increasingly seen as ensnared with underworld elements, Djindjić and the bulk of DOS were losing touch with a great part of the electorate. No effective dialogue had been launched after 2000 whereby Djindjić and the most committed of his allies sought to educate the electorate about the reform process.[54] The public was told of imminent progress on the European front that would produce economic deliverance as well as end Serbia's isolation, but the somewhat painful adjustments needed before Serbia could hope to join mainstream Europe were not spelled out.

Elections were a regular occurrence in the post-Milošević period and this increased the temptation for many in DOS to move closer to forces that promoted old-style Serbian nationalism. Not long after his election in 2000, Koštunica visited Hilander monastery on Mount Athos, accompanied by the federal prime minister and no less than seventeen ministers.[55] Trying not to be outflanked, Djindjić strengthened the position of the Orthodox Church in the Serbian state. Compulsory religious education was introduced in Serbian schools and large sums were donated from the state coffers to help complete the cathedral of St Sava in Belgrade.[56]

The army was the other pillar of conservative nationalism. In polls, it was the second most trusted institution after the Orthodox Church itself. Given the way it had been compromised under Milošević, liberal elements in DOS had a vested interest in trying to promote a revamped army that served the needs of society and citizens, but a debate about the role of the army never took off. Instead, Pavković, its head was able to play off rival DOS factions. It was interpreted as a victory for the forces of moderation when Pavković defected from the Koštunica camp, but the fact that Djindjić was prepared to offer political protection to this deeply tarnished figure showed how weak were the forces challenging authoritarian nationalism in Serbia.

Minorities and neighbours rebuffed

Except for the crucially-placed Presovo Albanians, no transformation occurred in the way the state responded to the minorities who may have comprised 20 per cent of Serbia's population. Rasim Ljajić, a Muslim from the Sandžak, proved an energetic minister for national and ethnic minorities in the federal government, but despite his efforts Serbia's minorities continued to be marginalised and disparaged. Goran Svilanović even felt compelled to criticise his DOS colleagues at the beginning of 2002 for ignoring, and in some cases, fuelling hate speech towards other ethnic groups.[57]

Irredentism was openly promoted by figures involved in unseating Milošević. Addressing an election rally on the Serbian side of the Drina river on 7 September 2002, Koštunica described the Republic of Srpska (RS) as 'a part of the family that is dear to us, near, temporarily split off, but always in our heart'.[58] Djindjić was far less provocative but in 2001 he expressed the view that Kosovo could be recovered after five years of internationally administered 'confidence-building'.[59] Shortly before his death, he was expressing the belief that 'borders in the region would have to be completely redefined'.[60]

The post-2002 Serbian policy towards Kosovo provided strong indications that separating the area around Mitrovica in the north and attaching it to Serbia was an active goal. The state at the federal level financed and controlled security forces – mainly elements from the controversial ministry of the interior police (MUP) operating inside northern Kosovo, a clear breach of the terms of the 1999 ceasefire. Nebojša Čović, the deputy premier responsible for Serbia's policy on Kosovo, admitted that funding even extended to 'the bridge-watchers of Mitrovica', hardliners who mobilised crowds for confrontation with Kosovo Force (KFOR).[61] Belgrade also maintained a parallel administration in some Kosovo municipalities.

Djindjić made no secret of the fact that his government wished to reinforce the Serbian state presence through the judiciary, schooling, health-care and security – at least in a portion of Kosovo.[62] International budgetary support to Serbia permitted Belgrade to set aside as much as €75 million annually for its partitionist strategy.[63] There were few, if any, confidence-building measures to try and overcome the deep suspicion of the Albanian majority towards Belgrade. Of the 630 Albanians from Kosovo detained in Serbia in 1999 after being tried in an often highly irregular manner, 162 were still in custody by March 2002. In Serbia, they were considered terrorists, but diplomatic sources in Belgrade considered at least seventy-eight of them to be political prisoners (*After Milošević* 2001: 51–2).

Turning to Bosnia, the RS's army, the Army of the Republic of Srpska (VRS) continued to be financed from Belgrade. The 1,700-strong officer corps was on the VJ payroll until formal ties were cut off early in 2003.[64] Serbia and the RS still maintained a common air defence network which prevented the establishment of an integrated Bosnian military command under civilian control and was in clear violation of the 1995 Dayton treaty.[65] Indeed until 2002 these were never ratified by Federal Yugoslavia and its President Koštunica openly supporting the Serbian Democratic Party (SDS) where close identification with the philosophy of its founder, Radovan Karadžić was not hard to find.[66]

Ultras fight back

Koštunica's unapologetic nationalism chimed in well with Serbian core beliefs. Any politician who hoped to enjoy electoral success would pay a cost if he overrode popular sentiment on emotive national issues. Political culture remained locked in blame and denial. Most Serbs saw themselves as blameless actors in the post-1991 Yugoslav upheavals when they became victims of a range of local and international forces, acting sometimes alone but usually in concert.[67] Milošević (who had few defenders when he was taken to The Hague in 2001), enjoyed a partial rehabilitation in the eyes of Serbian public opinion when he emphasised such themes in his defence. The analyst Srdjan Bogosajivić suggested in 2001 that at one end of the spectrum of public opinion was a 15 per cent grouping which asserted that both the objectives and methods of Milošević's wars were justified. Meanwhile, at the other end, 20–25 per cent believed the opposite, but in between were to be found the majority of Serbs, 'looking for a narrative of recent years that makes sense to them and has some continuation into the future'.[68]

It is likely that the 15 per cent of diehard nationalists grew considerably after 2001. From Djindjić down, politicians shied away from trying to alter public perceptions about controversial events in the recent and more distant past.[69] Zoran Živković, his successor as Prime Minister, appeared relaxed with the intransigent Serbian mindset when he was overheard at a Washington dinner declaring that 'there are three things Serbs cannot stand: an independent Kosovo, NATO, and the United States'.[70]

It remains to be seen if the shortlived era of Djindjić and DOS will (as the Serbian human rights lawyer Srjda Popović believes) be merely an interlude in a transfer from Milošević to non-communist but radical nationalist leadership.[71] Certainly military ultras found the political climate sufficiently conducive to mount an open challenge to Djindjić less than a year after DOS's electoral victory.

In November 2001, ex-members of Milošević's praetorian guard, the JSO (also known as the Red Berets) were arrested and later transferred to The Hague. When the JSO realised the implications for their unit, this heavily militarised force blocked the main road arteries through Belgrade for ten days. President Koštunica publicly endorsed their action. He believed that the JSO had 'understandable' and 'legitimate' demands... in their protest against the government's policy of cooperating with the war crimes tribunal.[72]

Hardliners showed their strength to even greater effect on 14 March 2002 when they brought down Momčilo Perišić, a deputy prime minister and former key military aide to Milošević until 1998. Perišić had been dining in a Belgrade motel with David Neighbour, a first secretary in the US embassy. Both men were seized by special task force agents from the VJ (some with Bosnian accents) and held for fifteen hours. It was widely believed that Neighbour had been looking for documents that would strengthen the case against Milošević. President Koštunica had barred The Hague investigators from access to military archives while Milošević had no difficulty in securing information for his defence from the same and other official sources.[73] Indeed, there is evidence that he was preparing for his trial since the 1999 indictment. He ordered the entire archives of the Yugoslav army's military intelligence to be transferred to his office, and after his overthrow, none of these archives were found.[74] Perišić, detained while allegedly in the middle of handing over information to the US diplomat was forced to resign soon after and no action appears ever to have been taken against his abductors.[75]

Popular disillusionment with reform in practice

The experience of the city of Kragujevac, the site of a once-flourishing car and arms industry, revealed the extent of the difficulties DOS had in keeping public approval.[76] In 2001 a restructuring programme for the loss-making arms producer soon saw the industry's work-force reduced from 30,800 to 15,400. In the local car industry, the cuts went even deeper with just 3,500 of the 11,300-strong work-force surviving. Redundant workers were offered $129 for each year worked to a maximum of $2,272. It was hoped that the severance pay would provide 'seed money' to grow new businesses locally. That proved to be a faulty calculation as the economy remained flat. Despite the presence of two agencies in the city dedicated to lending 'start-up' funding for new businesses – one state-run and the other agency belonging to the European Union – almost none were launched. Against a background of economic collapse which led to Kragujevac being nick-named 'the Valley of the Hungry', the view spread there that 'the agencies only serve to provide cushy jobs for a handful of bureaucrats, and cheap loans for their relatives and fellow party members'.[77]

Accumulating evidence of low standards in high places under DOS drained away much of its original support. The need for the governing parties to finance election campaigns gave the economic beneficiaries of the Milošević era plenty of scope to prolong their influence. Boguljub Karić, a leading tycoon defied government efforts to make him pay taxes on his pre-2000 gains. He bankrolled a range of parties that held fifty-five seats in parliament.[78] The pressure worked, leading to the resignation in September 2002 of the senior official tasked with drawing up a list of the companies that profited under the Milošević regime and owed back taxes. It was in fact government figures linked to the oligarchy who helped sabotage this attempt at ensuring fiscal probity.[79] Mladan Dinkić, the national bank governor was made of sterner stuff. He targeted money-launderers whom he claimed had sent up to $964 million out of the country through offshore banks. But one of the culprits belonged to a Belgrade gang, the Surčin clan, known to have been on close terms with Djindjić and members of his government.[80]

It was disingenuous for Djindjić to complain (as he did at the end of 2001) about the lack of substantial foreign investment, given the continued access of mafia elements to the politically powerful.[81] In March 2003 the European Union felt compelled to bar imports of sugar from Serbia and Montenegro after it caught several companies importing cheap foreign sugar and repackaging it to make it appear like a Serbian product. The sugar was then exported to EU countries, taking advantage of generous preferential trade conditions and subsidies. Belgrade had been warned for over a year but in that time no action had been taken, even though it was likely to adversely effect relations with the European Union.[82] The reason for such laxity was not hard to discover. Some of the companies involved financed parties in DOS.

Several leading DOS parties also hoped to fill their coffers by benefiting from the looming privatisation of the tobacco industry.[83] By 2002, smaller DOS parties sometimes even expected cash before they would turn up for key parliamentary votes.[84] Long forgotten was the 2001 announcement of the justice minister, Vladan Batić that 'members of the new Serbian government will not be allowed to have their own private businesses... or exert pressure on the media, the judiciary, the police, and public enterprises'.[85] Many of Serbia's self-styled reformers ignored this ethnical yardstick. Instead, a 'ubiquitous, dingy provincialism, endemic laziness, and a penchant for serious corruption' prevailed among important elements of the new political class.[86]

DOS rudderless after Djindjić

DOS was rudderless after the assassination of Zorin Djindjić in Belgrade on 12 March 2003. Beforehand, he had been starting to move against the Zemun clan, the biggest and most effective mafia clan in Serbia. Its main activities were killing and kidnapping, and the smuggling of drugs, cars, tobacco and alcohol.[87] One analyst has written: 'The possibility always loomed that if Djindjić crossed a line that endangered their revenues... by acting too aggressively against organized crime and in cooperation with the Tribunal, these elements might take active measures to remove him'.[88]

The record crowds that assembled for Djindjić's funeral on 15 March exemplified 'the indignation at the high-rate of crime in Serbian society rather than being a sign of personal affection for Djindjić'.[89] Amfilohije Radović, the Orthodox prelate who presided at his funeral, delivered an oration suffused with xenophobia and disregard for the slain prime minister, in which Djindjić was compared with Milan Obrenović, an earlier Serbian leader who like him was felt to have capitulated before foreign might.[90] Four of the six pallbearers, DOS notables, were either members, or else had been closely linked to, the oligarchy and even organised crime figures.[91]

Nevertheless, an energetic crackdown was launched during a six-week period when a state of emergency was imposed. Some 10,000 people were arrested, nearly 4,000 of whom were detained under the State of Emergency Act that allows for a 30-day detention.[92] Some 3,700 were charged with various crimes.

The Zemun Clan was targeted in what became known as 'Operation Sabre'. Most members were detained or killed with the exception of its leader, Milorad 'Legija' Luković (who later surrendered to police on 2 May 2004); on 1 April 2003 Pavković, the head of the army was arrested to answer allegations that the army colluded in an assassination attempt on prominent opposition figure Vuk Drasković while he was in charge of it.[93]

Western bodies were generally impressed by the scope of the crackdown. The Council of Europe quickly granted Serbia and Montenegro membership, partially out of sympathy with Djindjić's assassination. The United States, which had threatened to cut off all assistance by the end of March unless Mladić was apprehended, relented. Relations with Washington improved when leading suspects, Jovica Stanisić, former head of the state security service and officers implicated in massacres of civilians at the Croatian city of Vukovar were sent to The Hague.[94] NATO states still insisted on compliance with the war crimes tribunal in return for continued assistance, a stance that troubled Peter Schieder, President of the Council of Europe who publicly warned that this placed other leading reformers in danger.[95]

There were unsettling aspects to the crackdown which not only concerned well-documented reports that detainees had been subject to torture (an aspect which the OSCE played down in its report on the state of emergency).[96] The speed with which the police were able to bring charges against men accused of high-level assassinations in 1999–2000 indicated that much information was already available about them, perhaps even in government circles.[97] Indeed Operation Sabre revealed that most perpetrators of murders and kidnappings were members of special police units, the state security network, or else enjoyed close ties with them.[98] There was a suggestion that the crackdown had public relations aspects. On 4 April 2003 an arrest warrant was issued for Mira Marković, the wife of Milošević in connection with the killing in September 2000 of Ivan Stambolić, Milošević's patron in the 1980s. But by July an arrest warrant had yet to be forwarded to Moscow where Marković was believed to be.[99] Also, it gradually became apparent that allies of DOS in the shadowy interface of crime and politics were being treated lightly; only a small portion of the Surčin clan was attacked.

If DOS was trying to restore its credibility by being seen as taking the offensive against corruption and criminality, the effect was shortlived. The media alleged that Cedomir Jovanović, a vice-president in the Serbian government and a Djindjić protégé had enjoyed frequent contacts with members of both the Surčin and Zemun clans, including Legija.[100] Two warders at the Belgrade central jail publicly stated that on several occasions they saw Jovanović visit 'Siptar' Spasojević when he was in custody, indicating that he had helped to secure the release of this Zemun clan member.[101] Under public pressure, Jovanović admitted to the parliament's security and justice committee that he had indeed had contacts – but in good faith – with one of the crime bosses implicated in Djindjić's murder who had since died 'resisting arrest'.[102]

A fellow vice-president in the government, Nebojša Čović, complained that the government was not pursuing all those connected with the two clans. The new Prime Minister, Zoran Živković, tried to end the infighting and, on 27 May announced:[103]

> ...not one member of the government, not earlier or today, was connected... with any criminal or criminal group. Not one member of the government is a protector of any criminal or criminal group, nor is covering up criminal activities, and does not influence the work of the police. Also, state organs did not engage criminals or criminal groups to in a single instance to carry out their task.
>
> (*Serbian Reforms Stall Again*, p. 22)

The blanket assurance flew in the face of plenty of contrary evidence. It was also unfortunate that Jovanović was the minister in charge of integration with the European Union, a process that languished after 2002. Western diplomats were aware of the existence of a network of politicians, influential businessmen and media owners known as 'the business club' which appeared to enjoy important leverage over economic policy. In the spring of 2003, 'many perceived the group to be using the state of emergency...to "settle accounts" with its political opponents'.[104]

'Beba' Popović, the shadowy DOS figure whom the Djindjić circle used to control the media, tried to influence journalists coverage of the emergency by reading to them details from their own secret police dossiers.[105] The anti-Milošević media figure, Veran Matić, editor-in-chief of B-92 radio station, even found himself in the firing-line for adhering to an independent line after 2000.[106] There was even an attempt to silence the reporting of the ICG, an influential think-tank with a board of directors which had been strongly supportive of democratisation efforts in Serbia. On the eve of the publication of a report known to cast doubt on DOS's commitment to fundamental change, James Lyon, its author, director of the Serbia–Montenegro division of the ICG, was threatened with expulsion, allegedly because his visa expired. The authorities only backed down because of pressure from the EU's Chris Patten and senior diplomats in Belgrade.[107] There was further discomfiture when the US ambassador, William Montgomery, stated in June 2003 that he had been told by Djindjić himself that Popović, his communications chief, had instigated a smear campaign against Veran Matić at the instigation of the powerful TV Pink organisation which had switched from being a Milošević propaganda organ to working for the government.[108]

Hopes of gaining an electoral dividend from their leader's assassination made his political heirs in the DS contemplate holding a snap election. However, strong pressure was applied from the US embassy to abandon such an idea and concentrate on the reform agenda.[109] But coalition infighting increasingly took precedence over reform. G-17's Dinkić was forced out as the national bank governor in July 2003. He had been responsible for drastic financial house-cleaning that had cut an inflation rate previously at lethal proportions to under 20 per cent.[110] At least two factions opened up inside DOS, one pro-reform and the other pro-oligarchy. On 18 November 2003, the DOS coalition disbanded after announcing that it had completed its 'historic mission' and fresh parliamentary elections were set for 28 December.[111] Fewer and fewer believed the self-serving rhetoric. Instead, after the ending of the state of emergency on 22 April, it had been noticeable how quickly the government had renounced the battle against corruption and economic crime.[112] Djindjić, however flawed a figure, had recognised the urgency of moving in that direction. But he had left no successor capable of doing this effectively. Young people, the key support group of DOS in 2000, were disillusioned by its performance. More than 50 per cent in one 2003 poll stated they wished to emigrate.[113] The feeling that the governing elite had an agenda far removed from the needs of the common citizen was an impulse strongly felt by workers who had suffered the effects of factory closures. Aleksandar Beljaković, a trade-union officer in the stricken city of Kragujevac, complained that not a single Milošević-era director had been prosecuted in a city where fraud in state factories had grown notorious.[114] DOS was also accused of a lack of compassion towards workers who sometimes had not been paid in years, and families, 5,000 of whom in Kragujevac not having a single earner. In the city 35,000 people were dependent on charity from the Serbian Red Cross, yet their electricity was cut off due to their inability to pay their bills. Beljaković argued that this was unjust since the state owed many of these families money due to the arrears of wages from state companies. He compared DOS unfavourably in this respect with Milošević who looted the state at a time when nobody felt the need to pay utilities bills.[115] Milošević had sharper political antennae than perhaps most DOS figures and his populist skills had enabled him to stay in power longer than he might otherwise have done.

Polarised Serbia

A warning of the electoral fate shortly awaiting the reformers was provided in yet another attempt to elected a President of Serbia. It was the Radical Party's Tomislav Nikolić who emerged the clear winner in November 2003 with 49 per cent of the vote; however, the result was annulled due to a low turnout. In December Nikolić would say on TV that he was not sorry the anti-Milošević journalist, Slavko Ćuruvija had been killed in 1999.[116] But he was unable to outbid the party leader, Vojislav Šešelj, in the use of extremist language. He had gone voluntarily to the ICTY at The Hague, shortly before Djindjić's murder, prompting speculation about the timing of his move. He remained unapologetic about his role, especially in the 1991–2 confrontation with Croatia: 'I am proud that thousands of Serb Radical Party volunteers fought on almost all fronts where Serbdom was defended. Do they expect me to defend myself of this. I am proud of it and my sons, grand-children, and great-grand-children will be proud of this'.[117] Šešelj's gesture struck a chord with Serbs who were unaware or didn't want to know that the post-1991 wars had in fact witnessed few battles and had mainly been directed against civilians. But in its campaigning, the Serbian Radical Party (SRS) mainly addressed the economic woes of the population. Nikolić promised that if elected he would claim war reparations from NATO for the 1999 bombing. The Clinton administration in the United States had released figures, estimating that the direct damage to Serbia had been around $30 billion. The SRS indicated that if it made a successful claim to the International Court of Justice (also in The Hague), the Serbian economic recovery would be hastened. The appeal of the SRS rested in large part on the fact that it had usually been out of office in the preceding decade and therefore was not associated with government actions that left people worse off. It was aware that large numbers of voters, approximately 36 per cent according to one poll, were undecided so it projected a more moderate message in their direction.[118]

The ranks of the undecided had been swelled by a tide of media stories concerning the abuse of power by current office-holders. One usually realistic source expected that it was still possible for a party with 'a clean pro-reform, pro-European agenda' to pick up the majority of the undecided.[119] G-17 was seen as a potential new broom despite the fact that its pro-austerity image may have alienated as many people as were drawn to it by the anti-corruption measures its leaders had adopted in government. Another potential catalyst of change was Otpor which had never taken part in the DOS government and had been critical of its performance. Otpor decided to support candidates committed to its core programme of strengthening state institutions. It placed competence over party allegiance and threw its support behind candidates who were not its members. That was 'a novel approach in Serbia where parties are strictly hierarchical'.[120] But Otpor was a pale shadow of the movement at the head of the agitation in 2000 which toppled Milošević. At its 2001 conference there had been sharp dissension as provincial activists revolted against a manifesto drawn up by the Belgrade leadership which it was claimed had not been circulated to the membership for discussion.[121] Otpor seemed no better prepared than other civil society movements which had sprung to prominence opposing state tyranny in Eastern Europe about how to adjust to the challenge of remaining relevant in less heroic times.

Otpor failed to make much impact in the 28 December 2003 parliamentary elections and it was the Radicals who emerged as the clear victors with 28 per cent of the vote on a high turnout. Far behind in second place was Koštunica's DSS followed by its fierce rival the DS (formerly the lynchpin of DOS). The SRS did spectacularly well in economically depressed centres like Kragujevac, Serbia's fourth largest city where it obtained 35.2 per cent of the vote. Here nationalist concerns were not uppermost in most voters minds in centres where the fight for economic survival took precedence over most other things. Many experts concluded that 'the outcome of the vote was not a resurgence of nationalism, since the parties loyal to the Milošević regime actually won fewer votes in 2003 than in 2000'.[122] But of the 250 seats in parliament, 179 were taken by parties heavily critical of The Hague Tribunal. Most Serbs viewed it as unfair and humiliating and there had been a rising crescendo of criticism towards it during DOS's period in office.[123] The West had never presented a united front on the war crimes issue, which led to increasingly public squabbles between del Ponte and top officials from NATO and major states. She in turn was criticised for adopting a hectoring and self-righteous approach towards moderate Serbs which deepened their isolation at home.[124] At least memories of the Milošević era blighted the comeback hopes of the SPS. Denied ready access to the media and running low on funds, it barely made it into parliament. Nevertheless, it had the potential to exercise influence beyond its depleted numbers because the votes of smaller parties would be crucial in the search for a viable government.

Foreign and domestic observers were divided about how to respond to the rise of the SRS. Western spokesmen put undisguised pressure on moderate parties to shun the Radicals. Gert Weisskirchen, the German Social Democrat foreign policy spokesman, declared on 7 January 2004 that an all-party government in Serbia is 'absolutely unacceptable' to the European Union and Germany; he warned that parties still led by indicted war crimes suspects joined the cabinet, 'no more funds will be transferred from the rest of Europe for the reconstruction of the country'.[125] It is unlikely that this kind of stern lecture would impress the undecided Serbs who this time voted for the SRS. The reform camp in Serbia rejected the idea of an all-party government (in some cases perhaps out of concern not to alienate foreign donors who had supported their election campaigns). But the strength of the SRS derived from its oppositional character and it might have been better to test it out in government in ministries where it could not easily indulge in populist posturing. One analyst argued that 'it is much better to invite the SRS through a small door than to let them triumphantly enter through the main door alone in six months or in a year, if things do not radically change'.[126]

A government was finally formed under Kostunica in March 2004, the DSS ruling with minor parties. The Radicals and the SPS might have been formally on the sidelines, but their influence was strongly felt. Brakes were applied to legal reform and a Milošević-era figure took charge of state television. On 30 March, the Serbian parliament voted 141–35 to pay all Serbian war crimes indictees arraigned at the ICTY in The Hague 'compensation for lost salaries, plus help for spouses, siblings, parents, and children for flight and hotel costs, telephone and mail bills, visa fees and legal charges…'.[127] Thus, having illegally amassed a fortune of $1.6 billion, Milošević's own bills would be paid by the citizens of Serbia whose future had been mortgaged (along with that of other peoples in the former Yugoslavia) to pay for his cycle of wars.[128] This decision put neatly into perspective Kostunica's assurance that The Hague was unnecessary and Serbia had the means to carry out its own war crimes trials (a view seen as fanciful by nearly all Serbian and international legal experts).[129] It was debatable if the courts would be capable of dealing in a transparent manner with those charged with serious offences in the wake of Djindjić's killing (Gordy 2004: 15). The trial of 'Legija', due to begin in late 2004, would be a critical test for Serbian justice. The only bright note was the election of Boris Tadić as President of Serbia on 27 June 2004. The DS leader and former defence minister narrowly beat the SRS's Nikolić in a second-round contest (the rule requiring a 50 per cent turnout having been waived).

Conclusion

Nebojša Čović, a Serbian vice premier from 2000 to 2003, was quoted as saying in March 2003:

> I often stated that on October 5 2000, some people feared for their safety, on October 6 for their money, on October 7 for their status, and by October 8 they had already managed to enter somehow into our structures and that they are now getting their revenge.
>
> (Gordy 2004: 13)

The mafia structures which had flourished in wartime conditions and which had bent state institutions to their will were able to regroup after the October 2001 ousting of Milošević. Only a single-minded and swift effort to uproot them from the body politic and from the economic system could have resulted in a decisive victory over them. There were times when Djindić appeared to realise the titanic nature of the struggle he was engaged in. But he had few staunch allies in DOS, the Western international community often made unrealistic demands and he had numerous blindspots. It was wrong to assume that there was a clear dividing line between the 'reformers' of DOS and the nationalists, racketeers and communist-orientated figures who had dominated Serbia since the late 1980s. In fact the battle-lines were extremely blurred.

The remaining part of DOS until it folded in late 2003 was Velimir Ilić and the New Serbia Party. The mayor of Čačak, he had been instrumental in spearheading the anti-Milošević revolt in the autumn of 2000, but he made discriminatory comments against moderate colleagues for being allegedly lacking in Serbian patriotism or having Croatian or Muslim relatives. His party was also associated with proponents of fascism in pre-1945 Serbia.[130] Such contradictions were to be found in most countries of the region where politics often revolved around securing the spoils of office rather than championing specific political values or projects. But the schizophrenic nature of politics in Serbia placed it in a league of its own and those figures who tried to promote a course towards normality were on a difficult and dangerous road. Political renewal in Serbia depends on a reconfiguration of domestic forces resulting in a full-fledged effort to restore the rule of law and root out corruption. But such a modernising strategy also depends on the success of wider European integration processes and the wisdom of specific European strategies towards Serbia. Fresh thinking about how to breathe new life into a flagging reform process was far from evident either at home or in the capitals of the European Union as moderates struggled to retain the initiative against emboldened ultra-nationalist forces.

6 Bosnia
Redesigning a flawed peace process

How not to implement a peace agreement

The 1995 Dayton Peace Agreement (DPA) brought to an end a conflict mainly directed against civilians in which 200,000 people were killed and over 2 million were forced to flee their homes. It was a hastily arrived settlement meant to preserve a US-enforced armistice. Even before the ink was dry it was clear that its architects had given little serious thought about how Bosnia could be turned into a viable state. An international administration was to govern in partnership with local political forces. This hastily conceived experiment in political engineering was based on the assumption that the more complicated and multilayered the elected institutions were, the likelier it was that previously implacable rivals would discover the need to cooperate with one another.

A central state enjoyed nominal control only over a war-shattered country. It was a thin shell overlaying ethnically based layers of authority which was where real power resided. There were two ethnically based entities. The Federation of Bosnia–Herzegovina represented a union of the Bosniaks (or Muslims) and the Croats. But for the rest of the 1990s, Croat nationalists spurned the capital Sarajevo and, with the support of the Tudjman regime in Croatia, operated a para state known as Herceg–Bosna. Committed to unification with Croatia, this meant there was in reality a third unofficial entity which the UN authorities were slow to grapple with. The Federation was further weakened by the creation of ten cantons. They soon became centres of economic power as humanitarian aid flowed into Bosnia to begin its postwar reconstruction.

The second declared entity was the Republic of Srpska (RS). The breakaway Serbian statelet was allowed to remain in existence and indeed retain its own separate army.[1] Unlike the Federation, the RS was a highly centralised polity. It did not have intermediate levels of administration, and hardline nationalists rejoiced to see that the DPA did not represent a fundamental challenge to their rule. Indeed, the Serbian Democratic Party (SDS) of Radovan Karadžić cemented its hold on the RS in elections held throughout Bosnia in September 1996. Dayton's architects thought that early elections and the devolution of power to the entities and further down still to the cantons and the municipalities might provide the basis for trans-ethnic cooperation to get underway. Instead 'all the incentives were for the leaders of the three national groups to build three different polities and to ignore or weaken the central state'.[2] To imagine that multiple layers of decision-making would encourage cooperation between implacable enemies was profoundly misguided. No Stalin, Hitler or Saddam Hussein would have made such an elementary error. Prior to the 2003 US–Anglo intervention in Iraq, the DPA was the post-Cold War decision by Western policy-makers which most clearly exposed the shallow foundations on which a new democratic world order rested.

The DPA envisaged that conditions could return to some kind of normality relatively quickly, enabling the 60,000-strong NATO-led Stabilisation Force (SFOR) to be withdrawn by the end of 1996. Freedom of movement, the ability of people to return to their homes and inter-ethnic parity were enshrined by the DPA. But the NATO-led SFOR was reluctant to challenge the nationalists determined to allow none of this to prevail. A High Representative, appointed by the UN Secretary-General, had few powers to implement the key provisions of the DPA. A well-funded reconstruction effort did move forward from 1996 onwards which repaired much of the infrastructure and catered to the humanitarian needs of increasing numbers of people. But suspected war criminals indicted by the International Criminal Tribunal for Yugoslavia (ICTY) sitting in the Hague, defied the UN administration. Until 1997, there seemed to be no real will to detain them or reduce their influence, particularly in the RS. Indeed, by recognising the RS as a constituent element of the new Bosnia the DPA embraced a contradiction, for the RS had been founded in order to break up Bosnia and unite it with Serbia, the means towards this end being a series of atrocities directed against non-Serbs.[3]

Reinterpreting Dayton

The first real challenge to the forces of hardline nationalism occurred in 1997 when the Office of High Representative (OHR) and SFOR combined to wrest control of public broadcasting in the RS away from Karadžić loyalists.[4] Soon Karadžić went into hiding to begin a marathon attempt at evading the ICTY arrest warrant which made him a hero in the eyes of many Serbs. A wide network of lookouts and guards made him untouchable as he moved around outlying areas of Bosnia, Montenegro and Serbia. In 2001, it emerged that money was being diverted from RS institutions by Karadžić loyalists to provide this high level of protection (Festić and Rausche 2004: 29). The DPA had made it all too easy for those who had built a clandestine political economy in wartime to refine their operations in peacetime. Fiscal and regulatory agencies were administered by the two entities which enabled the nationalist parties to manipulate them to finance their activities. The architects of Dayton failed to ensure that wartime political figures were banned from assuming positions in customs, banking, telecommunications and tax administration posts, which gave them the means to create a shadow state of parallel structures which fed both their party and clandestine activities (Festić and Rausche 2004: 33).

A show of resolution by those in charge of the peace-building mission in Bosnia had been unavoidable to prevent what was the biggest ever UN post-conflict mission from collapsing into disarray and ridicule. Emboldened by the OHR's success in curbing 'hate speech' in the RS, the High Representative's powers were considerably expanded at the end of 1997. The Peace Implementation Council (PIC) which oversaw the OHR endorsed the High Representative's 'intention to use his final authority' regarding implementation of the civilian side of the Dayton agreement, 'in order to facilitate the resolution of difficulties'.[5] These 'Bonn Principles' laid down by PIC enabled the High Representative to impose numerous laws and dismiss hundreds of recalcitrant office holders in the years ahead.

The existence of major Western governments in the late 1990s who were persuaded of the need to build a durable peace in Bosnia silenced calls for a quick disengagement. A renegotiation of the DPA was unlikely but there was a growing determination to interpret its provisions in a way that would enable a stable and unified state to slowly emerge which might one day be able to enjoy a place in a European Union that embraced most of Europe. The main lever which the OHR enjoyed was the huge reconstruction budget; between 1996 and 2003 $15 billion in international funding was spent on the physical and political reconstruction of Bosnia.[6]

Initially, the RS was largely excluded from the aid programme. Instead, armed with new resolve, the OHR sought to weaken the grip of ultra-nationalists on the RS. In the first of a series of attempts to focus reform hopes around a prominent politi-cian, the International Community (IC) rallied around Biljana Plavšić in her attempt to oust her former colleagues in the SDS because of their pervasive corruption. The SDS split in 1997 but in 1998 it was the Serbian Radicals of Nikola Poplasen not moderate forces who were the beneficiaries. Poplasen was eventually removed as the RS President in March 1999 for open defiance of the DPA principles.

A heterogeneous non-SDS government, under Milorad Dodik, governed in the RS from the start of 1998 until January 2001. It was given access to reconstruc-tion funding and enjoyed regular infusions of budgetary support. But Dodik and his ministers only paid lip service to Dayton's goals. The OHR was far more exact-ing in the Federation than in the RS. Nevertheless, local leaders allied to The Bosniak Party of Democratic Action (SDA) benefited from the aid programme through control of local companies hired for specific projects and through the supply of goods and rented premises to international agencies. Acquiring the ability to direct aid according to political criteria strengthened its political influence substantially.[7] But the OHR enjoyed greater headway in bringing it to heel than it did in containing nationalists in Croatian or Serbian areas. There was a greater diversity of activists within the ranks of the SDA than in other nationalist parties.[8] In Sarajevo, remnants of a pre-war civil society survived, offering a platform for moderate political forces both inside and outside the SDA. In Croatian-dominated Herzegovina, a long period of obstructing reconciliation efforts by the Croatian Democratic Union (HDZ) persisted even after the conclusive electoral defeat in Croatia of its parent body at the start of 2000. The new Croatian leadership of

President Stjepan Mesić and Prime Minister Ivan Racić moved quickly to normalise relations with Sarajevo and remove backing for secessionist efforts around the city of Mostar, but the impact was not felt immediately.

Two successive High Representatives, Carlos Westendorp of Spain (1998–2000) and Austria's Wolfgang Petritsch (2000–2) sought to fill the administrative vacuum left in 1995 and strengthen the central state. Westendorp hailed from a country which had been turned into a successful quasi-federal state forty years after a civil war stemming in part from severe ethnic tensions. Petritsch came from the Austrian border city of Klagenfurt and was partly Slovene in background. From 1997 to 1999 he had been Austrian ambassador in Belgrade, for the last year of his appointment serving also as the EU's special envoy in Kosovo. Both of them used their powers to dismiss recalcitrant politicians with no interest in creating functioning state institutions. A common national flag, passport, driving licence and car number plates system, were introduced. In May 2000, the PIC set out an agenda for new institutions required to make a common state sustainable. They included a state treasury, court system, professional civil service, border police and agencies regulating procedures and standards over a wide area of the economy.[9] One central institution already in place, the Constitutional Court, delivered a ruling in July 2000 which had the potential of transferring substantial power from the entities. It ruled that the entity constitutions and other structures, established by the DPA, were unconstitutional as they failed to provide for the equal rights of all ethnic groups in both entities.[10] The court ordered that the constitutions of the Federation and the RS had to be amended accordingly. The RS in particular mounted stubborn resistance, prompting PIC to declare, in May 2000, that 'narrow nationalistic and sectarian political interests have impeded everything from refugee return to economic reform and the functioning of governing institutions. The Council urges the High Representative to use his authority . . . to ensure full and accelerated implementation in all sectors of civilian implementation, including removing obstacles that stand in the way of economic reform'.[11]

Finally, in the last days of his mandate, on 19 April 2002, Petritsch announced new constitutions for the entities. He stated, in the teeth of the evidence, that 'this is not an outright imposition . . . This is clearly a new approach . . . a partnership'.[12] The new constitutions set exact quotas for different ethnic groups to be represented at all levels of government and the public administration. By providing significant group rights in the decision-making processes of the entities, a deliberate attempt was being made to transform their remaining mono-ethnic character and promote a civic identity (Solioz and Petritsch 2003: 358).

No less than 264 laws designed to protect minorities and strengthen democracy were passed during Petritsch's tenure, only for many to be blocked at entity-level. Nevertheless, on leaving, he felt able to say that 'Bosnia has become a state but remains a relatively weak one'.[13] As proof, he could point to the transfer of the collection of customs dues and taxes, as well as institutions like defence, from the entity- to state-level. In the past, such moves might easily have triggered large-scale demonstrations and riots but the OHR was assisted by the brief rise of non-nationalist parties in the Federation.[14] From 2000 to 2002, a heterogeneous coalition known as the Alliance for Change governed in place of the SDA which had done badly in elections held in 2000. Dominated by the Social Democratic Party (SDP) often described as the only significant multi-ethnic party in Bosnia, it clamped down on corruption, established fiscal discipline and started army reforms, including the reduction of troop numbers.[15]

The OHR was committed to transferring wealth and influence power away from politicians, warlords and criminal bodies that had smashed their way to power in wartime. It would have been naïve to expect the latter to acquiesce in the creation of a new Bosnia that would result in their marginalisation and perhaps even detention. The SDA was more malleable than its Serbian counterpart, no doubt because its sins were of a much lesser order by comparison. But it tried (usually not by force but with bureaucratic obstacles) to impede efforts to create multi-ethnic institutions or spearhead refugee returns that were seen as against its electoral interests.[16]

From early 2001, the SDS was back in government in the RS as part of a coalition headed by another perceived reformer Mladen Ivanić. It had never lost power due to its domination of key civil and military bureaucracies as well as the municipalities. It remained determined to block any initiatives to strengthen the state even if they also proved beneficial to the inhabitants of the RS (many of whom lived in desperate poverty). It continued to try and alter permanently the ethnographic profile of many areas by expropriating public lands often illegally, often for the large-scale reconstruction of new housing.[17] The IC may well have grievously erred by failing to make the loans, grants and project funding provided to the RS from 1998 onwards, conditional on implementing the outstanding items on the state-building and indeed broader Dayton agendas.[18]

Return of refugees

Arguably, the most impressive international performance was shown in enabling increasing numbers of refugees to return to their original place of occupancy by the tenth anniversary of their dispossession in the 1992–5 Bosnian war. Ensuring large-scale refugee returns was arguably the key to making the DPA work.[19] Accordingly, the differing agencies charged with the implementation of the 1995 agreement, cooperated more effectively than in other areas to fulfil this goal. The Return and Reconstruction Task-Force, an inter-agency body led by the OHR, had been in existence since 1997.[20] In 1998, the Property Law Implementation Plan (PLIP) was unveiled. It succeeded in harmonising property repossession laws between the entities. Officials closely monitored the response of the local authorities in both entities. Often there was speedy intervention where resistance to the repossession of homes and property emanated from the judiciary, the police or local officials.[21] Petritsch dismissed more than seventy officials – mayors, housing officials and ministers – for blocking refugee returns (Solioz and Petritsch 2003: 361).

While the number of minority returns was 41,000 in both 1998 and 1999, in 2000 the number rose to 67,500, in 2001 to 92,000 and in 2002 reached a peak with 102,000 returns. During 2003, only 44,868 people returned to areas in which there were minorities (the decrease perhaps suggesting a draining of the pool of persons willing to return rather than a worsening of conditions that made it possible).[22] By the end of 2003, the United Nations High Commission for Refugees (UNHCR) reported that almost 1 million refugees, out of an original total of almost 2.2 million, had returned to their home districts. Only some 200,000 still wanted to return to what had once been their locality in Bosnia. In September 2002 the number of applicants who had managed to reclaim their property was 62 per cent of the total. By September 2003 this had gone up to 88 per cent of the total.[23]

There were few other aspects of the DPA where such impressive strides had occurred. But there was far less success in repossessing former business premises and usurped land.[24] It was also unclear how many people had returned only to sell or exchange homes and relocate elsewhere. Parents with young families faced numerous disincentives to return and try to restart their lives: a depressed economy (in a state where unemployment levels were massive outside a few major cities); discrimination and security worries; mono-ethnic institutions; even concerns over pensions and health insurance. The town of Foča in the Drina valley illustrated the scale of the problem. It was located in the east of RS where the level of returns was poor owing to the unbroken dominance of the SDS in its most hardline form. Bosniaks had been 52 per cent of the population before the war. The repression had been particularly severe here but 11 per cent of the pre-1992 population had returned by mid-2002. However, the economic basis for social recovery was almost non-existent. There was 70 per cent unemployment. 'A flea market, a small mine, and a few woodworking firms represented capitalism in Foča'.[25]

The picture was more encouraging in Prijedor, in north-west Bosnia. The arrest and conviction of high-profile war criminals in the late 1990s had created a sense of 'psychological security' for intending returnees, 20,000 of whom had returned by 2003.[26] A strong and highly visible Bosniak presence in the local economy, politics and society was established in an area which had witnessed systematic efforts to uproot and destroy a Muslim presence in 1992. However, only 3 Bosniaks were employed in the 150-member municipal administration.[27] Continued hardline social structures prompted returnees to establish a parallel existence separate from their Serb neighbours. Community leaders saw themselves as advocates on behalf of opposing interests. Nevertheless, the fertility of land and its proximity to Croatia meant that a chance of economic revival existed that might enable Prijedor slowly to put wartime enmities behind it.

The return of refugees reverses the ethnic homogeneity that was a primary nationalist war aim. The most well-organised attempts to discourage Bosniaks to return home occurred in May 2001. Rioters in Trebinje and in Banja Luka, the RS capital, prevented the laying of foundation stones for the rebuilding of two historic mosques razed by Serbs during the war.[28] Senior RS officials were removed by the OHR and the rededication of the mosques went ahead. But the following September, the Organization for Security and Co-operation in Europe (OSCE) chief of mission stated that the RS was 'devoting totally inadequate resources to support returns'. Indeed, obstruction of the return process was not being confronted in much of the RS, according to one think-tank writing in 2002, because it was felt to be too difficult.[29]

Police debacle

The weakness of the International Police Task Force (IPTF) until well into the returns process, proved to be a major impediment. It had a mandate merely to reform the existing police force rather than to create a new one, 'a tragic mistake' in the view of Richard Holbrooke.[30] This was the main responsibility entrusted to the United Nations and it was handled badly until the US official, Jacques Klein, took over in 2000. Klein had been Deputy High Commissioner in Bosnia since 1997 so this was a very senior level appointment. He had an uphill task. Many IPTF officials sent to Bosnia to teach police forces proper standards of policing came from countries with deplorable human rights records. They were poorly trained and had indeed paid bribes to gain what was seen as a lucrative posting to Bosnia.[31] 'Our biggest problem has been patrolling the IPTF', declared one UN field official in the Mostar area in 2001. He pointed out that a very senior IPTF official had been removed in 1999 for alleged corrupt practices; indeed, the same official was suspected of having passed on information to men accused of appalling crimes against local Bosniaks in Stolac, a Herzegovinan town firmly controlled by Croatian extremists long after 1995.[32]

In 2001, Human Rights Watch (HRW) claimed that eighteen IPTF monitors had 'engaged in illegal activities, either as customers of trafficked women or as outright purchasers of trafficked women and their passports'.[33] UN complicity in the burgeoning sex trade blighted the efforts of Jacque Klein, the IPTF's last head of mission (before it was replaced by the European Union in 2003) to strengthen its international performance in a critical area. In 2001, Steve Smith, a US police officer who became the IPTF's commander in Stolac, described some of his American colleagues in the IPTF in unflattering terms: 'They're making $85,000 in a place where everyone else is making $5,000 and they're chasing whores'. The Ukrainian contingent in Stolac made it abundantly clear that they had come to Bosnia to make money, not reform the local police, Smith said. He said that their compound was packed with cars they were reselling for a profit back home.[34] Recriminations erupted in 2002 when Kathryn Bolkovac, a UN police officer, was sacked for exposing the sexual abuse of women and children in Bosnia by her colleagues.[35] The high salaries IPTF personnel were paid (along with the immunity from prosecution that they enjoyed) encouraged low standards. Richard Holbrooke, the architect of the DPA, described the police mission as its weakest component.[36] Madeleine Rees, the UN High Commissioner for Human Rights in Bosnia described the involvement of UN personnel and international aid workers with prostitution rings in the Balkans as 'the biggest cover-up I have ever seen', adding that she believed 30 per cent of those visiting Bosnia's brothels were UN personnel, peace-keepers or aid workers.[37]

The price of neglecting the economy

Given inadequate international training in proper policing, it is not surprising that in many parts of Bosnia, the behaviour of the police reflected that of local political bosses. In both the RS and the Federation, politicians, from Prime Ministers downwards, looted their own budgets by offering their cronies and favoured firms exemptions from customs duties. The cost amounted to hundreds of millions of euros in lost revenue.[38] Customs was losing $200 million a year through fraud in 2002.[39] Illegal logging was also despoiling much of rural Bosnia and undermining the chances of a real economic recovery.[40]

Well into the Dayton era, little thought was given to the need for comprehensive economic reform that would replace communist-era forms of accountancy and try to counter the black economy that had thrived as a result of the war and high-level corruption. Instead, the channelling of massive amounts of aid through the complicated political structures imposed by the DPA proved itself to be a massive incentive for further corruption. Constitutionally, Dayton may have provided for a single economic space, but in reality economic power resides at entity-level (and at the cantons in the Federation and to a large extent in the municipalities in the RS where the SDS retained tight control). To make matters worse, a deeply inappropriate form of privatisation was imposed from 1998 onwards.[41] Privatisation legislation was hastily drawn up by USAID, the US aid agency, strongly influenced by the US treasury. Under a firmly neo-liberal economic agenda, it was assumed that privatisation would stimulate the economy and create accelerating social benefits. The approach of US advisers with little direct knowledge of Bosnia made this a virtual impossibility irrespective of what merits a neo-liberal agenda might have had. The USAID plan allowed for no less than twelve privatisation agencies, one for the RS, one for the Federation and another for each of its cantons.[42] Besides the opportunities for corruption, this unwieldy approach offered politicians the chance to confirm the effects of ethnic cleansing by means of ethnically exclusive privatisations. The voucher system, already discredited from the experience of the Czech Republic, was the method of privatisation chosen. The state liquidated its assets and paid debts that it owed citizens through distributing vouchers. The two entities were allowed to distribute disproportionate numbers of vouchers to war veterans, which discriminated against citizens who had fled or been forcibly removed from their homes in wartime. In both entities almost half the vouchers (by value) went to war veterans, many of whom were easily manipulated by nationalist organisations.[43]

Local economies remained under mono-ethnic control as privatisation gathered pace. The need to build up state competence was overlooked in an almost religious belief that deregulation would promote economic and political 'normalisation'. Instead, local nationalist elites quickly gained control of socially owned assets. Jobs and other economic goods were distributed by powerful magnates to favoured supporters, enhancing patron–client relations. The informal economy started to thrive as the socially owned one declined in the face of accelerating deindustrialisation. This enabled ethno-political leaders to strengthen their political hold over many Bosnians even as inter-ethnic tensions slowly began to recede (Pugh 2004: 55).

The worst effect of a clumsy privatisation, in which US ideologues matched the blindness of Soviet commissars when they had attempted to remake the political economy of the region two generations earlier, were most fully on display in the RS. Here, the SDS and the Serbian Radical Party (SRS) reinforced their control of the local economy by asset stripping small- and medium-sized state companies. These were sold off to cronies at absurdly low prices, minimising the proceeds from privatisation that could have cushioned job losses. The destruction of viable firms enhanced the importance of criminal structures in the economy, impeding refugee return and a transfer of power to moderate political forces. In 2002 67–68 per cent of the populace in the RS had insufficient income to acquire basic foodstuffs (Pugh 2004: 57). Meanwhile, a parasitic leadership grew even richer than it had been in wartime and acquired private title to much of the formerly socially owned economy. But its continued manipulation of nationalism, its ability to dispense patronage and the ease with which it could transfer blame for economic decline to international officials most of whom were completely out of their depth, meant that the looting of the economy resulted in no political backlash against the masters of the RS political economy. Soon it was clear in Bosnia as a whole, how misconceived the rush to privatisation had been. By mid-2001 industrial output had reached only one-third of its pre-war level. The Bosnian economy showed little sign of being able to recover and grow without further injections of external aid.[44] Increasingly, those Bosnians with the skills and outlook that made them capable of constructing a transparent economy, were voting with their feet by moving abroad.

But there were bright notes in a gloomy economic picture. The financial sector was effectively reformed due to a number of international agencies closing ranks to improve banking and regulatory practices.[45] Bosnia acquired some of the best private banks in the region under a strong state-level Central Bank. The communist-era payments bureaux (a huge drag on economic development) were abolished faster in Bosnia than in any other post-communist state (Solioz and Petritsch 2003: 363). But, approaching the tenth anniversary of the DPA, there was still an awful long way to go to build a national economy from effectively three economies in one state reflecting differing ethnic interests.

Judicial vacuum

Foreign investors could only be drawn to Bosnia, and local entrepreneurs encouraged to risk their capital in new transparent businesses, if clear progress was evident in establishing the rule of law. As with economic reform, the initial approach left a lot to be desired. From 1996, promoting the rule of law had been a top spending priority for the UN administration. No less than 200 foreign legal experts were assigned to improve the performance of Bosnia's 1,200 judges and prosecutors. But international agencies failed to devise a credible reform strategy that would seize the initiative from well-connected criminal networks with a proven ability to intimidate or bribe judges.[46] Their approach was very mediocre. By 1998, the judiciary was being swamped with invitations to seminars, workshops and training programmes at home and abroad, with very little effort being devoted to producing a strategy for comprehensive legal reform. Moreover, as with other branches of the international reconstruction and recovery effort, the performance of the legal reformers was not evaluated. They were accountable to increasingly disengaged bodies like the United Nations Security Council (UNSC), or the distant boards of directors or national government bureaucracies that were growing bored with Bosnia before the 1990s had ended.[47]

There was one part of Bosnia where the justice system appeared to have been transformed by 2003. This was the strategically placed district of Brcko in northeast Bosnia. It acted as a narrow land bridge linking the eastern and western parts of the RS. RS control over it was vital in order to accomplish the nationalist goal of unification with Serbia proper. Too contentious to settle at Dayton, it was placed under an international administration, both separate from, and more powerful than, the OHR. The Brcko Arbitration award of 1999 made it a neutral and demilitarised district whose elected government was overseen by an internationally appointed supervisor. In the years to come, a district previously seen as one of the likeliest flashpoints for renewed conflict in Bosnia acquired a positive reputation. Under a special regime, the reform process was more focussed and professionally executed than elsewhere in Bosnia. A comprehensive judicial and legal reform was carried out that created an efficient court structure and independent judiciary.[48] This proved to be a model for the rest of Bosnia and, in May 2002, Petritsch took the powers of appointment of judges and prosecutors away from elected politicians and awarded them to a council made up of local and international experts in order to ensure judicial independence.[49] Fiscal probity and a business friendly environment attracted a lot of foreign investment; Brcko easily outperformed both entities, but the unemployment level was still larger than the pool of permanently employed.[50]

Replicating the success of Brcko would involve a costly international effort, but the international experiment in Bosnia easily dwarfed any other peace-building initiative sponsored by the United Nations since 1945. Far more could have been done with the resources available to transform a wartorn society, rebuild its institutions and encourage a pattern of politics based on ethnic coexistence. Indeed, David Harland, a top UN official in Bosnia in the mid-1990s (later responsible for drawing up the UN's 1999 report on the Srebrenica massacre) wrote that 'Bosnia has taught much to all of us about how not to implement a peace agreement'.[51]

Bureaucratic failings

While the calibre of High Representatives has been consistently high, the same could not be said of the staff the holder of the post relied on to implement policy. OHR staff were seconded from home ministries or were specifically contracted persons. Secondees very often proved to be very junior or else were on the verge of retirement. The International Crisis Group (ICG) had no hesitation in writing that 'The rapid turnover of seconded staff limits expertise, dissipates momentum, and undermines institutional loyalty and memory. It means that the wheel needs regularly to be re-invented'.[52] As late as 2004, when many lessons had supposedly been learned about how to improve the quality of international engagement in the

Balkans, Gerald Knaus was still able to write: 'Across the region, most so-called institution-building and democratisation efforts are *ad hoc*, badly designed and ineffective. In the protectorates, fundamental strategy in most areas changes every two years (sometimes sooner) as key people in the international missions change. What is lacking is continuity'.[53] In the late 1990s, even the OHR proved deaf to proposals for strengthening its effectiveness. The main event in its calendar was a regular 'principals meetings chaired by the OHR and attended by the major organizations involved in the Bosnian peace effort: the OSCE, the UN, the UNHCR, the EU, aid donors, and international financial organizations'. The agenda was largely dictated by events and lacked strategic focus. 'Meetings would lurch from crisis to crisis, when there was no crisis, meetings were frequently cancelled'.[54] There was little enthusiasm for a 1997 suggestion that at principals meetings organisations should set their top five priorities for the next year.[55] The main organisational actors were funded and organised differently, had specific agendas and different degrees of openness. Communications between some agencies was so poor that occasionally there was no awareness that they were duplicating their own activities. Perhaps the most notorious example of overlap concerned the rivalry between two agencies mandated to clear Bosnia of mines. They were funded by two prominent international donors with their own policy agendas and they equipped themselves with lavish offices and fleets of vehicles while managing to clear very few mines.[56] Thus, a task vital for the normalisation of society, fell victim to bureaucratic infighting and empire-building.

OHR staff were predominantly international, Bosnian staff being mainly confined to support positions. (Specialist organisations such as the World Bank and the IMF, by contrast largely employed Bosnians.) For many years, the OHR was not the only international body which had a very casual approach to the recruitment of local staff. In some of the main cities, those working for internationals comprised a significant proportion of the employed population. In many instances, individuals were recruited through recommendations and no open competition exists for posts. The use of informal criteria for filling posts means that families could have 3–4 people working for the same international organisation. Inevitably, vulnerable groups like returnees from a minority background stood even less chance of gaining employment if international bodies failed to set a good example in the way that they recruit local staff.[57]

Significant duplication of field staff could occur between OHR, OSCE and the UN agencies. If there were dedicated people on the ground who understood the problems, cooperation was not a problem. There was a constant struggle to ensure coordination between agencies implementing peace in Bosnia (the United Nations, the OSCE, NATO, the European Union), each of whom had to report back to separate headquarters. Naturally, inter-agency rivalries often provided opportunities for opponents of peace-building efforts to confuse and divide international actors. The commitment of international staff to advance the Dayton agenda was often eclipsed by the determination of local political actors to sabotage their efforts. Their boldness increased after 1995 as they saw how mixed in terms of motivation and expertise were the international officials sent to implement the DPA's ambitious agenda. Many officials working for the United Nations were primarily in Bosnia to acquire brief experience in the field which would enable them to advance their careers in desk-based jobs away from conflict zones. The OSCE was in turn hampered by the need to accept sometimes unsuitable officials nominated by their national governments. Often, the coordination required between OSCE missions in Bosnia, Serbia and Croatia to promote refugee returns was conspicuous by its absence.[58]

In order to emphasise Bosnian ownership of the peace and recovery process, a lot of investment was directed towards the civil society sector. By 2002 a Civic Forum had been established by the OHR to allow voices drowned out by hierarchically organised parties to be heard. In wartime conditions local NGOs had mainly been concerned with humanitarian tasks and this was slow to change. After the war, many international NGOs engaged in reconstruction work often employed locals in secondary or menial positions. Despite their emancipatory goals, international NGOs were reluctant to put aside deeply competitive instincts and cooperate in order to maximise their effectiveness in Bosnia. The duplication, turf wars and semi-colonial attitudes towards locals noticeable in the behaviour of the international agencies was thus reflected in their NGO counterparts, but at least there was far greater variation and some NGOs offered excellent examples of good practice in their behaviour which punctured Bosnian cynicism (Sampson 2002).

By the end of the 1990s, the OHR was giving a lot of attention to the promotion of community initiatives that would transcend normal ethno-political divisions. Young people were seen as a vital target group. But the way community development was handled by international officials caused serious disillusionment. Many were seen as being in Bosnia to build their CVs. They spent little time in the field and made poor decisions based on a profound lack of knowledge of local conditions. Seminars built around external models that were often not applicable to Bosnia were a favourite way of imparting information and knowledge. This was usually seen as solely a one-way process which waived the need for the foreign experts to familiarise themselves with local conditions, history and language (Meyer 2001: 43). Decisions were made at OSCE headquarters in Sarajevo to focus on specific issues. Seminars and workshops might focus intensively on youth issues, to be followed by gender, or working with Roma. NGOs were often swamped with requests to attend a concentrated series of events which seemed to have no long-term purpose.[59] After 1999, the OSCE strongly promoted the idea of youth parliaments in different parts of Bosnia, drawn from youth branches of all political parties, NGOs and non-affiliated youth. They were meant to draw people into the political process who, hopefully, would then become familiar with a multi-ethnic approach to public affairs. However, the momentum was lost due to the frequent turnover of officials and the OSCE itself lost interest. Local youth activists who had striven to motivate disillusioned young people felt deep frustrations (Meyer 2001: 24). The short-term approach of OSCE officials who were transitory actors in Bosnia undermined long-term grassroots efforts to foster a local youth sector.

The poorly focussed international approach made it difficult for local NGOs to become self sustaining. Even in Prijedor, where youth initiatives were able to bridge the ethnic divide, international officials were seen as counter productive, arriving for a six-month contract and already working on their exit strategy: 'Just when one leaves, the next comes and completely changes the approach of his predecessor. Over the course of two years, we could start four new projects and finish none of them with this kind of turnover' (Meyer 2001: 45). Lacking a sense of empathy with the international administration, most NGOs in Banja Luka remained silent in the face of the 2001 attack on the dedication ceremony for the Ferhadija mosque, to the chagrin of international officials.[60] With civic-minded young people failing to obtain the backing that would enable them to transform conditions in Bosnia, it is not surprising that there was a huge exodus; 92,000 young people emigrated between January 1996 and March 2001.[61]

The Ashdown effect

Paddy Ashdown, the High Representative from May 2002 onwards, strove to improve the reputation of the international mission in Bosnia. A former professional soldier who had campaigned for a more decisive international response to the Bosnian war as the leader of the British Liberal Party, he was determined to move ahead more speedily with the state-building agenda inherited from his predecessor. His empathy with the country which he had visited many times before 2002 and his commitment to making radical changes that empowered ordinary citizens, helped his standing with Bosnians. An opinion poll published a year after his arrival showed that in the Federation 79 per cent supported the OHR and 16 per cent opposed it whereas in the RS, there were 42 per cent in support and 40 per cent in opposition.[62]

Ashdown faced two immediate challenges. One was the scaling down of the size of the international mission, particularly the SFOR. The withdrawal of US forces under President George W. Bush intensified. Chris Patten, the EU commissioner for External Relations had declared in December 2000, 'Europe will miss Bill Clinton. He has been a good friend to this continent. From Kosovo to Belfast millions of people have cause to be thankful for the contribution he has made' (Daalder 2001: 563). But the new Republican administration was focussed on the Americas and Asia in its first months in office. Long sceptical about being involved in the Balkans, the Department of Defence was occupied by a powerful figure, Donald Rumsfeld who echoed these sentiments. Confusion about US intentions towards the Balkans may have encouraged the internal unrest in Macedonia which flared up soon after Bush's inauguration and to which Washington was slow to respond. US Secretary of State Colin Powell ended speculation about the intentions of the United States when he declared on 11 April 2001 that the United States remains politically and militarily committed to an active role in the Balkans.[63]

Exactly five months later the devastating terrorist attacks launched by the Islamic terrorist group Al-Qa'eda in New York and Washington opened up a completely new foreign policy agenda for the United States into which it was hard to see how the Balkans fitted. The war on terrorism and NATO-led military intervention in Afghanistan, followed by preparations for a US-led invasion of Iraq, seemed to relegate Bosnia to the sidelines. The absence of conspicuous progress increased the pressure to cut budgets and programmes.[64] Al-Qa'eda operatives from the Middle East had been active in Bosnia during the mid-1990s and the violence of their onslaught against US targets may well have partly sprung from the belief that the West had shown its deep-seated hostility to Muslims by its inaction during the Bosnian war. The roots of Islamic fundamentalism in the Balkans were not, however, very deep. The presence of Mujahedin fighters who had failed to make a positive impact locally, was ended by 1998.[65] Most Muslims in the region tended to be more pro-American than their Orthodox neighbours and Bin Laden's operatives had found Bosnia and Kosovo poor recruiting grounds despite the suffering Muslims had encountered at the hands of nationalists who proclaimed their Orthodox beliefs (Dassù and Whyte 2001–2: 133). Following the gross policy failures that occurred in the wake of the 2003 occupation of Iraq, the United States even saw the need to strengthen its profile in the Balkans. Reviving efforts to capture the elusive war crimes suspect Radovan Karadžić was at least one way of partly redeeming America's tattered image in the eyes of moderate Muslims across the world.

So the fallout from the 9/11 attacks did not jeopardise the Bosnia mission and Ashdown was even able to convince multilateralists among US policy-makers of its continuing relevance. But his policy of strengthening central institutions in preparation for an eventual international pull out appeared to suffer a major setback due to the results of the elections in both of the entities, held on 5 October 2002. In the Federation, the Alliance for Change coalition succumbed to defeat. The SDP, its lynchpin, was overtaken by the SDA, which had lost office because of its poor governing record. However, the result was a verdict on the economic record of the SDP and the confrontational style of its leader, Zlatko Lagumdzija rather than an endorsement for the SDA.[66] He had decided to cave in to American pressure and force through the extradition of six suspected Arab terrorists to the United States (even though no evidence of wrongdoing was provided). This was despite the Federation's Supreme Court ruling that they should be released and brought much criticism from Madeleine Rees, the head of the Sarajevo office of the UN Commission for Human Rights.[67] The turnout was down nearly 10 to 54.6 per cent and the SDA had not fought on a radical platform. Meanwhile, in the RS, parties ranged against the SDS did well with Milorad Dodik's Alliance of Independent Social Democrats (SNSD) winning 30 per cent of the vote. In January 2003, a multi-ethnic RS government (including the SDS) was sworn in that included 8 Serbs, 5 Bosniaks and 3 Croats. The 2002 elections were the first postwar Bosnian elections held without international supervision. In May of that year the Council of Europe had decided to accept Bosnia as a full member because it seemed to fulfil the necessary criteria. At the start of the year, the leaders of the eight largest parties had met to discuss policy issues – the first such gathering in a decade without the participation of foreigners.[68]

Encouraged by these steps towards normalisation Ashdown stated that the newly ascendant nationalist parties were led by people with whom he felt he could do business.[69] The HDZ appeared a case in point. The Croatian nationalists had held their ground in Herzegovina and western Bosnia against a moderate challenge. But in February 2003, their hopes of consolidating their power in the city of Mostar were dashed when the OHR imposed a permanent status for the city that made it one undivided municipality. Back in March 2001 Ante Jelavić, the Croat president in the triparitite Bosnian presidency, had been removed after he had tried to turn Herzegovina into a third entity by getting HDZ parliamentarians to set up a constituent assembly. Widespread violence occurred when SFOR forces attempted to seize the headquarters of a leading bank which controlled companies in key sectors of the local economy that were the HDZ power base.[70] It took 5,000 troops and 400 armoured vehicles to accomplish this goal. The clandestine political economy that was the basis of Croatian separatism was brought under increasing control and in early 2004 Jelavić and key economic aides were charged with corruption and fraud. Western forces disrupted the financing of the nationalist para state that continued to undermine the Federation (Festić and Rausche 2004: 30–2).

Ashdown was a highly visible High Representative who appeared relaxed in the company of ordinary Bosnians. The policy of trying to secure change by working through a specific party or individual politicians was put aside and he emphasised the idea of a partnership with the Bosnian people.[71] A gradual transfer of responsibilities to elected institutions was planned but the pace of this power shift depended on the readiness of politicians to implement reform designed to make Bosnia a viable state. Ashdown hoped to get the nationalists to carry out these reforms which, by 2004, the OHR identified as having four main components: entrenching the rule of law; reforming the economy; strengthening the capacity of Bosnia's governing institutions, especially at the State level and 'embedding defence and intelligence sector reforms so as to facilitate…[Bosnian] integration into Euro-Atlantic structures'.[72] However, he knew Bosnia well enough to be aware that the success of such an approach would severely diminish the powers of patronage and illicit sources of wealth enjoyed by nationalist forces. Obstructionism did indeed intensify, requiring Ashdown to use the so-called Bonn powers and sack recalcitrant officials, impose laws and make administrative edicts. By July 2003 he was imposing 11 decisions or decrees every month, compared with an average of 4 in 1999.[73]

No senior international official with responsibilities in the Balkans worked as closely with the ICTY as Ashdown did. The promise was wrung from the RS government to join the search for the remaining major suspects. The first joint NATO–RS operation in search of Karadžić and his helpers took place in January 2004.[74]

In early 2004, laws were passed creating a single intelligence agency for the whole of Bosnia and providing it with a new defence structure based on civilian, state-level command and control, and a common defence ministry.[75] Powerful vested interests in the RS would need to be overcome before such proposals could become reality. But they were conditional on Bosnia joining the Partnership for Peace (PfP), a step required before membership of NATO became feasible. NATO was due to end its peace mission (whose size had fallen to 25,000) by the end of 2004. It was to be replaced by a 7,000-strong EU force known as Althea.[76] By early 2003, 85 per cent of SFOR was already composed of troops from EU states.[77] But much remained to be done: the new justice and security ministries remained 'empty shells, without staff or budgets of their own'.[78] Other ministries appeared in danger of breaking down into their nationalist components.

Ashdown's patience with the nationalists, at least in the RS, snapped on 30 June 2004 just after the NATO summit in Istanbul decided to withhold PfP status from Bosnia. He removed sixty people from public and party positions – all members of the SDS with several being its top leaders. Eleven were removed indefinitely, the rest being allowed to return to public life upon the detention of Karadžić. He said this decision stemmed from the continued willingness of 'a small band of corrupt politicians and obstructionists' to help Radovan Karadžić and other indictees to evade justice.[79]

Whither Bosnia?

Bosnia had considerably advanced beyond its 1995 position when the DPA gave nationalist leaderships strong incentives to refine their separatist agendas and ignore or weaken a central state which was more like a virtual state. The powers of the central state had been greatly augmented. Dayton had been rebuilt from within while retaining the outer shell of both entities. Croatian separatism had been tamed and the RS was being forced to give up a separate military and face severe sanctions if it did not cooperate in building a common Bosnian state. Some wanted to go much further by setting up a single state structure through a constitutional convention.[80] But there was no international consensus to completely rewrite Dayton. Even agreement to merge the OHR with the OSCE in Bosnia and save money and increase coordination proved impossible to secure. Neither was there much enthusiasm in Bosnia for a 2004 proposal emanating from a leading think-tank with Balkan concerns, the European Stability Institute (ESI) for the abolition of the country's two entities and the creation of a federal state similar to the Swiss model.[81]

Grudging acquiescence or covert resistance were the responses of nationalists, still very much in the political ascendancy, to an activist High Representative. Major sustainers of a powerful central state were in the doldrums, the multi-ethnic SDP still licking its wounds after its 2002 electoral defeat, and the Party of Bosnia–Herzegovina (SBiH) too bound up with its gifted but mercurial leader, Haris Silajdžić. A groundswell of popular support for a relaunched Bosnia with common institutions almost certainly depended on economic reforms benefiting the population. But privatisation had been completely mishandled in the late 1990s and it was difficult to undo the damage. Unemployment remained at 40 per cent (with just over half that figure working in the shadow economy, according to the IMF) (Pugh 2004: 57). Privatisation had not been linked to an anti-poverty or job creation strategy, nor was Ashdown's energetic attempt to move against the architects of wartime massacres and the godfathers of post-1995 corruption. It is difficult to see how he can mobilise strong popular backing for challenging illicit power structures while being burdened by this record of economic failure. Material improvements resulting from greater transparency in the financial realm are unlikely to be felt overnight. Muddle and inconsistency no longer summed up the OHR's approach in the Ashdown era but it was hard to see how a viable Bosnia could stand on its own feet if the international supervisory presence was effectively ended. Ashdown[82] himself struck a note of caution in February 2004:

> the speed of Bosnia–Herzegovina's progress . . . towards a reconfigured international presence that can relinquish its powers . . . will be determined not by rigid timelines, but by an ongoing assessment of the situation on the ground. Are the habits of stalemate and obstruction being replaced by a dynamic of compromise and reform? Is peace enduring? Has the rule of law been made secure? Is the state functional and viable? Is Bosnia–Herzegovina on track for European integration? Only when we are satisfied that sufficient progress has been made in these respects will we be able to declare our mission fulfilled.
>
> ('OHR Mission Implementation Plan 2004', p. 3)

Bosnia no longer faces a threat from a Croatia concentrating on joining the European Union and Serbian attitudes towards the RS have been ambivalent since the Milošević era. But nothing on the scale of the transformation of postwar Germany, Japan or Korea appears to have occurred there that would enable it to try and heal the wounds of the early 1990s. A flawed peace that allowed all but a few of the architects of ethnic cleansing to retain the levers of power and indeed expand their influence is the primary cause of the Bosnian malaise. Ashdown would be gone by Christmas 2005 while SFOR prepared to pull out in 2004 without having achieved two of its primary goals – completing the reform of Bosnia's armed forces and detaining the top war crimes suspects. In the event of a rapid international pull-out it is not unthinkable that efforts would be made to restore the mono-ethnic character of districts where large-scale refugee returns have occurred. By the middle of the first decade of the new century, it is likely to become apparent if Bosnia has acquired functioning state-level structures that will enable it to be drawn firmly into the mainstream of European affairs. If a decade of externally led state building, reveals that it is still a deeply fractured polity, then it is likely Bosnia will remain under international supervision. It is the European Union which has assumed control over both the civil and military aspects of the international mission to create a state fit for both EU and NATO membership. Whether a permanent political settlement emerges very much depends on the quality of the EU engagement with Bosnia.

7 Still a danger-point
Kosovo under international rule

Learning from Bosnia

The UN Secretary-General Kofi Annan had painful memories of the UN's role in Bosnia before and after 1995. His recommendations for the international presence in Kosovo sought to avoid elementary mistakes which blighted the international record in Bosnia. A clear chain of command was established to ensure that the civilian and military tasks of the international mission were effectively integrated. Moreover, unlike in Bosnia, the international mission was to act as the government with full executive, legislative and judicial powers.[1]

The UN Interim Administrative Mission in Kosovo (UNMIK), in fact, enjoyed more extensive authority than any previous mission in the history of the United Nations. It derived its legitimacy from Resolution 1244 which the UN Security Council (UNSC) passed on 10 June 1999. This was a compromise between the Western and Chinese and Russian positions. It endorsed the creation of an interim administration for Kosovo. UNMIK was tasked with launching a political process designed to determine Kosovo's future status. Substantial autonomy and self-government were promised, but the territory was still subject to the sovereignty of the Federal Republic of Yugoslavia (FRY). Indeed, Milošević had wrung an important concession from his NATO foes by insisting that his state would only agree to the United Nations replacing the Serbian administration not the Organization for Security and Co-operation in Europe (OSCE) or NATO. The International Crisis Group[2] (ICG) has written:

> Having had considerable experience with the United Nations in Bosnia, Milošević calculated that many of its characteristic traits – a political and bureaucratic culture which fosters caution and delay, chronic shortages of funds, and divisions among its leading members – would make it more difficult to overcome the climate of instability and turmoil on which Milošević has always relied to advance his own objectives.
>
> (*Kosovo Report Card*, p. 27)

Fateful early decisions

Under Resolution 1244, a Special Representative of the Secretary-General (SRSG) was to supervise the international civilian presence. The SRSG would also coordinate UNMIK's activities with the military force under the overall command of NATO, known as the Kosovo Force (KFOR). Its mandate was to deter fresh violence, maintain and, where necessary, enforce the cease-fire, demilitarise the Kosovo Liberation Army (UÇK) and work to establish a secure environment in Kosovo (*The Kosovo Report* 2000: 101). To facilitate peacekeeping, KFOR divided Kosovo into five zones, each under the control of a different NATO member. The north, in the region of Mitrovica was placed under the control of France which contributed 7,000 troops. The south, in the region of Prizren was to be Germany's responsibility (8,000). The region of Pec/Peja in the west was placed under control of Italy (6,000). The eastern area around Gjilan was to be the responsibility of the United States (6,000). Finally, the central area around Priština was patrolled by British forces (8,000) (*The Kosovo Report* 2000: 103). (A Russian peace-keeping contingent was distributed among three of these zones, finally leaving Kosovo in July 2003.)

KFOR was initially slow to make its presence felt. It had a firmer mandate than its military counterpart in the post-1995 Bosnia but was mainly concerned with overseeing the peaceful withdrawal of Serbian forces. Probably the most critical and early weakness was its failure to resolutely oppose revenge killings. Given the Bosnian experience, KFOR should have been prepared for this type of violence. There was a strong case for KFOR being mandated by the United Nations to use force against those who were aggressively threatening other people's lives. But in the summer of 1999, KFOR's presence only gradually made itself felt and, according to one source, its own security was its chief concern (*The Kosovo Report* 2000: 105).

Initially, KFOR was badly overstretched. With UNMIK even slower to get off the ground, the task of not only maintaining law and order, but also of repairing local infrastructure and even administering entire districts, fell to soldiers. Within three weeks, half-a-million Albanians had flooded back from camps in neighbouring countries.[3] The UÇK tried to fill the vacuum left by the departure of Serbian forces by setting up a 'provisional government' under its leader Hashim Thaçi. The UÇK was a very loosely run movement and high-handed actions carried out in its name by greedy or ruthless local figures backfired against it in future elections. The UN and NATO officials often responded ineptly to the initial post-conflict challenges confronting them, having underestimated the flow of returnees. Lacking an adequate intelligence-gathering capacity made it difficult for KFOR to halt the wave of crime that blew up in the second half of 1999, often linked to mafia elements based in Albania.

General Klaus Reinhardt, the German officer who was KFOR's first commander, acquired a good reputation for efficiency. But he had to negotiate with the defence ministries of the major governments involved in order to approve changes. Frequently, units reported for duty less than their total strength and sometimes NATO member states withdrew their contingents without any attempt at coordination (*The Kosovo Report* 2000: 106). The role of the French forces in the northern sector of Mitrovica became a real headache. A major mistake was the failure of the French to insist on an undivided city. Based on the past peace-keeping experience, especially in Bosnia, the strategy adopted was to separate Serbs and Albanians in the belief that this was the best way to maintain security (*The Kosovo Report* 2000: 109). Albanians were soon accusing the French of being biased in favour of the Serbs who were concentrated in the city's northern side. It took a long time before the KFOR commander secured an agreement that forces other than the French could be deployed in Mitrovica. In April 2002, when French KFOR troops stood aside, as the Serbian rioters attacked mainly the Polish UN police with grenades and small arms, wounding twenty-six and obstructed other police (mainly American) from coming to their colleagues' aid. This lack of coordination between international peace-keepers was revealed to be a glaring problem in this flashpoint area.[4]

KFOR's biggest success was to press ahead with the demilitarisation of the UÇK. As early as 21 June 1999, both signed an undertaking to this effect. Then approximately 20,000 strong, the UÇK was to be transformed into a civilian agency, the Kosovo Protection Corps (KPC) charged with providing emergency response and reconstruction services. The KPC was to have 3,000 members; only 200 would be authorised to carry weapons (*The Kosovo Report* 2000: 118). Many Kosovans hoped that the KPC would be the nucleus for a new army, but KFOR failed to build an effective relationship with it (as shown by the rioting of March 2004). But at least priority was being given to the need to prepare former insurgents for a role in a peace-time society.[5] Demilitarisation of the UÇK was officially completed on 20 September 1999, but future violence would be traced to ex-UÇK figures reluctant to lay down their weapons.[6] Moreover, the authorities were slow to make a move against underground-armed groups, while some of them often viewed it as the continuation of the UÇK in another guise.[7]

An initial spate of murders caused observers to fear that Kosovo would be overwhelmed by a wave of lawlessness. There were over 400 in the second half of 1999, with one-third of the victims Serb, one-third Albanian, and the rest mainly Roma (Naegele 2002). These attacks fuelled the exodus of Serbs, 180,000 of them had left Kosovo by the end of August 1999 and another 55,000 people, mainly Roma also departed. The number of political murders and attacks on civilians came down in 2000, murders being less than one-third of the figure for the previous year 1999 and arson attacks decreased by three-quarters (*The Kosovo Report* 2000: 107). But on leaving Kosovo in June 2000, after completing a one-year assignment there, the UN High Commission for Refugees (UNHCR) chief Dennis McNamara told the press: 'There was from the start an environment of tolerance for intolerance and revenge. There was no real effort or interest in trying to stop it'.[8]

The UN mission salvaged prestige from its ability to provide humanitarian relief over the winter of 1999–2000. The UNHCR won praise for providing adequate food, shelter and medical provision for over one million returning Albanians.[9] An UNMIK survey had found 120,000 houses damaged or destroyed by war, 250 schools in need of repair, the health care and banking systems in a state of collapse, roads in ruins, bridges destroyed; there was neither electricity nor mail service and the telephone lines were all down (*The Kosovo Report* 2000: 120). However, the funding and coordinating of the reconstruction effort (itself a more complicated task) was less successful. The European Union (EU) had a major role here, with its members providing about 70 per cent of all reconstruction assistance. But shortfalls in money and staff significantly delayed repairs to homes and roads.[10]

Funds pledged by donors totalled 2.6 billion DM, but known commitments were under half of this at 1.2 billion DM. The lengthy approval process needed to disburse EU funds inhibited the distribution of urgently needed assistance. Different committees, one in Brussels, another in Priština, administered the funds, which created unnecessary duplication for every single decision. Eighty different EU regulations had to be observed and the committees did not meet more than once a month (*The Kosovo Report* 2000: 124).

The sense of self-reliance shared in particular by many rural Kosovans was an important factor in preventing social collapse. Experience of coping in the shadow of a hostile political regime, had given many practical survival skills which they could put to effective use. Timothy Garton-Ash wrote: 'Fortunately Kosovan society is an unusual one: still firmly based on the extended family, and to some extent on the clans, with a strong code of mutual support and a capacity for improvisation that you no longer see in more developed societies like ours'.[11] But this reservoir of traditionalism in a mainly peasant culture would be more of a handicap when it came to building a new political life.

The reconstruction effort also concentrated on repairing schools: by the second half of 2000, 86 per cent of school-age children were attending school; universities and colleges had reopened (though the quality of education was extremely variable). UNMIK, along with the World Bank and the Food and Agriculture branch of the United Nations, started a major effort to revitalise agricultural activity. Fertilisers, seed, potatoes, maize and vegetable kits were distributed to farmers for the spring sowing season in 2000. The wheat harvest in July was able to meet the needs of over half the population.[12] The equivalent of a central bank was set up by 2000 along with a number of commercial banks and small credit institutions. The D-mark (from 2003 the euro) was introduced as the official currency.

UNMIK flaws

But UNMIK earned the reputation of being a near-insolvent organisation barely able to pay its bills. The Stability Pact for the Balkans set up at the height of the Kosovo conflict proved a phantom presence in Kosovo and certainly was unable to act as an effective aid-coordinating force in Brussels where it had its headquarters.[13] Bernard Kouchner, the first SRSG, has to spend long periods away from Kosovo touring donor countries in the search for additional funds. Kouchner, a medical doctor who had co-founded the well-known NGO Medecin Sans Frontiers before serving in the French government in the 1990s, would be the most popular of Kosovo's SRSGs. But chronic under-funding weakened his position. One source warned: 'for the price of a few days bombing we may be throwing Kosovo away'.[14]

Kouchner had left Kosovo after less than eighteen months as SRSG. This would be the longest period any of the five international officials appointed up to

2004 to run the territory, would remain in post. Before he left, Kouchner put in place tentative arrangements for co-governance between UNMIK and Kosovo representatives. A Joint Interim Administrative Structure for Kosovo took shape in February 2000. Twenty administrative departments were set up, each with an UNMIK and Kosovan co-head (Corrin 2002: 100). The departments were allocated to the political parties, with one exception. This was done without any wider consultation and bypassing civic organisations (*The Kosovo Report* 2000: 23). The local heads earned barely $250 a month while the internationals earned many times that amount (Corrin 2002: 100). These striking pay differentials made it difficult for an international-local partnership based on trust and easy rapport to develop. The almost complete absence of women in the governing structures led to tensions within UNMIK. Lesley Abdela, a British development specialist with long experience of seeking to champion women's interests in post-conflict situations, found that there was little interest in promoting women on the public bodies envisaged for a self-governing Kosovo: From her vantage-point working for the OSCE which was entrusted with UNMIK's democratisation 'pillar', Abdela tried to correct this attitude. But she wrote later: 'I was told women in leadership positions would be "alien to local culture and tradition" and, in any case, "no women in Kosovo are interested in participation in politics or public life" '.[15] By the end of 1999, Abdela had been summarily removed for being uncollegiate and too zealous in her approach in a dispute with Dan Everts, the head of the OSCE in Kosovo, which went all the way up to Kofi Annan.

The limitations of interim politics and government

A place for women was found on the interim transitional council and UNMIK encouraged the parties to put them on their lists for local elections held in October 2000, the first major step in restoring political autonomy. Ibrahim Rugova and the Democratic League of Kosovo (LDK) staged an astonishing political comeback. They won nearly 60 per cent of the vote on a huge turnout and 21 out of 30 municipalities. Previously, Rugova was widely felt to be finished because of his role in the 1999 conflict (see p. 65) When he returned to Kosovo afterwards, the newspaper *Koha Ditore* carried an icy headline: 'The Loser is Back'.[16]

The poor showing of the Kosovo Democratic Party (PDK), led by Hashim Thaçi, stemmed in large part from the behaviour of sections of the UÇK in mid-1999. The ex-fighters had squandered a lot of popularity by their arrogant behaviour. They seized businesses, homes and land and reacted badly if anyone objected. Ex-UÇK people were also sometimes associated with the burgeoning criminality of the post-1999 period. The local elections showed that most Albanians viewed NATO and not their own poorly armed and recently formed guerrillas, as their true liberators, so the UÇK only enjoyed uncritical support in areas where Serb oppression, and also opposition to it, had been strong for a long time, such as the Drenica valley.

Encouraged by the local elections result, Hans Haekkerup, the Dane who became SRSG at the start of 2001, announced a Constitutional Framework for

Provisional Self-Government in May 2001; this was only after limited consultation with local political actors. It allowed for the creation of an elected assembly in which minorities would have up to one-quarter of the seats, a President elected by the assembly and a Prime Minister and government chosen by the President. The government of Kosovo was entrusted with authority over domestic affairs – economy, education, transport, local administration, the judiciary, prisons and the media, but the SRSG enjoyed many reserved powers. He could dissolve the assembly and call new elections, set the 'financial and political parameters' for the budget, appoint and remove judges, control the KPC, the customs service, appoint all senior economic officials, oversee external relations and liase with KFOR in relation to internal and border security.[17]

So instead of the extensive self-government promised to Kosovo under UN Resolution 1244, what it actually got in 2001 was very limited autonomy. Elections for the Assembly took place on 17 November 2001 after an incident-free campaign. The LDK got 46 per cent of the vote, the PDK was far behind on 25.54 per cent and roughly half the 170,000 Serb voters participated under a Reform coalition that got 11 per cent of the vote and twenty seats in the 120-seat legislature. Rugova was elected President of the Assembly, a ceremonial position. After much grandstanding, he agreed to appoint a PDK deputy, Bejram Rexhapi as Prime Minister of a coalition government. Rexhapi would show himself to be a moderate and constructive figure who improved the image of the PDK which was slowly catching up on the LDK electorally.

By the end of 2001 much appeared to have been achieved by UNMIK. Violence had been substantially curbed. Important strides had been made in reconstruction. Two sets of elections had taken place in relative peace. The moderate choice had triumphed and minority representatives had agreed to sit in the new parliament. Compared with Bosnia after the peace imposed at Dayton in 1995, this was definitely progress. But Kosovan Albanians had the illusion of self-rule rather than the reality. There were in effect two governments after 2001, 'one democratic and legitimate but with limited powers, and one unelected and imposed, but with almost unlimited powers'.[18]

Javier Solana, the EU's security commissioner, was quick to remind Kosovans that independence was not on the agenda and that technically Kosovo was still part of Yugoslavia.[19] Milošević was now out of power and there was a growing tendency on the part of the European Union and NATO to make the strengthening of the Serbian reformers (with a tenuous grip on power) the cornerstone of the West's Balkans policy. Besides, within the United Nations, there was a deep reluctance to change boundaries or sovereignty unless it was absolutely necessary and it would be from New York that the international policy towards Kosovo would be increasingly drawn-up.

Standards before status

The message to Kosovo was that the new institutions would have to prove their worth and elected representatives and administrators would have to show competence and moderation before the final status of Kosovo could be decided. 'Standards before status' became the mantra of UNMIK, but the abrupt departure of Hans Haekkerup from his post over the Christmas holiday of 2001, suggested that he had little confidence that this new policy would bear fruit. After a hiatus, a new SRSG, Michael Steiner, took up his position in March 2002. He proved to be an autocratic and sometimes insensitive UN chief, but at least he had experience of the Balkans (having been deputy-High Commissioner in Bosnia in the mid-1990s). He was also at pains to disabuse Belgrade of the notion that it could re-acquire control of Kosovo by stealth. He stayed for seventeen months, a period in which a gulf opened up between UNMIK and what were known as the Provisional Institutions of Self-Governance (PISG). It was far from being entirely of Steiner's own making but his style definitely did not help. At public events, Kosovo politicians were relegated to the sidelines in what often proved to be photo opportunities for the SRSG. A sense of partnership failed to arise and no PISG representative was invited to the Security Council during the SRSG's presentation of the quarterly report on Kosovo. Steiner also had a tendency not to consult with Prime Minister Rexhapi on key initiatives. He sometimes indulged in posturing as when he told the public (in January 2003), that 'you the population should demand that all elected politicians and public officials make it crystal clear that they have absolutely no links with this underworld'. Critics pointed out that it was the responsibility of UNMIK to ensure that the links between politicians and organised crime were kept to a minimum and that UNMIK had far more power than the public.[20]

The ability of elected politicians to get on to the boards of public bodies, some of which were slated for privatisation, revealed that the tendency, noticeable elsewhere in the region of the emerging elite having a proprietorial attitude to public resources, was quite far advanced. The struggle against tyranny and ethnic aggression did not appear to have released a more ethical approach to public affairs. But UNMIK had not done much to strengthen the political standards by its own approach to the institutions of governance. The Prime Minister's office had serious weaknesses. It was unable to control its own limited budget and it lacked capable staff. The salaries on offer were unlikely to attract qualified officials and they were dwarfed by what UNMIK's principal officials could earn. No devices were put in place to encourage Assembly oversight of the government.[21] UNMIK made it clear that any anti-corruption drive would not include UN officials who, in fact, controlled most of the purse strings.[22]

No sense of common objectives, much less partnership emerged between Steiner-led UNMIK and the Kosovo institutions. In addition, tensions and frustrations often spilled over into a war of words in the media. By the fourth anniversary of UNMIK, it was impossible to conceal the shortcomings of the international administration. No planning framework was devised to determine priorities. 'The constant turnover and inexperience of staff in key positions undermined continuity and interrupted action on key initiatives'.[23] International communication was weak inside UNMIK. It had a '4-pillar structure under which police and justice along with civil administration were entrusted to the United

Nations, democratisation and institution-building to the OSCE, and reconstruction and economic development to the European Union. But there was plenty of evidence that this structure 'was created as much to reconcile the ambition of different international actors as to meet Kosova's needs'.[24]

The reluctance to try and resolve Kosovo's political status also suited a mission with a short-term perspective that reflected a staff that was frequently changing. The Independent Commission on Kosovo in a 2001 follow-up report had predicted a conflict over the SRSG's extensive reserved powers. A local political elite ratified by the ballot box was bound to press for more self-government while the international administration would try to hold on to its prerogatives.[25] Carl Bildt, an international official with abundant experience of the region, warned in July 2002 that Kosovo's future could not wait to be decided until stable institutions were in place. He insisted that a coherent road map for the territory's political future must be at the heart of the stabilisation process.[26] But all that was forthcoming from UNMIK was a promise in late 2003, that it would begin reviewing Kosovo's final status by mid-2005.

Local Albanian patience started to wear thin. UNMIK's high-handedness and its insistence that local forces must pass stiff political tests even though it held most of the political power, stoked frustrations. These were reinforced by deepening economic gloom. Kosovo's economy began to contract from 2003, as international assistance tailed off. Kosovo's lack of sovereignty meant it was unable to access funds from international financial bodies.[27] Their unwillingness to give it any kind of credit rating warned off most potential investors. Institutions were hardly going to exhibit high standards in an economic wasteland where a labour force already bursting at the scenes was augmented by 30,000–40,000 young people entering it each year. With agricultural and industrial activity very low, economic activity was concentrated in a small private sector consisting mainly of trade and services.[28] UNMIK showed little interest in long-term economic development. It was significant that the UN Development Programme, which might have been a channel for worthwhile ideas concerning the economic future, was left outside the pillar structure. The diplomats and administrators of UNMIK essentially had a short-term political focus. A West European diplomat stationed in Priština declared privately in November 2003: 'The rule of diplomats is killing Kosovo. Development doesn't come about through decreed standards, but from economics'.[29]

Property tangle

The way UNMIK resolved the complicated issue of state property was critical for Kosovo's economic future, which, under communism, was described as 'belonging to society as a whole'. UNMIK lacked the institutional resources to draw up an effective property register. From 1999 onwards, control of some of Kosovo's prime economic assets was 'determined outside the legal system, in countless individual power struggles in Kosovo'.[30] In June 2002, the Kosovo Trust Agency (KTA) had been set up as the trustee and landlord of Kosovo's most valuable assets. It found that the legal and institutional framework concerning social property had disintegrated into a free-for-all and numerous examples could be found of property occupied or leased out by private interests with no legal title whatsoever.[31] 'The absence of clearly enforceable property titles had created a market for private protection agencies, substituting for a weak state'.[32] Illegal construction mushroomed[33] and attempts to curtail it by the fledgling Kosovo government resulted in the murder of the architect, Rexhep Luci, one of the few people capable of solving Priština's chronic planning problems.[34] Any hopes that a privatisation process could get underway and would promote the rise of a transparent economy were dashed in October 2003. The United Nations declined to confer legal immunity on KTA staff which meant that few were prepared to take risks in order to do their jobs properly. Moreover, the United Nations declined to allow UNMIK to declare invalid in Kosovo, three Serbian laws of the 1990s under which state property had passed into the hands of Milosevic supporters and Albanian employees had been dismissed *en masse*. This was a sign of the backing that Serbia could rely on from members of the UNSC, who were prepared to shore up its interests in Kosovo. The KTA's director, Maria Fucci, had a bureaucratic approach to privatisation that seemed certain to lengthen the process interminably and she was only replaced following the crisis of confidence in UNMIK that erupted in March 2004.[35]

Ethnic enmities persist

An anarchic property regime and the legal vacuum in which the socially owned property regime operated, contributed to a growing atmosphere of disorder. The crisis in law-and-order had never been effectively tackled after the initial crescendo of violence from mid-1999 onwards. By the end of August 1999, 180,000 Serbs had left Kosovo along with 55,000 Kosovans from other minority backgrounds, mainly Roma (Amnesty 2004: 3). The main attacks had been directed against the Serbian minority and members of the Roma community, the latter deeply unpopular owing to the widespread perception that they had collaborated with the Serbs in the persecution of early 1999. The worst post-war incident occurred when a bus carrying Serbian civilians was blown up on 16 February 2001, killing seven. Veton Surroi, the best-known Kosovo journalist issued a forthright condemnation two days later, warning that the bombing was a boost for those who wished to partition Kosovo.[36] But there were some corners of Kosovo, usually places spared the worst affects of the war, where inter-ethnic relations exhibited some normal features. Gjilan, the largest town in south-eastern Kosova, acquired a progressive mayor, Lutfi Haziri who has tried to integrate the different ethnic communities. Serbs managed to retain 20 per cent of jobs in the municipality and in a 2002 interview the mayor proclaimed that they shopped in the centre of town and enjoyed freedom of movement.[37] At least some of the impetus for this relative normalisation may have stemmed from the trans-border smuggling networks that required a suspension of ethnic rivalries for them to be effective.

The local Orthodox leadership, Bishop Artemije and his assistant Father Sava, have been prepared to collaborate with UNMIK. They agreed to serve on its transitional council. Father Sava said publicly in the spring of 2000 that the Yugoslav army would never return to Kosovo and praised KFOR for its willingness to protect Serbs. [38] The only local Serb politician to speak in such conciliatory terms was Momčilo Trajković. At a UN-sponsored meeting with Albanian leaders in July 1999, he acknowledged the 'tremendous moral cost to the Serb nation caused by the tragedy which befell by the Albanians.... While some Serbs individually tried to prevent it, collectively we failed'.[39] But moderation has not been a passport for success in the embattled Serbian political community. In the inconclusive presidential election in Serbia held in September 2002, no less than 57.2 per cent of Kosovo Serbs supported the hardline nationalist Vojislav Šešelj.[40] By July 2002, even Father Sava had swung around to the view that 'Albanian terrorist groups act freely and with impunity in Kosovo today'.[41]

Intra-Albanian violence was increasingly noticeable. Probably the future of Kosovo would depend more on the extent that it was rooted out than on attacks against minorities which it would be difficult to curb given the level of bitterness in a fractured society. A string of senior and mid-level LDK officials were killed from 2000 onwards. Other killings stemmed from organised crime and business rivalries or even the tradition of blood feuds and clan rivalries that revived in a few places.

The search for the rule of law

Up until mid-2003, twenty-seven ex-officers and senior UÇK commanders had been charged with murder after investigations by KFOR and the UN police (eleven being released later for lack of evidence).[42] A functioning judicial system was vital in order to have effective policing and UNMIK directed considerable effort at creating one. Courts had to be built or repaired, judges and prosecutors hired and trained, and a decision made on the law to be used (it was decided to use the pre-Milošević era law of Yugoslavia). International judges and prosecutors sat in each district court as well as the Supreme Court in Priština. By 2001, there was a functioning justice system but one that faced stiff problems. UNMIK was trying to recruit not just judges but customs officials and teachers initially at salaries ranging from 100 to 500 DM a month. Some of these same people could earn 1,000–2,000 DM a month working as interpreters or drivers for the international organisations. Such salaries made it more likely that some judges and customs officials would boost their incomes through corruption. This would only strengthen the hold of the criminal underworld or political extremists who were often inter-changeable; and bribery was not the only action they were ready to contemplate in order to enforce their will on society.

Policing has been just as critical a challenge as creating a functioning justice system. NATO was able to bring in 30,000 troops in mid-1999, but it took three months for the United Nations to install the first 1,400 police. The UN peace-keeping mission in Kosovo was the first one in which international civilian police – drawn from over fifty countries – was given primary responsibility for policing. But by June 2000, the international police force had barely reached 77 per cent of its authorised strength. Some of the police were from countries where the police were not well known for efficiency and enjoying public respect and they were viewed by locals and colleagues as being in Kosovo primarily for the lucrative pay (Garton-Ash 2000: 5). Better-motivated police were prevented from serving in Kosovo because their national constitution prevented them doing so. France provided very few because the powerful Interior Minister, unlike his Prime Minister, was opposed to the 1999 NATO action. In others, policemen were not trained to use firearms, which they might be required to do in an environment like Kosovo. Most UNMIK police also suffered from a scant knowledge of local languages, geography and customs which also limited their effectiveness.

The slow build-up of the police presence in what was the UN's premier arena at the end of the 1990s showed the need for the creation of a permanent stand-by UN police unit, which national governments could put at the disposal of the UN Secretary-General (*The Kosovo Report* 2000: 112). But it also reinforced the urgency of training a local multi-ethnic police force. The police training college run by the OSCE has been one of the most clear-cut successes of the international effort in Kosovo. A multi-ethnic Kosovo Police Service (KPS) has emerged and by early 2003, 5,663 officers had graduated into its ranks.[43] At least 18 per cent of them were women and 15 per cent were from the minorities. Serbs and Albanians carried out their training together and were able to carry out joint patrols in some areas.[44] The KPS is taking over responsibility incrementally with a complete transfer of authority anticipated by 2004–5.

But the police and the courts lacked the ability to offer secure protection to witnesses in sensitive trials, which put them at a disadvantage against ruthless criminals. This was shown graphically in Pec/Peje in June 2003 when a high-profile UN witness and two of his family members were murdered in the centre of Kosovo's second city. Tahir Zemaj had been a key witness in the trial of 5 UÇK figures who were given lengthy jail sentences for the abduction and murder of 4 rivals. Among them was the brother of Ramush Haradinj, an ex-UÇK leader who is the head of Kosovo's third largest party, the Alliance for the Future of Kosovo. The Zemaj killings were a warning to those who would testify in Western Kosovo said a prominent human rights activist in a neighbouring town who wished to remain anonymous. The authorities were unable to relocate witnesses within Kosovo and what measures the police and the courts had devised, were not easily compatible with one another. Confidence in the rule of law plummeted in areas where those with guns still exercised real power. This was exacerbated by a longstanding reluctance of Albanians to testify against other Albanians in courts, which historically would have been controlled by their overlords or oppressors.[45]

UNMIK adrift

Michael Steiner left Kosovo in July 2003 with the words 'I am proud of the multiethnic climate I have developed during my mission here'.[46] But renewed violence on the day his successor arrived, which left two Serbs dead revealed the extent that rhetoric was failing to keep pace with reality (Amnesty 2004: 3). Against this background the European Union, at its Thessaloniki summit in June, decided that talks needed to be held between the main disputants. The European Union was slowly replacing the United States as the main international actor in the Balkans. Albanian leaders were unhappy: they felt that most Europeans were prepared to give too much credence to Belgrade's position. In particular, there was concern that this initiative had emanated from Javier Solana, the EU's security policy chief. He had been the architect of a union between two reluctant partners, Serbian and Montenegro. This, it was feared, might prove a precedent and EU leaders would attempt to push Kosovo and Serbia into a loose confederation.[47]

The lack of strong negotiators on the Albanian side was painfully felt though rarely admitted in public. Kosovo did not appear to be a state-in-the-making and its politics were parochial. An unreformed education system dominated by nationalist values was not producing talented young figures whom politicians welcomed to argue Kosovo's case in international arenas. The composition of the government showed that political loyalties and not a minister's capabilities, were the main criteria for selection.

Serbia had professional negotiators who cut a more impressive figure internationally. Nebojša Čović, a leading figure in the then still-ruling Democratic Opposition of Serbia (DOS) coalition, had made defence of Serbian interests in Kosovo, a top priority. Steiner had always disabused him of any hope that Serbia could recover what it had previously had in Kosovo. He had made this very plain in July 2002: 'While we cannot say now what... [Kosova's] future status will be, we can say what it will not be. There will be no partition, no cantonization, and no return to the status-quo' before 1999. He added that 'the outcome cannot be mono-ethnic but must be multi-ethnic'.[48] By 2003, Čović was branding Steiner as 'a factor of instability' in the region.[49]

Steiner's successor was Harri Holkeri, a former Prime Minister of Finland who had been associated with unsuccessful efforts to break the interminable peace logjam in Northern Ireland. Upon arrival, he said: 'My advantage over others is that I have never been to Kosovo'.[50] It did not seem to occur to the European Union that sending someone unfamiliar with Kosovo, the resolution of whose problems was crucial for the EU's Balkans strategy, might not be an inspired move. Holkeri lasted under a year and by the time he resigned on 25 May 2004, one high-ranking UN official was scathing of his boss, describing him as incompetent and complacent: 'He never read his briefs properly – just the bullet points'.[51]

Holkeri's ten-month tenure was marked by two main events. The first was undoubtedly an anti-climax. This was the Geneva meeting between Kosovan Albanian and Serbian officials on 14 October 2004. The talks were meant to resolve technical issues such as electricity supplies and car number plates, as well as enable safe returns for Serbian and Roma refugees and try to account for 3,700 missing persons from the 1998–9 conflict, mainly Albanians.[52] But the encounter proved to be a dialogue of the deaf in which prepared statements were read by both sides. By now Serbian deputies had withdrawn from the Kosovo assembly and the only regular Serbian–Kosovo encounters were proximity meetings chaired by neutral brokers, such as Eliamep, the Greek think-tank. Personal bonds may have been established but the talks did not lead on to any substantive settlement proposals.[53]

Albanian insecurity was rising as the size of KFOR was rapidly being scaled down from 45,000 to 17,500 and the initiative seemed to pass from an inexperienced SRSG to diplomats in New York. The UN's Department for Peace-keeping Operations succeeded in micro-managing UNMIK from New York by late 2003. It is negligent of development issues and often displays a conservative and legalistic interpretation of its Kosovo mandate.[54] The UN diplomats also carry a lot of weight. They may never have met Albanian political figures and often have stereotypical views of Albanians bound up with crime and terrorism. Michel Duclos, the deputy French ambassador to the United Nations, displayed an overbearing attitude towards the Rexhapi government when he said in June 2003 that its 'particular responsibility' was 'to establish a climate conducive to implementing the objectives of the international community...'. The ICG reminded him that it was an elected government primarily accountable to its electorate.[55]

Nerves had already been set on edge by the approach of General Fabio Mini during his one-year period as head of KFOR from October 2002. He proposed that a regional force could provide Kosovo's future security, including Serbian troops.[56] He also began to dismantle KFOR's partnership with the KPC, viewing this largely unarmed force with civil emergency tasks, and organised crime networks, as 'largely interchangeable'.[57] Holkeri tried to undo the damage after his departure, but the atmosphere was soured in the winter of 2003–4 when General Agim Ceku, the KPC's head was detained on Serbian Interpol warrants at European airports. The warrant had been issued against one of the Kosovan Albanians most popular figures by a Milošević-era judge.[58] Such events deepened the insecurity of Albanians and may even have suggested that the international community was turning its face against them as it had done for most of the 1990s.

Peace mission in crisis: the March 2004 violence

Shortly before his departure, Steiner had warned that Europe 'risks disaster' if it fails to help Kosovo rebuild and develop while the international community concentrates on Afghanistan and the Middle East.[59] These feelings were amplified when serious violence swept through parts of the territory on 17–19 March 2004, the second major event of Holkeri's governorship that led to his speedy departure. They had been provoked by at least two incidents. On 16 March several dozen Serbs in a village east of Priština had cut the city off from the south by erecting a roadblock which UNMIK police failed to move (following the fatal wounding of a local Serb).[60] This was followed by the unclarified drowning of three Albanian children whom media reports alleged had been chased into the river Ibar, near Mitrovica by Serbs.[61] Whether and to what extent, the Kosovo Albanian media, inflamed feelings was hotly disputed, with the OSCE damning its coverage and the International Federation of Journalists insisting that such claims were unfounded.[62] What followed is not in dispute. Thirty-three major riots involving an estimated 51,000 people, led to nineteen fatalities (Amnesty 2004: 2). Numerous Orthodox church buildings were targeted, the destruction being particularly widespread in Prizren. What were new were the attacks on UN police and KFOR soldiers. KFOR lacked the capacity to deal with the violent disorders. Even if its numbers had not been significantly reduced in the previous two years, the lack of a contingency plan or a centralised leadership would probably have left it struggling to respond effectively.[63] Some national contingents, notably those under French and German command, interpreted their mandates solely as the protection of people rather than property, the Swedes being a noteworthy exception (Amnesty 2004: 5). German troops in Prizren showed a passive response to mobs bent on destroying Serbian churches, monasteries and seminaries (Amnesty 2004: 5–6). The bad relationship between French KFOR in Mitrovica and local Albanians was confirmed. The KPC (under the command of KFOR) was assumed to be on the side of the rioters. Attempts were made by French troops to forcibly disarm KPC officers in the south of Mitrovica.[64] The demonisation of the KPC was overdone. In Vushtrri, a unit had stood by as rioters burnt the homes of recently returned Roma (Amnesty 2004: 7–8). But, elsewhere, there was no evidence of significant fraternisation with rioters and some units even tried to calm passions (even though they were not supposed to engage in a security role).[65]

President Rugova confirmed how increasingly out-of-touch he was with the situation by contenting himself with a statement to foreign radio stations calling for independence.[66] The Rexhapi government behaved more responsibly; on 20 March, of its own volition, it accepted responsibility for the financial repair of destroyed homes and other buildings (belonging mainly to Serbs). Holkeri's statements about the gravity of the violence fluttered erratically to the bafflement of his staff.[67] His characterisation of the violence as an extremist plot (one shared by other international spokespersons), was the response of a bureaucracy in disarray, one scrambling for a conventional explanation for events it found hard to comprehend. No formal organisation was evident; otherwise it was unlikely that the riots would have fizzled out so quickly. James Pettifer has written:

> The nature of the … events is familiar to students of inter-ethnic conflict in the Balkans and elsewhere. A series of random incidents links into a chain of causation that leads to a climate where street violence easily erupts, and patterns of 'tit for tat' revenge develop far from the original incidents. The large number of alienated jobless young people is a main factor in the scale and rapid spread of the protests.
>
> (Pettifer 2004: 2)

UNMIK retreated into denial. The serious charge was levelled by a major Brussels think-tank that UNMIK intimidated officers through the chain of command into acquiescing into a cover-up and sanitisation of the record during the period of rioting. Commanders, who had allowed mobs *carte blanche* to raze villages within hundreds of metres of major KFOR bases, received the plaudits of visiting international dignitaries.[68] The low state of morale in the international police was shown on 17 April when three officers were killed in a gunfight between the US and Jordanian members of the force.[69] The inadequacy of an international force supposed to be a beacon for peace and order, but barely able to conceal its own mutual animosities, was cruelly exposed by this incident. Holkeri had gone within ten weeks of the riots, briefed against by his own officials. His replacement, the Danish diplomat, Soren Jensen-Petersen, showed no sign of realising that the international obsession with standards when Kosova was economically moribund and its political class in extremely poor shape, was a road leading nowhere. Chris Patten, the EU foreign affairs commissioner, still threw his weight behind 'the standards before status' policy.[70] Some analysts believed that the high standards of governance Kosovo needed to acquire before its status could be resolved, were unrealistic even for stable ex-Yugoslavia states and they wondered how many EU states could even meet them.[71] Former US ambassador to the United Nations, Richard Holbrooke put the unrest down to the failure of the international community to resolve the status question.[72] Sharing this view, the ICG recommended that the SRSG role be divided between a chief administrator (liasing alongside the PISG) and a chief negotiator to handle the resolution of Kosovo's final status.[73] It reiterated the viewpoint of the 1999–2000 International Commission on Kosovo that a form of conditional independence was the best way forward. The conditions would need to include adhering to very high standards on minority rights before all the benefits of international recognition were bestowed.[74] For an unnamed diplomat working for Solana in Brussels, the Kosovo eruption was a sharp reminder that works in the Balkans 'requires huge investments in time and security. This is a real test case for the EU'.[75] Otherwise the territory had the capacity to rock the entire neighbourhood and undermine fragile constitutional experiments and peace building initiatives in Serbia–Montenegro, Macedonia and Bosnia. In response to the razing of Orthodox buildings in Kosovo, both Muslim and Orthodox churches were attacked in Serbia, Macedonia and Bosnia in the days after the March violence.[76]

What the future status of Kosovo might consist of, could be reduced to the following options according to the policy analyst Wim van Meurs (2004):

1 *Independent statehood*

 - conditional
 - unconditional

2 *Autonomy* within

 - Serbia
 - Serbia and Montenegro

3 *Reintegration* as third constituent part of the State-Union of Serbia and Montenegro
4 Permanent international *protectorate*
5 *EU integration.*

A sense of drift enveloped Kosovo in the summer of 2004. A soaring population, half of which is under twenty, with massive unemployment and the possibility of emigration foreclosed by the EU's tightly policed Schengen frontier, is a challenge to stability whatever political arrangements are in place. Economic misery is bound to fuel political extremism and reduce chances of an emerging Albanian leadership focussed on reconstruction and reaching a *modus vivendi* with the Serbs and Roma. One promising development was the decision on 14 July of Prime Minister Rexhapi and several leaders of the ethnic Albanian and Serbian communities, to issue a joint statement calling for the establishment of a new Kosovan ministry to deal with refugee and human rights affairs. The Serbian leader Oliver Ivanović declared that 'It's obvious we all expected too much from the international community . . . Basic issues must be resolved between the ethnic communities themselves'.[77]

Kosovo and Bosnia revisited

In 1999, the peace-building mission in Kosovo avoided elementary mistakes committed by the architects of its predecessor in Bosnia. Civilian and military tasks were integrated and the SRSG acted as a governor with more powers than Bosnia's High Representative. The political structures created to pave the way for multi-ethnic governance, were streamlined compared with the Byzantine edifice created at Dayton for Bosnia. Efforts were made to disarm combatants rather than allowing the existence of separate armies as in post-1995 Bosnia. Special care was taken to create a new police force from scratch that would command legitimacy across society. But the shortcomings and complexities of a multi-layered international force undermined UNMIK's performance in Kosovo. Lessons had been learned from the Bosnian experience but international organisations and participating major states were slow to discard their clashing agendas and management styles. The calibre of the international staff proved as variable as in Bosnia (except in some areas such as police training) and the turnover was just as rapid. International shortcomings had serious consequences for vital peace-building tasks, in particular the creation of a justice system that would offer genuine protection to citizens and reinforce the state. In a society, where ownership of weapons was far more widespread than in Bosnia, the rule of law proved difficult to consolidate. As in Bosnia, the international authorities made elementary mistakes in trying to decide the fate of socially owned property from the communist era.

The international administration in Kosovo may have enjoyed more power than its Bosnian counterpart, but it was greatly constrained by the fact that Serbia still enjoyed *de jure* sovereignty over the territory. It would have been advisable to try and decide Kosovo's final status in 1999–2000, when the attention of top-level leaders remained focussed on the question. It is quite likely that nationalism would not have proven as disruptive as it turned out to be in post-Milošević Serbia if sovereignty had been transferred into Kosovan hands with strong international guarantees that the rights of minorities be protected. Given the reduction in Albanian insecurity that might have been expected to follow, the prospects for minorities could have been considerably brighter than they have later become.

Ironically, given the risks taken by NATO in 1999 to reverse mass ethnic cleansing, Kosovo has become a more peripheral concern than Bosnia. Five years later, the European political figures who confronted Milošević were nearly all still in office, but the issue was rarely mentioned by Blair, Chirac or Schröder. A succession of governors has flitted in and out, with most of them leaving little imprint on the situation. By contrast, high-calibre figures have headed the international mission in Bosnia. Whether they succeed in the long-run, they have tried to rebuild from within a dysfunctional peace process and construct a common multi-ethnic Bosnia that can take its place in mainstream Europe. The symbolism of the Bosnian war, culminating in the Srebrenica massacre, appears to resonate more powerfully abroad than does the suffering Milošević inflicted on Albanians. The perception that Albanians are heavily involved in organised crime that threatens the cohesion of West European societies (however exaggerated at times) is a real one that was damaging the collective Albanian image even during the events of 1999. At least the dispute in Kosovo is not unduly sullied by religious animosities and the Albanians have shown a preference for moderate electoral options up to mid-2004. But the calibre of Rugova's LDK is low and the initiative is likely to swing towards its bitter rival, the PDK or perhaps a new force will seek to champion the interests of urban, educated and pragmatic Albanians.

UNMIK will be unable to overlook, for much longer, the final constitutional status of Kosovo, however difficult that will be to resolve because of differing positions in the UNSC. Not only does being stuck in political limbo give the initiative to radical forces but it also rules out any prospect of economic recovery. It is quite possible that the huge scale of Kosovo's economic problems will eclipse its political status as the key challenge for Europe in the time ahead. A young population confined to Kosovo by rigid emigration laws and facing a life of unemployment, would be a combustible element without the territory's ethnic divisions and recent bloody history. The resolution of the Albanian–Serbian standoff will be a major turning-point in South-East Europe if it can be accomplished. A much higher calibre in the international approach to resolving the problem will be needed from the European Union in particular, the present chief international agency in the region. The ability of the Kosovo dispute to destabilise Macedonia and Southern Serbia (Presovo Valley) can still all too easily be overlooked. But the resolution of its disputed constitutional status is likely to be only one step on a long journey towards a sustainable political and economic future.

8 The European Union in search of Balkan answers

The European Union emerged from the Cold War as a force that seemed capable of reinforcing peace and security in a continent that had witnessed the deadliest violence seen anywhere on the planet during the twentieth century. But it sunk into introspection when faced with a challenge from ethno-nationalist forces in the Balkans. During the 1991–5 wars in parts of the former Yugoslavia, major West European states had largely recoiled from the problems of the region. The European Union had acquired a foreign policy arm at the 1991 Maastricht Summit but there was not the common ground required to take purposeful initiatives in the Balkan region, either in states that had remained at peace (the majority) or new states (Croatia and Bosnia) and disputed territories (Kosovo) caught up in conflict. But from the late 1990s the European Union acquired far greater visibility in the Balkans. There was a belated consensus that the region could not be ring fenced from the rest of Europe and debased political standards more reminiscent of Europe from 1933 to 1945 be allowed to prevail. After equivocating during the wars in Croatia and Bosnia when it singled out as a key negotiating partner Serbia's Slobodan Milošević, widely viewed as the chief architect of the post-1991 conflicts in Yugoslavia, the European Union adopted a fresh approach. It actively intervened in the escalating confrontation between Milošević and most of Serbia on the one hand and the Albanian population of Kosovo on the other that rejected Serbian overlordship. Belgrade was warned that forced transfer of populations and warfare mainly directed against civilians would no longer be tolerated. Not only was it morally repugnant but the resultant upheavals also undermined the security of West European states. In 1999, the European Union showed impressive solidarity with NATO when it militarily confronted Milošević over the skies of Kosovo and Serbia. The solidarity showed no signs of cracking despite the ill-planned and sometimes insensitively conducted operation. Afterwards, a sign of the good relations between two multilateral entities sometimes viewed as rivals was the transfer of Javier Solana from his post as NATO Secretary-General to a new post as the EU's High Commissioner for Security. The holder was meant to coordinate the EU's Common Foreign and Security Policy.

Solana's colleague, Chris Patten, the EU's Commissioner for External Relations admitted that the Balkans would be a critical test for this new policy departure.[1] When the European Union published its long-awaited Security

Strategy on 12 December 2003, a number of the threats it identified – regional conflicts, failing states and organised crime – applied with particular meaning to the Balkans.[2] The 1999 conflict in Kosovo, which ranged most of the EU states (as members of NATO) against the Milošević regime in Serbia, had starkly brought home the nature of the threat and the unpreparedness of the European Union. At the end of 1999 the European Union reached agreement to establish a European Security and Defence Policy (ESDP). There was a commitment to be 'able, by 2003, to deploy within 60 days and sustain, for at least one year, military forces of up to 50,000–60,000 persons'.[3] But by 2003 the ESDP was still in the melting pot. The overseas commitments of leading EU states, Britain in Iraq, Germany in Afghanistan and France in the Ivory Coast had caused delays.[4] So had the shortage of funds caused by the slow down of the West European economy and the fact that integration of national armies proceeded more slowly than had been hoped.

American and European distrust

The realisation that US political leaders and particularly the defence establishment were unenthusiastic about long-term involvement in the Balkans strengthened the need for the European Union to be ready to fill Washington's shoes in the region. In the first months of George W. Bush's administration, influential voices described US engagement in the Balkans as a drain on resources which overstretched the United States as it faced potential and actual difficulties in Latin America and north-east Asia. There was scant enthusiasm for the 'state-building' agenda that was seen as crucial for stability in the Balkans. US interest in the region was revived after the 11 September 2001 terrorist attacks in New York and Washington because parts of it were adjacent to the Middle East. But the deepening military involvement in Iraq from the spring of 2003 onwards renewed calls for the US military pull out from the Balkans to free up troops for a far more critical theatre of operations.

Before the US occupation of Iraq, the Pentagon had been reluctant to accede to EU overtures to take over the military mission in Bosnia. When the European Union took over part of a small military mission in Macedonia in March 2003, the Pentagon had done its best to delay it getting off the ground, according to one NATO ambassador.[5] US officials argued for a US presence in order to hunt down Islamic militants in the region.[6] But its worsening problems in Iraq allowed a sense of rivalry with the European Union and its new defence arm to be shelved. When news of the US retreat spread locally there was dismay. Both Bosnian Muslims and Kosovo Albanians had a tendency to view the United States as the only serious military force in the region.[7] The Europeans were seen in many quarters as 'often avoiding the tough issues, preferring to postpone difficult decisions in the hope that they will become easier to solve at some later, better time'.[8] As late as December 2001, Wolfgang Petritsch, the High Representative in Bosnia had complained of the European Union being 'too bureaucratic' and lacking 'enough vision' to be of effective assistance to Bosnia.[9] In October 2003,

Richard Holbrooke and Bernard Kouchner, who had cooperated in Bosnia and Kosovo as representatives of the US and French governments wrote of the need to continue what they believed had been a successful transatlantic partnership in the Balkans.[10]

NATO leaders finally agreed at their Istanbul summit on 28 June 2004 to replace their Stabilisation Force (SFOR) with a new peace-keeping mission led by the European Union. It was given the name Althea and would be the same size as SFOR – 7,000-strong. By now, 85 per cent of the SFOR was already drawn from EU armed forces.[11] Since 2002, officials from EU states held all of the top three offices in the Bosnia mission led by Paddy Ashdown. But the United States had not entirely yielded leadership to the Europeans in the Balkans. A NATO mission was to remain, primarily US-led, whose main task would be to actively search for war crimes suspects.[12] The commanders of both missions were meant to have a parallel, not a hierarchical relationship, and their commanders to cooperate on a daily basis.[13] One sign of added effectiveness was that Althea was required to support the implementation of civilian aspects of the Dayton agreement, an element missing from SFOR's mandate.[14] But there were lingering concerns that a failure in coordination (the bane of many previous international operations) might open up a security vacuum in Bosnia; the European Union had taken charge of the international police mission in Bosnia in December 2002. There were differing views about how pro-active it should be. In the light of evidence that the United States was far more concerned with using its intelligence strength in Bosnia to monitor suspect Islamic groups a danger existed that the hunt for Karadžić would not really be seen as anyone's principal responsibility.[15]

The Stability Pact: a German mirage in the Balkan desert

The European Union had been the primary international agency which had worked to prevent Macedonia plunging into a full-scale civil war in 2001, and in 2002 the European Parliament had worked effectively behind the scenes to prevent Albanian's tenuous political calm being shattered by renewed internecine warfare. Doris Pack, who was the Parliament's Rapporteur for Albania, had worked hard to find a compromise candidate to be the country's new president. Fatos Nano, the Socialist party leader was contested by modernising elements within his own party and reviled by the opposition Democratic Party led by his long-time foe Sali Berisha. Pack successfully intervened to promote a consensual figure, a 74-year-old retired general, Alfred Moisiu whom the protagonists agreed to accept. Here was a sign of how a relatively weak body in the EU hierarchy was able to successfully deploy soft power in order to head off a potentially destructive collision in a still unstable Balkan state.[16] But the European Union had contributed to the failure of a much more crucial international initiative in the region which was being quietly buried just as Brussels flexed its muscles in a range of actual and potential Balkans trouble spots. This was the Stability Pact (SP) for the Balkans announced at a meeting of EU Foreign Ministers in Cologne on 10 June 1999. Germany then held the EU Presidency and it was very much the creation of its Foreign Minister,

Joschka Fischer, the leader of the Green Party. More than forty countries and organisations agreed to take 'a comprehensive and coherent approach' to reinforce the countries of South-East Europe 'in their efforts to foster peace, democracy, respect for human rights, and economic prosperity' (*After Milošević* 2001: 239). The rhetoric of the declarations at the ceremonial launch in Sarajevo on 31 July, attended by some forty world leaders, suggested that the SP would be a dynamic forum for transforming the Balkans into a genuine part of Europe rather than an uncomfortable appendage.

The idea had emerged during the nerve-wracking confrontation with Milošević over Kosovo when NATO badly needed the cooperation of neighbouring Balkan states. The SP was promoted as a belated Marshall Plan for the region but Germany's motives were also bound up with concerns about domestic security. By 1998 Kosovan Albanians were the second biggest ethnic group involved in German organised crime. German diplomats were ready to concede that it was the possible flow of an even greater volume of refugees from the territory and the wider region that 'was driving the country's Balkans policy'. Accordingly, Germany was ready to contribute over $600 million via the SP between 2000 and 2003.[17]

Early pronouncements indicated that the SP would coordinate the work of the states and international agencies working in the Balkans and provide the synergy, the absence of which had dissipated much of their efforts. Martti Ahtisaari, President of Finland – the country that held the EU Presidency in the second half of 1999 – hoped that the dawning of the SP would result in proposals for reform being 'generated within the region. It is no longer sufficient to respond to each crisis on an *ad hoc* basis'.[18] But these hopes were soon dashed. The headquarters of the SP were in fact in Brussels. Neither Bodo Hombach, the German politician appointed to implement the pact, nor most of his staff of twenty-eight people had any real familiarity with South-East Europe. Hombach was criticised for being a political appointee unqualified for his position and as one who has 'been more concerned with his own salary and perks than with the Balkans', according to the *Frankfurter Allgemeine Zeitung* newspaper.[19] Many of the organisations asked to draw up projects for the SP had little experience of design and implementation projects in the Balkans. Soon the European Commission started treating it as a rival rather than as a coordinating agency which could give the West's Balkan strategy a much-needed sense of direction. Indeed much effort was wasted in institutional fighting, the European Union being quick to launch its own 'Stabilisation and Association Process' for the region as soon as the SP loomed into view. A well-publicised fund-raising conference occurred in Brussels in March 2000 which raised $2.3 billion. But very little of it was new. It 'was simply smoke and mirrors, because they're not donating a single new dollar or euro...of funds for the SP. What they're doing is they're taking funds that have already been allocated and they're putting a new label on them'.[20]

The SP failed to galvanise donors or attract officials able to devise original proposals that could be the basis of an effective peace and security agenda in the Balkans. Two-thirds of the money raised was to be spent on infrastructure, of which 71 per cent would be on roads alone. The motives for this were obvious. Donor agencies could point to visible results for their investment and most of the contracts went to EU-based firms which meant that a great deal of the money never in fact got to the region.[21] Undoubtedly, improving the local infrastructure was worthwhile but it was unclear whether the improvements would be sustainable ones. There was no provision for financing the maintenance of these projects. There was the danger that insolvent states would fail to carry out routine maintenance. Indeed, by late 2002 it was being claimed that 'despite the massive international investment, infrastructure across the region is steadily de-capitalising'.[22]

The approach of Hombach and his team was in the best tradition of remote international bureaucrats. Micro-level assistance that might stimulate local economic and social recovery was rejected because the results were likely to be too slow in appearing. Physical reconstruction, perhaps based on rebuilding a set number of houses for returning refugees, was prioritised over broader projects meant to make the returns process sustainable. Privatisation was seen as the answer to the lack of economic progress by the World Bank which was implementing much of the economic side of the SP. In a region where very often the only well-organised and lucrative domestic economic entrepreneurs were engaged in the underground black economy, this approach risked transferring control of much of the economy from the state to mafia elements. The World Bank failed to prioritise restarting businesses in depressed or postwar localities – a process that required a longer term focus rather than one requiring rapid results.[23]

Claims that the SP would be part owned by the people of the region quickly evaporated into thin air. Local NGOs were swept aside which prompted a consortium of Balkan NGOs to set up a 'Stability Pact Watch'. In the period 2000–1, it hosted several conferences and also published a regular newsletter urging Hombach to consider alternative approaches, warning that authoritarian and corrupt forces would regroup upon the failure of the SP.[24] Hombach departed in the autumn of 2001 amidst an exchange of recriminations with EU's Chris Patten (who declared, 'I wish all those luck who now have to work with Bodo Hombach').[25] The EU Commission pondered whether to dissolve the SP but decided to redirect its work towards promoting concrete projects based on cross-border cooperation.[26] The SP had enjoyed some success in providing a forum where regional leaders could regularly meet. Erhard Busek, the Austrian politician, who became its new head talked of the need for it to get 'back down to earth':[27] 'viable solutions can only be achieved through enhanced local ownership. We will aim to transfer much more of the Stability Pact functions to the region'.[28]

The European Union and peace building in Macedonia

But there was often a deep-seated unwillingness for EU representatives with key Balkans responsibilities actually to base themselves in the region. The EU's special representative in Macedonia from July 2004, Michael Sahlin from Sweden, was originally going to be a non-resident representative until events on the ground compelled him to be based permanently in Skopje.[29] Escalating disagreements over an ambitious and highly charged decentralisation scheme threatened to plunge relations between ethnic Macedonians and Albanians back into crisis. In 2001, the European Union had played a crucial role in containing serious ethnic strife and had since worked to produce a constitutional settlement for more balanced ethnic relations. The decentralisation package was indeed the last major element of the 2001 Ohrid Agreement brokered by the European Union that needed to be voted into law.[30] Moderate political forces in both communities had been in the ascendancy since 2002, but radicals committed to ethnic separation were active in both communities. They were able to exploit emotive issues since it was clear that in some parts of the country the changes were bound to result in a redistribution of ethnic power.

The decentralisation plan was meant to reverse the centralisation of power in Macedonia which many in both main communities complained of. It had stifled initiative, disempowered local authorities and produced alienation (particularly among Albanians) towards a distant bureaucracy. Under the new law, control over a range of services including schools, health, construction, local economic development, and some taxes would pass from the centre to local authorities.[31] But the shake up would involve the reduction of the number of municipalities from 123 to 70. The key question was which municipalities would be merged, and, in particular, which mainly Macedonian ones would become part of enlarged ones with an Albanian majority. The fact that presidential elections had been held early before the issue came to the boil, owing to the untimely death in a plane crash of President Boris Trajkovski on 26 February 2004, was fortunate. Prime Minister Branko Crvenkovski was elected President and the multi-ethnic coalition endured. But any new law that alienates citizens in specific localities could turn out to be a Pyrrhic victory for the authorities.[32] The difficult nature of the decision encouraged some officials to search for international mediation, but the omens for Macedonian stability are not good if local forces do this as a matter of course.[33]

The European Union has made timely interventions meant to consolidate peace that don't involve interference in domestic politics. In February 2004 Macedonia became the third country in the region to receive an EU 'blacklist' of people accused of hampering peace efforts. The list contained 10 ethnic Albanian names and 2 ethnic Macedonian names, individuals being sought by the police on serious criminal charges or on the basis of having leadership roles in the underground Albanian National Army (AKsh).[34] But the ability of the European Union to successfully promote reforms that will provide the efficient and growth-orientated state which can transcend ethnic divisions remains in question.

A 2002 report by independent consultants commissioned by Brussels found that between 1991 and 2001, €500 million worth of EU aid designed to foil corruption and build a strong civil society in Macedonia failed to accomplish its goals. The report found that a much larger sum, €1.5 billion sent to the region as a whole with these objectives was to a large degree wasted. Both Brussels and the government in Skopje were at fault. The authorities had no development strategy and thus no idea how and where to target the flow of funds. The usual bureaucratic difficulties involving Brussels also came into play and EU representatives seemed prepared to continue the funding programme even though they knew that it was often being spent inappropriately.[35]

There are few signs that the European Union is aware of the degree to which corruption threatens its objectives in Macedonia – the regional cornerstone of its peace-building strategy in the Balkans. It assumed critical levels and had reached the very top of government by the late 1990s. Macedonia was both a source and transit area for human trafficking and smuggling of weapons, drugs, fuel and cigarettes. In many ways this corruption was a cross-community enterprise; there were high levels among the Albanian minority partly because it was excluded from the official state in many respects.

The international strategy crafted by the European Union since 2001 emphasises 'process' and 'capacity building' – the passing of laws and the training of officials so as to reduce opportunities for corruption. It relies on local bodies, an Ombudsman and a planned Anti-Corruption Commission, or the media and civil society, in order to challenge an elite of which large sections are corrupt. If huge amounts of international aid are poured into Macedonia without the international community being able to oversee how it is spent, then it will probably feed the corruption process. According to the International Crisis Group (ICG), a serious anti-corruption effort would involve having international watchdogs in the key spending ministries as well as in the customs service, the prosecutor's office and the judiciary. Aid would need to be conditional on serious anti-corruption reform. The ICG's report of 2002 warned that no international actor believed that leading the fight against corruption in Macedonia was its responsibility. If this issue was ducked, it feared that the Framework Agreement would end up as a paper peace.[36]

Balkan States on the fast-track to EU membership

From 2001 to 2005, the European Union was due to channel €4.6 billion to Romania, a country whose reputation for state-level corruption exceeded even Macedonia's.[37] Directing such a large sum with the proviso that it needed to be spent quickly in order to prepare the country for full membership of the European Union increasingly appeared to be a major stimulus for corruption. In its report for the period from 1 July 2002 to 30 June 2003, the European Office for Combatting Fraud (OLAF) reported that of the 125 dossiers investigated from 13 candidate countries no less than 49 involved Romania.[38]

Both Romania and Bulgaria had received invitations at the EU's Helsinki summit in December 1999 to open talks for full membership. The implications were obvious. If the negotiations were successful, two post-communist Balkan states would be at the heart of the EU integration process, not just countries that spasmodically flitted into the EU's zone of vision. It is worth recalling the reasons why Bulgaria and Romania were invited to become full players in the mainstream Europe of the European Union. The impetus did not stem from a perception in

Brussels that both of them were able to fulfil the membership terms. Indeed, at the start of 1999, when an armed rebellion of coal miners was only narrowly contained by a jittery government, Romania appeared to have all the hallmarks of a fissile Balkan state.[39] Bulgaria was also still recovering from a financial collapse in 1996 which saw a switch in power from post-communists, who had diverted state resources to their business cronies on a massive scale, to centre-right reformers (Giatzidis 2002: 68–70).

However, in 1999, the seventy-eight-day Kosovo conflict had briefly transformed Romania and Bulgaria from Balkan 'backwaters' to states crucial for NATO security in a confrontation with Serbia whose outcome by no means appeared a foregone conclusion until its very final stages (Gallagher 1999: 301–2). Both states overcame past suspicions of one another and synchronised their efforts to assist NATO. The Bulgarian President Petur Stoyanov declared in April 1999 that the conflict in Yugoslavia was one 'confronting the democratic world with the last communist regime in Europe'.[40] Along with Romania, it denied Russia permission to overfly its airspace to reinforce and supply troops it had rushed to Priština at the end of the NATO campaign. Aligning with the West over Kosovo placed Bulgaria sharply at odds with Russia, often seen as its longstanding ally; in 2001, Bulgaria expelled three Russian diplomats with the Foreign Minister Solomon Pasi declaring that 'Bulgaria is prepared to pay the price for its national sovereignty'.[41]

The 1999 Helsinki decision was widely viewed as a reward for the high-level support they had extended to the West over the Kosovo crisis. Tony Blair, on his way to Sofia and Bucharest in May 1999 to address the respective national Parliaments, astonished his advisers by deciding to promise Romania and Bulgaria early membership in return for their support in this high-risk conflict (Kampener 2003: 55). Britain and Germany, hitherto unenthusiastic about supporting their entry because of the impediments they faced in meeting EU conditions, dropped these reservations. The European Commission, which had previously indicated its opposition to including them in the next round of enlargement, also fell into line (Phinnemore 2001: 259–61).

As will be seen, it has been security issues not ones central to the EU entry process that have continued to provide the momentum behind negotiations, above all, in the case of Romania.

The European Union considered that Romania and Bulgaria were countries whose problems were so similar that they deserved to be grouped in a single category during the accession process and be given an identical entry date which, by 2002, was 2007. But five years of deepening EU engagement with these countries has seen growing discrepancies between them. Despite its economy staging a partial recovery after 2000, Romania has fallen clearly behind Bulgaria in its ability to meet entry conditions. These centred around the Copenhagen criteria, agreed at a 1993 EU summit in Denmark. The criteria emphasised: (1) the stability of institutions guaranteeing democracy, the rule of law and human rights; (2) a functioning market economy as well as the capacity to cope with competitive pressure and market forces within the European Union and (3) the ability to take on the obligations of membership including adherence to the aims of political, economic and monetary union.[42]

In retrospect, it became possible to see that Stalinism had been less intense in Bulgaria than in Romania before 1989 and that authoritarian forces had been far less successful in colonising the political and economic space in the post-communist era (Gallagher 2003: 16–22). Overall, the reform constituency has been stronger in Bulgaria right through the transition period that is in its fifteenth year at the time of writing. The election of Bulgarian reformers with a secure majority and committed to structural change in 1997 coincided with the willingness of the West to step up the inclusion of the Balkans in Euro-Atlantic integration efforts. A different set of reformers belonging to the party set up by ex-King Simeon won the 2001 elections and have been pursuing broadly similar policies. By contrast, in Romania, the centre-right suffered a catastrophic defeat in 2000 and ceased to be a serious force. Avowed reformers were in office but not in power. From 1996 to 2000, a heterogeneous four-party coalition presided over tumbling living standards which had created growing impatience in the population with the democratic process (Gallagher 2004: 244–50). Disunited reformers were dependent upon a state machine attuned to the needs of the post-communists in charge from 1990 to 1996. Parallel structures had been created under Nicolae Ceauşescu (1965–89) and, in many cases, refined under his successor, Ion Iliescu (1989–96, 2000–4) which meant there were blocking mechanisms in the judiciary and the security services that thwarted unwelcome change. The 1991 Constitution had also created a parliament with two chambers whose powers were virtually identical, a recipe for legislative gridlock.

The ex-communists, soon to be renamed the Social Democratic Party (PSD) swept back to power in 2000 with ultra-nationalists in a strong second place. It soon became impossible for the European Union to ignore the emergence of an oligarchy based around the ruling PSD. It had taken shape during the government's first extended period in office until 1996, when a wealthy new class had emerged, as state property was informally transferred to private hands, lucrative contracts were granted to government supporters and virtually interest-free bank loans were awarded to PSD and state officials.

After 2001, some 70 per cent of elected representatives had their own businesses to which they often devoted more attention than to their parliamentary duties.[43] The economic upturn and the arrival of EU funds failed to erode deep-seated poverty. Romania remained a low-wage, high-tax economy in which purchasing power had fallen by nearly 50 per cent since 1990. In 1989 Romanians had been weighed down by shortages, but household costs such as rent and heating usually did not exceed 10 per cent of an average income. Fifteen years later, these costs exceeded the average salary or pension on which most citizens tried to subsist.[44]

A clique around the PSD, at national and local-level, grew steadily richer as millions of Romanians started to flock abroad to work in menial jobs in order to support their families. The PSD was willing to pursue energetic reform measures only if strongly pressed by Brussels. It strongly resisted pressure to reform the legal system and took steps to tighten its hold on the public administration.

Anti-corruption prosecutors were taken off sensitive cases and top officials supposedly protected by a law guaranteeing security of tenure (that had been introduced under EU pressure in 2000) were marginalised if not dismissed outright.[45] The PSD failed to convert itself into a social democratic party comparable to the Socialist Party in Hungary or the Democratic Left Alliance in Poland. It bore closer resemblance to the parties in different parts of the former Soviet Union which had smartly dumped the communist ideology while retaining a monopolistic approach to politics and a desire to channel state assets towards party leaders and their business allies.

But Romania's hopes of joining the European Union steadily brightened and it was quickly invited to join NATO in 2002 having previously been seen as an unlikely member because of issues of economic weaknesses and problems of governance and human rights. The Al-Qa'eda's attacks on New York and Washington on 11 September 2001 had changed the accession criteria. The Bush administration in Washington chose to single out military reform and a demonstrable willingness to help counter the threat of global terrorism as the key criteria which ought to determine whether an applicant state was ready to join NATO.

The United States also suddenly found itself needing countries in the Black Sea region ready to provide bases, overfly rights and even local troops for terrorist threats further east. Romania (along with Bulgaria) proved willing to fulfil such roles when existing NATO members in South-East Europe, Greece and Turkey, were reticent or unwilling. Even before 11 September, President George Bush had been re-evaluating the USA's strategic objectives. Growing American interest in the vast oil and gas supplies of the Caspian Sea and on securing pipelines for delivery of these energy sources was starting to raise the profile of this part of South-East Europe in the White House.[46]

No other European state was as forthright in its backing for the US occupation of Iraq as Romania. By the end of September 2002, Romania had made it clear that it would provide all that was necessary for the United States other than Romanian combat troops. On 1 August, Romania had become one of the first countries in the world to sign a bilateral agreement with the United States giving American soldiers and diplomats immunity from prosecution by the International Criminal Court (ICC), a global war crimes court under the jurisdiction of the United Nations. The United States was then in dispute with most of its European allies over this and the European Commission told Bucharest on 9 August: 'we would have expected a future member state to have at least coordinated with us on such an important issue'.[47]

The government faced a barrage of accusations in the eleven months prior to the Prague summit that it was trying to muzzle the media, hound independent prosecutors serious in their approach to dealing with corruption cases involving PSD notables and disable those parts of the opposition most ready to energetically challenge it. That it was disinclined to rectify these matters suggested that, by now, NATO membership was virtually in the bag. Indeed, the Foreign Minister Mircea Geoana declared on 29 August 2002 that NATO membership was 'a done deal'.[48]

The government was able to furnish abundant information to Washington since Romania had built a large part of Iraq's infrastructure in the 1980s.[49] Moreover, close ties had been maintained well into the 1990s between acting and former members of the Romanian intelligence services and counterparts from Middle Eastern states, some of whom settled in Romania after 1989 to become important businessmen. Washington seemed untroubled that such intelligence figures would have access to sensitive NATO information and in April 2004 Romania joined as a full member.

Romania's ties with the European Union were ultimately not harmed by its close identification with the controversial Middle East strategy of the Bush administration. A powerful consortium of EU states also wanted Romania inside the European Union by 2007. Its most vocal backers – Britain, Italy and Spain – are also the EU states which (until 2004) gave strongest support to President Bush's military aims in the Middle East. These Atlanticist states (dependent on Middle East oil supplies for their economic viability) had been impressed by Romania's readiness to act as a bridgehead for US-led operations there. For Italy and Germany, which had stagnant economies, Romania also represented an important economic prize. Tariff barriers have been lowered in line with EU requirements. The deepening relationship with the European Union coincides with a flood of imports against which Romanian producers, whether agricultural or commercial, find it very difficult to compete. It appears hard to envisage how Romania will become a functioning market economy if one of the main results of EU entry is a flood of cheaper and better-produced goods which Romanian producers will be powerless to match for years to come.

Romania made very slow progress in closing negotiations for thirty-one 'chapters' of EU law known as the *acquis communautaire*. The ones concerning the transparency of the justice system, the effectiveness of regulatory state agencies and the ability of industry and agriculture to compete effectively with EU partners raised stark challenges. Unlike Bulgaria which received it in 2002, Romania was denied the status of being a functioning market economy. Indeed, it was the only candidate country failing in this respect despite being the second-largest recipient of EU funding designed to prepare it to withstand the rigours of full membership.

The European Union had failed to devise a customised strategy for Romania that took into account the problems arising from the nature of its totalitarian legacy, with a political class largely composed of individuals who (despite, or because of, the communist backgrounds of many) were essentially concerned with acquiring personal fortunes courtesy of the state and subsequently the European Union.[50] The accession process is largely identical to that for the candidate countries joining in 2004 and indeed for those who joined in earlier rounds centring on the need to absorb the entire body of regulations of the European Union which have been accumulated and revised over the last forty-five years. Thus, the *acquis communautaire* consists of:

- the contents, principles and objectives of the EU treaties;
- the legislation adopted in application of the treaties and the case law of the European Court of Justice;

- the declarations and resolutions adopted by the Union;
- measures relating to the Common Foreign and security policy;
- internal agreements concluded by the European Union and among the member states themselves in the field of the Union's activities (*After Milošević* 2001: 255).

Thirty-one chapters need to be opened and completed before a candidate country can be deemed to have fulfilled the entry terms. These terms are far weightier and complex than those Spain, Portugal and Greece had been required to fulfil in the 1980s because the powers of decision-making and regulation of the European Union have vastly increased in the subsequent two decades. Their public administrations, which escaped the corrosive effects of communist decision-making, nevertheless struggled to complete the much less demanding EU road map of the 1980s. It would be interesting to know if a debate ever occurred inside the relevant EU departments about whether a specific accession strategy that addressed the specific needs of a country like Romania was required. If it did, the advocates of 'the one size fits all' strategy prevailed.[51]

The way the EU's pre-accession instruments – Phare, Ispa and Sapard – have sometimes been implemented does not provide convincing proof that they are adequate ones for overcoming massive problems inherited from communism and a decade of non-reform. They are supposed to modernise the country's infrastructure and economy and prepare Romania for competing with existing members in the economic marketplace. But the allocation of funding was often in the hands of local politicians who dominated regional development agencies and were more concerned with profiting personally from the largesse than in using it to try and transform the country's prospects. Moreover, OLAF, the anti-corruption arm of the European Union, was hardpressed to track the fate of pre-accession money. Indeed, the decision whether to take action against those who had corruptly handled EU funds was left to the government official who monitored the spending of state money. He was also a vice-president of the ruling party and in mid-2004 he agreed not to pursue a case against senior members of his own party whose handling of Phare funds OLAF had investigated and found to be seriously wanting.[52]

The Romanian justice system was particularly impervious to reform.[53] As the main instrument to support institution building in candidate states, the European Union promoted 'twinning': Romanian officials would go to the Justice Departments, prosecutors officers and courts of EU states, learn good practice and return to Romania to implement all the good examples. Civil servants and consultants would be seconded from EU states, usually in lager numbers, to work in receiving institutions such as the Justice Ministry. Ultimately, the European Union was relying on the willingness of the government not to take reprisals against officials who wished to substitute the goal of public service for that of acting primarily in the ruling party's interest. By early 2002 there were no less than 503 twinning projects in the 12 candidate countries. They ran on average for eighteen months and cost €1 million each. The European Court of Auditors produced a damning assessment of the twinning programme in 2003, finding that the projects had produced scant progress in the implementation and enforcement of EU laws and practices.[54] One drawback was the payment of EU experts at a daily rate that often exceeded the monthly salary of the officials among whom they were working, sometimes on very sensitive issues. Ill feeling and resentment would be hard to avoid if assistance proclaimed by Brussels as being intended for the recipient country was in fact 'serving as a system of outdoor relief for already rich foreigners'.[55] With the Western Balkans in mind, where such practices appeared likely to be replicated from 2004 onwards, the ICG argued that it is vital 'the money invested should be seen to benefit local civil-servants: enhancing their skills and knowledge, and providing them with vital experience of professional and disinterested administration'.[56]

Bulgaria made much more impressive progress in meeting the conditions for EU membership than Romania had done. It was also less strident in its backing for US policy in the Middle East (though Bulgarian troops were in Iraq by 2003), and it preferred to align with the EU over the 2003 ICC controversy. In 2001 visa restrictions on Bulgarian nationals intending to visit EU states had been lifted but would remain in place for Romanians until 2002 because the European Union failed to be convinced that Bucharest could easily prevent illegal immigration. A much bigger prize for Bulgaria was acquiring the status of a functioning market economy from the European Union in 2002. This accolade was withheld from Romania in 2002 and 2003 (Prime Minister Năstase initially claiming that there had been a mistranslation in the EU's Progress Report and Romania had indeed been upgraded).[57]

The temptation to get carried away with Bulgarian progress should be avoided. Ivan Kostov, prime minister from 1997 to 2001, was dogged by accusations of 'nepotism, corruption and of having links with organized crime structures'.[58] Police corruption was a major problem, judicial reform got bogged down in turf-wars and trafficking in children also surfaced as a disturbing issue. But the Bulgarian state appeared to satisfy the European Union with a more energetic response to most of its problems than its Romanian counterpart. An Adoptions Council was set up in 2003 which decides on each application for adoption brought before it. Moreover, in 2003, nearly 400 police were dismissed after being caught in the act of taking a bribe.[59] Only justice was a cause of real worry in Brussels as inter-departmental disputes slowed down the pace of reform and weakened the struggle against organised crime.[60]

The stronger capacity of the state and the greater willingness of the government to carry out EU recommendations was shown by the much faster progress of Bulgaria in completing the EU road map. In July 2002 Bulgaria had concluded negotiations for 21 out of 31 chapters of the *acquis communautaire*. Romania at that time had still to open 3 and had completed only 13.[61] By February 2004 Bulgaria had completed 27 chapters but Romania still had 10 to successfully complete, including several of the most difficult ones.[62] The chief Bulgarian negotiator with the European Union along with the finance, transport and labour ministers were also graduates of prestigious Western universities while nobody remotely like that could be found in the post-2000 Romanian government.[63] Around seventy young technocrats who had been the backbone of the Romanian negotiating team were promptly dismissed in 2001 and substituted by a larger group of inexperienced appointees whose only real qualification often appeared to be their personal closeness to PSD notables.[64] The Romanian minister of European Integration, Mrs Hildegard Puwak, was eventually forced from office in September 2003 after it emerged that firms belonging to her husband and son had obtained 150,000 euros from the Leonardo Da Vinci vocational training programme.[65] She was later cleared of any personal wrongdoing but there were numerous allegations that funding in this programme was being mishandled.[66]

Romania's application ran into unexpected trouble in January 2004. Baroness Emma Nicholson, the European Parliament's Rapporteur for Romania, released a highly critical report. In it she raised fresh concerns about children in state care and warned that 'if Romania is serious about EU membership, the trade in children must stop completely'.[67] Soon after, the wind was rather taken out of her sails when it emerged that EU notables, including Romano Prodi, the Commission President and Alvaro Gil-Robles, former President of the European Parliament, had lobbied for the right to allow exemptions for the country's moratorium on international adoptions – brought in during 2001 largely thanks to strong EU pressure![68] But Romania's difficulties were added to when the Dutch Christian Democratic politician, Arie Oostlander, called for negotiations with Romania to be suspended because of its inability to make progress in meeting entry terms. Oostlander was the Rapporteur for Turkey and Prime Minister Năstase publicly suggested that he was acting to strengthen Turkey's membership claim at Romania's expense.[69] Both Nicholson and Oostlander joined forces to table a motion for debate at the Parliament's Foreign Affairs committee on 19 February that called for the suspension of negotiations. It had been expected that Romania's sponsors would ensure that it was thrown out, but instead the committee agreed to recommend that the European Union 'reorientate' its approach towards Romania. Nicholson's draft report was endorsed and passed with only minor amendments by the full plenum of the European Parliament on 11 March 2003. It warned that 'Romania faces serious difficulties fulfilling the [membership] requirements . . . and becoming a member in 2007 is impossible' unless Romania implements anti-corruption measures, ensures the independence of the justice system and also the freedom of the press.[70]

The official Romanian reaction was a complacent one. Năstase complained that there was a hidden EU agenda, that the European Union had had a fit of nerves or that it was normal for Brussels to issue warnings to countries nevertheless doing well at this stage of the accession process.[71] He and his colleagues talked about 'a counter-offensive' or 'an action plan' in order to undo the damage.[72] In a hasty cabinet reshuffle no less than five people were given positions of responsibility for EU integration. Ioan Talpes, the former head of foreign intelligence and head of President Iliescu's office was placed in overall charge, despite having no evident expertise in EU matters.[73] Upon returning from Brussels on 26 February, Năstase promised that 3 years of reforms would be carried out in

4 months.[74] Brussels was increasingly wary of such inflated claims because by now it was well aware that even if the political will was there bureaucratic failures meant it would be difficult to act on such promises. Between October 2001 and spring 2003, the government had mapped out, launched and then relaunched its anti-corruption strategy without any noticeable decrease in the level of corruption.

By contrast, Bulgaria in 2004 made steady progress towards its accession goal. The report submitted to the European Parliament's Foreign Affairs committee by its Rapporteur for Bulgaria, Geoffrey van Orden, also a British Member of the European Parliament (MEP), adopted a tone contrasting markedly with that of Baroness Nicholson in her report on Romania. In summary, it 'congratulates Bulgaria on having been able to provisionally close twenty-six out of the thirty-one negotiation chapters; requires timely proposals from the Commission, the Presidency, and the Member States to enable Bulgaria to complete negotiations early in 2004'; these were completed in June 2004.[75]

In October 2002, Bulgarian frustrations about being linked with slow moving Romania had spilled out in public. The European Affairs minister, Megleva Kuneva declared that this arrangement hindered Bulgaria's chances of joining in 2007.[76] In response, Vasile Puskas, the Romanian chief negotiator, complained that Bulgaria's wish to disassociate itself from Romania in the accession process was 'Machiavellian' and 'Byzantine'.[77] Here was evidence that the EU desire to adopt common procedures for dealing with both countries in the accession process had not encouraged warmer ties between them.

Bulgaria appeared assured of being accepted into the European Union in 2007. In February 2004, the European Commission had announced that it would be receiving the most generous allocation of funds proportionately ever given to any post-accession state.[78] Between 2007 and 2009 Bulgaria would receive funding amounting to 7 per cent of its GDP. Romania was due to receive a higher amount but in population terms it was proportionately less than Bulgaria's allocation.[79] The respective allocations were no doubt influenced by the persistent difficulties Romania had had in absorbing EU funds due to poor administrative capacity. Prime Minister Jan Peter Balkenende of the Netherlands – the country which held the Presidency of the European Union in the second half of 2004 – expressed uncertainty about whether Romania could emulate its neighbour and complete accession talks by the end of 2004.[80] Nevertheless, the PSD government of Adrian Năstase continued to enjoy important backing among powerful member states. Italy's Prime Minister Silvio Berlusconi had announced in 2002 that he would be Romania's 'special ambassador' with the European Union and NATO and his support continued to be unstinting. Italy, along with Germany, had important investments in Romania and enjoyed preferential trading links. France hoped that Romania would be a powerful ally within the European Union because of its traditional Francophone outlook while Britain, under Tony Blair, remained influenced by Năstase's strong support for Anglo-American security interests in the Middle East. With such high-level advocates the tougher re-orientation strategy for Romania, promised in Brussels, failed to materialise.

Romania, by now the largest country in the Balkans, and increasingly important in strategic terms, had important advocates who judged its fitness to join the

European Union on these strategic, commercial and political considerations and not on its ability to complete the arduous EU roadmap. Flexible entry terms were agreed which would not be available for the countries of the Western Balkans.[81]

What to do about the Western Balkans?

In June 1999, a time when the degree of West European involvement with the region was at its height owing to the recently ended Kosovo conflict, the European Union appeared to significantly reassess its approach to the Western Balkans. Statements from Brussels indicated that the main motivating force behind reform would be the offer of a credible prospect of EU membership once a country had fulfilled minimum political and economic conditions.[82] The new approach was branded the Stabilisation and Association Process (SAP). It involved assisting Albania, Bosnia, Croatia, Macedonia and Serbia-Montenegro to meet the conditions for EU entry (*acquis communautaire*). The emphasis would be on fulfilling core elements of the *acquis* 'in easily digestible pieces' rather than swallowing a formidable mass of conditions at the pace required by Bulgaria and Romania after 2000 when their engagement with the European Union began in earnest (*After Milošević* 2001: 256). Stabilisation and Association Agreement (SAA) were to be signed by countries intending to join the European Union which set out an agenda for training, modernisation, regulatory systems, institution building, good practice and exchange of information. The SAP gave special emphasis to issues such as combating crime and improving the justice system which the European Union felt had real implications for the security of Western Europe. Another key element was strengthening bilateral relations among the countries of the region by promoting trade relations, harnessing of energy, common infrastructural projects and joint measures to combat trans-border crime. The European Union in its turn liberalised its trade regime with the countries of the Western Balkans from September 2000 onwards. It offered duty-free access for most goods with the exception of some agricultural products. From late 2001, the European Union also drew up a new assistance programme for the region designed to anchor it to the EU enlargement process. This was the Community Assistance for Reconstruction, Development and Stabilisation (CARDS). Its total budget for aid to the Western Balkans was €4.65 billion up to 2006.[83]

The prospect of EU membership was explicitly offered at the EU summit in Feira, Portugal in June 2000 and agreed at the EU Balkan summit held in Zagreb the following November.[84] The European Union had come a long way from the mid-1990s when clean elections had been viewed as the main indicator of political progress in the Balkans. Institution building was now seen as the key to sustainable development (allied with the privatisation of much of the state economy). David Chandler, a stern critic not just of the international approach in the region but what he saw as the interference of international agencies in the sovereign affairs of Balkan states, decried the absence of active participation from local states in shaping the SAP and CARDS agenda. He wrote, not without reason, that 'the stress upon EU managerial control...leaves little doubt that the

SAP process is far from one of partnership'.[85] But there was no sign that ruling elites had many alternative proposals to enable Western money to make a stronger impact on the ground. Economists like Vladimir Gligorov and policy analysts from think tanks like the European Stability Institute (ESI) were wary of approaches already tried out elsewhere being applied in the Balkans without its special conditions and problems being taken into account. Gligorov argued that the Balkans should be treated as an underdeveloped region not as one which requires the application of the macrostabilisation programmes tried out in Central Europe in a bid to create market-based economies.[86] Privatisation programmes from the World Bank and the IMF carried out in partnership with the European Union were seen by the ESI as sometimes being responsible for profound economic and social dislocation. The sudden closure of the main employer in towns dependent on a single industry could increase crime and also affect inter-ethnic relations for the worse if the locality was an ethnically mixed one. In March 2003, Chris Patten described organised crime as 'a cancer, which could eat away the potential success of south-east Europe', but there was often a lack of awareness in Brussels about how economically insensitive policies that devastated local communities could enable such criminality to flourish.[87] The energetic Sofia-based think-tank, the Centre for Liberal Strategies, proposed 'a human security approach' to the problems of the Balkans based on strengthening human security. It could be defined as 'safety from such chronic threats as repression, oppression, hunger, disease, and protection from sudden and hurtful disruptions in the patterns of daily life'.[88] Measures which strengthened economic and social development, rather than ones that led to economic and social disruption (however virtuous were the longer term aims of radical economic surgery), were seen as the only likely precursors of effective democracy and long-term stability.[89]

The European Union signed a Stabilisation Agreement with Macedonia in April 2001 and with Croatia in September that year, but with none of the other countries did it appear that a similar breakthrough was likely. Croatia made rapid progress. It applied to join in 2003 and in April 2004 Brussels issued a positive opinion on its readiness to begin negotiations.[90] The nationalist Croatian Democratic Union (HDZ) which had returned to power in November 2003 under Ivo Sanader successfully repackaged itself as a modernising conservative force and promised to cooperate with the International Criminal Tribunal for Yugoslavia (ICTY) at The Hague and with easing the return of Serbian refugees.[91] Macedonia regressed due to the effects of the serious crisis of 2001 and only applied to join the European Union in March 2004. Albania seemed to be far from reaching that stage. The 2004 SAP report expressed disappointment that its previous recommendations 'had not been properly implemented'. It pointed to tensions between the main parties, and within the ruling Socialist Party itself, as being barriers to reforming the justice system, modernising the administration and combating corruption. The government was told by Brussels in March 2004 that 'it is crucial that it demonstrates political will, determination and the capacity to address the key issues identified in [the latest SAP] report without delay'.[92]

Turning to Bosnia–Herzegovina, Commissoner Patten felt that it needed to behave like a unified state before it could enter the SAP. 'We would like to see a self-sustaining state acting like a country not like "two and a bit countries" and that is an imperative', were his words in March 2003.[93] A year later progress had been identified but it was still felt that 'structural weaknesses persist and implementation of an SAA would be a major challenge'.[94] Serbia–Montenegro was also far behind, owing to the fact that relations with the European Union had only begun to be normalised in late 2000 and progress was dented by the killing of Prime Minister Djindić nearly thirty months later. It was only in the autumn of 2003 that Brussels started to work on a feasibility study on opening SAA negotiations with Belgrade.

The bulk of the CARDS assistance was concentrated in the years from 2000 to 2004. From 2004 to 2006, the countries of the Western Balkans were due to receive 'relatively little aid from the EU irrespective of their progress up the Stabilisation and Association ladder'.[95] The Balkans would find itself competing with the countries of the Southern Mediteranean and the Middle East for Brussels assistance. Most EU aid would be extended to the new accession states (twelve of them mostly from former communist East-Central Europe) which joined in 2004, and on Bulgaria and Romania, due to join in 2007. The ICG believed it was wrong that 'the countries which are the most unstable and the most in need of development assistance should be penalised in terms of lower assistance precisely because they are so problematic'.[96] There was a glimmer of hope that the European Union would retain its focus on the Balkans when the region's only EU full member, Greece, held the EU Presidency in the first half of 2003. It announced that the Western Balkans would be a key priority of its Presidency but no memorable initiatives emerged from this period.[97] The only significant breakthrough concerned Croatia which, under the nationalist HDZ from 2003, abandoned obstructive policies concerning cooperation with the Hague tribunal and the return of Serbian refugees. This raised hopes that Croatia could be in the European Union by 2009. But the other countries in the region were menaced by political instability, corruption and a range of economic problems. The problem did not just stem from the shortcomings of local political elites. Bosnia and Kosovo, whose affairs were supervised by a UN-mandated mission, were protectorates in all but name. In some eyes Macedonia qualified as a semi-protectorate given the strong international oversight of its affairs provided by the 2001 Ohrid Agreement. Serbia–Montenegro was a loveless union forcibly arranged in 2002–3 by the EU High Commissioner for Security Javier Solana. The road map for recovery and reform laid down by the European Union for each of these countries was dauntingly similar. 'One size fits all' seemed to be the watchword of Brussels. But the assistance appeared to have no significant impact on reducing the underdevelopment of the region. Sectors such as education, crucial for strengthening human capital, were neglected by the European Union not just in the Western Balkans but also in the two candidate countries of Bulgaria and Romania. A new European Commission headed by President Jose Manuel Barroso from Portugal – a country far removed from the problems of the region – took office in the autumn of 2004. It was far from clear if the new team would show the degree of engagement with the region's problems exhibited by Prodi, Solana and Patten. If attention were focussed on other challenges – mending relations with the United States, integrating the new accession states or reforming the EU and strengthening its existing powers – then it was likely to be only a matter of time before those at the top were forcefully reminded that there were states and territories in the Balkans that remained islands of acute instability in the new Europe.

Conclusion

The European Union (and indeed NATO) were slow to get involved in the Balkans even as its problems became dominant factors in European affairs from the early 1990s onwards. A deep-seated instinct was to adopt minimalist measures to contain its problems and particularly to prevent a large flow of refugees into the European Union. Boundary changes and an exchange of populations were initially favoured. These were answers from the second quarter of the last century when they seemed the only way to deal with implacable bilateral disputes from the Aegean to the Alps and the Franco-German borderlands. But redrawing borders only appeared to be an incentive to the intransigent parties in ethnic disputes and an invitation for new movements to press their claims violently. A period of drift characterised by a tendency to appease ethnic hardliners because they appeared to represent mainstream popular opinion, gave way to a less cynical and more optimistic outlook about what could be done in the Balkans. Kosovo was the catalyst. In 1999 there was sufficient transatlantic resolve to prevent Milošević completing a strategy of ethnic cleansing more audacious even than the ones perpetrated in Croatia and Bosnia. A new team took over in the European Commission that year which showed impressive common ground about the need to prioritise the Balkans and give the countries and territories of the region the chance to eventually find a place in the European Union as full members. The removal of Milošević in 2000 and the need to support a fragile successor regime with a tenuous pro-Western agenda, followed by the 2001 crisis in Macedonia, kept the attention of the European Union focussed on the region. Aid programmes were geared towards reconstruction of war-affected states, the rebuilding of infrastructure and the transformation of institutions. This was wrapped around the SAP, unfurled in 2000–1, which was meant to be a gateway for EU membership for the states of the Western Balkans. But the results have been mixed. Concentrated assistance has not provided a strong momentum behind economic recovery or the emergence of states with the capacity to effectively tackle major structural problems. The approach of the European Union has all too often been poorly coordinated and over-bureaucratised. The reliance on neo-liberal strategies encapsulated by rapid privatisation all too often gives additional leverage to predatory elements who have acquired wealth by their involvement in war or by looting the publicly owned economy. Corruption and organised crime are increasingly recognised as scourges that threaten not just the well-being of South-East Europe but the security of its western neighbours, yet the broader economic strategy promoted by the European

Union, the World Bank and IMF has failed to effectively confront these twin menaces. Only Croatia appeared to be well-advanced in the EU integration process by 2004. A range of internal problems prevented Albania, Macedonia and Serbia–Montenegro making significant headway. Under international supervision, Bosnia and Kosovo remained aid dependent territories whose political futures remained unclear (particularly in the latter case). From 2004, a new EU team, under Portugal's José Barroso had plenty of non-Balkan preoccupations. Its predecessor despite showing rare consistency and dedication in trying to overcome some of the region's problems had not devised strong instruments to do this effectively. There was a risk that the pressure of events (such as a new crisis in Macedonia or recurring unrest in Kosovo) might revive the appeal of old solutions such as border changes and transfers of population (still being promoted by Russia up to the present).[98] If Bulgaria and Romania successfully acceded to the European Union around 2007, what would be the fifth enlargement of the Union might provide welcome momentum for their Western neighbours. But, particularly in the case of Romania, the enlargement process has not been well-handled. It approaches the European Union as a weak and under-performing state with worrying authoritarian tendencies which, to put it mildly, has not made the best use of pre-accession funds from Brussels. Bulgaria has made more effective progress and could be a model for its western neighbour Macedonia, with which it shares close links. The European Union is more closely intertwined with the Balkans than it could have imagined it would be in 1994, but the process still remains an *ad hoc* one despite the unfurling of common strategies after 1999. Accordingly, there are still real dangers that it could be blown off course.

Conclusion
An uncertain political future
for the Balkans

The former communist states of South-East Europe face particular difficulties as efforts are made to embrace competitive systems of politics and economics, which they had scant familiarity with for two generations or more. The legacy of dictatorship is one that is hard to overcome although communist party states were more totalitarian and repressive in some places than in others. Forced industrialisation was taken to extreme lengths in Albania and Romania, being accompanied by rigid methods of political control influenced by the East Asian models of North Korea and Mao's China. The squandering of human and material resources on a gigantic scale in pursuit of obsolete heavy industrial goals saddled these countries (and also Bulgaria and parts of Yugoslavia) with colossal debts, unwanted factories, environmental degradation and a poorly utilised workforce. A heresy-hunting secret police was employed in most places to punish critics of this aberrant system. But a more calculating attempt was also made to reshape the popular consciousness. A political culture based around collectivism was promoted, in which, attitudes associated with freedom and individualism were screened out. People became accustomed to having their political thinking done by others. Taking initiatives, even in spheres far removed from politics, was discouraged. A conformist population encouraged to be dependent on the state and distrustful of any other source of influence or example, had emerged by the 1960s. In much of the region, societies were indoctrinated in an openly nationalist direction by communist elites seeking to mask policy failures or acquire freedom of action from Moscow. A political culture emphasising suspicion of the outside world and putting the blame for reverses on foreigners and, in some cases, local minorities or adjacent states, created a strongly nationalistic outlook. This was particularly the case in sections of the population caught up in the industrialisation process and who were left vulnerable by its collapse when the communist era drew to a close at the end of the 1980s.[1]

The legacy of intense authoritarian rule, colossal policy errors in the economic realm and a powerful sense of collectivism shading over into intolerant nationalism, was an ominous one for the region. The state boundaries of South-East Europe were relatively recent and there was plenty of potential for ethno-nationalist antagonisms to be rekindled across those borders or indeed within them. It was in Yugoslavia that this potential was realised with the most destructive effect in the 1990s. This is supremely ironic, not to say tragic, because communist Yugoslavia appeared to have avoided the worst policy failings of its Stalinist neighbours. Collectivisation of agriculture had been reversed in the early 1950s, central planning dismantled later in the decade and borders opened in the early 1960s allowing workers to migrate abroad and tourists to arrive in increasing numbers. An increasingly elaborate federal system was designed to manage ethnic differences, which had resulted in furious bloodletting during the Second World War. But the political system remained an autocratic and a closed one, however much it was decentralised. Economic failures enabled rivalries to be revived, especially between Serbia and some of the other republics and provinces in the federation. The successful manipulation of ethno-nationalism by the Serbian leader, Slobodan Milošević drove the federation over the cliff from 1989 onwards. Except for Slovenia in the far north-west, all the rest of Yugoslavia suffered a deep regression. Warfare and economic collapse resulted in the decline of the middle class, often the emigration of the most capable members of the younger generation and the rise of new social formations that had obtained their wealth through violence, extortion and wholesale theft. Nearly all the states and internationally administered territories that had emerged from the ashes of Tito's federalist state would find themselves far behind Bulgaria and Romania, Balkan countries that had previously been looked down upon.

Communist successor parties tried with varying degrees of success to manage the transition from one-party rule to competitive politics on their own agenda of usually limited change (Gallagher 2000: 106). The existence of majority–minority tensions or uncertainty over state boundaries led to a heightened sense of nationalism and this often made their task easier. In Romania and Serbia, the post-communists ruled with the assistance of ultra-nationalist formations for long periods after 1990. But in Bulgaria and Macedonia, the post-communist parties avoided making explicit nationalist appeals, despite the presence of Turkish and Albanian minorities who were regarded with suspicion by a majority of opinion. So the relationship between post-communist parties and nationalism was more complicated than it might appear at first sight. Sometimes, an external danger, such as that posed by Serbia towards Macedonia, could outweigh domestic nationalist preoccupations; sometimes, centre-right parties were able to seize the initiative from the social democratic successor of the pre-1989 ruling party. This happened in Albania and Croatia in contrasting conditions of economic collapse and engulfment in the first of the full-scale wars fought on Yugoslav soil. In Bulgaria, political conditions were ambiguous as power passed back and forth between the left and a strong centre-right challenger, neither of which proved able to decisively supplant the other. But in Bulgaria all the main political challengers refused to mobilise nationalism since this strategy was indelibly associated with the last phase of the discredited Zhivkov regime.

By the time Milošević was forced from office in the year 2000, all the states in the region had experienced a transfer of power to opposition forces. But it was easier for post-communist forces to stage a comeback than for self-styled reformers to consolidate their position and win re-election. The centre-right parties found it difficult to maintain broad popular support. Their reformist rhetoric lacked conviction if citizens who had turned to them experienced further economic hardship and with no tangible proof that the state was offering them higher-quality service. In Romania, the disappointment with the main foe of the ex-communists, the National Peasant and Christian Democratic Party (PNTCD) led to its elimination from parliament in 2000. Bulgaria once again proved an exception since disappointment with the austere measures of the Union of Democratic Forces ((UDF), elected in 1997) led to the victory of another centre-right formation, the Simeon II National Movement (SNM) under the former king. But arguably, Simeon secured his victory on populist terms by appearing to be a providential political figure capable of rapidly boosting personal living standards. The resulting disappointment with his record among many who flocked to the SNM makes the return of the Bulgarian Socialists in 2005 increasingly likely (despite the financial chaos associated with their last period in office).

The conditioning of communist times and the fact that the democratic era has resulted in falling living standards for most citizens of the region has instilled a powerful distrust of politics. Parties are nearly always among the most despised institutions in polls evaluating political attitudes. Parliament was often viewed as an arena where highly placed figures fulfilled their appetite at the public expense and even as a haven for individuals wishing to evade justice by acquiring parliamentary immunity. Parties lacked a strong local presence and the elected representatives usually did not feel the need to stay close to those who had elected them. Legislators were seen as more willing to champion the interests of powerful economic interests who subsidised their parties or helped to ensure that they had acquired a lifestyle that their constituents could only dream of. In the 1990s, ultra-nationalists were well-placed to exploit the failings of conventional parties. But except in Serbia and territories whose disputed status was the cause of acute uncertainty – Kosovo and the Republic of Srpska (RS) – their power tended to be on the wane after 2000. Businessmen attempted to fill the political vacuum by promising that, if given power, they could make the general populace more prosperous. Bogoljub Karić and Dan Voiculescu, two economic moguls from Serbia and Romania who enjoyed electoral success in 2004, [provided the clearest examples of a type of politics modelled on Silvo Berlusconi's Forza Italia]. More promisingly, independent-minded figures who promised effective local government have carved out a power-base separate from conventional parties. The best-known examples are Edi Rami in Tirana (though a member of the Socialist Party), Klaus Johannis in Sibiu, and Stefan Sofianski in Sofia. Effective local politicians able to deliver good public services are a vital requirement, especially in regions and districts where national parties have delivered simplified appeals, often by trading on ethnic tensions.

It is difficult to relaunch parties that have grown stale and out-of-touch in the grasp of old-guard figures. Albania is probably the best example of that, after 2000. Two ageing confrontational figures, Fatos Nano of the Socialists and Sali Berisha of the Democrats, have managed to repulse more capable and consensual younger figures, but at the cost of vastly increasing public disillusionment with politics. Ruling parties like Nano's Socialists which are dominated by narrow cliques, are doubly handicapped when confronted with the scale of the challenges they face. These involve rebuilding the economy along competitive lines, creating a pluralist political system, an administration with the capacity to shoulder these challenges and integrating with global and regional institutions. In the case of most of the states and territories of ex-Yugoslavia, recovering from the effects of warfare has to be added to this formidable list.

Not only in parts of ex-Yugoslavia, do states find it difficult to impose their authority on recalcitrant regions. The informal or underground economy is often beyond their reach (resulting in a low tax-base) and organised criminals are often able to openly defy or suborn law-enforcement agencies. This is particularly true in parts of the Balkans where communications are poor or different state jurisdictions have vied for control. The mainly hilly or mountainous regions between the Albanian coastal plain and the plain of Thrace (mainly to be found in Bulgaria) are perhaps the best example of recalcitrant regions that have tried to go their own way over a long historical period. The southern stretches of the Dinaric mountain chain and the Rhodope Mountains meet in the uplands of Albania, Kosovo and Macedonia. Here, there was much greater scope for the politicisation of ethnic differences than further north, in areas today comprising Croatia, Bosnia and Serbia. There were sharper linguistic contrasts: Greek, Albanian, Slavophone languages and Turkish were widely spoken. South Slavs shared and later competed for territory with Albanians and Greeks. The Ottomans Turks were wholly in control of this part of the Balkans for longer than elsewhere in the peninsula. Hanging on was a greater priority because of its proximity to Constantinople.

There were more enforced conversions in the southern Balkans than further north, which led to a greater number of Slavic or Albanian Muslims, as well as Turks, being located there. When active resistance to Ottoman rule got underway in the early nineteenth century, Christian–Islamic conflicts became more intense and bloodier than further north. They were soon accompanied by rivalries between the different national Orthodox churches enlisted by their states to legitimise claims to territory. The ill-defined territory known as Macedonia suffered terribly, owing to the determination of insecure young states to extend their territory to the maximum extent irrespective of the desires of the local inhabitants. Present-day Macedonia, Albania, Kosovo and parts of northern Greece centred on Thessaloniki were in fact the last part of 'Turkey in Europe' to be surrendered. The 1912–13 Balkan Wars created bitter enmities between those seeking to snatch as much of the remaining Ottoman inheritance as they could. The victorious states did not behave in ways designed to inspire respect or trust among the local inhabitants. The imposition of boundaries made life difficult for groups that didn't readily embrace a national identity. The Vlachs, pastoralists who moved from the plains to the mountains in line with the seasons, suffered badly in various conflicts extending from the First and Second Balkans Wars to the Greek Civil War of the late 1940s.

Internecine South-Slav enmities had scarred the Western Balkans during the Second World War. But the Tito regime strove to foster reconciliation through promoting rapid modernisation, with very little of this being seen in most of the communist-ruled southern Balkans. Inter-marriage, increasingly commonplace in the cities of Bosnia was hardly evident in parts of the southern Balkans where Slavophones and Albanians existed in uneasy proximity. The massacre of Albanians, which occurred when Serbian armies took possession of Kosovo in 1912, left little prospect that both ethnic groups could share it in amity. Further pacification of Kosovo in 1944–5 by Tito's Partisans gave fresh cause for hatred to fester. Foreign visitors to the Presovo valley of south-west Serbia in 2000, discovered that 'oral histories of expulsion and atrocity can readily be found in households throughout the area', ones that circulated from at least the late nineteenth century.[2] State frontiers often coincided with rugged or inhospitable terrain that was ideal for smuggling. During the 1990s, when UN economic sanctions were imposed on Serbia and Serbia in its turn closely watched what went in and out of Kosovo, old smuggling routes were re-opened. Clandestine economies sprung up, controlled by men who owed no allegiance to any state and never paid their taxes. The smuggling of cigarettes, hard drugs and weapons coupled with the trafficking of illegal immigrants and women sold into sexual slavery, created fiefdoms which conventional state and trans-national agencies found it difficult to subdue. Albanians were to the fore in developing this underground political economy of crime. For elaborate explanation, it is necessary to look to the fact that they were the biggest losers in the state formation process that ensued between 1878 and 1945. Accordingly, they had less cause to give loyalty to states, which they felt treated them badly. This also applied to the repressive state controlled by Enver Hoxha in Albania as well as its post-communist successors. The impetus to emigrate was greater, which meant that a large Diaspora community had sprung up on both sides of the Atlantic. The existence of an Albanian Diaspora enabled fruitful links to be made with drug trafficking gangs from South America looking for means to transport drugs into Western Europe.[3] It is the need to contain such criminal networks and prevent them wreaking devastation in West European cities which is likely to encourage the European Union to remain an active player in the Balkans even if its post-conflict strategies are not blessed with early success.

Most Albanians have no links with the crime barons and the most thoughtful ones can see only too clearly the damage they cause to the reputation of a national group which has only advanced painfully and slowly from positions of subordination in Kosovo and Macedonia with international backing. Organised crime is even closer to the centre of power in Serbia and led to the killing of Prime Minister Djindjić in 2003, President Gligorov of Macedonia narrowly escaping death as a result of crossing criminal interests in 1995. Both were consensual figures with a post-nationalist agenda. Gangsters and mafia figures have a vested interest in ensuring that international conventions and laws do not impede their activities. Therefore, a natural tendency exists for them to patronise chauvinist politicians and parties who insist that only nationalist norms should shape state policy. Their influence is likely to wane, only if a new economy emerges which supplants the abnormal one that flourished in the shadow of war, economic sanctions and the debilitating long-term effects of the communist system. War and its attendant disruptions even in places which remained at peace, prevented the growth of economies which supply the needs of the domestic market, employ large numbers of citizens in productive as opposed to speculative or criminal activities and earn revenue from legitimate trading abroad. It was probably in post-2001 Macedonia that the struggle for supremacy between those who preferred a weak state unable to supervise the economy and other forces committed to a state able to gradually bring to heel criminal structures which diverted revenues and enforced property rights according to its own values, was at its most intense. The ex-guerilla fighter Ali Ahmeti made common cause with moderate ethnic Macedonians to try to enforce a political settlement based on ethnic power-sharing. But they were confronted by Ljubčo Georgievski, the ex-Prime Minister defeated in the 2002 elections and also by Albanian parties which had lost positions in the government. What this alliance of ethnic Macedonian radicals and opportunist Albanians had in common was that, the leading figures had grown wealthy during the crisis years in which the Macedonia economy had suffered owing to acute regional instability and low political standards in high places. The emergence of politically settled times threatened to marginalise them. The outcome of this struggle could well determine not only whether a fragile peace was consolidated in Macedonia but also whether the often-combined forces of radical nationalism and underground crime could be stopped in their tracks in neighbouring Kosovo and Serbia.

The appeal of the Orthodox Church and the military was high in post-war Macedonia among a majority distrusting its own politicians and often unhappy at the extent of concessions made to ethnic Albanians. These institutions and the traditional values they encapsulated, enjoyed high standing across much of the rest of the region. Even in Greece, which escaped the destructive communist experience, the Orthodox Church and the armed forces, outstrips Parliament, the Justice system, political parties and the European Union in popular esteem.[4] It is hardly encouraging for democratic prospects across the region, that two hierarchical bodies whose performance is not related to social and economic policy and whose internal standards of behaviour often fall short of their perceived image, score so highly (Stan 2003: 16). There is no sign of the military asserting its influence in politics (except in Serbia) but there are increasing signs that the dominant religion is not afraid to exploit its popularity. This is true of Croatia where the Catholic Church threw its weight against cooperation with the International Criminal Tribunal for Yugoslavia (ICTY) in The Hague, Serbia where the Orthodox Church did likewise and acquired important educational and financial concessions from post-Milošević governments and also Macedonia where the Orthodox Church became a rallying ground for nationalism, especially after the destruction of venerated religious monuments.

Traditional institutions enjoy their greatest appeal among the elderly, who turn out to vote in larger numbers than the rest of the population and also rural dwellers. It is easy to mobilise the rural poor and the elderly, on a dependency basis. Millions of pensioners depend on a tiny state allowance and, although they live below the threshold of poverty, they still strongly incline towards rhetorically leftist parties like the Bulgarian Socialist Party (BSP) and Social Democratic Party (PSD) in Bulgaria and Romania, which have failed to safeguard them when in power. The number of subsistence farmers has swelled wherever heavy industry has been in retreat and they also depend on parties that exercise power at local or national level. The control, political bosses have over licences and permits to collect wood or over social welfare grants envelops vulnerable social groups in a web of informal and formal arrangements that influences their voting behaviour.[5] This is even true of residents who live in the peripheral suburbs of major Balkans cities. Their size has mushroomed due to the social engineering policies of communist states or the need to escape from war. In some cases, the suburbs, characterised by overcrowded housing, minimal amenities, packs of dogs and the music with plangent oriental sounds that enjoys popularity from Herzegovina to the Black Sea, appear in danger of overwhelming the more historic and refined urban core.

Many of the political figures who have come to prominence in the Balkans since 1989 have mobilised the traditional, dependent sectors of the population who have low expectations and a pre-disposition for authoritarian solutions. Among their number are former communists like Iliescu, figures from the professions, particularly medicine, like Berisha who has built up a large clientele among rural people (something that doctors can easily do owing to the skills they possess and their access to scarce medication), intellectuals in ethnically divided territories (Georgievski and the intransigent Albanian educationalist, Fadil Sulejmani in Macedonia, as well as Karadžić in Bosnia) but also figures from the underground economy or organised crime, adept at consolidating power through patron-client relations. Parties very often have a nebulous ideology and are based around a powerful individual and a retinue who follow him unconditionally unless his power to deliver electoral rewards and the spoils of office begins to desert him. A Romanian, writing in 2004, observed that in such parties the leader acts like a gypsy chieftain or 'bulibasa'. His subordinates do all that they possibly can, to ingratiate themselves with him. Nobody dares to take an initiative so as not to risk entering into conflict with 'şeful' (the chief).[6]

The inner life of these parties is often non-existent. Much energy is devoted to capturing the state and diverting its revenue to party figures and their business allies. What Lavinia Stan has written about Romania applies to a greater or lesser degree to most other countries discussed here: 'A vast share of government revenue leaks into the pockets of well-connected businessmen who choose to lend financial support to sympathetic political parties' (Stan 2003: 15). Even states that experience significant privatisation of the economy can witness the rise of a limited number of parties who try to channel the resulting proceeds towards their supporters in order to exercise a monopoly over the political system. Nowhere has this succeeded absolutely, since all countries in the region have witnessed substitutions in office. But oligarchic tendencies, involving the transfer of economic and political power to a limited few, are strong. In Bulgaria, Albania and Romania just under a quarter of national income and consumption belonged to 10 per cent of the population in 2004. This compares well with the Czech Republic (22.4%),

Hungary (22.8%) and Poland (27.4%).[7] But the crucial point to note is that, there had already been a higher income differential in the Central European communist states before 1989 thanks to policies that encouraged the emergence of a middle-class. The Balkan states mentioned had been rigidly egalitarian yet, in the space of fifteen years population, inequality in income had already reached or surpassed the Central European states. This suggested that there was a much higher upward redistribution of income taking place in the Balkans than in Central Europe and there is nothing to suggest that the trend will not continue or even intensify.

These economic trends make it more difficult for more genuine democratic alternatives and modern-minded people behind them to break through into front-rank politics. They represent the better-educated, younger and largely urban sectors of the electorate. In no Balkan country have they managed to establish their ascendancy. Ex-King Simeon's SNM, has gone further in pursuing structural reforms than any other government recently in office but this party has failed to rally younger modernising elements and is, instead, dominated by regional and local powerbrokers with lawyers strongly to the fore. The tendency of young, politically aware Balkan city dwellers is to steer clear of politics and achieve professional fulfilment in business or hi-tech pursuits that often means emigrating. Often only the media, particularly the press and radio stations, offers a creative outlet for politically minded young people but journalism is often a frustrating and even dangerous occupation and the electronic media is kept under tight state control wherever possible.

Women have not been to the fore in Balkan politics. They are numerous only in the internationally supervised states and territories of Bosnia and Kosovo with their proportional systems. In both cases, this is due to the insistence of the Office of High Representative (OHR) and UN Interim Administrative Mission in Kosovo (UNMIK), that the parties place women in electable positions on their lists and that voters can only select party candidates in descending order and not vote for them at random. It means a block of women is found in the parliaments of both territories (but at the price of giving centrally run parties absolute control over the selection of candidates, preventing any prospect of renewal from the grassroots or the provinces). In Bulgaria, the former foreign minister Nadezhda Mihailova became leader of the main centre-right opposition force, the UDF after 2001 but this was too much for the party's domineering ex-leader Ivan Kostov to bear and in 2004 he launched a new party on a macho platform, promising strong rule. In Romania, women are conspicuous by their absence from mainstream politics, but here some women who have shown the patience and resilience to survive adversity and build up a cohesive team of activists have guided some of the most effective NGOs.

Everywhere, much of the struggle for material survival falls on women's shoulders, leaving little room for political activism. Statistics from Albania show why political activism is a very narrowly based profession. Almost a quarter of Albanians are registered as unemployed; many more do not earn a living wage. Only 18 per cent of the population enjoy a regular electricity supply and only 1 in 6 household has constant running water.[8] In this and many other Balkans countries, the income of the urban middle-classes is swallowed up by food and utility payments, which means they don't have the leisure time or the freedom to consider the long-term investment of time and energy that politics requires. The Human Development rankings produced annually by the UN Development Programme (UNDP), for the years between 1993 and 2004, show some Balkans countries making progress from very low-base-lines (Albania, Croatia and Macedonia) but others stagnating (Romania was ranked seventy-fourth in 1995 but had only gone up to the sixty-ninth place in 2004, having been overtaken by all states in the region previously ranked lower).[9] In the Balkans by the end of the 1990s, total fertility rates (the average number of children that a woman would have during her lifetime) were among the lowest in the whole of Europe. Bulgaria's remained at 1.2 through the second half of the 1990s (one of the lowest figures in the world).[10] The decrease was in fact most dramatic in Albania where the fertility rate fell from 4.7 in the early 1970s to a still high 2.3 in 2002. Sometimes birth rates differ between ethnic groups whose relations are strained. The Albanian populations in Kosovo and Macedonia have higher birth rates than the local Slav populations. It might only be the high reproduction rate of the Roma (gypsy) population in Romania that kept the fertility rate in 2000 (1.4) above the Bulgarian one. With the flight of young enterprising citizens to the West, an ageing population finds itself dependent on a shrinking pool of regular wage-earners in countries like Romania and Bulgaria, which has uncomfortable implications for the future. (In Romania, by 2004, there were 4.5 million wage earners but 6.11 million pensioners.)[11] Populations are projected to fall substantially across much of South-East Europe in the next thirty years. This raises awkward geopolitical issues since not far away, in the Middle East, are much larger populations trying to subsist on much poorer-quality land.

Country	Human Development rankings	
	HDI rank 2004	*HDI rank 1995*
Slovenia	27	37
Czech Republic	32	39
Poland	37	52
Hungary	38	47
Croatia	48	76
Bulgaria	56	67
Macedonia	60	80
Albania	65	105
Romania	69	74

Source: *UNDP Human Development Report*, 1995 and 2004, New York: United Nations.

The European Union does not appear to have asked to what extent the policy prescriptions it insists must be followed (closure of unviable industries, rationalisation of agriculture to phase out unproductive smallholdings, reduction in social welfare to balance the budget), will effect the ominous demographic picture emerging across much of South-East Europe. The depletion of human capital has continued as the EU's engagement with the region has intensified. Except for elite groups in Romania (and to a much lesser extent in Bulgaria), there is a lack of popular excitement in those countries about approaching EU membership. It seems unlikely to transform a gloomy economic and social picture for a long time. Indeed, children in these two Balkan accession states will have to reach extreme old age before there is any hope that living standards will approach the current EU average (and for that to happen both countries will have to enjoy uninterruptedly high rates of growth).

It remains to be seen if the unimaginative approach of the European Union towards Romania and Bulgaria can avoid reproducing (at the European level) the dependency relationships that already exist inside these countries between powerful political and economic forces and the rest of the society. The European Union was unfamiliar in dealing with weak states until forced to try and contain the worst crises in the former Yugoslavia. Along with the United Nations and other trans-national bodies, it has presided over a dysfunctional peace process, first in Bosnia and then in Kosovo. Both territories have remained deeply fractured polities despite being the object of expensive and complicated experiments in state-building directed from outside, with Brussels increasingly to the fore. Neither has the economy revived nor have new forces successfully managed to fill the political space. Particularly in Kosovo, there is a strong disinclination on the part of the majority to share social space with other ethnic groups (Mungiu-Pippidi 2004: 66–7). Ethnic polarisation could also become a feature of Macedonia if the internationally crafted peace process suffers the same degree of failure. There are countervailing examples (notably the steady improvement in relations between Romanians and Hungarians in Transylvania and between ethnic Bulgarians and Turkish and Slavic Muslims south of the Danube) but economic recovery will be the essential requirement if inter-ethnic relations are to be normalised in trouble-spots and a form of politics intimately bound-up with protecting human security is to get off the ground in the rest of the region. But it remains to be seen how enlightened and successful a political and economic patron the European Union will prove to be as its influence over the Balkans deepens in the first decade of a new century. Its attention span is now much greater than it was, but it still reacts mainly to events and its policy prescriptions are often devised by officials with little knowledge of Balkan realities. Low-grade approaches risk allowing the initiative to pass from radical ethno-nationalists to socially entrenched criminal forces who might prove a far deadlier enemy.

Notes

1 Greece: a peace-making role lost and re-found

1 Quentin Peel, 'Too late for cold feet over Turkey', *Financial Times*, 12 November 2002; Timothy Garton-Ash, 'A bridge too far', *The Guardian*, 14 November 2002.
2 The press release issued by this Canadian group on 9 June 2003 and carried by the Greek Helsinki group, on www.greekhelsinki.gr
3 Christina Rougheri, 'Traditional Greek nationalism breeds new display of intolerance', Alternative Information Media Network, 24 June, www.greekhelsinki.gr/english/articles/AIM24-6-98.html (consulted July 1998).
4 International Helsinki Federation for Human Rights, 'Greece Annual Report 1998', p. 5, www.ihf-hr.org/reports/ar98/ar98gre.htm (accessed July 1998).
5 Leonard Doyle, 'Row over report on "true" Greeks', *The Independent*, 19 August 1993.
6 Tony Barber, 'Macedonian republic flags its differences', *The Independent*, 7 April 1993.
7 Takis Michas, 'Greece's major, yet incomplete change in its policy towards Macedonia', Alternative Information Media Network, 14 April 2001, www.greekhelsinki.gr
8 Ibid.
9 Ibid.
10 2 May 1999, www.greekhelsinki.gr
11 Yugofax, 1 August 1992, p. 10.
12 John Palmer, 'EC loses patience with Greek moves to block the recognition of Macedonia', *The Guardian*, 14 January 1993.
13 John Palmer, 'Greece infuriated by EC attack over Macedonia', *The Guardian*, 21 January 1993.
14 Ibid.
15 'Roll out the welcome mat', *The Economist* (A Survey of Greece), 12 October 2002, p. 8.
16 Tony Barber, 'Athens leans hard on Albania', *The Independent*, 21 July 1993.
17 Robert Kaplan, 'The next Balkan war', *The Guardian*, 22 December 1992.
18 Jim Hoagland, 'America can't approve Greece's Balkan mischief', *International Herald Tribune*, 28 March 1994.
19 Leonard Doyle, 'Greek outburst enrages Germans', *The Independent*, 27 November 1993.
20 Helena Smith, *The Guardian*, 30 November 1993.
21 Tad Szulc, 'Scenes in a Greek tragedy', *The Guardian*, 17 November 1992.
22 Leonard Doyle, 'Academic uproar at banned book', *The Guardian*, 2 February 1996. See also Panayote Dimitras, 'Greece's "Hate Media" breeds popular "Hate Culture"', Alternative Information Media Network, Athens, 21 February 1998, www.greekhelsinki.gr/english/articles/AIM21-2-98.html (accessed March 1998).

23 Leonard Doyle, 'Academic uproar at banned book'.
24 John Palmer, 'Greece under attack for violating human rights', *The Guardian*, 12 May 1994.
25 Leonard Doyle, '"Macedonian Patriot" faces trial in Athens clampdown', *The Independent*, 11 May 1994.
26 Leonard Doyle, 'Nationalist Greece muzzles dissidents', *The Independent*, 16 August 1993.
27 International Helsinki Federation (IHF) for Human Rights, 'Greece Annual Report 1998', p. 2, www.ihf-hr.org/reports/ar98/ar98gre.htm (accessed July 1998).
28 Panayote Dimitras, 'Pangalos, the torch-bearer of the Greek consensus against national minorities', Alternative Information Media Network, Athens, 21 February 1998, www.greekhelsinki.gr/english/articles/AIM26-12-98.html (accessed January 1999).
29 Panayote Dimitras, 'Non-Governmental Organizations in Greece', Alternative Information Media Network, Athens, 8 October 1999, www.aimpress.org/dyn/trae/archive/data/199910/91008-001-trae-ath-htm (accessed in 2001).
30 Helena Smith, 'Mitsotakis says the Serbs not the only culprit in Bosnia', *The Guardian*, 9 June 1992.
31 Serbian radio, 19 December 1994, quoted in BBC World Service, Survey of World Broadcasts, 21 December 1994.
32 Tony Barber, *The Independent*, 30 June 1995.
33 Panayote Dimitras, 'Efforts to rationalize Greece's Balkan policy: the Kosovo case', Alternative Information Media Network, Athens, 25 July 1998, www.greekhelsinki.gr/english/articles/AIM25-7-98.html (accessed January 1999).
34 Takis Michas, 'Greek complicity in Serb wars', Institute for War and Peace Reporting (IWPR), 10 August 2002, www.iwpr.net/index.pl?archive/bcr2/bcr2_20020792_2_ir_eng.txt (accessed August 2002).
35 Ibid.
36 Helena Smith, John Palmer and Jabir Derala, 'Athens cuts trade links with Skopje in name dispute', *The Guardian*, 17 February 1994.
37 Helena Smith and John Palmer, 'Defiant Greece threatens to close border with Macedonia', *The Guardian*, 18 February 1994.
38 Helena Smith, 'Greece faces shame of role in Serb massacre', *The Observer*, London, 5 January 2003.
39 Stephen Castle, 'Major calls for Serbia blockade', *The Independent*, 18 April 1993.
40 Takis Michas, 'Vladimir Bokan, Milošević's front man in Greece, killed after his revelations', Alternative Information Media Network, Athens, 26 October 2000.
41 Kerin Hope and Stefan Waystyl, 'Defiant Cyprus banks that helped fund wars', *Financial Times*, 24 July 2002.
42 Daniel Howden, 'Cypriot leader's law firm "broke" Milošević sanctions', *Financial Times*, 17 April 2003.
43 Ian Traynor, 'Search for missing millions', *The Guardian*, 29 March 2001.
44 Smith, Palmer and Derala, *The Guardian*, 17 February 1994.
45 Halberstam, *War in a Time of Peace*, p. 304.
46 Mark Mazower, 'Classic errors in the Balkans', *The Guardian*, 12 April 1994.
47 Matthew Kaminski, 'Greece's identity crisis', *Wall Street Journal*, 11 April 2002.
48 Radio Free Europe/Radio Liberty (RFE/RL), *South-East Europe Newsline*, 19 January 2004.
49 Dionyssis Goussetis, 'National identity and civil society in Greece', AIM, Athens, 23 May 2000, www.aimpress.org
50 Goussetis, 'National identity and civil society in Greece'.
51 Nicos Chrysolaras, 'Unorthodox politics: the most religious political culture in Europe', Greekworks com., 15 January 2004, www.greekworks.com/english/balkans/2004/0115_chrysolaris.asp

52 Chrysolaras, 'Unorthodox politics'.
53 Alexei Barrionuevo, 'On a divided island, decades of hate begin to melt amid goodwill', *Wall Street Journal*, 24 July 2003.
54 George Wright, 'Greek Cypriot leaders reject Annan plan', *The Guardian*, 22 April 2004.
55 Helena Smith, 'Separate and unequal', *The Guardian*, 30 April 2004.
56 RFE/RL, *South-East Europe Newsline*, 23 August 2001.
57 'L'Espansione Economica Della Greci Nei Balcani', *Notizie Est*, No. 376, 5 December 2000, www.notizie-est.com/printer/php?at id=569 (accessed December 2003).

2 The road to war in Kosovo

1 Malcolm, p. xxvii on utilitarian attitude to formal religion. See also Judah, *Kosovo*, pp. 18–19.
2 A summary of the pogroms carried out in Kosovo in 1912 is found in Malcolm, *Kosovo: A Short History*, pp. 253–4.
3 There is a discussion of these events in Gallagher, *Outcast Europe*, pp. 115–16.
4 Malcolm, *Kosovo: A Short History*, p. 290.
5 But for the claim that many were in fact deported, see Fischer, *Albania at War*, p. 60.
6 'Profile of Ibrahim Rugova', *The Economist*, 4 November 2000.
7 Phil Davidson, 'Expelled despite his campaign to end bloodshed', *The Independent*, 9 June 1999.
8 World Bank figures for 1990, quoted by Neier (1994).
9 'Rugova's difficult road to Tirana', AIM, Tirana, 18 May 1999, distributed by Greek Helsinki Monitor, www.greekhelsinki.gr (accessed May 1999).
10 Guy Dinmore, 'A long and bloody trail', *Financial Times*, 8 March 1998.
11 Violeta Oroli, 'Targetting the moderate', IWPR, Balkan Report, No. 32, 13 May 1999.
12 José Cutileiro, 'Kosovo is a political problem, not just a moral crusade', *International Herald Tribune*, 21 April 1999.
13 Ahrens and Owen differ over whether Kosovo was sidelined by the International Conference on the Former Yugoslavia. See Bellamy (2001: 22).
14 The Conference for Security and Cooperation in Europe (CSCE) was the OSCE's name up to December 1994.
15 See Fred Hiatt, *International Herald Tribune*, 1 September 1998.
16 See Veton Surroi, 'The Albanian national question: the post-Dayton pay-off', *Balkan War Report*, No. 41, May 1996, p. 45.
17 RFE/RL, *Newsline*, 9 February 1998.
18 Ibid., 31 December 1997.
19 Frank Csongos, 'Yugoslavia: US moves to punish Belgrade over Kosovo', RFE/RL, 6 March 1998.
20 RFE/RL, *Newsline*, 4 March 1998.
21 Burton Gellman, 'The path to crisis', *International Herald Tribune*, 19 April 1999.
22 Marcus Tanner, 'US fails to unite warring Kosovo factions', *The Independent*, 15 August 1998.
23 Sadako Ogata, 'Prevent a Kosovo catastrophe before it's too late', *International Herald Tribune*, 17 August 1998.
24 Burton Gellman, 'The path to crisis', *International Herald Tribune*, 19 April 1999.
25 Mark Brannock, 'Milošević has breathing-space and a deal that suits', *Irish Times*, 14 October 1998.
26 RFE/RL, *Newsline*, 6 January 2003.
27 Ibid., 9 February 1998.
28 Willem van Eekelen, 'Recognise Kosovo', *International Herald Tribune*, 19 June 1998.

29 This phrase was included in the statement on Kosovo issued by the Contact Group after it met in Washington on 1 August 1998.
30 Radio B92, Daily News Service, 27 June 1998, quoted by Caplan (1998: 758).
31 See also Guy Dinmore, 'Through a glass darkly', *Financial Times*, 1–2 May 1999.
32 Stacy Sullivan, 'Milošević's willing executioners', *The New Republic*, 10 May 1999.
33 Large excerpts from this 1995 article were republished in Fintan O'Toole, 'Nato stopped genocide in its tracks', *Irish Times*, 19 June 1999.
34 Press Release of Secretary-General found at www.un.org/News/Press/docs/1999/19990128.sgrm6878.html (consulted 3 May 2003).
35 See interview with Veton Surroi, IWPR, Balkan Crisis Report, No. 50, 23 June 1999.
36 See John Pilger, 'Acts of murder', *The Guardian*, 18 May 1999.
37 Letter from Alex Bellamy, *The Guardian*, 22 May 1999.
38 Letter from Ian Black, *The Guardian*, 18 May 1999.
39 Paul Goble, 'Yugoslavia: analysis from Washington – when warnings are ignored', RFE/RL, 29 January 1999.
40 Martin Woollacott, 'How the man we could do business with is becoming the man we must destroy', *The Guardian*, 3 April 1999.

3 Milošević and NATO collide over Kosovo

1 Philip Stephen, 'Staying power', *Financial Times*, 21 May 1999.
2 Rupert Cornwell, 'Has Milošević Won?', *The Independent On Sunday*, 23 May 1999.
3 Hugh Davies, 'Air assault is enough to halt Milošević', *Daily Telegraph*, 5 April 1999.
4 'Russia rules out force in response to NATO', Reuters, 25 March 1999.
5 Fred Halliday, 'Are NATO actions prudent and are they legal', *Irish Times*, 1 April 1999.
6 Ibid.
7 Sonja Biserko, 'Balkan endgame', *Bosnia Report* (New Series), Nos. 9/10, April–June 1999.
8 David Owen, 'A lukewarm NATO risks humiliation in Kosovo', *International Herald Tribune*, 23 March 1999.
9 Carlos Westendorp, 'A reply to Lord Owen', *Bosnia Report*, 10 April 1999, www.bosnia.org.uk (accessed June 1999).
10 'Left behind: the American Left and Kosovo', *Human Rights Review*, Vol. 1, No. 2, January–March 2000 (from *Bosnia Report*), 11 May 2000, www.bosnia.org.uk (accessed June 1999).
11 AIM, 21 August 1999, 'Crimes in Kosovo: taking turns in violence', www.greekhelsinki.gr (accessed May 2003).
12 'Balkan Report', RFE/RL Research Report, 6 August 1999, www.rferl.org/balkan-report.html (accessed August 1999).
13 AIM, 21 August 1999, 'Crimes in Kosovo . . .'.
14 Stephen Castle and Rupert Cornwell, 'General admits failure of airstrikes', *The Independent on Sunday*, 5 May 1999.
15 James Rubin, 'Countdown to a very personal war', *Financial Times*, 30 September/1 October 2000.
16 *Irish Times*, 27 May 1999. See also Takis Michas (2002), *Unholy Alliance: Greece and Milošević's Serbia*, Austin, Texas: A&M University Press, pp. 77–86.
17 The view of Senator Joseph Biden who was interviewed on the programme.
18 Steven Erlanger, 'Serbs set ceiling for Kosovo population', *International Herald Tribune*, 26 April 1999.
19 Slavoljub Scekić, 'Between the Bombs and Belgrade', IWPR, Balkan Crisis Report, No. 14, 1 April 1999, www.iwpr.net
20 Zeljko Bajcic, 'Nato brawling upsets Macedonians', IWPR, Balkan Crisis Report, No. 134, 20 April 2000, www.iwpr.net

21 Iso Rusi, 'Fighting breaks out in Macedonia', IWPR, Balkan Crisis Report, No. 7, 19 March 1999, www.iwpr.net
22 'Difficult Serbian–Albanian dialogue', 'Balkan Report', RFE/RL Research Report, Vol. 3, No. 18, 12 May 1999, www.rferl.org/balkan-report.html (accessed May 1999).
23 Peter Luković, 'The Media War, Round 2', IWPR, Balkan Crisis Report, No. 7, 19 March 1999, www.iwpr.net
24 Jovo Curuvija, 'New Serbia "shields" Curuvija Killers', IWPR, Balkan Crisis Report, No. 385, 26 November 2002, www.iwpr.net
25 Robert Fisk, 'Murdered in cold blood: the editor whose sin was to criticise Milošević', *The Independent*, 13 April 1999.
26 Carlotta Gall, 'The advocate', *Bosnia Report*, New Series, Nos. 9/10, April–June 1999.
27 Sonja Biserko, 'Balkan endgame', *Bosnia Report*, New Series, Nos. 9/10, April–June 1999.
28 Andrew Gumbel, 'Voices were raised in protest, now the silence is deafening', *The Independent On Sunday*, 18 April 1999.
29 Ibid.
30 Daniel Goldhagen, 'Why NATO must take Belgrade', *The Guardian*, 29 April 1999.
31 Janusz Bugajski, 'Stability pact or status quo', Nacional, Zagreb, 26 April 2000 (from *Bosnia Report*), 24 May 2000, www.bosnia.org.uk (accessed May 1999).
32 Steve Boggan, 'NATO is warned on war crimes', *The Independent*, 5 May 1999.
33 Andrew Rawnsley, 'Can Blair walk on water', *The Observer*, London, 2 May 1999.
34 Hansard, 23 March 1999.
35 www.fco.gov.uk
36 Philip Stephens, 'Europe's choice', *Financial Times*, 21 May 1999.
37 David Hoffman, 'In symbolic move, Duma endorses a loose union with Yugoslavia', *International Herald Tribune*, 17–18 April 1999.
38 'A toothless growl', *The Economist*, 1 May 1999.
39 Vlado Vurušic, 'Report from Moscow', *Globus*, Zagreb, 30 April 1999 (from *Bosnia Report*), 13 May 2000, www.bosnia.org.uk (accessed May 1999).
40 Interview with Andrei Piontkowski, director of the Moscow Centre for Strategic Research, *Globus*, Zagreb, 30 April 1999 (from *Bosnia Report*), 13 May 2000, www.bosnia.org.uk (accessed May 1999).
41 Vurušic, 'Report from Moscow'.
42 Reuters, 25 March 1999.
43 Interview with Andrei Piontkowski...
44 Peter Gowan, 'From Rambouillet to the Chinese Embassy', from www.igc.apc.org, quoted by Bellamy (2001: 187 and accessed by him on 16 February 2000).
45 James Gow believes that the one area in which the question of war crimes might be raised concerned the use of cluster munitions. See Gow (2003), p. 287, n. 13.
46 Robert Fisk, 'NATO deliberately attacked civilians', *The Independent*, 7 June 2000.
47 Victor Chernomyrdin, 'Impossible to talk peace with bombs falling', *Washington Post*, 27 May 1999.
48 Zbigniew Brzezinski, 'Why Milošević capitulated in Kosovo', *The New Leader*, 7 October 1999.
49 See Tariq Ali, 'Opinion', *The Guardian*, 19 June 1999.
50 Fintan O'Toole, 'NATO stopped genocide in is tracks', *The Irish Times*, 19 June 1999.
51 Anthony Knight of Billericay, Essex, 'Letter', *The Guardian*, 18 June 1999.
52 Maurice Hill, Alicante, Spain, 'Letter', *The Guardian*, 18 June 1999.
53 Timothy Garton-Ash, 'Vivid, dark, powerful and magnificent – but wrong', *The Independent*, 6 May 1999.
54 Fergal Keane, *The Independent*, 17 April 1999.
55 Timothy Garton-Ash, 'No we're right to fight this war', *The Independent*, 20 April 1999.

56 Marko Attila Hoare, 'Nothing is left', *Bosnia Report*, New Series, No. 36, October–December 2003, p. 34.
57 Quoting Noam Chomsky and Edward S. Herman, 'Distortions at fourth Hand', *The Nation*, 25 June 1977.
58 Colm Breathnach, 'Letter', *The Irish Times*, 14 April 1999.
59 Timothy Garton-Ash, 'No we're right to fight this war', *The Independent*, 20 April 1999.
60 Susan Sonntag, 'An evil that makes the Balkan war just', *The Observer*, London, 16 May 1999.
61 'Editorial', *The Observer*, 28 March 1999.
62 Christopher Caldwell, 'A war between strategists and humanitarians', *Financial Times*, 7–8 June 2003.

4 Macedonia: internal dangers supplant external ones

1 *Fact-finding Missions Regarding the Ongoing Crisis and Human Rights Violations in the Republic of Macedonia*, Oslo: International Helsinki Federation for Human Rights, 2001, pp. 2, 5.
2 Jolyon Naegele, 'Macedonia: how the nation's Albanians and Slavs perceive one another (Part 2)', RFE/RL, 28 June 2001.
3 Jolyan Naegele, 'Macedonian census due by year's end', RFE/RL, 10 July 2001.
4 'The other Macedonian conflict', Berlin: European Stability Initiative, 2002, www.esiweb.org (consulted February 2002).
5 Ibid.
6 *Ahmeti's Village: The Political Economy of Interethnic Relations in Macedonia*, Skopje and Berlin: European Stability Initiative, 1 October 2002, p. 22.
7 Internal Macedonian Revolutionary Organization (VMRO) was in alliance with the smaller Democratic Party for Macedonian National Unity (DPNE).
8 Kim Mehmeti, 'War whirlwind in the peace oasis', AIM, Skopje, 16 March 2001, distributed by Greek Helsinki Monitor, www.greekhelsinki.gr (accessed March 2001).
9 'The other Macedonian conflict', Berlin: European Stability Initiative, 2002.
10 Ferid Muhic, 'The devil of perversity', IWPR, Balkan Crisis Report, No. 246, 11 May 2001, www.iwpr.net
11 Kim Mehmeti, 'Futile dialogue exposed', IWPR, Balkan Crisis Report, No. 228, Part 2, 21 March 2000.
12 Stefan Krause, 'Tito takes the first round in Macedonia', IWPR, Balkan Crisis Report, No. 90, 5 November 1999.
13 Ibrahim Mehmeti, 'A new chance for inter-ethnic relations', IWPR, Balkan Crisis Report, No. 102, 15 December 1999.
14 Zeljko Bajić, 'Macedonia locked in cycle of corruption', IWPR, Balkan Crisis Report, No. 126, 21 March 2000.
15 *Macedonia's Public Secret: How Corruption Drags the Country Down*, Brussels: International Crisis Group (ICG), Balkan Report, No. 133, 14 August 2002, p. 23.
16 'Macedonia Divided', RFE/RL, Balkan Report, Vol. 5, No. 33, 4 May 2001.
17 Zeljko Bajić, 'Scandals rock Macedonian army', IWPR, Balkan Crisis Report, No. 145, 2 June 2000.
18 Dragan Nikolić, 'Against the West and against the new President in Macedonia', IWPR, Balkan Crisis Report, No. 104, 21 December 1999.
19 Zeljko Bajić, 'Nato brawling upsets Macedonians', IWPR, Balkan Crisis Report, No. 134, 20 April 2000.
20 'Our neighbourhood – an attempt to prevent conflict', Macedonian Information and Liaison Service (MILS) News, 17 August 1999.
21 Zeljko Bajić, 'Macedonian languages dispute', IWPR, Balkan Crisis Report, No. 142, 23 May 2000.

22 MILS News, Skopje, 17 August 1999, www.greekhelsinki.gr (accessed August 1999).

23 'The other Macedonian conflict'.

24 *Ahmeti's Village: The Political Economy of Interethnic Relations in Macedonia*, pp. 22, 25.

25 'The other Macedonian conflict'.

26 Ibid.

27 The International Monetary Fund (IMF) noted in 2000 that: 'With the privatisation process nearing its end, the outcome has been below expectations'. Quoted in *Ahmeti's Village: The Political Economy of Interethnic Relations in Macedonia*, p. 9.

28 Kim Mehmeti, 'Futile dialogue exposed', IWPR, Balkan Crisis Report, No. 228, Part 2, 21 March 2000.

29 'The other Macedonian conflict'.

30 *Ahmeti's Village: The Political Economy of Interethnic Relations in Macedonia*, p. 23.

31 For the preceding two paragraphs, see Jolyon Naegele, 'The Tanusevci Story', RFE/RL, Balkan Report, Vol. 5, No. 18, 9 March 2001.

32 Vladimir Gligorov, 'The *Modus Vivendi* collapses', *Central European Review*, Vol. 3, No. 25, 10 September 2001, www.ce-review.org (consulted September 2001).

33 RFE/RL, *Newsline*, 19 March 2001.

34 See Edward Luttwak, 'From the Oval Office you can't see Europe', *The Sunday Telegraph*, 12 November 2000.

35 *Macedonia's Public Secret: How Corruption Drags the Country Down*, No. 133, Brussels: ICG, Balkan Report, 14 August 2002, p. 25.

36 Naegele, 'The Tanusevci Story'.

37 *Macedonia's Public Secret*.

38 Ibid.

39 See 'The net of the Albanian Mafia', *Welt am Sonmtag*, 25 March 2001, an English translation appearing in 'Euro-Balkan briefing on the Macedonian crisis', Euro-Balkan Institute, 26 March 2001, www.greekhelsinki.gr/bhr/English/organizations/eurobalkan/br 26 03 01.html (accessed 11 October 2003).

40 Robert Alagjozovski and Altin Raxhimi, 'Ethnic partition revisted', *Transition Online*, 14 May 2003, www.balkanreport.tol.cz

41 For a summary of this argument, see Tom Gallagher, *Outcast Europe: The Balkans From the Ottomans to Milošević*, London: Routledge, 2001, pp. 264–5.

42 Veton Latifi, 'Storm over Macedonian partition plan', IWPR, Balkan Crisis Report, No. 253, Part 1, 6 June 2001.

43 Ibid.

44 Euro-Balkan Institute, 31 March 2001, www.greekhelsinki.gr/bhr/English/organizations/eurobalkan/br 31 03 01.html (accessed 11 October 2003).

45 Jolyan Naegele, 'Macedonia: UÇK insurgency shifts focus to Tetovo', RFE/RL, 16 March 2001. Actually, an attack on a police station in the Tetovo region on 23 January 2001 is widely seen as the first Albanian insurgent action. See Rusi (2002: 20).

46 Ibid.

47 Philip O'Neil, 'Kosovo leaders urge Montenegro negotiations', IWPR, Balkan Crisis Report, No. 230, 28 March 2001.

48 Euro-Balkan Institute, 27 March 2001, www.greekhelsinki.gr/bhr/English/organizations/eurobalkan/br 27 03 01.html (accessed 11 October 2003).

49 Karina Johansen, 'West should step up Macedonia support', IWPR, Balkan Crisis Report, No. 228, Part 1, 21 March 2001.

50 Mehmeti, 'War whirlwind in the peace oasis', AIM, Skopje, 16 March 2001.

51 Euro-Balkan Institute, 24 March 2001, www.greekhelsinki.gr/bhr/English/organizations/eurobalkan/br 24 03 01.html (accessed 11 October 2003).

52 Euro-Balkan Institute, 5 May 2001, www.greekhelsinki.gr/bhr/English/organizations/eurobalkan/br 24 05 05 01.html (accessed 11 October 2003).

53 Gordana Stojanovska, 'New Skopje coalition calms nerves', IWPR, Balkan Crisis Report, No. 245, Part 1, 10 May 2001.
54 Jane Perlez, 'Powell, on Balkan trip, warns against fresh violence', *The New York Times*, 14 April 2001.
55 Pax Christi, 'Disarmament in Macedonia: a delicate job for NATO', 11 July 2001, www.reliefweb.int (accessed 11 October 2003); also, *Macedonia: The Last Chance for Peace*, Brussels: ICG, Balkan Report, No. 113, 20 June 2001, p. 14.
56 RFE/RL, *Newsline*, 25 June 2001.
57 Ibid.
58 *Macedonia: Still Sliding*, Balkan Briefing, Brussels: ICG, 27 July 2001, p. 2.
59 *Macedonia: The Last Chance for Peace*, p. 15.
60 Nexhat Aqifi, 'Kumanovo braced for war', IWPR, Balkan Crisis Report, No. 244, 5 May 2001.
61 Veton Latifi, 'Kumanovo holds together', IWPR, Balkan Crisis Report, No. 268, 3 August 2001.
62 Ibid.
63 Letter from the National Liberation Army (NLA) to heads of various international organisations dated 24 April 2001.
64 Laura Rozen, 'NLA Autonomy Goal', IWPR, Balkan Crisis Report, No. 228, Part 1, 21 March 2001.
65 Saso Ordanoski, the editor of *Forum* in Skopje who has a long track-record of activities fostering civic-minded NGOs in the Balkans has been associated with this viewpoint.
66 RFE/RL, *Newsline*, 29 May 2003.
67 Henrik Villadsen and Whit Mason, 'Find Out Just What Macedonia's People Think of Each Other', *International Herald Tribune*, 8 June 2001.
68 Ibid.
69 *Macedonia: The Last Chance for Peace*, p. 11.
70 Bobi Hristor, 'Two-way traffic in Aracinovo', IWPR, Balkan Crisis Report, No. 271, Part 2, 14 August 2001.
71 R. Jeffrey Smith, 'Ethnicity distorts truth in reporting', *Washington Post*, 3 July 2001.
72 Zlatko Dizdarević, 'Mass Media's war', IWPR, Balkan Crisis Report, No. 284, 28 September 2001.
73 Iso Rusi, 'Non-Governmental Organizations in Macedonia: they exist, but little good do they do', Alternative Information Media Network, Skopje, 23 September 1999, www.aimpress.org/dyn/trae/archive/data/1999909/90927-002-trae-sko.htm (consulted October 1999).
74 RFE/RL, *Newsline*, 22 June 2001.
75 Ibid., 25 June 2001.
76 Justin Huggler, 'Macedonians blast rebels as talks falter', *The Independent*, 23 June 2001.
77 RFE/RL, *Newsline*, 25 June 2001.
78 Ahto Lobjakos, 'Macedonia, EU taking a tougher diplomatic line', RFE/RL, 25 June 2001.
79 Lobjakos, 'Macedonia, EU taking a tougher diplomatic line'.
80 RFE/RL, *Newsline*, 25 June 2001.
81 Ibid., 26 June 2001.
82 Vlad Jovanovski, 'Skopje politicians sober up', IWPR, Balkan Crisis Report, No. 261, 4 July 2001.
83 *Macedonia: Still Sliding*, Balkan Briefing, Brussels: ICG, 27 July 2001, p. 4.
84 RFE/RL, *Newsline*, 26 June 2001.
85 *Macedonia: Still Sliding*, p. 4.
86 EIU Country Report for Macedonia, May 2001, London: Economic Intelligence Unit, p. 19.
87 Lobjakos, 'Macedonia, EU taking a tougher diplomatic line'.
88 RFE/RL, *Newsline*, 29 June 2001.

89 Ibid., 31 May 2001.
90 For Trajkovski, see Judy Dempsey, 'Under siege', *Financial Times*, 3 July 2001.
91 Ana Petrusuva, 'Macedonian peace deal in Jeopardy', IWPR, Balkan Crisis Report, No. 269, 9 August 2001.
92 Borijan Jovanovski, 'Macedonia's labour pains', IWPR, Balkan Crisis Report, No. 22, June 2001.
93 Cecile Feuillatre, 'Ethnically mixed Macedonian village strained by ongoing clashes', Agence France-Presse, 27 May 2001.
94 *Macedonia: Still Sliding*, p. 5.
95 Saso Ordanoski, 'Reading between the lions', IWPR, Balkan Crisis Report, No. 278, 10 September 2001.
96 *Macedonia: Still Sliding*, p. 5.
97 EIU Country Report for Macedonia, May 2001, London: Economic Intelligence Unit, p. 14.
98 Ulrich Büchsenschütz, 'Macedonia: peace talks successful, civil war inevitable', RFE/RL, Balkan Report, Vol. 5, No. 55, 7 August 2001.
99 *Macedonia: Still Sliding*, p. 5.
100 Ibid., p. 5.
101 Ibid., p. 6.
102 RFE/RL, *Newsline*, 25 July 2001.
103 Ibid., 19 July 2001.
104 Justin Huggler, 'New Macedonian demands hamper peace deal', *The Independent*, 7 August 2001.
105 See EIU Country Report for Macedonia, November 2001, London: Economic Intelligence Unit, p. 13; also *Moving Macedonia Towards Self-Sufficiency: A New Security Approach for NATO and the EU*, Brussels: ICG, Balkan Report, No. 135, 15 November 2001, p. 2.
106 Ana Petruseva, 'Macedonian doubts over peace deal', IWPR, Balkan Crisis Report, No. 277, 4 September 2001.
107 Jolyan Naegele, 'Macedonia: UÇK insurgency shifts focus to Tetovo', RFE/RL, 16 March 2001.

5 Serbia from 2000: Milošević's poisonous legacy

1 Tom Walker, 'Milošević faces $10 billion fraud trial', *The Sunday Times*, London, 15 October 2000.
2 Noel Malcolm, 'Welcome Koštunica – but with serious reservations', *The Daily Telegraph*, 7 October 2000.
3 'Belgrade's lagging reform: cause for international concern', No. 126, Washington/Brussels: ICG, Balkan Report, 7 March 2002, p. 2.
4 Sonja Biserko, 'Anti-European vertical scores off in Serbia: Serbia turns the clock back again', *Helsinki Charter*, November–December 2003.
5 'Djindjić attacks west's hollow promises', *B92 News*, Belgrade, 29 November 2001.
6 'Salvaging Yugoslavia', *Business Central Europe*, London, November 2000.
7 *Current Legal Status of the Federal Republic of Yugoslavia (FRY) and of Serbia and Montenegro*, No. 101, Washington/Brussels: ICG, Balkan Report, 19 September 2000, p. 29.
8 'Yugoslavia', *East European Constitutional Review*, New York, Vol. 9, No. 2, Winter/Spring 2000, www.law.nyu.edu/eecr
9 *Montenegro: In the Shadow of the Volcano*, No. 89, Podgorica/Brussels: ICG, Balkan Report, 21 March 2000, pp. 9, 30.
10 RFE, *South-East Europe Newsline*, Prague, 16 October 2000, www.rferl.org
11 Ibid., 5 February 2001.
12 Ibid., 23 January 2001.

13 Michael Emerson *et al.* (2001), 'A European solution for the constitutional future of Montenegro', in Nicholas Whyte (ed.), *The Future of Montenegro: Proceedings of an Expert Meeting*, Brussels: Centre For European Policy Studies.

14 Emerson (2001),'Closing Remarks', in Whyte (ed.), *The Future of Montenegro*, p. 94.

15 Jolyon Naegele, 'Yugoslavia: Serbia and Montenegro create new state', RFE, *Newsline: End Note*, Prague, 14 March 2002.

16 'The Federal Republics', *Central and South-Eastern Europe 2003*, London: Routledge, 2003, p. 627.

17 Ines Sabalić, 'Montenegro: Brussels U-turn on the new state', IWPR, Balkan Crisis Report, No. 250, 12 July 2002.

18 RFE, *South-East Europe Newsline*, Prague, 20 August 2002.

19 Peter Palmer (2002), 'The European Union and Montenegro', *Bosnia Report*, New Series, No. 29–31, June–November, London: The Bosnian Institute.

20 *A Marriage of Inconvenience*, No. 142, Podgorica/Brussels: ICG, Balkan Report, 16 April 2003, p. 11, n. 67.

21 *Thessaloniki and After (III): The EU, Serbia, Montenegro and Kosovo*, Brussels: ICG, Balkan Report, 20 June 2003, p. 7.

22 *Serbia's U-turn*, No. 154, Belgrade/Brussels: ICG, Balkan Report, 26 March 2004, p. 9.

23 Steve Erlanger, 'Yugoslavs bicker over army and secret police', *The New York Times*, 8 November 2000.

24 'Belgrade's lagging reform', p. 17.

25 RFE, *Newsline*, 27 October 2000.

26 Timothy Garton-Ash, 'Can this gloomy man save Yugoslavia', *The Independent*, 6 October 2000.

27 *Serbia After Djindjić* (2003), No. 141, Brussels: ICG, Balkan Report, 18 March 2003.

28 Noel Malcolm, 'Milošević was doomed by press freedom', *Sunday Telegraph*, 1 July 2001.

29 *Serbia's Transition: Reforms Under Siege*, No. 117, Brussels: ICG, Balkan Report, 21 September 2001, p. 10.

30 *Belgrade's Lagging Reform: Cause for International Concern* (2002), No. 126, Brussels: ICG, Balkan Report, 7 March 2002.

31 RFE, *Newsline*, 29 November 2001.

32 *Serbian Reforms Stall Again*, No. 145, Brussels: ICG, Balkan Report, 17 July 2003, p. 5.

33 *Belgrade's Lagging Reform*, pp. 15–16.

34 Ibid., p. 17.

35 'Possibilities of Democratic Development in Serbia and the OSCE's Possible Role', Belgrade, Centre for Human Rights: 17 January 2001.

36 *Belgrade's Lagging Reform*, p. 17.

37 *Serbian Reforms Stall Again*, p. 15.

38 Ibid., p. 19.

39 Alison Freebairn, 'Obituary: Zorin Djindjić', IWPR, Balkan Crisis Report, No. 414, 13 March 2003.

40 *Serbia After Djindjić*, p. 7.

41 *Serbian Reforms Stall Again*, p. 23.

42 Vincent Boland, 'Paris Club to write off much of Yugoslavia's debt', *Financial Times*, 17–18 November 2001.

43 EIU Country report for Serbia and Montenegro, January 2004, London: Economic Intelligence Unit, p. 24.

44 *Serbian Reforms Stall Again*, pp. 24–5.

45 *Serbia After Djindjić*, p. 8.

46 John Sweeney, 'Serbs cover up deadly secret', *The Observer*, London, 3 December 2000.

47 *Serbia After Djindjić*, p. 8.

48 *Belgrade's Lagging Reform*, p. 20.

49 Ibid., p. 14.
50 *Serbian Reforms Stall Again*, p. 17.
51 *Serbia's Transition*, p. 14.
52 Ibid., p. 3.
53 EIU Country Report for Yugoslavia, London: Economic Intelligence Unit, January 2003.
54 *Serbia's Transition*, p. 10.
55 Aleksandar Cirić, 'The Church and the state, the state and the borders', AIM, Belgrade, 13 December 2000.
56 *Serbia after Djindjić*, p. 16.
57 *Belgrade's Lagging Reform*, p. 10.
58 *Serbia after Djindjić*, p. 14.
59 Patrick Moore, 'Hard-headed détente', RFE, *Endnote*, 5 January 2001.
60 *Serbia after Djindjić*, p. 14.
61 *Belgrade's Lagging Reform*, p. 23.
62 Ibid.
63 *Serbia after Djindjić*, p. 12.
64 *Belgrade's Lagging Reform*, p. 20.
65 *Serbia after Djindjić*, p. 14.
66 *Belgrade's Lagging Reform*, p. 22.
67 Patrick Moore, 'Incorrigible Serbia', RFE, *Endnote*, 11 December 2003.
68 Martin Woollacott, 'Milošević's transfer was the price that had to be paid', *The Guardian*, 6 July 2001.
69 *Serbia after Djindjić*, p. 17.
70 Patrick Moore, 'Failed states in the Balkans', RFE, *Endnote*, 8 August 2003.
71 Moore, 'Incorrigible Serbia'.
72 RFE, *Newsline*, 16 November 2001.
73 Aleksandar Radić, 'Anti-Hague army unit abolished', IWPR, Balkan Crisis Report, No. 424, 17 April 2003.
74 Tim Judah, 'Serbs won over by Milošević's TV trial tactics', *Guardian Weekly*, 7–13 March 2002.
75 Aleksa Todorović, 'A smoking bag', *Transition Online*, 21 March 2002.
76 Sasha Grubanović, 'A Serbian Labyrith', *Transition Online*, 8 January 2004.
77 Milovan Mracevich, 'How the DOS bungled it', *Transition Online*, 8 January 2004.
78 *Serbian Reforms Stall Again*, p. 19.
79 Ibid., p. 20.
80 Ibid., p. 23.
81 *B92 News*, 29 November 2001.
82 Siljka Pistolova, 'Serbia: Eu may extend sugar ban', IWPR, Balkan Crisis Report, No. 445, 18 July 2003.
83 *Serbian Reforms Stall Again*, p. 26.
84 *Serbia After Djindjić*, p. 5.
85 RFE, *Newsline*, 12 January 2001.
86 'Serbia's election merry-go-round', British Helsinki Human Rights Group, www.bhhrg.org
87 'Serbia and Montenegro', *East European Constitutional Review*, Vol. 12, No. 1, Spring–Summer 2003, p. 45.
88 *Serbia After Djindjić*, p. 4.
89 Patrick Moore, 'Which way for Serbia', RFE, *Endnote*, 28 March 2003.
90 A text of the funeral address was published by the Serbian Helsinki Committee on 21 March 2003, see www.helsinki.org.yu (accessed in March 2003); see also Sonja Biserko, 'The political aspirations of the Serbian Orthodox Church', 8 April 2003, www.helsinki.org.yu (accessed in April 2003).
91 *Serbian Reforms Stall Again*, p. 18.

92 Milos Vasić, 'Patriots by trade, criminals by persuasion', *Transition Online*, 15 May 2003 (accessed May 2003).
93 Aleksandar Radić, 'Anti-Hague army unit abolished', IWPR, Balkan Crisis Report, No. 424, 17 April 2003.
94 *Serbian Reforms Stall Again*, p. 5.
95 Ibid., p. 12.
96 Ibid., p. 14.
97 Ibid., p. 2.
98 Ibid., p. 14.
99 RFE, *Newsline*, 7 April 2003; *Serbian Reforms Stall Again*, p. 15.
100 *Serbian Reforms Stall Again*, p. 18.
101 Ibid., p. 22.
102 *The Economist*, 26 June 2003.
103 *Serbian Reforms Stall Again*, p. 22.
104 Željiko Cvivanović, 'ICG affair shakes Serbia–West relations', IWPR, Balkan Crisis Report, No. 442, 8 July 2003.
105 *Serbian Reforms Stall Again*, p. 11.
106 Gordana Igrić, 'Dark side of Serbia's revolution', IWPR, Balkan Crisis Report, No. 420, 20 April 2003.
107 Cvivanović, 'ICG Affair Shakes Serbia–West relations'.
108 Ibid.
109 Željiko Cvivanović, 'Serbia: Shaky government truce', IWPR, Balkan Crisis Report, No. 435, 6 June 2003.
110 Biljana Stepanović, '500 days of Djindjić', IWPR, Balkan Crisis Report, No. 363, 30 August 2002.
111 RFE, *Newsline*, 19 November 2003.
112 *Serbian Reforms Stall Again*, p. 3.
113 Ibid.
114 Milovan Mracevich, 'How the DOS bungled it', *Transition Online*, 8 January 2004.
115 Ibid.
116 *Serbia's U-turn*, p. 5.
117 RFE, *Newsline*, 12 November 2001.
118 *Serbian Reforms Stall Again*, p. 27.
119 Ibid.
120 Ivan Marović, 'Otpor…', IWPR, Balkan Crisis Report, No. 471, 5 December 2003.
121 Brian Pozun, 'Planning for an uncertain future', *Central Europe Review*, Vol. 3, No. 8, 26 February 2001, www.ce-review.org (accessed February 2004).
122 Patrick Moore, 'Serbia's uncertain future', RFE, *Endnote*, 12 January 2004.
123 Sasha Grubanović, 'A Serbian labyrinth', *Transition Online*, 8 January 2004.
124 See 'Playing tough to a scornful gallery', *Transition Online*, 16 February 2004, www.tol.cz (accessed 17 February 2004).
125 RFE, *Newsline*, 8 January 2004.
126 Grubanović, 'A Serbian labyrinth'.
127 RFE, *Newsline*, 31 March 2004.
128 'Creeping restoration', Helsinki Charter, April 2004, www.greekhelsinki.gr
129 *Serbia's U-turn*, p. 15, n. 44.
130 Ibid., p. 7.

6 Bosnia: redesigning a flawed peace process

1 The General Framework Agreement for Peace in Bosnia and Herzegovina was initialled in Dayton, Ohio, USA on 21 November 1995. The full text can be found in *Bosnia and Herzegovina Essential Texts*, Sarajevo, 2000, 3rd edn, pp. 23–63.
2 Gerald Knaus and Nicholas Whyte, 'The internationals and the Balkans: time for a change', IWPR, Balkan Crisis Report, No. 505, 2 July 2004.

3 *The Wages of Sin: Confronting Bosnia's Republika Srpska*, Sarajevo/Brussels: ICG, Balkan Report, No. 118, 8 October 2001, p. 1.
4 *Reshaping International Priorities in Bosnia and Herzegovina, Part II: International Power in Bosnia*, Sarajevo: European Stability Institute (ESI), 30 March 2000, p. 3.
5 *Bosnia and Herzegovina Essential Texts*, p. 199.
6 Tobias K. Vogel, 'Responsible disengagement: the international community in Bosnia–Herzegovina', *European Balkan Observer*, Vol. 1, No. 1, April 2003.
7 *Reshaping International Priorities in Bosnia and Herzegovina, Part II*, p. 14.
8 *Reshaping International Priorities in Bosnia and Herzegovina: Bosnian Power Structures Part I*, Sarajevo: ESI, 1999, p. 20.
9 *In Search of Politics: The Evolving International Role in Bosnia–Herzegovina*, Sarajevo: ESI, November 2001.
10 See *Bosnia and Herzegovina Essential Texts*, pp. 116–43.
11 Ibid., p. 228.
12 RFE, *South-East Europe Newsline*, 22 April 2002.
13 Ibid., 24 May 2002.
14 Janez Kovac, 'Bosnia's British bulldozer', IWPR, Balkan Crisis Report, No. 383, 18 November 2002.
15 *Bosnia's Nationalist Governments: Paddy Ashdown and the Paradoxes of State Building*, Sarajevo/Brussels: ICG, Balkan Report, No. 146, 22 July 2003, p. 7.
16 *Reshaping International Priorities in Bosnia and Herzegovina, Part I*, p. 14.
17 *The Wages of Sin*, p. 30.
18 Ibid., p. 48.
19 *Is Dayton Failing? Bosnia Four Years After the Peace Agreement*, Sarajevo/Brussels: ICG, p. 83.
20 *Reshaping International Priorities, Part I*, p. 5.
21 Interview with the Director of the Human Rights Department of the Organization for Security and Co-operation in Europe (OSCE) in Sarajevo, 17 September 2001.
22 B. Ivanisevic, 'Legacy of war: minority returns in the Balkans', Human Rights Watch, World Report 2004, available online at www.hrw.org (accessed February 2004).
23 *The Continuing Challenge of Refugee Returns in Bosnia and Herzegovina*, Sarajevo/ Brussels: Balkan Report, No. 137, p. 1; Communique of PIC Steering Board, ICG, 26 September 2003.
24 Ibid., p. 2.
25 Ibid., p. 23.
26 Ibid., pp. 5, 26.
27 Ibid., p. 27.
28 *The Wages of Sin*, p. 2; RFE, *South-East Europe Newsline*, 9 May 2001.
29 Ibid., p. 5.
30 *Policing The Police in Bosnia: A Further Reform Agenda*, Sarajevo/Brussels: ICG, Balkan Report, No. 130, 10 May 2002, p. 58.
31 *Is Dayton Failing?*, p. 121.
32 Interview with senior UN official based in South-West Bosnia, 19 September 2001.
33 Julie Poucher Harbin, 'Bosnia: UN handover causing concern', IWPR, Balkan Crisis Report, No. 393, Part 1, 23 December 2002.
34 Colum Lynch, 'Misconduct, corruption by US police mar Bosnia mission', *Washington Post*, 29 May 2001.
35 Dominic Hipkin, 'Bosnia sex trade shames the UN', *Scotland On Sunday*, 9 February 2003.
36 Lynch, 'Misconduct, corruption'.
37 Hipkin, 'Bosnia sex trade'.
38 *Bosnia's Precarious Economy: Still Not Open For Business*, Sarajevo/Brussels: ICG, Balkan Report, No. 155, 7 August 2001, p. 36.

39 Paddy Ashdown, 'Bosnia wants change – not nationalism', *Financial Times*, 10 October 2002.
40 Tim Judah, 'Half-empty or half-full towns', *Transition Online*, 5 February 2004.
41 Haris Silajdžić, the wartime Prime Minister of Bosnia, singled out faulty privatisation as one of the prime factors prolonging the influence of nationalist elites in an interview on BBC World Service, *Hardtalk*, 13 July 2004.
42 *Bosnia's Precarious Economy*, p. 18.
43 Ibid., p. 19.
44 *Bosnia and Herzegovina Country Profile, 2001*, London: The Economist Intelligence Unit, p. 24.
45 *Bosnia's Precarious Economy*, p. 27.
46 *Courting Disaster: The Misrule of Law in Bosnia–Herzegovina*, Sarajevo/Brussels: ICG, Balkan Report, No. 127, 26 March 2002, p. 1.
47 Ibid., p. 11.
48 Ibid., p. 16.
49 RFE, *South-East Europe Newsline*, 28 May 2002.
50 *Bosnia's BRCKO: Getting In, Getting On and Getting Out*, Sarajevo/Brussels: ICG, Balkan Report, No. 144, 2 June 2003, pp. 16–17.
51 David Harland, 'What has not happened in Bosnia', *International Herald Tribune*, 27 January 2004.
52 *Bosnia: Reshaping the International Machinery*, Sarajevo/Brussels: ICG, Balkan Report, No. 127, 29 November 2001, p. 6.
53 Knaus and Whyte, 'The internationals and the Balkans'.
54 *Bosnia: Reshaping the International Machinery*, p. 4.
55 Ibid.
56 Personal observation.
57 Ibid.
58 Ibid.
59 Interview with OSCE Democratisation officer in Mostar, September 2001.
60 Interview with Project Officer for Human Rights, European Commission Delegation to Bosnia, 18 September 2001.
61 N. Ahmetasevic and Julie Poucher Harbin, 'Bosnia's brain drain gathers pace', IWPR, Balkan Crisis Report, No. 385, 26 November 2002.
62 *Bosnia's Nationalist Governments*.
63 RFE, *South-East Europe Newsline*, 12 April 2001.
64 *Bosnia: Reshaping the International Machinery*, p. 9.
65 See *Bin Laden and the Balkans: The Politics of Anti-Terrorism*, ICG, Balkan Report, No. 119, 9 November 2001.
66 'A victory not a triumph', *Transition Online*, 7 October 2002.
67 'Bosnia–Herzegovina', *East European Constitutional Review*, Vol. 11, No. 3, Winter–Spring 2002.
68 RFE, *South-East Europe Newsline*, 28 January 2002.
69 *Bosnia's Nationalist Governments*, p. 1.
70 Janez Kovac, 'Bank closure provokes Croat wrath', IWPR, Balkan Crisis Report, No. 237, 12 April 2001.
71 *Bosnia's Nationalist Governments*, p. i.
72 'OHR Mission Implementation Plan 2004', p. 2, Office of High Representative (OHR) General Information, 23 March 2004, www.ohr.int
73 Ian Traynor, 'Ashdown running Bosnia like a Raj', *The Guardian*, 5 July 2003.
74 *Bosnia and Herzegovina Country Report*, April 2004, London: The Economist Intelligence Unit, p. 16.
75 'OHR Mission Implementation Plan 2004', p. 2.
76 RFE, *South-East Europe Newsline*, 13 July 2004.
77 Ibid., 25 February 2003.

78 *Bosnia's Nationalist Governments*, p. ii.
79 OHR Press conference statement, 30 June 2004.
80 See Patrick Moore, 'What to do about Bosnia?', RFE/RL, *Newsline*, *Endnote*, 8 September 2003.
81 Nerma Jelacić, 'New reform plan fails to unite Bosnians', IWPR, Balkan Crisis Report, No. 476, 15 January 2004.
82 'OHR Mission Implementation Plan 2004', p. 3.

7 Still a danger-point: Kosovo under international rule

1 *Kosovo Report Card*, Priština/Brussels: ICG, Balkan Report, No. 100, 28 August 2000, p. 22.
2 Ibid., p. 27.
3 Ibid., p. 15.
4 See *UNMIK's Kosovo Albatross: Tackling Division in Mitrovica*, Priština/Brussels: ICG, Balkan Report, No. 131, 3 June 2002.
5 Ismet Hadjari, 'Ex-fighters shovel snow', IWPR, Balkan Crisis Report, No. 117, 18 February 2000.
6 See Naser Mitfari, 'Policing the protectors', IWPR, Balkan Crisis Report, No. 440, 30 June 2003.
7 *Kosovo Report Card*, p. 3.
8 Steve Erlanger, 'UN official warns of losing the peace in Kosovo', *The New York Times*, 3 July 2000.
9 *Kosovo Report Card*, p. 41.
10 Ibid., pp. 34, 39.
11 Timothy Garton-Ash, 'The nightmare ahead', *The Independent*, 8 June 1999.
12 *Kosovo Report Card*, p. 2.
13 Ibid., p. 41.
14 Timothy Garton-Ash, 'Kosovo: was it worth it?', *NewYork Review of Books*, 21 September 2000, p. 52.
15 Lesley Abdela, 'Men with a mission: no women', *The Guardian*, 2 March 2000.
16 Laura Rozen, 'The short unhappy return of Ibrahim Rugova', *Salon Times*, 16 July 1999, www.salon.com/news/features/1999/07/16/rugova
17 *Two To Tango: An agenda for the new Kosovo, SRSG*, Priština/Belgrade/Brussels: ICG, Europe Report No. 148, 3 September 2003, p. 3.
18 Martin Woollacott, 'There is a dangerous lack of clarity on Kosovo's future', *The Guardian*, 9 November 2001.
19 RFE, *South-East Europe Newsline*, Prague, 19 November 2001, www.rferl.org
20 For Steiner's relations with the Provisional Institutions of Self-Governance (PISG), see *Two To Tango*, pp. 3–6.
21 *Two To Tango*, pp. 5–6.
22 Fron Nazi, 'The need for accountability', IWPR, Balkan Crisis Report, No. 488, 23 March 2004.
23 *Two To Tango*, p. 2.
24 *Collapse in Kosovo*, Priština/Belgrade/Brussels: ICG, Europe Report No. 155, 22 April 2004, p. 36.
25 The Independent Commission on Kosovo, Follow-Up Report, 2001, www.kosovo.org.com (accessed in January 2002), p. 10.
26 RFE, *South-East Europe Newsline*, 31 July 2002.
27 *Kosovo Report Card*, p. 34.
28 *Collapse in Kosovo*, p. 37.
29 Ibid.
30 *The Ottoman Dilemma: Power and property relations under the United Nations mission in Kosovo*, Priština: Lessons Learned and Analysis Unit of the EU Pillar of UN Interim Administrative Mission in Kosovo (UNMIK) in Kosovo, 2002, p. 2.

31 Ibid., p. 10.
32 Ibid.
33 Letter from Rudolf Hoffmann, Outgoing Regional Administrator of Prizren, published in *Focus on Kosovo*, October 2002 (UNMIK's monthly newsletter).
34 Veton Surroi, 'Kosovo tributes', IWPR, Balkan Crisis Report, No. 172, 15 September 2000.
35 *Collapse in Kosovo*, pp. 6, 39.
36 RFE, *South-East Europe Newsline*, 19 February 2001.
37 RFE/RL, Focus Kosovo.
38 RFE, *South-East Europe Newsline*, 30 March 2001.
39 Jonathan Steele, 'Confused and still in denial, Serbs have a long way to go', *The Guardian*, 9 July 1999.
40 RFE, *South-East Europe Newsline*, 19 February 2001.
41 Father Sava, 'Kosovo extremists out of control', IWPR, No. 355, 2 August 2002.
42 Naser Mitfari, 'Policing the protectors', IWPR, Balkan Crisis Report, No. 440, 30 June 2003.
43 Information from Dr Tamara Duffey of the Kosovo Police Service School.
44 Information from Arber Gorani of the Kosovo Police Service School.
45 For the Zemaj killing, I used Hugh Griffiths, '(UN) Protected witnesses', *Transition Online*, 19 June 2003, www.tol.cz
46 *Southeast European Times*, 14 July 2003.
47 Alma Lama, 'Albanians still wary of dialogue', IWPR, Balkan Report, No. 443, 11 July 2003.
48 RFE, *South-East Europe Newsline*, 31 July 2002.
49 'The status issue looms', *Transition Online*, 19 May 2003.
50 Marcus Tanner, 'Hunt for successor grips Kosovo after Governor resigns', *The Independent*, 26 May 2004.
51 Ibid.
52 RFE, *South-East Europe Newsline*, 14 October 2003.
53 'Hopes flare in the Aegean', *The Economist*, 28 June 2004.
54 Alex Anderson, 'UN Chief faces uphill battle in Kosovo', IWPR, Balkan Report, No. 506, 8 July 2004.
55 *Two To Tango*, p. 6.
56 *Collapse in Kosovo*, No. 34, p. 8.
57 Ibid., p. 8.
58 Ibid., p. 9.
59 RFE, *South-East Europe Newsline*, 11 March 2003.
60 *Collapse in Kosovo*, p. 14.
61 'Impunity for ethnic violence in Kosovo and Serbia must end', International Helsinki Federation For Human Rights, 29 March 2004.
62 RFE, *South-East Europe Newsline*, 23 April 2004, 3 June 2004.
63 *Collapse in Kosovo*, p. 19.
64 Ibid., pp. 20–1.
65 Ibid., p. 41. The EU Foreign Affairs Commissioner, Chris Patten said on 30 March 2004 that the evidence about the KPC's role was mixed. See *Europe South-East Monitor*, No. 53, March 2004, Brussels: Centre of European Policy Studies (CEPS).
66 Veton Surroi, 'Now all Kosova is a hostage', IWPR, Balkan Report, No. 488, 23 March 2004.
67 *Collapse in Kosovo*, p. 28.
68 Ibid., p. 19.
69 RFE, *South-East Europe Newsline*, 19 April 2004.
70 See *Europe South-East Monitor*, Brussels: CEPS, No. 53, March 2004.
71 Patrick Moore, 'Which way for Kosova', RFE/RL, *Newsline*, 29 March 2004.
72 RFE, *South-East Europe Newsline*, 29 March 2004.
73 *Collapse in Kosovo*, p. 36.

74 Ibid., p. 43.
75 RFE, *South-East Europe Newsline*, 29 March 2004.
76 'Impunity for ethnic violence in Kosovo and Serbia must end', International Helsinki Federation for Human Rights, 29 March 2004.
77 RFE, *South-East Europe Newsline*, 15 July 2004.

8 The European Union in search of Balkan answers

1 See Chris Patten, 'A European vision for the Balkans', *Nato Review*, Vol. 48, No. 2, Autumn 2000, pp. 13–15.
2 *EUFOR-IA: Changing Bosnia's Security Arrangements*, Sarajevo/Brussels: ICG, Europe Briefing, 29 June 2004, p. 4.
3 Dana Allin, Nato's Balkan interventions (Adelphi Papers) (2002), Oxford: Oxford University Press, p. 66.
4 RFE, *South-East Europe Newsline*, 25 February 2003.
5 Judy Dempsey, 'Operation in Macedonia will test European security policy', *Financial Times*, 31 March 2003.
6 RFE, *South-East Europe Newsline*, 17 September 2003.
7 Ibid.
8 *EUFOR-IA: Changing Bosnia's Security Arrangements*, p. 6.
9 RFE, *South-East Europe Newsline*, 8 December 2000.
10 Ibid., 10 October 2003.
11 Ibid., 25 February 2003.
12 *EUFOR-IA: Changing Bosnia's Security Arrangements*, pp. 4–5.
13 Ibid., p. 6.
14 Ibid., p. 5.
15 Ibid., p. 7, n. 30.
16 Nicholas Whyte, 'The European Parliament flexes its muscles in Albania', *Europe South-East Monitor*, Brussels: CEPS, No. 35, June 2002, pp. 2–3.
17 Leon Mangasarian, 'Domestic concerns fuel goals', *Balkan Eye*, Vol. 1, No. 1, June 2000 for the preceding sentences.
18 BBC news, 29 July 1999.
19 RFE, *South-East Europe Newsline*, 29 March 2000.
20 Alexandra Poolos, 'Balkans: money pledged is not money spent', RFE, *Endnote*, 31 March 2000.
21 Janusz Bugajski, 'Stability pact or status quo?', Bosnia Report, 24 May 2000, www.bosnia.org.uk/binews/24050%5Fi.html (accessed July 2000).
22 *Western Balkans 2004, Assistance, Cohesion and the New Boundary of Europe: A Call for Policy Reform*, Berlin: ESI, 3 November 2002, p. 9.
23 Vladimir Gligorov, 'Strategies and instruments', *Balkan Eye*, Vol. 1, No. 1, June 2000.
24 Saso Ordanoski, 'Will the king get the kingdom', *South-East Europe Information Network*, Vol. 2, No. 5, 17 March 2000.
25 RFE, *South-East Europe Newsline*, 4 January 2002; 'Balkan pact boss Hombach slams European Commission', Reuters, 18 December 2001.
26 *Europe South-East Monitor*, Brussels: CEPS, No. 29, November 2001.
27 RFE, *South-East Europe Newsline*, 16 December 2002.
28 *Europe South-East Monitor*, Brussels: CEPS, No. 32, March 2002.
29 RFE, *South-East Europe Newsline*, 13 July 2004.
30 'Reshaping Macedonia', *Transition Online*, 19 July 2004.
31 Nevena Angelovska, 'Macedonia: move to break decentralisation impasse', IWPR, Balkan Crisis Report, No. 503, June 2004.
32 Ulrich Büchsenschütz, 'Macedonia's decentralization talks deadlocked', *South-East Europe Newsline*, 2 July 2004.
33 Angelovska, 'Macedonia: move to break'.

34 Biljana Stavrova, 'Macedonia: the blacklist as peace tool', *Transition Online*, 10–16 February 2004.
35 Svetlana Jovanovska and Gordana Icevska, ' Macedonia: EC aid Under fire', IWPR, Balkan Crisis Report, No. 310, Part 2, 21 January 2002.
36 *Macedonia's Public Secret: How Corruption Drags the Country Down*, Skopje/ Brussels: ICG, Balkan Report, No. 133, 14 August 2002, pp. 32–5.
37 In the Corruption Perceptions Index produced by Transparency International Romania fell from sixty-ninth to seventy-seventh and then to eighty-third position between 2001 and 2003, only Russia, the Ukraine and Moldova occupying lower positions in the European category. See www.transparency.org
38 Marius Ghilzean, 'Campioni la fraude din banii Europei', *Evenimentul Zilei*, 4 December 2004.
39 See Tom Gallagher, *Theft of a Nation: Romania Since Communism*, London: Hurst, 2004, chapter 6.
40 *Nine O'Clock*: 19 April 1999 (Bucharest), www.nineoclock.ro
41 Monitorul: 22 March 2001 (Iasi, Romania), www.monitorul.ro
42 See *Thessaloniki and After (1): The EU's Balkan Agenda*, Brussels: ICG, Balkan Report, 20 June 2003, p. 3.
43 Valerian Stan, *A Few Remarks About the Transparency and Integrity of Public Administration in Romania*, this text was sent to international bodies and institutions on 1 June 2001.
44 Liviu Ioan Stoica, *Cotidianul* (Bucharest), 5 August 2002.
45 See Gallagher, *Theft of a Nation*, chapter 10. See also Christian Levant, 'Justiţia "mortul din fereastra"', *Dilema* (Bucharest), No. 12, April 2004.
46 See Tom Gallagher, 'Balkan but different: Romania and Bulgaria's contrasting paths to NATO membership 1994–2002', *Journal of Communist Studies and Transition Politics*, Vol. 2, No. 3, 2004, pp. 9–10.
47 Reuters, 9 August 2002.
48 RFE, *South-East Europe Newsline*, 30 August 2002.
49 Ibid., 25 February 2003.
50 For the personal uses, one of the PSD's most powerful regional barons found for EU Phare funds, see Dan Cristian Turturica, 'Old barons, new barons', *Evenimentul Zilei*, (English language online edition), 2 May 2004.
51 In June 2001 at the Gothenburg EU summit, the Swedish Presidency stated that both Romania and Bulgaria deserved special attention from member-states so as to be able to catch up, but the advice seemed to have fallen on deaf ears. See Mungiu-Pippidi, 'European integration, a moving target?', *Romania after 2000*, p. 158.
52 *Evenimentul Zilei* (Bucharest), 31 May 2004.
53 See for instance Marian Chiriac, 'Romania: reform failure threatens EU bid', IWPR, Balkan Crisis Report, No. 501, 3 June 2004.
54 Special Report No. 6/2003, 'Twinning as the main instrument to support institution building in candidate countries', 21 May 2003, www.eca.eu.int
55 *Thessaloniki and After (1)*, p. 6.
56 Ibid.
57 Enrico-Pasquarelli, the chief EU negotiator with Romania publicly refuted Năstase's claim. See *Evenimentul Zilei*, 8 November 2003.
58 Ulrich Büchsenschütz, 'Bulgarian Conservatives go on without former leader', RFE, *Endnote*, 25 February 2004.
59 For both examples see *Evenimentul Zilei* (Bucharest), 21 February 2004. Ion Rus, the Romanian Interior Minister when told about the success of anti-corruption measures, declared: 'We don't need to learn from the Bulgarian example'.
60 Albena Shkodrova, 'Bulgaria faces EU entry hurdles', IWPR, Balkan Crisis Report, No. 503, June 2004.

61 EIU Country Report for Romania, October 2002, London: Economic Intelligence Unit, p. 18.
62 *Evenimentul Zilei*, 21 February 2004.
63 Sorin Pislaru, 'Why are Bulgarians better rated than Romanians?', *Ziarul Financiar* (Bucharest), 23 February 2004.
64 Zoe Petre, *Ziua*, 19 March 2004.
65 *Ziarul de Iasi*, 28 August 2003.
66 One of the lesser ones arose from the fact that a call for tenders was published in the Official Gazette on 5 February 2004 with the closing date being the thirteenth. See *Evenimentul Zilei*, 13 February 2004.
67 RFE, *South-East Europe, Newsline*, 20 February 2004.
68 Ibid., 9 February 2004; *Ziarul de Iasi*, 9 February 2004.
69 *Adevărul*, 5 February 2004.
70 Mediafax (Bucharest), 19 February 2004; for the plenum debate, see *Ziarul de Iasi*, 11 and 12 March 2004.
71 *Ziarul de Iasi*, 20 February 2004.
72 RFE, *South-East Europe Newsline*, 27 February 2004.
73 *Evenimentul Zilei*, 9 March 2004. Talpes, whose influence extended back to the communist era, found it difficult to answer questions about the respective positions of Romania and Bulgaria in the EU integration process at his first encounter with parliamentarians as a government member. See *Adevărul*, 10 March 2004.
74 Cornel Nistorescu, 'We will do this and that', *Evenimentul Zilei*, 27 February 2004 (English language edition).
75 *Draft Report on Bulgaria's Progress Towards Accession*, Brussels: European Parliament, 18 December 2003.
76 RFE, *South-East Europe Newsline*, 3 October 2002.
77 *Ziarul de Iasi*, 4 October 2002.
78 Velina Nacheva, 'Reading Room', *Sofia Echo*, 7 March 2004.
79 RFE, *South-East Europe Newsline*, 11 February 2004.
80 Ibid., 22 July 2004.
81 From the end of the 1990s, the EU identified as 'the Western Balkans' all of ex-Yugoslavia, excepting Slovenia, plus Albania.
82 *Belgrade's Lagging Reform: Cause for International Concern*, Brussels/Belgrade: ICG, Balkan Report, No. 126, 7 March 2002, p. 7.
83 *Europe South-East Monitor*, Brussels: CEPS, No. 31, January–February 2002.
84 David Chandler, 'European Union and governance in the Balkans: an unequal partnership', *European Balkan Observer*, Vol. 1, No. 2, November 2003, p. 5; ICG, No. 126, 7 March 2002, p. 7.
85 Chandler, 'European Union and governance in the Balkans'.
86 Vladimir Gligorov, 'Strategies and instruments', *Balkan Eye*, Vol. 1, No. 1, June 2000.
87 Interview with Chris Patten, 26 March 2003.
88 Human Security Report: Inventing South-East Europe, Sofia: Centre for Liberal Strategies, 2002.
89 See *Western Balkans 2004, Assistance, Cohesion and the New Boundary of Europe: A Call for Policy Reform*, Berlin: ESI, 3 November 2002.
90 EIU Country Report for Croatia, London: Economic Intelligence Unit, June 2004, p. 7.
91 'Slouching towards respectablity', *Transition Online*, 24 November 2003, www.tol.coz (accessed 29 November 2003).
92 *Third Annual Report of the Stabilisation and Association Process for South-East Europe*, Brussels: European Commission, 30 March 2004, p. 34.
93 Interview with Chris Patten, 26 March 2003, www.europa.eu/ml/comm/external relations/news/paten/sap260303.htm (accessed July 2004).
94 *Third Annual Report of the Stabilisation and Association Process for South-East Europe*, p. 7.

95 *Western Balkans 2004, Assistance, Cohesion and the New Boundary of Europe: A Call for Policy Reform*, p. 11.
96 *Thessaloniki and After (1): The EU's Balkan Agenda*, p. 7.
97 Georgana Noutcheva, 'How much EU involvement is enough', *Europe South-East Monitor*, Brussels: CEPS, No. 42, January 2003.
98 RFE, *South-East Europe Newsline*, 24 September 2003.

Conclusion: an uncertain political future for the Balkans

1 *Romania in 2004: Prognoze*, Bucharest 2004: Romanian Academic Society, p. 71.
2 *Peace in Presovo: Quick fix or long-term solution*, Priština/Belgrade/Brussels: ICG, Balkan Report, No. 116, 10 August 2001, p. 2.
3 *Albania: The State of the Nation in 2001*, Tirana/Brussels: ICG, Balkan Report, No. 111, 25 May 2001, p. 21.
4 'Prometheus unbound: a survey of Greece', *The Economist*, 12 October 2002, p. 19.
5 *Romania in 2004: Prognoze*, pp. 4–5.
6 These points were eloquently made by Stefan Bârsan, a contributor to the 'Reader's Forum' of the Romania newspaper, *Evenimentul Zilei* on 15 July 2004.
7 *UNDP Human Development Report, 2004*, New York: United Nations, pp. 188–9.
8 Neil Barnett, 'Traffickers risk death in Albania's high seas', IWPR, Balkan Crisis Report, No. 479, 5 February 2004.
9 *UNDP Human Development Report, 2004*, New York: United Nations.
10 Ibid., 'Eastern Europe: demographic trends', Oxford Analytica Daily Briefs, 29 May 1998.
11 *Cotidianul* (Bucharest), 29 July 2004.

Bibliography

Broadcasting sources

The Fall of Milošević, Part 3 (Brook Lapping productions, BBC 2, 2001).
War In Europe (Channel 4, 2001).

Books and academic articles

Ackermann, Alice (2000), *Making Peace Prevail: Preventing Violent Conflict in Macedonia*, Syracuse, NY: Syracuse University Press.

Ackermann, Alice (2003), 'International intervention in Macedonia: from preventive engagement to peace implementation', in Siani-Davies, Peter (ed.), *International Intervention in the Balkans Since 1995*, London: Routledge.

After Milošević: A Practical Agenda For Lasting Balkans Peace (2001), Brussels: International Crisis Group.

Ahmeti, Sevdije (1994), 'Forms of apartheid in Kosovo', in *Conflict or Dialogue: Serbian–Albanian Relations and Integration of the Balkans*, Subotica: European Centre for Conflict Resolution.

Ahtisaari, Marti (2001), *Misija U Beogradu*, Belgrade: Filip Višnić.

Albright, Madeleine (2003), *Madame Secretary: A Memoir*, London: Macmillan.

Ali, Tariq (2000), *Masters of the Universe: NATO's Balkan Crusade*, London: Verso.

Amnesty International (2000), *NATO/Federal Republic of Yugoslavia: Violations of the Laws of War by Nato during Operation Allied Force*, London: Amnesty International. www.amnesty.org/library/Index/ENGEUR7001182000?open&of=ENG-YUG

Amnesty International (2004), *Serbia and Montenegro (Kosovo/Kosova), The March Violence: KFOR and UNMIK Failure to Protect the Rights of Minority Communities*, 8 July.

Baltsiotis, Lambros and Embiricos, Leonidas (2001), 'Speaking in tongues', *Index on Censorship*, No. 2.

Belgrade's Lagging Reform: Cause for International Concern (2002), Brussels: International Crisis Group, No. 126, 7 March.

Bellamy, Alex (2002), *Kosovo and International Society*, Houndsmill: Palgrave.

Bozo, Alba (2001), 'Kosovo refugees in Albania: the emergency response', in Waller, Michael, Drezov, Kyril and Gokay, Bulent (eds), *Kosovo: Myths, Conflict & War*, London: Frank Cass.

Buckley, Mary (2001), 'Russian perceptions', in Buckley, Mary and Cummings, Sally (eds), *Kosovo: Perceptions of War and its Aftermath*, London: Continuum.

Bugajski, Janusz (1994), *Ethnic Politics in Eastern Europe*, New York: M.E. Sharpe.

Caplan, Richard (1998), 'International diplomacy and the crisis in Kosovo', *International Affairs*, Vol. 74, No. 4.

Chomsky, Noam (1999), *The New Military Humanism*, London: Pluto Press.

Clark, Howard (1998), 'I still want to follow the non-violent way but...', *Peace News*, June.

Clark, Howard (2000a), *Civil Resistance in Kosovo*, London: Pluto Press.

Clark, Martin (2001b), 'Italian perspectives', in Buckley, Mary and Cummings, Sally (eds), *Kosovo: Perceptions of War and its Aftermath*, London: Continuum.

Clark, Victoria (2000b), *Why Angels Fall: A Journey Through Orthodox Europe*, London: Macmillan.

Clark, Wesley (2001a), *Waging Modern War: Bosnia, Kosovo and the Future of Combat*, Oxford: Public Affairs Ltd.

Cohen, Lenard J. (2001), *Serpent in the Bosom: The Rise and Fall of Slobodan Milošević*, Boulder and Oxford: Westview Press.

Collin, Matthew (2001), *This is Serbia Calling*, London: Serpent's Tail.

Constas, Dimitri and Papasotiriou, Charalambos (1999), 'Greek policy responses to the post-Cold War Balkan environment' in Coufoudakis, Van *et al.* (eds), *Greece and the New Balkans: Challenges and Opportunities*, New York: Pella Publishing Company.

Corrin, Chris (2002), 'Developing democracy in Kosova: from grassroots to government', *Parliamentary Affairs*, Vol. 55, No. 1.

Coufoudakis, Van *et al.* (1999), *Greece and the New Balkans: Challenges and Opportunities*, New York: Pella Publishing Company.

Cowan, Jane K. (2000), *Macedonia: The Politics of Identity and Difference*, London: Pluto.

Daalder, Ivo H. (2001), 'Are the United States and Europe heading for divorce?', *International Affairs*, Vol. 77, No. 3.

Daalder, Ivo and O'Hanlon, Michael (2000), *Winning Ugly: NATO's War To Save Kosovo*, Washington, DC: Brookings Institute.

Dannreuther, Roland (2001), 'War in Kosovo: history, development and aftermath', in Buckley, Mary and Cummings, Sally (eds), *Kosovo: Perceptions of War and its Aftermath*, London: Continuum.

Debray, Regis (2000), 'An open letter from a traveller to the president of the republic', in Ali, Tariq (ed.), *Masters of the Universe: NATO's Balkan Crusade*, London: Verso.

Deighton, Anne (2000), 'The European Union and NATO's war over Kosovo: towards the Glass Ceiling', in Martin, Pierre and Brawley, Mark R. (eds), *Alliance Politics, Kosovo, And NATO's War: Allied Force Or Forced Allies?*, Houndsmill: Palgrave.

Doder, Dusko and Branson, Louise (1999), *Milošević: Portrait of A Tyrant*, New York: Free Press.

Dragović-Soso, Jasna (2002), *Saviours of the Nation: Serbia's Intellectual Opposition and the Revival of Nationalism*, London: Hurst & Co.

Drezov, Kyril (ed.) (2001), 'Collateral damage: the impact on Macedonia of the Kosovo war', in Waller, Michael, Drezov, Kyril and Gokay, Bulent (eds), *Kosovo: Myths, Conflict & War*, London: Frank Cass.

Dyker, David (2003), 'The Serbian economy', *Central and South-Eastern Europe, 2003*, London and New York: Europa Publications.

Elsie, Robert (1997), *Kosovo: In the Heart of the Powder Keg*, Boulder, CO: East European Monographs.

Europe Enlarged: Understanding the Impact (2003), London: Economist Intelligence Unit.

Festić, Amra and Rausche, Adrian (2004), 'War by other means: how Bosnia's clandestine political economies obstruct peace and state-building', *Problems of Post-Communism*, Vol. 51, No. 3, May/June.

Fischer, Bernd J. (1999), *Albania at War, 1939–1945*, London: Hurst.

Fouskas, Vassilis (2003), *Zones of Conflict: US Foreign Policy in the Balkans and the Greater Middle East*, London: Verso.

Gaber, Natasha (1997), 'The Muslim population in FYROM (Macedonia): public perceptions', in Poulton, Hugh and Taji-Farouki, Taji (eds), *Muslim Identity and the Balkan State*, London: Hurst.

Gallagher, Tom (1999), 'The West and the challenge to ethnic politics in Romania', *Security Dialogue*, Vol. 30, No. 3, September.

Gallagher, Tom (2000), 'Nationalism and democracy in South-East Europe', in Gallagher, T. and Pridham, G. (eds), *Experimenting with Democracy: Regime Change in the Balkans*, London: Routledge.

Gallagher, Tom (2002), 'Minorities in Central and South-Eastern-Europe', in *Central and South-Eastern-Europe 2003*, London: Taylor & Francis.

Gallagher, Tom (2003), *The Balkans after the Cold War: From Tyranny to Tragedy*, London: Routledge.

Gallagher, Tom (2004), *Theft of a Nation: Romania since Communism*, London: Hurst & Co.

Garton-Ash, Timothy (2000), 'Kosovo: was it worth it?', *New York Review of Books*, 21 September.

Giatzidis, Emil (2002), *An Introduction to Post-Communist Bulgaria: Political, Economic and Social Transformation*, Manchester: Manchester University Press.

Gligorov, Kiro (1995), 'Macedonian model of peace and security in the Balkans', *Balkan Forum*, Vol. 3, No. 12, September.

Gordy, Eric (2004), 'Serbia after Djindjić: war crimes, organized crime, and trust in public institutions', *Problems of Post-Communism*, Vol. 51, No. 3, May/June.

Gow, James (2003), *The Serbian Project and its Adversaries*, London: Hurst.

Gowan, Peter (2000), 'The Euro-Atlantic origins of NATO's attack on Yugoslavia', in Ali, Tariq (ed.), *Masters of the Universe: NATO's Balkan Crusade*, London: Verso.

Gruevski, Nikola (2004), 'Secretive, unprincipled law sows public distrust', IWPR's Balkan Crisis Report, No. 510, 5 August.

Guicherd, Catherine (1999), 'International law and war in Kosovo', *Survival*, Vol. 41, No. 2.

Halberstam, David (2001), *War in a Time of Peace: Bush, Clinton and the Generals*, New York: Scribner.

Hendrickson, Ryan (2002), 'NATO's Secretary General Javier Solana and the Kosovo crisis', *Journal of International Relations and Development*, Vol. 5, No. 3.

Henrikson, Alan K. (2000), 'The constraints of legitimacy: the legal and institutional framework of Euro-Atlantic security', in Martin, Pierre and Brawley, Mark R. (eds), *Alliance Politics, Kosovo, And NATO's War: Allied Force Or Forced Allies?*, Houndsmill: Palgrave.

Hislope, Robert (2004), 'Crime and honor in a weak state: paramilitary forces and violence in Macedonia', *Problems of Post-Communism*, Vol. 51, No. 3, May/June.

Hoare, Marko Attila (2003), 'Genocide in the former Yugoslavia: a critique of Left revisionism's denial', *Journal of Genocide Research*, Vol. 5, No. 4.

Ignatieff, Michael (2000), *Virtual War: Kosovo and Beyond*, London: Chatto and Windus.

International Helsinki Federation (IHF) (1999), *Responses to Human Rights and Humanitarian Law Violations in Kosovo*, New York: International Helsinki Federation, 1999, www.ihf-hr.org (consulted May 2001).

Ioakimidis, P.C. (1999), 'Greece, the European Union and Southeastern Europe: past failures and future prospects', in Coufoudakis, Van *et al.* (eds), *Greece and the New Balkans: Challenges and Opportunities*, New York: Pella Publishing Company.

Islami, Hivzi (1994), 'Demographic reality of Kosovo', in *Conflict or Dialogue: Serbian–Albanian relations and integration of the Balkans*, Subotica: European Centre for Conflict Resolution.

Janev, Goran (2003), 'Kosovo independence and Macedonian stability: is there any alternative to the nationalistic discourse?', in Bieber, Florian and Daskalovski, Židas, (eds), *Understanding the War in Kosovo*, London: Frank Cass.

Jelavich, Barbara (1983), *History of the Balkans: Eighteenth and Nineteenth Centuries*, Cambridge: Cambridge University Press.

Job, Cvitejo (2002), *Yugoslavia's Ruin: The Bloody Lessons of Nationalism, a Patriot's Warning*, Lanham, MD: Rowman & Littlefield.

Judah, Tim (2000), *Kosovo: War and Revenge*, New Haven, CT: Yale University Press.

Kampener, John (2003), *Blair's Wars*, London: Free Press.

Karakasidou, Anastasia (1997), *Fields of Wheat, Hills of Blood: Passages to Nationhood in Greek Macedonia, 1870–1990*, Chicago, IL: Chicago University Press.

Kaufman, Joyce P. (2002), *NATO and the Former Yugoslavia: Crisis, Conflict and the Atlantic Alliance*, Lanham, MD: Rowman & Littlefield.

Kemp, Walter A. (2001), *Quiet Diplomacy in Action: The OSCE High Commissioner on National Minorities*, The Hague/London/Boston, MA: Kluwer International.

King, Robert R. (1973), *Minorities Under Communism*, Cambridge, MA: Harvard University Press.

Kitromilides, Paschalis (1999), 'The Greek cultural presence in the Balkans', in Coufoudakis, Van *et al.* (eds), *Greece and the New Balkans: Challenges and Opportunities*, New York: Pella Publishing Company.

Kofos, Evangelos (1989), 'National heritage and national identity in nineteenth- and twentieth-century Macedonia', *European History Quarterly*, Vol. 19, No. 2.

Kofos, Evangelos (1999), 'Greek policy considerations over FYROM independence and recognition', in Pettifer, James (ed.), *The New Macedonian Question*, Houndsmill: Macmillan.

Kola, Paulin (2003), *The Search For Greater Albania*, London: Hurst & Co.

Koliopoulos, John and Veremis, Thanos (2002), *Greece The Modern Sequel: From 1831 to the Present*, London: Hurst.

The Kosovo Report: Conflict, International Response, Lessons Learnt (2000), Oxford: Independent International Commission on Kosovo.

Kostovic, Denisa (1998), 'The trap of the parallel society', *Transitions*, Vol. 5, No. 5, May.

Kostovičová, Denisa (2001), 'Albanian schooling in Kosovo 1992–1998: "Liberty Imprisoned"', in Waller, Michael, Drezov, Kyril and Gokay, Bulent (eds), *Kosovo: Myths, Conflict & War*, London: Frank Cass.

Leurdijk, Dick and Zandee, Dick (2001), *Kosovo: From Crisis To Crisis*, Aldershot: Ashgate.

Loza, Tihomir (1998), 'Kosovo Albanians: closing the ranks', *Transitions*, Vol. 5, No. 5, May.

McInnes, Colin and Wheeler, Nicholas (2002), *Dimensions of Western Military Intervention*, London: Frank Cass.

Macleod, Alex (2000), 'France: Kosovo and the emergence of a new European security', in Martin, Pierre and Brawley, Mark R. (eds), *Alliance Politics, Kosovo, and NATO's War: Allied Force or Forced Allies?*, Houndsmill: Palgrave.

Malcolm, Noel (1998), *Kosovo: A Short History*, London: Macmillan.

Maliqi, Shkëlzen (1994), 'Self-understanding of the Albanians in non-violence', in *Conflict or Dialogue: Serbian–Albanian relations and integration of the Balkans*, Subotica: European Centre for Conflict Resolution.

Maliqi, Shkëlzen (1998), *Kosova: Separate Worlds*, Priština: MM Society & Dukagjini Publishing.

Margaronis, Maria (2001), 'Acropolis now: fast forward', *Index on Censorship*, No. 2.

Marmullaku, Ramadan (2003), 'Albanians in Yugoslavia: a personal essay', in Djokić, Dejan (ed.), *Yugoslavism: Histories of a Failed Idea*, London: Hurst & Co.

Mazower, Mark (2001), 'High political stakes', *Index on Censorship*, No. 2.

Mehmeti, Kim (1998), 'Separate dreams', *War Report*, February–March, No. 58.

Mertus, Julie (1999), *Kosovo: How Myths and Truths Started a War*, Berkeley, CA: University of California Press.

Meyer, Amy (2001), Perceptions of Bosnia–Herzegovina Youth of the International Community, MA dissertation, Budapest: Central European University.

Michas, Takis (2002), *Unholy Alliance: Greece and Milošević's Serbia*, Austin, TX: A&M University Press.

Morelli, Umberto (2001), 'Italy: the reluctant ally', in Weymouth, Anthony and Henig, Stanley (eds), *The Kosovo Crisis: The Last American War in Europe?*, London: Pearsons Education/Reuters.

Mungiu-Pippidi, Alina (2004), Milošević's voters: explaining grassroots nationalism in postcommunist Europe', in Mungiu-Pippidi, Alina and Krastev, Ivan (eds), *Nationalism After Communism: Lessons Learned*, Budapest: Central European University Press.

Naegele, Jolyon, 'Yugoslavia: assessing the effects of NATO's air strikes three years on', *RFE-RL Features*, Prague: Radio Free Europe, 25 March 2002.

Neier, Aryeh (1994), 'Kosovo survives', *New York Review of Books*, 3 February.

Ordanoski, Saso (2002), 'Lions and tigers: the militarisation of the Macedonian right', in *Ohrid and Beyond: A Cross-Ethnic Investigation into the Macedonian Crisis*, London: Institute for War and Peace Reporting.

Perry, Duncan (1997), 'The Republic of Macedonia: finding its way', in Dawisha, Karen and Parrott, Bruce (eds), *Politics, Power, and the Struggle for Democracy in South-East Europe*, Cambridge: Cambridge University Press.

Perry, Duncan (2000), 'Conflicting ambitions and shared fate: the past, present, and future of Albanian Macedonians', in Roudometof, Victor (ed.), *The Macedonian Question: Culture, Historiography, Politics*, New York: Columbia University Press (East European Monographs).

Petruseva, Ana and Devaja, Shpend (2002), 'War crimes and the Hague', in *Ohrid and Beyond: A Cross-Ethnic Investigation into the Macedonian Crisis*, London: Institute for War and Peace Reporting.

Pettifer, James (1999), 'The new Macedonian question', in Pettifer, James (ed.), *The New Macedonian Question*, Houndsmill: Macmillan.

Pettifer, James (2004), *Kosovo March 2004: The Endgame Begins*, Sandhurst: Conflict Studies Research Centre, April, www.csrc.ac.uk

Phillips, John (2004), *Macedonia: Warlords and Rebels in the Balkans*, London: IB Tauris.

Phinnemore, David (2001), 'Romania and Euro-Atlantic integration since 1989: a decade of frustration', in Light, Duncan and Phinnemore, David (eds), *Post-Communist Romania: Coming to Terms with Transition*, Houndsmill: Palgrave.

Pollis, Adamantia (1994), 'Strangers in a strange land', *Balkan War Report*, No. 25, March/April.

Poulton, Hugh (1995), *Who are the Macedonians?*, London: Hurst & Co.

Poulton, Hugh (1999), 'Non-Albanian Muslim minorities in Macedonia', in Pettifer, James (ed.), *The New Macedonian Question*, Houndsmill: Macmillan.

Pugh, Michael (2004), 'Rubbing salt into war wounds: shadow economies and peacebuildng in Bosnia and Kosovo', *Problems of Post-Communism*, Vol. 51, No. 3, May/June.

Ramet, Sabrina P. (2001), 'Kingdom of God or the kingdom of ends: Kosovo in Serbian perceptions', in Buckley, Mary and Cummings, Sally (eds), *Kosovo: Perceptions of War and its Aftermath*, London: Continuum.

Ramet, Sabrina P. and Lyon, Phil (2001), 'Germany: the Federal Republic loyal to NATO', in Weymouth, Anthony and Henig, Stanley (eds), *The Kosovo Crisis: The Last American War in Europe?*, London: Pearsons Education/Reuters.

Rawnsley, Andrew (ed.) (2001), *Servants of the People: The Inside Story of New Labour*, London: Penguin.

Reuter, Jens (1999), 'Policy and economy in Macedonia' in Pettifer, James (ed.), *The New Macedonian Question*, Houndsmill: Macmillan.

Richardson, Louise (2000), 'A force for good in the world? Britain's role in the Kosovo crisis', in Martin, Pierre and Brawley, Mark R. (eds), *Alliance Politics, Kosovo, and NATO's War: Allied Force or Forced Allies?*, Houndsmill: Palgrave.

Rieff, David (2002), *A Bed for the Night: Humanitarianism in Crisis*, London: Verso.

Roberts, Adam (1999), 'NATO's Humanitarian War Over Kosovo', *Survival*, Vol. 41, No. 3, Autumn 1999.

Robertson, Lord (1999), *Kosovo: An Account of the Crisis*, London: Ministry of Defence.

Romania in 2004: Prognoze (2004) Bucharest: Romanian Academic Society.

Roudometof, Victor (1996), 'Nationalism and identity politics in the Balkans: Greece and the Macedonian question', *Journal of Modern Greek Studies*, Vol. 14.

Roudometof, Victor (ed.) (2000), *The Macedonian Question: Culture, Historiography, Politics*, New York: Columbia University Press (East European Monographs).

Roudometof, Victor (2001), *Nationalism, Globalization, and Orthodoxy: The Social Origins of Ethnic Conflict in the Balkans*, Westport, CT and London: Greenwood Press.

Rudolf, Peter (2000), 'Germany and the Kosovo conflict', in Martin, Pierre and Brawley, Mark R. (eds), *Alliance Politics, Kosovo, and NATO's War: Allied Force or Forced Allies?*, Houndsmill: Palgrave.

Rusi, Iso (1998), 'Beyond Gligorov', *War Report*, No. 58, February–March.

Rusi, Iso (2002), 'From army to party: the politics of the NLA', in *Ohrid and Beyond: A Cross-Ethnic Investigation into the Macedonian Crisis*, London: Institute for War and Peace Reporting.

Salitu, Astrid (1998), 'An education in profit', *Transitions*, Vol. 5, No. 3, May.

Sampson, Steven (2002), 'Weak states, uncivil societies and thousands of NGOs', in Resic, S. and Tornquist-Plewa, B. (eds), *The Balkans in Focus: Cultural Boundaries in Europe*, Lund: Nordic Academic Press.

Schwartz, Jonathan Martin (2000), 'Civil society and ethnic conflict in the Republic of Macedonia', in Halpern, Joel and Kideckel, David (eds), *Neighbours at War: Anthropological Perspectives on Yugoslavia's Ethnicity, Culture and History*, University Park, PA: Pennsylvania State University Press.

Schwartz, Stephen (2001), *Kosovo: Background to a War*, London: Anthem Press.

Sell, Louis (2002), *Slobodan Milošević and the Destruction of Yugoslavia*, London: Duke University Press.

Smith, Helena (2001), 'Acropolis now: Church V State', *Index on Censorship*, No. 2.

Solioz, Christopher and Petritsch, Wolfgang (2003), 'The fate of Bosnia and Herzegovina', *Journal of Southern Europe and the Balkans*, Vol. 5, No. 3.

Stan, Lavinia (2003), 'Fighting the demons of the recent past: prospects for Romanian Reconstruction and Development', paper presented at the conference on 'Southeastern Europe: Moving Forward', 23–24 January: Ottawa.

Surroi, Veton (1998), 'Kosova and the constitutional solutions', in Veremis, Thanos and Kofos, Evangelos (eds), *Kosovo: Avoiding another Balkan War*, Athens: ELIAMEP.

Svolopoulos, Constantinos (1999), 'Cooperation and confrontation in the Balkans: a historical overview', in Coufoudakis, Van *et al.* (eds), *Greece and the New Balkans: Challenges and Opportunities*, New York: Pella Publishing Company.

Swire, Joseph (1971 reprint), *Albania: The Rise of a Kingdom*, New York: Arno Press.

Szajkowski, Bogdan (2000), 'Macedonia: an unlikely road to democracy', in Pridham, Geoffrey and Gallagher, Tom (eds), *Experimenting With Democracy: Regime Change in the Balkans*, London: Routledge.

Talbott, Strobe (2002), *The Russia Hand: A Memoir of Presidential Diplomacy*, New York: Random House.

Thomas, Robert (1999), *Serbia Under Milošević: Politics in the 1990s*, London: Hurst & Co.

Thompson, Mark (1999), *Forging War: The Media in Serbia, Croatia, Bosnia and Herzegovina*, Luton: University of Luton Press.

Triantafyllou, Dimitrios (1999), 'Recent developments in Greece's Balkan diplomacy networks', in Coufoudakis, Van *et al.* (eds), *Greece and the New Balkans: Challenges and Opportunities*, New York: Pella Publishing Company.

Trotsky, Leon (1980), *The Balkan Wars 1912–1913*, Sydney: Pathfinder Press.

Under Orders: War Crimes in Kosovo (2001), New York: Human Rights Watch.

van Meurs, Wim (2004), *Kosovo's Fifth Anniversary – on the Road to Nowhere*, Munich: Bertelsman Foundation and the Center for Applied Policy Research (CAP), www.cap.lmu.de/publikationen/cap/kosovo.htm

Veremis, Thanos (1999), 'Greece and the Balkans in the Post-Cold War era', in Coufoudakis, Van *et al.* (eds), *Greece and the New Balkans: Challenges and Opportunities*, New York: Pella Publishing Company.

Veremis, Thanos and Kofos, Evangelos (1998), *Kosovo: Avoiding another Balkan War*, Athens: ELIAMEP.

Vickers, Miranda (1998), *Between Serb and Albanian: A History of Kosovo*, London: Hurst & Co.

von Kohl, Christina and Libal, Wolfgang (1997), 'The Gordian Knot of the Balkans', in Elsie, Robert (ed.), *Kosovo: In the Heart of the Powder Keg*, Boulder, CO: East European Monographs.

Waller, Michael, Drezov, Kyril and Gokay, Bulent (eds) (2001), *Kosovo: Myths, Conflict & War*, London: Frank Cass.

Weller, Marc (1999), 'The Ramboiuillet Conference on Kosovo', *International Affairs*, Vol. 75, No. 2.

Wheeler, Nicholas (2000), *Saving Strangers: International Intervention in Humanitarian Conflict*, Oxford: Oxford University Press.

Yahuda, Michael (2001), 'Chinese perceptions', in Buckley, Mary and Cummings, Sally (eds), *Kosovo: Perceptions of War and its Aftermath*, London: Continuum.

Young, Antonia (2000), *Women Who Become Men: Albanian Sworn Virgins*, Oxford: Berg.

Index

226   *Index*